In August 1914, the South Midland was numerically the second strongest division in the Territorial Force (TF); three months later it was considered to be the second most efficient of the TF's fourteen 1st Line formations. In the same way as other TF divisions, its pre-war officers and other ranks came from a variety of urban and rural backgrounds, trades and professions but, in contrast to the Kitchener formations, all of its units had a history and tradition dating back to at least the mid-19th century. It became the third TF division to be despatched to the Western Front and, having spent 30 months in France and Belgium, it deployed to Italy as one of the British formations tasked to support the Italian Army. Like the majority of British divisions, 48th (South Midland) Division was not an especially spectacular formation, with no particular or outstanding success to its name. It did suffer the indignity of having its commander sacked, but on the whole, it earned a reputation as a good, solid, reliable formation.

This volume explains the division's pre-war difficulties in trying to raise, equip and train efficient units; it also assesses those units' successes and failures in their major engagements. It examines the extent to which the TF ethos and the division's local character were maintained during the course of the war and how well its various constituent units adapted to the tactical and operational evolution apparent within the British Army. The key elements of command and leadership – and what in modern conceptual doctrine is known as 'fighting power' – are analysed across the component units, with considerable attention also being paid to the essential roles played by the supporting arms.

The book offers a comprehensive study of the character and activities of a reasonably typical TF division, but also of a formation which although competent and efficient, received few of the plaudits enjoyed by many of its fellow 'Saturday afternoon soldiers'.

Dr Bill Mitchinson is a lecturer with King's College London at the Joint Services Command and Staff College, Shrivenham. He has written and lectured extensively on the Great War for over 40 years and has a particular interest in the work of the Territorial Force. His books include the well-received trilogy on the Territorial Force and the Volunteer Training Corps, *Defending Albion, England's Last Hope* and *The Territorial Force at War 1914-1916*. These volumes offer an examination of the often difficult and tense relationship between the War Office and the auxiliaries and assessments of the competence of TF formations in the first half of the war. He regularly leads staff rides to the battlefields of Europe and is a member of both the British Commission for Military History and the Royal Historical Society.

The 48th (South Midland) Division 1908-1919

K.W. Mitchinson

Helion & Company Limited

Helion & Company Limited
26 Willow Road
Solihull
West Midlands
B91 1UE
England
Tel. 0121 705 3393
Fax 0121 711 4075
Email: info@helion.co.uk
Website: www.helion.co.uk
Twitter: @helionbooks
Visit our blog http://blog.helion.co.uk/

Published by Helion & Company 2017
Designed and typeset by Mach 3 Solutions Ltd (www.mach3solutions.co.uk)
Cover designed by Paul Hewitt, Battlefield Design (www.battlefield-design.co.uk)
Printed by Lightning Source Limited, Milton Keynes, Buckinghamshire

ISBN 978-1-911512-54-7

British Library Cataloguing-in-Publication Data.
A catalogue record for this book is available from the British Library.

For details of other military history titles published by Helion & Company Limited contact the above address, or visit our website: http://www.helion.co.uk.

We always welcome receiving book proposals from prospective authors.

Contents

List of Illustrations

List of Maps

List of Abbreviations

Unless otherwise stated, all TF battalions mentioned in the text are 1st Line. They are written as, for example, "7/Worcester" rather than "1/7th Worcester". If a 2nd or 3rd Line battalion or unit is mentioned, it is written as, for example, "2/5th Norfolk" or "3/5th Norfolk". For further clarification on unit designations, see the Introduction.

A&Q	Adjutant and Quartermaster
AA&QMG	Assistant-Adjutant and Quartermaster-General
AAG	Assistant Adjutant-General
AC	Army Council
ACI	Army Council Instruction
ADMS	Assistant-Director Medical Services
ADVS	Assistant-Director Veterinary Services
AG	Adjutant-General
AOD	Army Ordnance Department
AQMG	Assistant Quartermaster-General
ASC	Army Supply Corps
BEF	British Expeditionary Force
Bde	Brigade
Bde Maj	Brigade Major
BG	Brigadier General
BGGS	Brigadier General General Staff
BGRA	Brigadier-General Royal Artillery
CCS	Casualty Clearing Station
CIGS	Chief of the Imperial General Staff
C-in-C	Commander-in-Chief
CRA	Commanding Royal Artillery
CRE	Commanding Royal Engineers
CO	Commanding Officer
DAAG	Deputy Assistant Adjutant-General
DAC	Divisional Ammunition Column
DDMS	Deputy Director Medical Services
DRS	Divisional Rest Station
F.Amb	Field Ambulance

F.Coy	Field Company
FM	Field Marshal
FOO	Forward Observation Officer
GHQ	General Headquarters
GS	General Staff/ General Service
GSO	General Staff Officer
GOC	General Officer Commanding
Lt.Col.	Lieutenant Colonel
Lt.Gen.	Lieutenant General
LGS	Limber General Service
Maj.Gen	Major General
MG Coy	Machine-Gun Company
MGGS	Major General Staff
MO	Medical Officer
MVS	Mobile Veterinary Section
NCO	Non-Commissioned Officer
OP	Observation Post
ORs	Other Ranks
Pdr	Pounder
QMG	Quartermaster-General
RAMC	Royal Army Medical Corps
RASC	Royal Army Supply Corps
RAVC	Royal Army Veterinary Corps
RE	Royal Engineers
RFA	Royal Field Artillery
RHA	Royal Horse Artillery
SAA	Small Arms Ammunition
SMLE	Short Magazine Lee Enfield
TEWT	Tactical Exercise Without Troops
TF	Territorial Force
TM	Trench Mortar
WO	War Office

Acknowledgements

The National Archives has granted permission to quote from corps, division and unit war diaries and the Trustees of the Liddell Hart Centre for Military Archives at King's College London have kindly allowed the use of General Sir Ian Hamilton's papers.

Thanks are due to my colleagues at the Joint Services Command and Staff College at Shrivenham and to the Defence Academy's librarians for their interest and help. Several individuals have been of particular help during the preparation of this work. They include David Tattersfield and Tom Thorpe, both of whom provided some important source material and David Thistlethwaite, who loaned me a copy of his father's recollections. Following a photographic disaster on my part, Lt.Col. Paolo Capanni and Simon Jones very generously granted me permission to use their photographs of the Asiago. Finally, my appreciation, as always, goes to JB for her patience and understanding.

Introduction

Representatives of the victorious Allied nations had barely returned from the peace conference at Versailles when the first of the histories of Territorial Force (TF) divisions appeared in print. This volume and its successors were concerned to provide a record of the activities and achievements of that particular formation primarily for the benefit of those who fought with it. In the same way as most of the regimental and battalion histories which appeared at about the same time, it is rare to find any real criticism or analysis of how the division, its commanders and its troops behaved and fought. Understandably, the authors concentrated on the formations' successes and sacrifices and wanted their particular volumes to stand as testament to both. Volumes detailing the work of 55th (West Lancashire) and 46th (North Midland) Divisions[1] were published in the same year as the peace treaty was signed and another three histories appeared in 1920. The volume covering 50th (Northumbrian) Division was not published until the Second World War began, but with the exception of 43rd (Wessex) and 44th (Home Counties) Divisions, which did not retain divisional structures once they had sailed for India in 1914, 54th (East Anglian,) and 48th (South Midland), all 1st Line TF divisions had a history published by 1927. Even 74th (Yeomanry), which had been formed only in March 1917, and some 2nd Line divisions had also seen their war records appear in print during the first decade after the war.[2] Indeed, by 1940 almost 40 divisional histories of the 75[3] British regular, territorial and new army divisions which existed during the war had been published.

There appears to be no recorded decision as to why 48th (South Midland) Division did not have a history written after the war. It is possible that the six county associations which administered the division's units agreed to support the publication of battalion histories rather than a volume covering the entire formation. This does seem, however, unlikely as many unit histories of other TF divisions appeared alongside

1 Strictly speaking, R.Priestley's *Breaking the Hindenburg Line* (London, 1919) was a record of the division's stunning attack on the *Seigfried Stellung* in September 1918 rather than a complete history of the formation's activities in France and Belgium.

2 Full details of the authors, titles and publication dates of the TF divisional histories will be found in the bibliography.

3 This total includes the 2nd Line Territorial Force divisions, several of which did not serve overseas and which were broken up before the war ended.

those of their parent formation. Neither does it seem likely that there was disunity or a lack of cooperation within the division's county associations about whether a volume should be compiled. While 47th (2nd London) Division had only one association responsible for its administration, the relatively geographically compact six associations involved in running the South Midland were paltry compared to, for example, the 20 involved in organizing 51st (Highland) and the 15 contributing to the 52nd (Lowland) and 53rd (Welsh) Divisions. These more numerous groups managed to coordinate their efforts to contribute to the production of their formations' histories; it is probable that had there been the will amongst the South Midland's associations to publish a single volume, the objective could have been achieved.

Several of the 1st Line divisions had something special to celebrate or describe and this may have been one of the motives for their decision to have their war record written up. 48th (South Midland) did not have the triumph or tragedy of a Riqueval, a High Wood, a Gommecourt, a Thiepval or a Krithia to remember but it had been among the first TF divisions to go abroad and it was the only one to fight in Italy. It was a workhorse division which had fought and suffered on the Somme and at Ypres but without having achieved any really significant success. In this it was no different from many other divisions of the BEF; nonetheless, several of those did subsequently have their activities published. If there was discussion between the chairmen of the six county associations about the issue, even if only after the division had been reformed as part of the Territorial Army in 1920, it seems either to have been informal and thus unrecorded, or the minutes have not survived. It may have been that individual units opted independently to have a history written of their exploits and the issue of a divisional volume was, for whatever reason, never raised.

Several of 48th (South Midland) Division's constituent parts did have their story told in post-war regimental volumes. There is no complete history of the Royal Warwickshire's work during the war although some of its new army battalions have a volume dedicated to their existence. There is also a short history of 143 (Warwickshire) Brigade and two of the regiment's four 1st Line TF battalions also have their own volume.[4] The Buckinghamshire Battalion of the Oxford and Buckinghamshire Light Infantry, 1/4th Oxford and Buckinghamshire Light Infantry and 1/4th Royal Berkshire all have their own separate volumes.[5] None of the three 1st Line battalions of the Gloucestershire Regiment have a discrete volume and receive only fairly

4 T.Carter, *Birmingham Pals: 14th, 15th and 16th (Service) Battalions of the Royal Warwickshire Regiment* (Barnsley: Pen&Sword, 1997); P.Caddick-Adams, *'By God they can fight'. A History of 143rd Infantry Brigade 1908-1995*, (Shrewsbury, 1995); Carrington, *The War Record of the 1/5th Battalion, the Royal Warwickshire Regiment*, (Birmingham: Cornish Bros,1922) ; Compiled, *The History of the 1/6th Battalion the Royal Warwickshire Regiment*, (Birmingham: 1922)

5 P.Wright, *The First Buckinghamshire Battalion 1914-1919* (London, 1920); P.Pickford, *The War Record of the 1/4th Oxfordshire and Buckinghamshire Light Infantry*, (Banbury: 1919); F.Petrie, *The Royal Berkshire Regiment* (Reading: 1925)

brief mentions in Wyrall's regimental history.[6] The two 1st Line battalions of the Worcestershire Regiment are well covered in Stacke's monumental work on the regiment and, in addition, 1/8th Battalion has its own volume.[7] The pioneers of 1/5th Royal Sussex have a short history published but the division's other supporting arms, with the exception of the signal company, appear to have had little if any of their work in print.[8]

These histories served the purpose of recording the units' years of active service and sometimes also its pre-war development through the period of the rifle volunteers. Although primarily intended for those who had fought and for the soldiers' families, they were also aimed at a wider audience. The Territorial Force was disbanded in 1919 but many of those who had served in the active service units or on the committees of the county associations which administered them, campaigned for the force to be reconstituted. They viewed the publication of unit histories, often with a roll of the fallen and a list of honours awarded to the personnel, as a means of conveying the importance of the auxiliary to imperial and home defence. Although published soon after the Territorial Army had been formed, the uncompromising Foreword in Barnett's book, written by the division's last wartime commander, served the same purpose. Lieutenant General Horace Walker warned the nation that it must "look upon the Territorial Army as its main support for defence against aggression."[9] By emphasizing how the TF had so willingly supported the Regular Army in the early years of the war, how its later service had been a crucial factor in the eventual defeat of Germany and its allies, and its continuing importance in an uncertain world, the TF's supporters aimed to demonstrate to the post-war government that its existence remained indispensible to national security.

Like any source, battalion and regimental histories have to be approached with a degree of caution. The speed with which those volumes written for units of 48th Division appeared precluded any real analysis of the actions in which the units had been engaged. That, was not the purpose of the books. Furthermore, the authors of many of them had themselves served in the battalions and, quite naturally, were reluctant to criticize their fellow officers or the men they commanded. There was a slightly different scenario for the relatively small number of authors engaged by regimental committees to write regimental histories. Most of the would-be authors had had some experience of nineteenth century imperial military service and circulated the many regimental committees with a curricula vitae, essentially touting for business. They were usually interviewed before any contract was awarded to ensure the

6 E.Wyrall, *The Gloucestershire Regiment in the Great War 1914-1918* (Methuen, 1931)

7 H.Stacke, *The Worcestershire Regiment in the Great War* (Worcester: Cheshire & Sons, 1929); E.Corbett, *War History of the 1/8th (Territorial) Battalion the Worcestershire Regiment*, (Worcester: 1921)

8 E.Fazan, *The Cinque Ports Battalion*, (Chichester: 1970); F.W.Dopson, *The 48th Division Signal Company in the Great War* (Bristol: Arrowsmith, 1938)

9 G.H.Barnett, *With the 48th Division in Italy* (Edinburgh, 1923) p.xi

story they would tell aligned with the committee's wishes. In contrast, authors of battalion histories were often self-appointed former officers who wanted to see their unit restored and asked for contributions from their colleagues; if an old comrades' association had already been formed they were also likely to seek information from their former soldiers. The authors were concerned to relate the facts as they and their former comrades remembered them in order to demonstrate the identity and wartime comradeship of the unit. This was particularly important to regular and territorial battalions, all of which had long-standing traditions and important local or regional affiliations. If, as it looked possible when the authors were compiling their volumes the Territorial Force was to be reformed, it was assumed it would appear in a different shape and form. With their history dating back to at least the mid-nineteenth century the infantry battalions wanted to remain as infantry battalions and had no wish to be converted to engineers or anti-aircraft units.[10] By stressing in the new age of financial austerity the unit's past wartime successes it was hoped the War Office might be convinced of its continuing worth.

The style and content of the South Midland Division's battalion histories vary. Corbett's account of 1/8th Worcestershire is divided into short sections, contains a number of anecdotes and in places is almost light-hearted in tone. The volume covering 1/6th Warwick was 'compiled' so presumably has contributions from several former soldiers. The prose is in places purple and heroic, while Pickford's work on 1/4th Oxford & Buckinghamshire is workmanlike, factual and with little elaboration. Some of the books are rather more egalitarian than others in their coverage of the officers and other ranks, but this probably reflected the differing offers of assistance and the financial contributions required to get the book published. Like Wright's volume on the Buckinghamshire Battalion, Carrington's work on 1/5th Royal Warwickshire is not all factual gloom and straightforward narrative. Both offer realistic descriptions of the hardships and trauma faced by the troops but also put emphasis on how the local identity and belief in purpose maintained battalion cohesion and morale in the darkest times. The most critical and analytical of the volumes, however, is Cruttwell's work on 1/4th Royal Berkshire. It appeared in 1922, two years later than most of the other volumes and does distance itself from them in its view of how certain aspects of the war were conducted. The book makes full use of the battalion war diary, which is in itself one of the more extensive of the division's units and, like volumes covering other formations which were to be published in the 1920s, wants to ensure the reader understands that if the battalion failed to achieve an objective it was not the fault of the officers and men. The troops did all that was asked of them and more: they attacked when ordered, behaved with courage, resourcefulness and humanity and withstood the privations and horrors of trench warfare with stoic humour and endurance. If they failed, it was because the staff work was faulty or because the objectives

10 This was the 'fate' suffered by several TA battalions in the 1920s. After the Munich Agreement of 1938, several more battalions were converted to armoured or motorized units.

set were beyond the capacity or ability of *any* unit. This was particularly important to territorial units who had for years before the war been subject to the derision and ridicule of certain sections of the Regular Army and the War Office. The territorials had had a point to prove and wanted the volumes to underline the fact that it had, indeed, been proven. The way the battalion had performed in the cauldron of war was also, of course, important to the relatives of those who had fallen and to the men who had fought and survived.

With varying degrees of haste, individual officers and soldiers also began to produce their own memoirs. Some of these did offer an alternative view on the war. Most retold, often with a degree of humour, their author's particular experiences while others were more critical of the politicians and generals and of the strategy and tactics adopted by the leadership. Former members of some of the more fashionable or exclusive TF battalions published, often privately, their reminiscences, but a great many other battalions and units, apart from diaries and memories written and deposited in local or national archives,[11] had nothing publically recorded about them for decades. 48th (South Midland) Division had its share of former officers, such as Barnett, Greenwell, Eberle, Carrington and Vaughan, as well as a small number of other ranks who published their memoirs either privately or publically.[12]

This divisional history does not offer long and detailed descriptions of the ground conditions experienced on the Western Front. Many readers will be readily conversant with the often appalling physical conditions so references to them in this volume are generally only made when necessary to explain a particular tactical or operational situation. It has also deliberately made only limited use of the published battalion histories mentioned above and of the personal diaries deposited elsewhere. Instead, the study has purposefully depended very largely on the war diaries of the division's own units and the corps and armies within which the division fought. As is widely known, the quality, detail and usefulness of war diaries varies considerably from unit to unit; depending upon who wrote them and the circumstances in which they were completed, some have considerably more utility than others. Several include anecdotes and asides while others are excessively brief in content and fact. Despite their flaws and limitations, this present volume does utilize them extensively in order not just to produce a record of what the division did during the war but also to offer some assessment of its worth and quality. Analyzing success or failure is replete with problems, especially when it involves making judgements on the quality of decisions made by human beings. War and man's behaviour in it is an emotive topic and it is dangerous to sit in the safety of peace and security and criticise the actions of men who 100 years

11 The Department of Documents at the Imperial War Museum holds the papers and diaries of about a dozen former members of 48th (South Midland) Division. They range from Brigadier General R.A.Broderick, former OC of 2/(South Midland) Field Ambulance and later Consulting Dental Surgeon to the Army at Home 1944-1952, and Lieutenant Colonel R.J.Clarke, formerly commanding officer of 4/Berkshire, to privates.

12 Full details of these volumes will be found in the bibliography.

ago lived in an environment of fear and filth which can barely be imagined. The role of the historian is not always easy but it is his or her task to be fair and to come to conclusions based on evidence and just consideration. In order to assist in the analysis, regular reference is made to the concepts and vocabulary of current British military doctrine. These include, for example, the need to establish and maintain momentum and tempo, sustainability, flexibility, concentration of force and fighting power.[13]

For reasons of production certain modifications have been agreed. 48th (South Midland) Division was a 1st Line formation of the Territorial Force. As all its component units were 1st Line they are simply referred to throughout as, for example, 4/Berkshire rather than the technically correct 1/4th Royal Berkshire. Where 2nd Line units are mentioned, they are referred to as, for example, 2/4th Berkshire. The Warwickshire, Berkshire and Sussex Regiments all enjoy the prefix 'Royal'. This is omitted in references to them in the text but no slight is, of course, intended. The Buckinghamshire Battalion The Oxford and Buckinghamshire Light Infantry is referred to either as 'the Bucks' or '1/Bucks'. The division's field companies, artillery brigades and field ambulances were all originally known by the area from which they were raised or simply by a number with 'South Midland' as part of its title. In 1915, the titles were changed to numbers so, for example, I South Midland Brigade RFA became CCXL (240) and 2/South Midland Field Company RE became 475th (1/2nd South Midland) Field Company RE. The new designations for the Royal Field Artillery (RFA) brigades are used in the text from June 1915 and for the Royal Engineer (RE) field companies from February 1917 but the original familiar numbers are retained for the Royal Army Medical Corps (RAMC) field ambulances. Hence, 1/2nd (South Midland) Field Ambulance is listed simply as 2/Field Ambulance.

In order to avoid an inordinate and overwhelming number of footnotes, direct quotations from war diaries of division level and below are not referenced. In addition to army and corps war diaries there are almost 40 separate diaries written by divisional units. The decision not to cite the source for every short quotation in the text may raise eyebrows among some readers but it is often evident from the prose as to where the origin of the source actually lies.[14] The decision to adopt this practice for the war diaries has been made entirely on practical grounds but where quotations from secondary sources are used they are fully referenced. Similarly, quotations from primary sources, such as War Office papers and corps or army war diaries rather than those of units belonging to the division itself, are also referenced.

13 In modern British doctrine, fighting power provides the army with its ability to operate and fight. It consists of a conceptual component (the ideas behind how to operate and fight), the physical component (the means to operate and fight) and the moral component (the ability to get people to operate and fight). Military effectiveness in battle comes from harmonizing all three components.

14 A full list of The National Archives (TNA) War Office reference numbers is given in the bibliography.

1

The Pre-War Division

Like the other 13 divisions of the Territorial Force (TF), the South Midland Division came in to existence as a result of an extensive series of reforms undertaken by the Liberal administration during the first decade of the twentieth century. Richard Haldane, the Secretary of State for War, initiated the reforms with the objective of improving the efficiency of both the regular and the auxiliary forces. Changes to the regular forces were developed from earlier reforms, but the battalions, artillery, engineer companies and other units of the old Volunteer movement were swept away and replaced by the newly created Territorial Force. The new units were to be administered, clothed, equipped and partially horsed by TF County Associations but, in a bid to make them considerably more militarily efficient than the Volunteers they replaced, the new organization was to be trained by permanent staff of the regular forces working under the authority and supervision of the War Office.

The number of units to be raised and administered by each county association depended on the size of the particular county's population. With an establishment of over 18,000 men, a TF division was composed of 12 battalions of infantry, four brigades of artillery, two field companies, three field ambulances and several other supporting arms. The component units of the South Midland Division were to be raised by the Gloucestershire, Worcestershire, Warwickshire, Oxfordshire, Buckinghamshire and Berkshire associations. Each association was to raise a regiment of yeomanry while, among other units, Warwickshire was to provide one infantry brigade of four battalions, four batteries of Royal Horse and Field Artillery (RHA and RFA), a brigade of heavy artillery (RGA), one mounted and two other field ambulances; Gloucestershire was to provide three battalions, three RFA batteries, two field companies of engineers and the remaining field ambulance; Worcestershire two battalions, and three batteries of RFA. The remaining three battalions were raised by each of the other three associations with the ammunition columns, the transport and supply columns of the Army Supply Corps (ASC), the various signal companies, clearing hospitals and other assorted units being distributed across the six associations.[1]

The county associations officially assumed their responsibilities in April 1908. Supporters of the new force, however, knew there were many in the War Office, the Regular Army and the public in general who wanted the experiment of a volunteer auxiliary for home defence to fail. Originally, Haldane had intended the TF to be the means by which the Regular Army could be reinforced and expanded but for reasons of political expediency he was forced to compromise. The result was that the TF was designated only for home defence. The detractors, a disparate group of substantial size and influence which included many who had been intimately involved with the Volunteers and who now resented the creation of the TF, believed the money allocated to the auxiliary would be far better spent on the regular forces. The unfortunate and mistrustful beginning to the relationship between the War Office and the county associations continued and remained one of the principal reasons why in the years before the war the TF's efficiency was regarded with such suspicion.

If the South Midland Division was to become an efficient and capable formation, able to play its part in defeating any invasion of the East Coast, the country associations and their men knew it had to be adequately clothed, booted, equipped, horsed and militarily trained. There were several issues which repeatedly soured relations with the military authorities and which regularly helped to convince many in the TF that the War Office thought little of the auxiliary's worth. The War Office was notoriously slow to reply to associations' letters and queries, an issue which consistently caused anxiety and annoyance among the local committee members. Many such members were local businessmen, used to receiving immediate replies from customers or suppliers; tardy responses were, to them, anathema. Delays in War Office administration caused the Warwickshire Association, for example, to lose the opportunity to obtain a good site for a drill hall and Gloucestershire Association had long, heated and inconclusive exchanges with the War Office concerning accommodation for the field ambulances in Bristol. There were frequent disagreements over who should pay for facilities and manning at brigade headquarters and over what salary associations could pay their secretaries and permanent staffs. Warwickshire became so incensed with the War Office's apparent reluctance or inability to furnish sufficient wagons for its units that it eventually decided to defy the authorities' strictures and bought far more of their own than the regulations allowed. It also declined a rather insensitive and clumsy War Office invitation to raise a cyclist battalion on the very reasonable grounds that the unit was not intended for use with the South Midland Division.

1 Most of the following examples of the work undertaken by the county associations are taken from the minute books of the six associations. Details of their locations and collection references will be found in the bibliography. For further discussion of the trials and tribulations of the pre-war Territorial Force in its relationship with the War Office, see, K.W. Mitchinson, *England's Last Hope* (Basingstoke: Palgrave Macmillan, 2008).

An earlier pre-war request by the War Office for the South Midland Division's TF county associations to raise a cyclist company had been refused by the associations. The company was finally raised in December 1914. (Private collection)

Another very contentious issue was the supply of horses. Like other industrial, and to a lesser extent rural, areas of the United Kingdom the South Midlands was undergoing the slow transition towards mechanical transport. The War Office was keen that whenever possible TF supply columns should adopt motor transport. Useful as they were, however, it was accepted that motor vehicles would be unable to replace horsed transport in all units for many years to come. The horse establishment of an infantry division such as the South Midland was close to 4,200 animals. Even infantry battalions needed 74 horses, a RFA brigade a little under 300 and a field ambulance 70. County association committees consequently devoted a considerable amount of their time and energies in attempting to identify horses in their areas which could be requisitioned on mobilization. In addition, and in order to try to ensure they had a nucleus of trained horses, many associations bought a number of animals and either kept them in riding schools or contracted them out for work and care to local farmers and dealers. There were constant disputes between associations and the farmers over the amount of money paid and the quality of the variable accommodation they provided.[2] Individual associations tried different methods and means of establishing a nucleus but were often foiled by a shortage of custodians, the apparent obduracy of the War Office, and a lack of money. Following the success of using their own, trained horses at camp, Gloucestershire Association congratulated itself for having the foresight to buy sufficient horses for its two RE field companies but when it proposed to buy 36 as a nucleus for the Bristol RFA batteries, the War Office refused it permission. In anger, the association minuted, "Any inefficiency in the Royal Field Artillery will be the responsibility entirely of the War Office."

Money was always a difficult issue. Many in the Regular Army thought grants to the auxiliary were too generous and frequently accused the counties of profligacy. This was rarely, in fact, the case because the businessmen in the associations understood the need for prudence and for living within a budget. Although many unit commanding officers regularly and at times irresponsibly badgered the association treasurer for grants for weekend camps and new uniforms or kit, most associations even managed to establish a reserve. Gloucestershire Association did, however, admit that it had been too "extravagant" in its provision for bands, prizes and officers' camp baggage. In a testy letter the War Office complained that in financial terms the association was very near to the bottom of association league tables and stressed the "urgent necessity of retrenchment." In response, the association declared that it would "clear ourselves of the reproach that we are more extravagant than our neighbours."

Annual camp was another issue riven with difficulties. The South Midland attempted to arrange a divisional camp in 1908, but unless it could be held on Salisbury Plain the administration of organizing such a huge affair was almost beyond the means of associations. The most that could normally be expected was a brigade camp of a fortnight but it was more usual for individual battalions to go off to camp alone. It was rare even for the four Royal Warwickshire battalions in the Warwickshire Brigade to be able to agree on dates which suited them all; it was even rarer for the artillery and yeomanry to be available at the same time as the infantry and thus be able to take part in joint exercises. The number of horses required for a brigade camp and the number of farmers and tenants who needed to agree to their land being used or crossed made such events all but impossible. Trying to get the disparate units of the South Midland and the Gloucestershire and Worcestershire Infantry Brigades to agree on dates was also virtually impossible. Employers were often reluctant to release employees for a fortnight and the men themselves had to be prepared to sacrifice almost their entire holiday entitlement if they were to attend for what was meant to be

2 Whenever they could, associations tried to hire horses from the same providers every year. For example, Gloucestershire hired 100 yearly from the Birmingham Omnibus Company. It was always pleased with the quality of the animals but, with regret, felt it had to look elsewhere when the bus company decided to join a horse traders' association which aimed to increase the prices they charged associations.

a compulsory period. The reported sacking of men, such as five of II South Midland Brigade RFA by their employers because they had had the temerity to attend camp, was not unusual.[3] Oxfordshire Association declared that employers in its area had a "satisfactory" attitude to camp attendance but did also attempted to arrange its camp dates to suit the Clarendon Press, one of the largest employers in the county and one which raised a company of 4/Ox&Bucks. Worcestershire acknowledged the county's borough and municipal authorities were extremely sympathetic in their attitude while Gloucestershire was grateful for its employers' "considerable concessions." Regular Army brigade commanders, such as the General Officer Commanding (GOC) South Midland Brigade, could add to the difficulties of trying to get the full two weeks attendance by the insensitive practice of announcing at short notice that the date of the camp was being changed unilaterally. There was little which annoyed the county committees more than this total lack of understanding of the difficulties faced by associations. If the target number of animals required for camp could ever actually be realized, the cost of horse hire alone for the fortnight amounted to almost £7,000 for the Warwickshire Association. To have to lose that amount of money and incur a multitude of other cancellation costs was too much for the associations and it is little wonder they accused the War Office of crass arrogance.

The Regular Army frequently reported on what was described as the dreadful standard of TF musketry. Territorials took a less demanding test than their regular counterparts, which added to the criticism, but it was only in 1912 that associations were allowed to pay travel expenses and provide rations for troops who had probably given up an afternoon's overtime to attend a range practice. South Midland territorials were generally not lacking in enthusiasm to shoot; the problem was finding sufficient range accommodation to allow them to shoot regularly. Local residents close to existing ranges objected to Sunday firing and the difficulties encountered when attempting to acquire land to build a new range at times seemed insurmountable. Warwickshire struggled for years to obtain permission to construct a 1,000 yard range at Kingsbury, Gloucestershire eventually had to rely on the local council rather than the War Office to buy land for a range near Tewkesbury, while Worcestershire was grateful for the generosity of a landowner who offered to lease his land for a nominal sum. After four years of disappointing negotiations over rights concerning existing footpaths and access across other fields, Oxfordshire Association finally abandoned its proposal to build a range at Noke.

Shooting arrangements, horses and the provision of facilities at drill halls consumed great tranches of committees' time but the issue which usually dominated meetings of General Purpose Committees was the question of recruitment and retention. Many county associations had been disappointed by the low number of Volunteers who

3 Worcestershire Association wrote to the men's respective employers to complain of their action. One man was re-employed, two were found not to have been sacked and the employers of the other men did not respond to the letter.

opted to transfer to the new TF in April 1908. Former Volunteers were offered special terms of service if they did transfer but Birmingham, like most areas, suffered from the Volunteer movement's sense of betrayal by the military authorities. It is probable that only 30 percent of the city's approximately 2,700 Volunteers did decide to transfer but within 15 months, the four battalions of the Warwickshire Brigade were not far from establishment.[4] This, again, echoed what was occurring across the country. The largely tabloid press induced "invasion scare" of 1909 acted as a major stimulus to TF recruitment but by 1912-13 those men who had joined at the peak of the "scare" would have served their four year term of enlistment. County associations realized the need to retain both as many of these trained men as possible and also to continue to recruit new volunteers.

County associations tried a huge and varied number of schemes designed to improve recruitment and retention. Most of these involved financial outlay but were considered to be a necessary and worthwhile expense. The associations of the South Midland Division were not the most innovative but were prepared to experiment with schemes which ranged from a constant effort to improve drill facilities and ceremonial parades through the local towns, to notices in parish newsletters and advertisements in factories and post offices. Oxfordshire Association thought it would be useful if the patriotic play, *An Englishman's Home*, which had done so much to encourage recruiting in the capital, could be performed in Oxford. The committee also proposed that as there were continuing problems in recruiting in the county's larger towns, the War Office should allow the formation of more rural companies and detachments. Warwickshire wanted to go a stage further and suggested the creation of local recruiting committees working under the authority of the central administration. Given the amount of time and energy devoted to the recruitment issue, what was especially galling was any unjustified criticism from the military authorities. Gloucestershire Association was particularly annoyed when the division's GOC, Major General Raitt, condemned the quality of two of the county's battalions and what he perceived to be poor recruiting methods employed by the committee. In 1914, Worcestershire believed a golden opportunity to improve the profile and status of the TF had come when it was announced Regular Army manoeuvres were to be held in the county. Eager to exploit the opportunity, the association petitioned the War Office to allow units of the Worcestershire TF to take some part alongside the regulars. The proposal was,

4 R.D. Williams, *A Social and Military History of the 1/8th Battalion The Royal Warwickshire Regiment in The Great War.* (Unpublished MPhil, University of Birmingham, 1999) The infantry were also doing quite well in the other associations of the South Midland Division. In September 1909, the Warwickshire battalions were at 98 percent, Worcestershire and 4/Berkshire at 91 percent and 1/Bucks at 87 percent of establishment. With 85 percent of establishment, 8/Worcestershire had the dubious honour of being the lowest of any battalion in Southern Command. Worcestershire RO: 004.6 BA5204/5, 17 Sep. 1909.

however, promptly snubbed by the War Office. This left the association to minute its disappoint at the lack of official "encouragement" for the TF.[5]

The frustrations with the attitude of the War Office experienced by associations across the country came to head in 1913. Among others, the West Riding Association circulated a list of proposals aimed at improving terms of service for TF soldiers. The scheme was far-reaching and imaginative and attracted a great deal of interest among associations as well as the military authorities. Worcestershire Association quickly announced its support for the scheme but Warwickshire submitted its own series of amendments. In the same way, however, as the associations believed the War Office was less than cooperative and largely unappreciative of the work done by the county committees, the War Office interpreted the existing discontent as yet more evidence that associations were failing to understand what a drain the inconvenient TF had on the Army Estimates. The other essential problem was that the army was unused to working with civilians. There was certainly a lack of empathy at times on the part of both camps but the enthusiasm and determination of the associations to fulfil what they regarded as their civic and patriotic duty meant the War Office was constantly bombarded with suggestions and complaints by amateurs who, the Regular Army thought, had little understanding of how things should be done. Although the county associations did have military members, these members were officers commanding the various units and were, very largely, former Volunteers rather than former Regular Army. The bulk of the other members were professional men and entrepreneurs who were used to making decisions quickly and having them swiftly acted upon. While improvements had been made since the Boer War in the way the War Office worked, the process of implementing new policy or ideas remained inherently slow. The resulting mistrust and suspicion between the two sides did little to enhance the status of the TF or to impress the Regular Army with its efficiency.

The War Office and regulars used the annual reports on TF camps as evidence that the force would be of little use in an invasion of the UK.[6] Since its formation there had been an expectation that a six month mobilization period would allow training to be completed and new recruits absorbed. The danger expressed by many was that a putative enemy might not allow this mobilization period to be enjoyed untroubled by serious amphibious raids or even a full-scale invasion. The South Midland Division came under the control of Southern Command, the GOC of which, General Douglas, appeared to endorse the view of the doubters. He considered the infantry under his command led such a sedentary life they were incapable of enduring any prolonged periods of hardship and also believed they would be more susceptible to disease than the regulars. Reports suggested their physique was poor and would require a concentrated period of PT to get them fit and, as evidence that they marched badly, described the road to camp as usually littered with those who had fallen out. The

5 The Worcestershire Yeomanry was eventually allowed to attend the manoeuvres.
6 TNA: WO32.9192: Efficiency of Territorial Force compared to Regular Army, 1911.

yeomanry were assessed as superior in class and intellect to the regular cavalry but it was thought they would probably fail to care adequately for themselves and their horses. They rode well but were condemned for apparently lacking initiative. The usual regulars' complaint about the poor quality of TF NCOs was frequently reiterated; artillery units were thought to show potential, if the enemy allowed them time to train and develop, but the belief persisted that real improvement would only be achieved if regulars were appointed to command brigades and batteries. Much the same assessment was also made about the quality of the division's officers. "Most" of the junior regimental commanders were condemned as "not fit to command in war, either to lead their men or to look after their comfort and supply in bivouac." Unit commanding officers (COs), however, were considered to be keen and would improve further once the policy of appointing regulars as brigade commanders and brigade majors had had time to take effect. They were, thought General Douglas, "as good as we can hope to obtain."

The issue of who should be appointed to command TF divisions and brigades had long exercised the minds of senior officers in the War Office. A report of January 1912 considered there had been "little, if any, increase in TF value during the last two years."[7] There was a general consensus within the War Office, however, that once the policy of appointing Regular Army colonels from the Active List to command TF infantry and cavalry brigades, as well as regular lieutenant colonels to TF artillery brigades and batteries, improvements would soon become evident. In accordance with this policy, by mid-1912 the South Midland Division had received a new divisional GOC, three new infantry brigade commanders and new commanders for the divisional artillery and engineers. Only one of these men, Lieutenant Colonel Sinnott, the commander of the Royal Engineers, (CRE) was a territorial. Major General Thorneycroft, who had replaced Brigadier General Raitt, the division's first GOC, was despatched to the Retired List and replaced by Major General Keir of the Royal Artillery. Keir had been commissioned in 1876 and had spent the previous seven years before his appointment in India. His knowledge and understanding of the TF and its soldiers was, therefore, somewhat questionable. Keir's brigade commanders, all full colonels, were already in post when he arrived at the division. Colonels James, Daubeney and McClintock were commissioned between 1878 and 1882 and were appointed to command from the Half Pay List. The first two had previous experience of working with either the Militia or Volunteers and all three had spent time in imperial service. Colonel Prinsep, commanding the Royal Artillery (CRA) was a contemporary of the infantry brigade commanders and had previously spent six years as adjutant to a Volunteer artillery unit. The size and number of the staffs appointed to these commanders is unclear but if the regulations were followed the three infantry and artillery commanders would each have had a regular soldier as their brigade major and a small administrative staff. It was the task of these commanders to weld a division with six independently minded

7 TNA: WO32.9192: Aug.1912.

county associations and nearly 40 disparate and dispersed units equipped with obsolete weapons into an efficient formation capable of playing its part in defeating any invasion or raid. The units were commandeered by officers unused to taking orders from regulars, junior officers and NCOs who were generally considered to be inadequate for their task and a fairly transient body of indifferently trained other ranks.

The 12 infantry battalions comprised about two-thirds of the South Midland Division's personnel. Being a mixture of both urban and rural units they were typical of most TF divisions. Their men were drawn from the artisan class, the working class and a sprinkling of white collar clerks and student teachers. Between them they possessed a wide cross section of civilian trades and skills, but there was a general shortage of wheelwrights, smiths and farriers. Three of the Warwickshire battalions were recruited from within Birmingham and Aston, with two sharing the same central drill hall. The 7th Battalion was a more dispersed unit, with four companies drawn from Coventry and the other four from elsewhere in the country. Two of the Gloucestershire battalions were concentrated in Bristol with the other, like 7/Warwick and the two Worcestershire battalions, recruited from a much wider and area which encompassed rural and urban settlements. 4/Ox&Bucks and the Buckinghamshire Battalion each had several dispersed companies with further attached drill stations, as did 4/Berkshire, whose drill halls and stations were spread over the entire county. Those battalions which had a central drill hall where men could parade together regularly and enjoy communal messing and recreation could more easily develop a unit identity. Although the company or platoon remained the main focus for these urban troops, the nature of the isolation on drill nights and even sometimes musketry sessions and route marches meant soldiers in the dispersed units were even more company and platoon orientated than their centrally based colleagues. TF companies of battalions based in city centres were often composed of men who worked in the same factory, office or for the same firm. These could include, for example, a local brewery, the town corporation, a teacher training college or the area's coal and gas supplier. This was indeed the case for 8/Warwick. In rural companies men were often drawn from the same large estate or small companies working within similar trades or industries. Reports by the Inspector-General did often criticize the officers of this type of company as men who only happened to be in command because they were the employer or landlord of many of the other ranks. Nonetheless, their admittedly often flawed leadership and sometimes eccentric personalities did help to build their platoon or company into a bonded and cohesive unit. What was crucial to this development was, of course, their ability to retain their men for at least their initial term of four years.

Unit commanders of both town and rural battalions were generally men who enjoyed high status in local and provincial society: Lieutenant Colonel Martineau of 6/Warwickshire, for example, was a solicitor and former Lord Mayor of Britain's second city; Sir John Barnsley, until April 1914 CO of 5/Warwickshire, ran a huge building and engineering concern. The majority were drawn from the upper middle-class and included such professions as architects, lawyers and factory owners. With the exception of yeomanry regiments, which could often contain a few sons of Lords of the Realm and a smattering of MPs, most TF COs generally came from the same social class as their junior officers. Indeed, most commanders of units in the South Midland Division had been commissioned into their battalion, battery or field company and, over many years of Volunteer and TF service, had been promoted to CO. In July 1914, this applied to the four battalion COs comprising the Gloucestershire and Worcestershire Brigade, all of whom had been in post since at least April 1911; it was the same story for two COs in the South Midland and one in the Warwickshire Brigades. The five COs who had been appointed since 1912 had all served as majors in their respective battalions. The majority of these COs, like Lieutenant Colonel Young of 3/South Midland Field Ambulance, had served 20 years or more with the same unit. As commanding officers they sat by right on their county association General Purposes Committee and were thus intimately involved in the decision making of their association. This did not, however, preclude them from sometimes showing what their associations and the War Office considered an alarming independence when it came to ordering equipment and demanding building alterations.[8]

The same consistency of service is also apparent in the service of the (usually) two majors in each battalion and the supposed eight company commanders. All of the division's 21 majors in post in July 1914 had been promoted from within their own battalion. Furthermore, in the South Midland Brigade, for example, all but one of the 28 serving company commanders had been promoted from within. A similar picture also appears in the three brigades of RFA and the two field companies RE. In the RFA, the three brigade and nine battery commanders, as well as the nine second-in-commands, had been with their unit since at least 1910; in the RE, seven of 11 officers in July 1914 had been with their unit for at least three years. The support and service of these high profile civic figures, together with the Lord Lieutenant as President and often a member of the local aristocracy as Chairman, were seen as crucial to the development and strength of the TF.

Of the 14 TF divisions on the eve of war, only the North Midland Division was closer to establishment than the South Midland. The South Midland's infantry brigades were 83 percent and 90 percent of establishment in officers and other ranks. The six yeomanry regiments administered by the six county associations were even closer to full strength and the other supporting arms had also been recruiting well. The associations had, despite the tension sometimes experienced between them and the divisional commander, provided the men with kit and equipment and had a system of separation allowances in place should mobilization ever be called. They had made difficult decisions about how their men should be equipped, for example Worcestershire had opted to buy Mills webbing by reducing the amount spent on recreation rooms, and there remained potentially disruptive obstacles such as the

8 For example, in 1911 the CO of 4/Gloucestershire made a unilateral decision to alter the previously agreed plans for his drill hall. Annoyed at not having been consulted, Gloucestershire Association refused to pay the additional cost of £37 10s.

provision of transport to be overcome. In July 1914, Warwickshire Association was financing a number of building and improvement projects which ranged from new drill halls and riding schools to the construction of several firing ranges. This scale of activity was nothing exceptional. Some of the associations had trialled the mobilization process and had envelopes already addressed; commanding officers knew the location of their units' war stations and the timetable by which they would be reached; the official *War Book* identified how and where the units would be resupplied and accommodated. What remained unanswered, however, were the crucial questions of how well trained the units would prove to be and how quickly they would respond if an enemy launched a swift invasion or large scale raid.

Nationally, the TF was accused of being plagued by the youth and inexperience of its personnel. Only a very small percentage of the four-year men re-enlisted in 1912 and 1913 but it was assumed that if mobilization were ever called these trained men would quickly re-appear. That assumption had still to be proved. Haldane's earlier hope that the TF would be the means of expanding the army if an expeditionary force left the shores showed little sign of materializing. The South Midland Division might have been close to establishment but the number of men who had agreed to serve overseas was minimal. In 5/Warwickshire and 7/Warwickshire, a combined total of only one officer and 15 other ranks (ORs) had agreed to what was called "imperial service"; in the entire Gloucestershire and Worcestershire Brigade the total was a mere 14 officers and 333 ORs. The yeomanry showed slightly more enthusiasm but the three regiments of 1st South Midland Mounted Brigade could muster a total of only 31 officers and 199 ORs who had agreed to serve overseas. The surviving returns of the other units made for similarly depressing reading for the authorities. Being a member of the TF entailed financial loss, considerable time commitment and, if married, a disrupted home life. The men had, after all, enlisted for home defence. To expect them to volunteer for overseas service in addition to their other responsibilities was expecting rather too much. That was why, for example, Lieutenant Colonel Innes, CO of 8/Warwickshire, was one of many senior TF officers who were heavily involved in their local branches of the National Service League, a pressure group which aimed to conscript men for home and possible foreign service. Nonetheless, there was a great deal of enthusiasm and commitment within all ranks of the TF. Officers and probably many of the longer serving men knew the Regular Army thought little of the force's worth and were aware of the frequent jibes in the press about its alleged deficiencies. The men had sacrificed their leisure time and often their own money to achieve a degree of efficiency which they believed would be the foundation on which to build should mobilization be called. As the units and personnel of the South Midland Division prepared for camp in early August 1914, many would have known that the Precautionary Period, in which TF cyclists and some other personnel were put on alert, had been announced. The South Midlanders possibly had little idea about the actual respective strengths of the other 13 TF divisions but probably did know their own units were close to establishment and, weapons apart, had been generally well equipped by their county associations.

2

Mobilization & Trench Acclimatization

During the afternoon of 4 August the telegram announcing the embodiment of the TF arrived at drill halls across the country. Many TF units, including most of the infantry of the South Midland Division, were away at camp when the orders arrived. The Gloucestershire and Worcestershire Brigade, for example, had only recently arrived at Minehead, and the Warwickshire Brigade had just detrained at Rhyl. When the mobilization orders were received, TF units at camp returned quickly to their home towns and put into effect the plans locked away in the COs' safes. The mobilization schemes for the infantry brigades were to embody at their drill halls before marching to war stations. There, in theory, they would spend about six months getting up to establishment and completing their training. If an invasion ever did take place, the South Midland Division was part of the Central Force's Third Army.[1] The division was scheduled to assemble at Swindon, although 5/Gloucestershire was detailed to spend a few days on the Isle of White before joining the rest of the division in Wiltshire. After a few days digging and reorganization, the units travelled by train and march route to villages deep in the Essex countryside around Chelmsford. This move was in itself a severe test of the stamina of the troops and of their ability to transport a motley collection of impressed wagons and horses to the war stations. This initial trial, difficult as it was would, however, prove to be less demanding than those which were to follow in subsequent weeks and months.

With units and companies dispersed over a wide area of southern Essex, the difficulties of ensuring proper medical and veterinary care for men and animals were significant. In peacetime, TF COs complained regularly of the inadequate number of medical officers and vets, with the result that in this initial period of mobilization provision for men and beasts was at times less than satisfactory. Any man suffering from an ailment which could not be dealt with adequately by a field ambulance was likely to be sent to a civilian hospital. After treatment the hospital, which was usually in London, might decide to send the man on sick leave but its doctors had no

1 Third Army HQ was in Luton.

responsibility to inform the soldier's battalion of the decision. COs were thus often in ignorance of what had happened to the man and railed against the perceived "slip-shod" administration of the hospitals. There was no proper provision for the effective isolation of infectious cases, although by January 1915, 4/Gloucestershire had hired a cottage for the purpose of accommodating those men who were not sufficiently ill to be admitted to hospital. There were occasional cases of cerebra-meningitis and the poor billeting in barns and empty houses caused regular outbreaks of flu and mumps. Medical officers were short of drugs and other necessities and at times became reliant on charitable donations from Bristol and Birmingham. This was appreciated but also condemned as having been necessary in the first place. It was not until February 1915 that more than half the infantry were actually housed in huts; their less fortunate comrades who were still in scattered barns and houses continued to suffer from a lack of heating and drying facilities. Lanterns and stoves were bought from private and regimental funds but overcrowding remained a problem and did little to improve discipline or to build group identity.

The shortage of vets led to calls that individual units should at least be supplied with a veterinary chest containing basic necessities for horse care. It was argued that should there be men in an infantry battalion who had some idea of horsemanship, the contents of the chest and the men's rudimentary knowledge might at least be able to help the stricken animal until professional help was secured. Cast horses were slow to be replaced and those few units which did receive a reasonable number of light and heavy draught animals were frequently forced to stable them in poor conditions. The lack of horsemanship and adequate stabling caused more casualties and thus, the eventual arrival of replacements which were barely trained. Ten days before it embarked, II South Midland Brigade RFA, for example, was forced to send away 82 horses for various reasons. Twenty-one remounts arrived four days later with the remaining beasts being received even closer to the date of departure. 3/Field Ambulance had a similar experience, with 11 of its heavy draught horses arriving only four days before departure. In the infantry, three battalions of one brigade were still short of heavy and light draught animals in late March; in another brigade nearly 40 percent of its establishment of almost 340 horses only arrived within 10 days of embarkation. The provision of riding mounts was equally difficult. One staff captain complained bitterly that ponies of a mere 12 hands were being supplied as chargers for officers who were over six feet tall. The arrival of riding horses did on the other hand offer some amusement to the troops. Two battalion histories recall the "many amusing episodes" concerning attempts by officers to learn to ride, and the introduction of a "new game" which involved guessing the number of times the company commander would fall from his mount.[2] The shortage of all types of horses, however, meant that even if a

2 P.Pickford, *The War Record of the 1/4th Oxford & Buckinghamshire L.I.* p. 2; Compiled, *History of 1/6th Warwickshire*, p. 6.

unit or formation did possess a good proportion of its wagons and other vehicles it was probably unable to have them all on a route march at the same time.

Route marches for horsed units were an essential part of the training process. It was not only the familiarity that came with working with new animals and vehicles but also the need to practise the secure packing of loads and maintenance of working wagons. Unsurprisingly, the eclectic armada of wagons which had wended its untutored way across Southern England to Essex was found to be totally inadequate for the purposes required. When they arrived at their war stations most vehicles, including the essential water carts, were immediately condemned and indents for replacements dispatched. COs made repeated requests for these to be sent as swiftly as possible particularly because unit transport sections were having to cover miles between their dispersed companies. It was not, however, until well into the new year that even small numbers of replacement wagons began to appear. Even when they did arrive they usually came without harness and saddles for their animals. This caused a fresh flurry of dire warnings by COs that if these crucial pieces of equipment were to appear only on the eve of departure, chaos would ensure as inexperienced men and horses attempted to make sense of complicated harness. This did, in fact, prove to be the case. One brigade commander subsequently asserted that attempting to get men and animals used to new harness in such a short time was "one of the greatest difficulties" of the mobilization period. Units only received their full quota of harness within a week or so of departure which meant that time which could have been better spent in training was necessarily devoted to spending hours greasing harness and then trying to fathom how to fit them to often reluctant animals. It was only in February 1915 that infantry brigade transport columns were able at least to begin supplying their outlying units with rations drawn from central depots. This had the futher advantage of helping to reduce the number of complaints about the filthy state of Army Supply Corps wagons, their perpetual unpunctuality and the casualness of drivers who took little care in how they delivered rations. It also meant that at least a proportion of the division's crews could engage in practical training.

The rations themselves were not particularly inadequate, but simply monotonous. Unit commanders complained of the inordinate quantities of jam, much of which was deemed to be of poor quality, and requested supplies of butter and potatoes. Bread was often delivered sodden and fresh meat and vegetables were frequently in short supply. Unlike the wealthier families of men in some battalions of several other TF divisions, those of the South Midland could generally ill-afford to send their men parcels to supplement their army rations. Comforts committees were established by the county associations and although they did provide vital help were never as financially well endowed as, for example, some of the more fashionable London or Liverpool battalions. Appeals for additional comforts were also made through official channels but the TF had long experience of the length of time it took central authority to respond to requests. The War Office was, of course, also trying to house, feed and equip the expanding New Armies and, in a strange reversal of roles, its insistence on immediate replies to its administrative demands was extremely frustrating for TF commanders.

There were constant complaints about the "endless" bureaucracy which cascaded from Whitehall. Among the most annoying was, despite showers of associated forms, a lack of clarity about how men should physically be paid. In addition to frustrating adjutants and paymasters this also affected troops' morale. Requests from units to higher authority for copies of Army Orders in book form went unheeded; this added to the problems of understanding what it was the authorities actually expected or wanted. Frequent references were made in correspondence from Whitehall to orders in the books but without copies of the volumes unit officials had no idea to what the demands referred. In ironic vein, the CO of one unit decided, "The only simplification [in administration methods] is that correspondence for Third Army now goes not in duplicate but in quadruplicate."

The traditional belief among TF members that the War Office evinced little sympathy with the movement as a whole was exacerbated when the New Armies were formed. The perception was that Kitchener formations received priority in the issue of kit and equipment. The CO of 8/Worcestershire spoke for many when he complained, "It seems unfair that we should not receive the same facilities for training as the New Army." Rather than being able to conduct what it considered to be more suitable training, the Gloucestershire and Worcestershire Brigade resented the time it spent digging the London Defences. This was a task, it believed, which should have been allocated to reserve units rather than to battalions preparing for deployment.[3] It accepted that digging itself was a useful activity but felt that it should not have had to finish work abandoned by other units and argued that if the Royal Engineers had supplied proper tools and equipment the task would have been finished sooner, This, it protested, would have allowed more time for other types of training. The lack of equipment, kit, serviceable rifles and artillery pieces, as well as the seemingly interminable cold and wet weather, severely hampered training during the winter months. It seems likely that the RFA brigades had only one period of nine days training on Salisbury Plain, and those were spent in the depths of January. The acute shortage of shells meant that the 15 pdr and 5 inch batteries were allocated only 50 shells and the 4.7 inch guns even fewer. When they returned to their Essex billeting areas they could usually undertake only trial 'alarm' exercises with skeleton crews and batteries. The CRA conducted a few tactical exercises with brigade and battery commanders and delivered the odd lecture but most of the men's time was spent in drills, specialist training and, from March when the gunners were rearmed with rifles firing Mark VII ammunition, on musketry courses. Officers went on courses about cooperation with aerial spotting but there is only one recorded exercise which involved more than one battery working with an infantry brigade.

3 The Gloucestershire and Worcestershire Brigade, comprising 4/ and 6/Gloucestershire and 7/ and 8/Worcestershire, is fairly unusual in that it has left a war diary of the period before it deployed overseas. Many of the quotations and points which follow are taken from this war diary. TNA: WO95.2757.

The field ambulances did certainly undertake some field exercises with the infantry and were also responsible for assessing the fitness for overseas service of the division's officers. The ambulances spent most of the time, however, on route and concentration marches, kit inspections, practising how to erect and dismantle tents, on basic drills, listening to lectures on "Discipline", "The War", care of the wounded and general hygiene. As an adjunct to the ambulances the divisional sanitation section was formed in February 1915. Its officer commanding (OC), Captain Dale, visited all divisional units inspecting their water carts and lecturing on sanitation procedures. He worked under the direction of the Assistant Director of Medical Services (ADMS), who was sometimes joined on his tours of the units' billeting areas by the Assistant Director of Veterinary Services (ADVS). Although their war diaries are silent on what training they undertook, it is probable that the Royal Engineer (RE) field companies concentrated on rapid wiring, excavating trenches and dugouts, drainage, water supply and constructing hard standings and ablution facilities.

Like the other arms, the infantry trained as best as they could with their existing kit and facilities. Initially, division and brigade HQs laid down what they wanted battalions to do and then let them get on with it, albeit subject to inspections and observations by senior commanders. Because battalions remained in their eight company format until January 1915, the company commanders under whom their men had often enlisted were responsible for the training process. As one officer remembered, "Training started in earnest from the very bottom."[4] Adjutants, with their Regular Army background and experience, were supposed to supervise but there were constant complaints that they were so over-burdened with administrative work they could not devote adequate time to training. Besides, several adjutants returned to their own units in September together with many if not all of the permanent staff (PS). The loss of these trained soldiers was another blow to battalions attempting to absorb new recruits and improve existing skills. To heighten the sense of grievance felt by many TF supporters, rather than rejoining their own battalion some PS were sent instead to train the New Armies. To add further fuel to the dissatisfaction, the TF was told that as there were sufficient former teachers within their ranks used to giving drill instruction in schools, the territorials could look after themselves.[5] Until January, when brigade training began to take precedence over company and then battalion training, OC companies and platoons did what they could from *Field Service Regulations 1* and other training manuals published by former Regular Army officers. The problems they faced were severe: not least was the issue of where they could actually train. Most farmers and land owners were reported to be generally sympathetic to requests for their land to be used, but at least one seemingly unpatriotic Essex farmer refused to allow his estate to be used in case the troops disturbed the covers of his game birds. As winter wheat and barley began to sprout there were further restrictions on which areas

4 Compiled, *The History of 1/6th Warwickshire,* p. 5.
5 TNA: WO70/48: Territorial Force Misc Letters 351-700, 27 Jan. 1915.

could be used. To add to the overall problems, the wet winter weather caused much of the low-lying ground which was available to flood.

Uniforms soon began to wear out and county associations quickly found replacements virtually impossible to secure. New webbing began to arrive in the New Year but ammunition fell from inadequate pouches and the quality of manufacture was poor. Blankets and other personal items remained in short supply all through the winter and calls for men to be issued with two suits and two pairs of boots went unanswered. The South Midland associations had all employed similar policies for providing boots in the pre-war period but now in competition with the forming New Armies they found them difficult to obtain through their former suppliers. In addition, the quality of those they could secure was variable. The GOC Gloucestershire and Worcestershire Brigade recorded his dissatisfaction at the quality of boots the county associations had provided and after 2/Field Company had been issued with "carefully fitted boots" from the Army Ordnance Department the men complained that even a short route march left them painfully footsore. This was something, they asserted, which boots supplied by their association had never done.

When the ground or equipment was unusable or unavailable, the South Midlanders route marched along the lanes of Essex. The pre-war shortage of firing ranges which the regulars believed had so adversely affected the standard of TF musketry persisted for the first months. What ranges were available were used until new ones were constructed, but even after Woodham Mortimer was commissioned, the markers' gallery flooded in winter and the range was unusable for many days. There was hope that TF units would be quickly rearmed with the Short Magazine Lee Enfield (SMLE) but the hope proved false and when they did eventually lose their Long Lee Enfields the battalions and supporting arms received equally elderly weapons as replacements. These had been modified to take Mark VII ammunition but most of these "new" rifles had corroded and worn barrels. An enduring lack of armourers, about which the brigadiers complained regularly from August until January, did little to improve the weapons' condition. Even the Regular Army GOC of the three brigades had some sympathy with the plight of their TF infantry when it came to firing musketry courses. It was deemed "manifestly unfair" that the TF should be trying to secure proficiency pay when firing these old weapons. Furthermore, regulars had traditionally fired their qualification courses during summer months whereas the territorials were shooting in blustery winter gales. For these reasons, the brigadiers believed, the results should not have been compared with those of pre-war regulars. Moreover, there was not only a shortage of ammunition to fire, but also of dummy cartridges with which to practise rapid loading. In March 1915, the same month as the division sailed, each battalion was allocated 100 dummy cartridges for a period of only two days with which to practise.

Another issue which affected the continuity of training was that of inoculation. As Commander-in-Chief Home Forces, General Sir Ian Hamilton asserted that the education of many TF soldiers made them "specially susceptible to the bigotry of cranks and faddists." This, he thought, caused them to have "something almost amounting to a religious conviction" on inoculation.[6] Inoculation was voluntary but the army wanted it done and pressured unit COs, who had no power to insist on it, to force their men to accept the injection. The matter was regarded as so important that the history of 5/Warwickshire suggests it was made clear to the men that those who refused were unlikely to travel abroad.[7] The unhappy CO of 8/Worcestershire appears to have spoken for many when he asserted, "To a certain type of man it is a great satisfaction to be able to insist on his freedom to flout" the CO's wishes. For those who did accept the procedure, and the majority of TF troops did, it was so painful that it often incapacitated the man for up to three days. When the whole battalion or unit was done at the same time, it could be managed relatively easily but as Lieutenant Colonel Butler, CO of 4/Gloucestershire noted, men coming from the depot had not been inoculated and so could not begin immediate training when joining the Imperial Service battalion.[8]

The questions of promotion of NCOs and the composition and quality of drafts were other burning issues as the division attempted to get itself ready for overseas deployment. Kitchener's August invitation to the TF to agree to foreign posting was met with varying responses across the country. The units of the South Midland were fairly typical in that an average of around 80 percent of infantry other ranks who were already members or August recruits seem to have accepted the invitation. Battalion histories often skate over the issue and avoid giving precise figures. The actual figures could vary widely, but it is likely that about 20 percent of the membership decided for personal or medical reasons that they could not go overseas with their battalion.[9] The manpower establishment of units was not altered once the division had been accepted for foreign service, but the units continued to spend their training period working on home service TF mobilization rather than expeditionary force tables. This caused some confusion and resentment on the part of, for example, the CO of 8/Worcestershire

6 Liddell Hart Centre for Military Archives (LHCMA), Hamilton Papers, 6/4, Hamilton to Sclater, 10 Oct. 1914.

7 C.Carrington, *The War Record of the 1/5th Battalion the Royal Warwickshire Regiment*, p. 5.

8 There was a strange corollary to the issue of inoculations in 4/Gloucestershire. In May 1915, the ADMS of the South Midland's 2nd Line wrote to his counterpart in the 1st Line, who passed the wire on to Capt Clayton, MO of 4/Gloucestershire. The 2nd Line wanted to know if Sgt Harris, late of 1/4th Gloucestershire and now in an asylum had been inoculated and, if so, did his insanity follow the inoculation. Clayton replied that he believed the inoculation had brought on acute symptoms of melancholia. 'I was then told he had been melancholic and strange for a week. Had I known this before, I wouldn't have inoculated him. I have no doubt in my mind that the inoculation made him worse.' TNA: WO95.2748: 7 May 1915.

9 I.F.W.Beckett, 'Territorial Force in the Great War' in P.Liddle (ed) *Home Fires and Foreign Fields* (Brassey, 1985) p. 23, estimates that 42 percent of 4/Ox&B and 30 percent of 1/Bucks did not go, but some other TF units had well over 90 percent acceptance. Carrington, *War Record of 1/5th Warwick*, p. 4 avoided giving numbers but claims the response was 'gratifying in the extreme.'

and the Adjutant of 6/Gloucestershire. These officers requested clarity on certain issues and equality with New Army units who were working to the same *Field Service Manual* and mobilization tables as the Regular Army. Newly-commissioned platoon commanders relied for training guidance on their long-serving NCOs but TF NCOs had traditionally been accused of lacking military knowledge and confidence in asserting command. Immediately on mobilization some battalions had accepted National Reservists,[10] a good percentage of whom had been former Regular Army and Volunteer NCOs. Although some of these experienced men soon proved to be "difficult", others did become very useful. The often dispersed nature of a battalion's eight companies in the early days of mobilization meant, however, that promotion to NCO usually had to come from within that same company. This insular practice, therefore, limited the use to which these former NCOs could be put. The practice was abandoned fairly quickly at the war stations but a new problem arose when the division's units training for overseas deployment were forced to retain NCOs who had opted for home service. COs repeatedly insisted that home service personnel should be posted back to their 2nd Lines which since September and October had been forming at their home depots. These men should then have been replaced at the war stations with 2nd Line recruits who had accepted imperial service; this would have enabled units destined to go overseas to train together with the personnel who would actually be sailing. The GOC of one brigade described the situation as "chaotic" and insisted that although efficiency was improving, it would become even more marked if his battalions could separate their home service and imperial service men. Some battalions did put their home service troops into discrete companies within the imperial service unit but relations between the home and imperial service units were soured when COs of the 2nd Line were accused of sending only their older and less useful imperial service recruits and retaining for themselves the younger and fitter men for the day when their own battalion would be sent abroad.[11] Brigadier Daubeney of the Gloucestershire and Worcester Brigade made his dissatisfaction about the attitude of the 2nd Line clear in a memorandum written in November. This was a cry soon echoed by similar missives from GOC of other TF brigades and divisions.

It was not only the alleged selfishness of the 2nd Line COs which so disrupted the flow of imperial service recruits to the 1st Line; many of the 2nd Line imperial service troops were themselves also thought to be holding back because they had heard reports of poor conditions at the war stations. Moreover, men were not supposed to be sent to the 1st Line until they were fully trained and the reserve battalions possessed few facilities for training and even fewer rifles. This created a vicious circle because

10 Membership of the National Reserve was open to any man who had served for a year or more in virtually any uniform. Its members had not been armed and had not trained. For a lengthy discussion on the formation and use of the National Reserve, see K.W. Mitchinson, *Defending Albion* (Basingstoke: Palgrave 2005).

11 TNA: WO95.590: I Corps WD. Report by Major General Barter, 20 Mar.1915.

men could not be fully trained by the 2nd Line and thus, in theory, could not be sent to the imperial service battalion. Whatever the cause, the result was the same: the flow of partly trained recruits was intermittent and disrupted the progressive training programmes which operated in the imperial service brigades. As more men were deemed unfit to travel and as the division formed new units to bring the formation to overseas establishment,[12] this disruption continued well into the month of departure. In March, for example, 4/Gloucestershire sent nearly one quarter of its strength to its 2nd Line in exchange for a similar number, while 8/Warwickshire dispatched about one tenth. HQ of the Warwickshire Brigade recorded the arrival of a draft with apparently little knowledge of musketry and which was "very backward in all other forms of training." In the RFA formations, I and II South Midland Brigades exchanged or received about one fifth and one tenth of their strengths respectively with their 2nd Lines.

The departure of longer-serving men and the arrival of new and probably unknown faces were also bound to affect the cohesion of the South Midland units. Regular Army inspectors had long thought TF discipline to be unsatisfactory and believed that before units could serve effectively overseas they would require a substantial injection of rigour. To the army, "discipline" meant more than just how many men overstayed their leave or the attitude of troops towards their superiors; it also embraced the whole scope of what was known as 'internal economy'. This term involved aspects of what is today referred to as fighting power and includes elements ranging from unit and individual morale, ethics, attitudes and approaches to training, group cohesion and a willingness to learn and adapt in the light of experience. Those TF units which recruited their battalions, batteries, field companies and ambulances from one town or city had a more recognizable identity that those more dispersed units. In his battalion war diary, Lieutenant Colonel Harman, CO of 7/Worcestershire reflected on the difficulties he and his officers faced in trying to weld his eight companies into an efficient and unified battalion. During the first few months of its time in Essex, Harman believed there was "little facility for the internal economy essential to the smooth running, and discipline of the battalion." He advocated the issuing of guidance on TF discipline by the War Office especially, so he said, for battalions such as his which suffered from having "eight distinct Units who, with the exception of the Annual Training, have never been concentrated. The result is, there is no cohesion, and what is worse a certain element of rivalry, almost antagonism, exists between the various Companies." It was the responsibility of company, battery and section officers to exploit the rivalry in order to encourage skills improvement but also ameliorate the antagonism to promote a wider efficiency. In the early days of training the established TF members and the August recruits generally worked under the officers they knew

12 The Divisional Cyclist Company, Ammunition Column and Mobile Veterinary Section were formed while the formation trained in Essex, largely from men already serving with units within the division.

but, with the introduction of the four-company system and the decision by officers, whether for business or medical reasons not to accept imperial service, there was a significant turnover in the commissioned ranks of several units.

It would not have made much if any difference to most troops in the division to learn they had a new GOC Division appointed the day mobilization began. Major General Heath, a former GOC of 11 Brigade, assumed command from Major General Graham, who went off to join the Adjutant-General's Department. Two of the three existing brigade commanders were to sail with their command, the exception being Brigadier General James. He was probably considered to be medically unfit to deploy and was replaced two days before departure by Brigadier General Nicholson. Like James, Nicholson had previously served as adjutant to a militia battalion so did perhaps have some idea of how auxiliary formations worked. The General Staff Officer 1(GSO1), Lieutenant Colonel Clarke, oversaw the division's departure from the UK and was then immediately replaced by Lieutenant Colonel Simpson-Baikie. He supervised its arrival at the front before moving on towards the end of April 1915 to be replaced by Lieutenant Colonel Baumgartner. The Assistant Adjutant-Quartermaster General (AA&QMG) Captain Law, had been replaced on the first day of mobilization by Colonel Reilly, a 'dugout' who had retired from the Army Supply Corps in 1905; Reilly remained in post until August 1915. The division's senior artillery commander (CRA), Brigadier General Butler of the Regular Army, had only been appointed in July 1914. The officer in overall command of the divisional engineers (CRE), Lieutenant Colonel Sinnott, remained the only TF officer in a senior divisional staff position. Both Butler and Sinnott sailed with the division but Sinnott was to be replaced within three weeks of arrival in France.

Unlike several other TF divisions, the South Midland had not suffered significant changes in its commanding officers between mobilization and departure for France. In peacetime, and especially in dispersed battalions, the CO was to most of the other ranks a fairly remote figure. Once at the war stations, however, he would have been seen regularly observing the exercises and route marches. Yet, the replacement of Lieutenant Colonel Parkes in February, described by the chronicler of 5/Warwickshire as a "bitter blow",[13] was probably more of a psychological 'blow' rather than one which had any great lasting impact on battalion morale. Of the 12 infantry battalions, six left the UK with their August 1914 CO, most of whom had been in command for at least one year before the declaration; two sailed with COs who had been majors in their battalion for several years before promotion to command. Two-thirds of the battalions, therefore, left with COs who knew and understood the character, idiosyncrasies and composition of their unit. Three of the remaining COs were regulars who were drafted in during early 1915; the last, Anderson of 6/Gloucestershire, another regular, arrived 10 days before departure. A similar picture emerges for the supporting arms. Two of the three RFA brigades sailed with their

13 Carrington, *The War Record of the 1/5th Warwick*, p. 8.

long-standing CO, an identical proportion to the three field ambulances. One of the RE field companies had a CO appointed from elsewhere and the other promoted its experienced major to replace the CO who could not sail.[14]

There was impressive continuity of service within the same unit for the other officers of the division but because so many of the South Midland battalions were below officer establishment in August 1914 many of those who were already serving in their unit were very quickly promoted. The number of July 1914 officers who finally sailed nearly seven months later, however, varied between the battalions. To take four examples. The CO and the only major in 7/Worcestershire serving in August did not sail, and only three of the eight captains left with the battalion in March. Five of the eight lieutenants sailed, three as captains, and six of the seven second lieutenants deployed. Three of these went as lieutenants. When it left the UK, the battalion sailed with 10 new second lieutenants, an identical number to that taken by its sister battalion 8/Worcestershire. This battalion departed, however, not only with its existing CO and two majors but also with four of the seven captains and eight of the nine lieutenants. In the Warwickshire Brigade, 7th Battalion had eight subalterns in August but probably only three of them left with the unit in March 1915. Seven new second lieutenants and four lieutenants had joined by late February and another seven subalterns, four of whom had been commissioned from the Inns-of-Court, joined during the month the battalion sailed. At the start of August, 5/Gloucestershire of the South Midland Brigade, had only four of its establishment of eight captains and 13 of its intended 16 subalterns. Two of the captains and three of the subalterns did not sail. Various promotions were awarded but it still embarked with only six captains and five lieutenants; 10 entirely new second lieutenants had been appointed between August and March. As with all battalions which had appointed a large number of new subalterns, 5/Gloucestershire had to train its new officers at the same time as the officers themselves were trying to train and become familiar with their platoons. Young boys of 18 years were expected to impose discipline on, and to earn the respect of, often older more worldly-wise and more experienced men. With usually only the knowledge gained from their school cadet corps, these youngsters, without the historic and structured support of a regular battalion, faced a daunting task. With little confidence in the military abilities and knowledge of his own officers it was understandable that Lieutenant Colonel Harman requested the War Office produce a text to help the process of developing TF discipline.

The War Office did not, in fact, issue any specific guidance on discipline for TF units. As, however, the provision of hutted accommodation progressed, and the companies

14 The division seems to have been fortunate in the COs who did arrive. The quality of the 'dug outs' appointed to some TF and new army units varied considerably. Some were certainly enthusiastic and competent but others were less so. For a particularly bitter description of one, see A.P. Herbert, *The Secret Battle* (Collector's Library, 2016) pp. 125-129.

could begin messing and parading as a battalion, discipline improved and a more unified identity developed. Nonetheless, the situation was not ideal because the slow progress made by the hutting contractors meant two companies of 4/Gloucestershire remained in scattered billets almost until the division marched out of Essex. The slightly better spring weather did auger well for training but, on 13 March, units received a wire declaring they were likely to be going to France in the near future. This was followed by one on 19 March suggesting the division would begin moving in four to five days' time. Small advanced parties from the 2nd Line had already begun arriving at the war stations to relieve the 1st Line and brigade majors and a selection of adjutants had been in France for two days' trench experience earlier in the month. On 24 March, four officers from each of the infantry brigades set off for France to supervise the future landing, entraining and billeting of the division; at home, the final rush of kit and equipment flooded into units' stores. Warwickshire Brigade HQ claimed that because the flow was so intense any thought of training was abandoned; there was no time to do anything except fathom how all the new equipment fitted and worked. Final move orders began to arrive at brigade and then unit HQs around 24 March. Staffs were instructed to liaise with local railway officials to determine the time they needed to have their men at stations and to confirm what rolling stock would be available.

The South Midland Division was the third TF division in a matter of weeks to travel to the Channel for deployment to the Western Front. The North Midland and 2nd London Divisions had gone in February and early March to join the TF units despatched since October 1914 independently of their divisions. The three complete formations had all been elements of Central Force's Third Army under the overall command of General Sir Ian Hamilton. While on tours of inspection in August 1914, Hamilton had noted the above average physique of the Warwickshire Brigade troops and recorded his bemusement in December as to why the War Office had selected the North Midland to be the first to depart.[15] The decision was probably Kitchener's but was also likely to have had much to do with the incessant pressure placed on the War Office by the North Midland's GOC, Major General Montagu-Stuart-Wortley. The authorities' decision came as a surprise to Hamilton who believed the South Midland to be "clearly above the rest" in its training and preparations. "Some of the battalions", he thought, "especially the South Midland Brigade [were] superb."[16] In a letter to Winston Churchill he wrote of the "immense Divisional *esprit de corps*" in the South Midland, and also assumed the decision to send it abroad behind the North Midland and 2nd London had been taken by Kitchener or Major General Kiggell, the Director of Home Defence.[17] Major General Heath appears to have been under the impression that the South Midland would be leaving early in the mobilization period as he told the division's officers in the

15 LHCMA: Hamilton Papers: 6/4, Hamilton to Wolfe-Murray, 9 Dec.1914.
16 Ibid.
17 Ibid, 6/8, Hamilton to Churchill, 6 Jan. 1915.

second week of September that it would go abroad within six weeks.[18] The winter, in fact, saw only independent battalions and units leaving for France with a result that, for example, 5/Warwickshire felt there was a feeling of "staleness and impatience" creeping into the battalion.[19] Similarly, the historian of 4/Ox&Bucks later recalled the battalion being "haunted by the fear of not getting to France before the war was over" and of its jealousy at the plaudits showered upon the London Scots and other "favoured Territorial Force battalions."[20] Hamilton's faith in the auxiliary remained undiminished and in February 1915, he again expounded the virtues of the TF. He claimed it had developed and trained so efficiently that he had "never seen finer divisions than two or three of my best. Thirty miles with full pack and ammunition is nothing to them, or to their transport units."[21] Given the problems the South Midland and other TF divisions had experienced in trying to obtain equipment, training areas, decent weaponry, horses and vehicles it is difficult to take seriously all the praise Hamilton bestowed on the TF. It is evident, however, that despite the many obstacles strewn in its path when the South Midland entrained for Southampton in late March 1915, it was reasonably well trained in the theory and nature of war but naïve in its practicalities and character. Nonetheless, one officer thought his battalion was in "the most excellent fighting trim", with all unfit men having been weeded out. The troops were, he recalled, very different from the "somewhat pasty-faced individuals who had left Birmingham on 4 August 1914."[22]

Disembarking at Le Havre, the Warwickshire Brigade had been the first of the three infantry brigades to leave the UK. Most of the rest of the infantry and supporting arms travelled to Boulogne but much of the transport landed at Le Havre and was then sent by rail to Boulogne. The inexperience of the troops and animals in loading trains and ships appears not to have delayed sailings to any significant degree.[23] There was the odd hiccup, for example, when the combination of a vessel riding too high in the water and an exceptional spring tide meant 240 horses had to be slung rather than led off and, despite a report from the movements officer claiming there were no accidents or damage incurred during transit, 2/Field Company needed two wagons replaced on arrival. The main criticism of the division's transit was its lack of clarity in telegrams about which units were to be accommodated in which vessels. Rather than accommodate all of one unit in the same ship, there was a tendency to split them up between several which then sometimes berthed at separate quays. This caused delays, especially for wheeled units as they tried to reassemble on the congested dockside. There was also some criticism of the staff work and internal organization of battalions which allowed several ships

18 Heath's statement may, of course, simply have been a means of encouraging his officers during the early training period.
19 Carrington, *War Record of 1/5th Warwick*, p. 8.
20 Pickford, *War Record of 1/4th Ox&Bucks*, p. 2.
21 LHCMA: Hamilton Papers: 6/17, Hamilton to Lowther, 8 Feb.1915.
22 Compiled, *History of 1/6th Warwickshire*, p. 7.
23 The evidence used for this paragraph is taken from 48th Division unit war diaries and TNA. WO95.2745, DAQMG Embarkation Report, Apr.1915.

to carry other ranks with little or no officer supervision and for not sending sufficient numbers of men and officers with transport sections to load three days' rations on the docks. Simple errors and misjudgements such as these are understandable in the novel experience of embarking on active service and for what was the first major move by the division. The disembarkation officer at Boulogne thought the South Midland's planning and procedures were an improvement on the other two TF divisions which had passed through his hands and praised the condition of its horses and vehicles. The units themselves were also generally content with the way they had managed the exercise: 3/Field Ambulance noted several times in its diary how efficiently it had entrained and detrained; 8/Warwickshire thought it should have all been together on one ship and 2/Field Ambulance thought the overcrowded conditions made the journey rather "uncomfortable." The only regret felt by 4/Gloucestershire appears to have been that it managed to leave the censor's stamp behind when it left Danbury.

The next stage of the journey was not without incident because the division was reliant upon the vagaries of the French rail system. The difficulties began early because there were delays in reuniting the horses from Le Havre with their units at Boulogne; there were then problems in persuading inexperienced horses and their nervous drivers to ascend the steep hill to the rest camp. One horse was killed and two drivers injured in the Warwickshire Infantry Brigade when a wagon went out of control and a sudden departure by one train almost stranded two lieutenants of I South Midland Brigade RFA in Abbeville. Divisional HQ opened at St Omer on 31 March and the various brigades moved into the area between Cassel and Hazebrouck. From there they moved towards Bailleul and Armentières, a journey which again caused some difficulties. In one truck carrying horses of 2/Field Company three of the exhausted and stressed four animals fell and remained down for two hours. One died and another was removed to a veterinary hospital. The Deputy Assistant Director of Medical Services (DADMS) and the second-in-command of 4/Gloucestershire were sent to hospital within days of arrival and three men of 6/Warwickshire and five of 1/Bucks were also admitted before the march began towards the assembly areas. During the march a reasonably small number of men fell out and one of the first tasks of the ADMS was to visit billets to inspect the men's feet. A few more deficiencies in equipment became apparent as the division moved forward: the sanitary section was without its lorry, the Adjutant and Quartermaster Branch (A&Q) assumed some ammunition had been left behind at Southampton and the South Midland Infantry Brigade recorded it was short of a vet and of eight machine guns. Nevertheless, and despite the inevitable difficulties with inadequate and insufficient accommodation, by early April the units were in the areas where they were to be attached to the regular 4th and 6th Divisions for their trench acclimatization.[24] While the senior officers

24 Ploegsteert village lies approximately nine miles south of Ypres (Ieper) and four miles north of Armentiéres. The wood which bears the same name lies to the north and north-east of the village.

attended conferences held by army, corps and divisional HQ, the troops first spent a few days digging in the rear and sitting through the odd lecture on sanitation and trench warfare. The worst of the winter was over but the trenches in the Ploegsteert sector remained waterlogged and the Germans enjoyed a clear superiority during artillery exchanges. The South Midlanders were to be taught the rudimentary but essential aspects of how to survive the rigours of trench warfare. Ironically, many of their new tutors had received a much shorter time in training in the UK than had their now students. The tutors had, however, at least a little more experience in how to keep weapons clean in mud-filled trenches and brew tea in an old tin can.

The arrival of the TF divisions had caused corps and divisional commanders to consider how best they could train the auxiliaries whilst they were attached for trench acclimatization. Notes and memos had already been circulated to regular divisions warning them of what to expect when the TF arrived. Brigadier General Whigham of I Corps noted that TF officers and NCOs "are apt to fail, not only in their methods of giving orders, but to an even greater degree in seeing them carried out." He believed the interchange of regular with TF officers and NCOs within his corps had achieved "excellent results" and suggested this procedure could be adopted by all.[25] From London, the Chief of the General Staff, Major General William Robertson warned that territorials needed "hardening up" by plenty of route marching, had little knowledge of telephone communications, billeting procedures and maintenance of transport, and also lacked a "proper sense of discipline and the correct chain of responsibility."[26] The South Midland was to be instructed by 4th and 6th Divisions and plans had already been suggested by GOC brigades of those formations as to how the task might best be achieved. Brigadier General Hunter-Weston, GOC 11 Brigade, advocated the posting of GOC TF divisions, brigades and their staff to regular formations for a few days, with two battalions being attached to each regular brigade for 16 days. TF battalions would be put into the trenches by platoons but each territorial should be attached to a regular soldier who would teach him the basics of trench survival. Each man should have, Hunter-Weston suggested, an initial 48 hours trench instruction, which would thus need eight days for the two battalions. Those awaiting their 48 hours, and those who had completed them, would be employed in construction, pumping and sanitation duties under TF officers, with those officers themselves being supervised by regular officers and NCOs.[27] The CRE, CRA and ADMS of 4th Division submitted similar proposals as to how they would instruct the territorials under their supervision.

Hunter-Weston's suggestions, although not quite his proposed time scale, were adopted by 4th Division and the South Midland began its acclimatization in the Ploegsteert sector around 5 April. When not undergoing instruction in what were very wet trenches and breastworks the troops were engaged in digging elsewhere,

25 TNA: WO95.590: Whigham, BGGS I Corps, to 1st and 2nd Divisions, 8 Feb. 1915.
26 Ibid: Robertson to First Army, 4 Feb. 1915.
27 TNA: WO95.669: III Corps WD. Hunter-Weston to 4th Division, 6 Feb. 1915.

carrying and wiring parties and being taught about trench mortars, grenades and sanitation. 8/Warwickshire noted it was trained "as per the syllabus" and, together with the other three Warwickshire battalions, became the first of the division's brigades to assume command of their own front trenches. The Warwickshire Brigade was followed shortly by the other brigades in adjoining sectors and they all quickly discovered the difficulties of preventing the collapse of trenches with little reveting material and few sandbags. Trench foot and other ailments began to make their impact with 6/Gloucestershire, for example, losing one officer and 61 men in the month.[28] Lieutenant Colonel Schofield of 4/Ox&Bucks was the first CO to lose his command overseas when he was posted down the line to become OC of a depot at Le Havre; Lieutenant Colonel Collett of 5/Gloucestershire became the first CO to be wounded, albeit only slightly. Second Lieutenant Barnett, who had enlisted on 4 August, became the division's first officer fatality and, like several other deaths from that first month, was buried in Ploegsteert Wood Cemetery.

The graves of the first officer and other rank of 48th (South Midland) Division to die directly as the result of enemy action: Second Lieutenant Charles Barnett, 5/Gloucester, is buried in Ploegsteert Wood Military Cemetery; Pte W.Holland, 1/Buckinghamshire Battalion, lies in Strand Military Cemetery. (Author)

28 This total included 4 dead and 13 wounded.

Like the infantry, the three RFA brigades were paired with regular brigades. In common with other similar units in other divisions, however, the Warwickshire Heavy Battery was swiftly detached from the division and grouped with Second Army's artillery. The CRA and his brigade major spent most of the time driving around trying to locate senior Royal Artillery (RA) personnel as well as their own batteries, often with little success, and narrowly escaped death or injury when a shell burst near their car. The CRA recorded the death of Driver Tooth who shot himself "while of unsound mind" and, with the relief of the regular brigades, became responsible for the artillery of the divisional sector on 17 April. His brigades had been put to work improving the pits and covers of existing positions but once the regulars had gone the gunners had to dig entirely new or deepen existing pits because the shields of their obsolete 15 pdrs were of a different size than those of the regulars' 18 pdrs. Each gun was allowed a mere three rounds per day which meant that once they had conducted registration they had virtually no shells left to fire. The batteries were accused of shelling the Warwicks' trenches (but managed to establish that the culprits were the adjacent North Midland Territorials) complained about the poor quality of the rations ("so good under 4th Division, so bad under South Midland Division") kept watchful eyes on certain buildings thought to be the haunt and signalling positions of Belgian spies and discovered to their chagrin the exceedingly erratic and "abominable" nature of British shells and fuses. I South Midland Brigade recorded that the majority of its shells and fuses had been made between 1899 and 1902. It noted laconically "occasionally we find a shell of 1906." Often, only one in 10 shells fired would actually burst and, in obvious anger, the diarist of II South Midland Brigade declared No.63 fuses "should never have been ordered to be fired. Sheer waste." There was little he and his men could do other than to resign themselves to the reality of the situation. The BEF was critically short of all types of ammunition and with their ancient field guns the only significant increase in supplies the TF batteries could expect were those which might be discovered lying forgotten in the dark depths of magazines at home. Second Army dispatched a frosty reply to III Corps' April request to increase the daily allotment: "No special grant of ammunition can be made to the artillery of TF Divisions for training purposes."[29] For the time being at least, the North and South Midland Divisions, both currently in III Corps, would have to combine practice shoots with firing in earnest.

While his field companies worked under instruction from the regulars, the division's long-serving CRE, Lieutenant Colonel Sinnott, and his adjutant were attached to 4th Division. 2/Field Company cooperated with 9/Field Company on razing an already semi-ruined villa on Hill 63, digging and repairing trenches and screening crossroads from observation by Germans perched in Messines church. They were visited by the ADMS who was doing the rounds of the division's billets, field ambulances and

29 TNA: WO95.670: III Corps WD. From MGGS Second Army to II and III Corps, 5 Apr. 1915.

convalescent depot. His ambulances were distributed by sections to those of 4th and 6th Divisions and his three OCs were busy inspecting the advanced dressing stations (ADS) and regimental aid posts (RAP) with the DADMS. They also attended lectures on and consulted with GOC brigades and others about the best way of countering the poison gas which had just made its appearance at Ypres. Lieutenant Colonel Young of 3/Field Ambulance motored to Bailleul in the hope of questioning gas victims who may have been evacuated there and also accompanied the Assistant Provost Marshal on an investigation of one of the division's 12 cases of venereal disease. One priority as far as the ADMS and general hygiene were concerned was to establish a divisional baths; until one could be opened the South Midlanders were dependent on sharing the "very badly organized" baths of other divisions. Possibly the least happy of the division's senior officers was Lieutenant Colonel Harris, the Assistant Director of Veterinary Services (ADVS). Harris vented his frustration by complaining about the shortage of officers and men in his unit, railing about having to rely on incompetent NCOs, bemoaning the lack of a car and the removal of his second charger, criticizing the units' poor stable management and was aghast at the seeming inability of the Director of Veterinary Services (DVS) at GHQ to appreciate his difficulties. The fuming Harris believed that to ensure continuity of welfare provision, rather than trail along in their wake the Mobile Veterinary Section (MVS) should move with advanced units when the division marched to a new sector. He also argued that the DVS's decision to cancel the scheme by which Harris had been paying French farmers to care for the recovery of sick horses until they were fit enough to rejoin the division would hamper efficiency and cause a greater number of horses to be cast.

Armed still with old weapons and many untrained horses, the South Midland Division became responsible for its own sector of front line. As it did, heavy and continuous gunfire was heard to the north. What later became known as the 2nd Battle of Ypres had begun and as it lasted well into May it seemed likely the South Midlanders would be drawn into the furnace. Until then, if that indeed was to be its fate, the division would attempt to hone its skills and prepare for what might come. The efficiency and keenness of the territorials had come as an unexpected surprise to many regulars and, like the North Midland and 2nd London Divisions, the South Midland had received encouraging reports from its Regular Army tutors. One report of April passed on by III Corps praised the division which had "created a very favourable impression by their appearance on the march and in billets…Their general bearing has inspired every confidence in the future."[30]

While the guns to the north around Ypres thundered, soon to be joined by those to the south of the division close to Festubert and Aubers, the South Midlanders were to undergo nearly four months of trench warfare and intermittent training. The division occupied trenches and breastworks to the north and south of Plugstreet Wood, a sector which by that time was relatively quiet. Forty-five field kitchens arrived in late

30 TNA: WO95.670: III Corps WD. Report, Apr. 1915.

A row of 5/Gloucester in Ploegsteert Wood Military Cemetery. The plot of graves in the left distance by the entrance gate contains men of 1/Buckinghamshire Battalion. (Author)

April but the division's lack of appropriate equipment soon became apparent when it experienced great difficulty in obtaining sandbags, reveting materials and timber. Pumps were almost unknown, gum boots rationed and although when relieved the brigades of 4th Division generously left their ration carts and telephones wires for use by the South Midlanders, they took their telephones with them. The CRE held regular meetings with staff captains to try to ensure a supply of engineering materials for the front trenches and bricks and timber for improving the roads and tracks towards the rear. Men and officers of the field ambulances were engaged in cleaning former schools in preparation for their conversion to hospitals, lecturing sanitation squads, advising on the prevention of food contamination, chairing conferences with regimental MOs and sending some of their men to labour under the RE in constructing RAP dugouts.

The RE also spent a considerable portion of their time building huts, sinking wells, making trench boards and wire knife rests and mining. Both sides were industriously burrowing towards each others' lines but the damage done and the casualties inflicted by the explosions were limited. The psychological impact is difficult to assess but there were fairly regular detonations combined with ruses performed in order to draw enemy garrisons to the front trenches before mines was fired. Batteries would drop some of their restricted supply of shells in the craters in the hope of inflicting casualties on the enemy troops moving up to reoccupy the damaged front. On one occasion when the artillery was asked to destroy a particularly strong enemy breastwork, gunners and infantry alike were angry, frustrated and bemused when the first shell burst prematurely, the second fell in the British trenches, the third landed on the division's wire and the fourth "reached if it did not seriously disturb its objective."[31] The guns were rather more successful when a small mountain gun was manhandled through Plugstreet Wood to destroy at almost point blank range a sandbag "tower" used as a sniping post.[32] Trench periscopes were in short supply and a favourite target of German snipers; the CO of 5/Gloucestershire was one of several men slightly wounded by glass when periscopes were hit. So accurate were the German snipers that the diarist of 4/ Gloucestershire bemoaned the battalion's inability to replace the increasing number of smashed viewers and the difficulties and dangers their loss involved. Small nocturnal patrols were sent beyond the wire and occasionally encountered similar groups of Germans. Lieutenant Ward of 4/Gloucester established something of a reputation in the Gloucestershire and Worcestershire Brigade for his frequent excursions into no man's land. Casualties in such encounters were usually light but prisoners were sometimes taken or the occasional fatality left to be recovered later. The Germans quickly discovered which sections of the division's line were inadequately covered by RFA batteries and launched sudden localized bombardments with rifle and hand-thrown grenades against the poorly protected stretches. The most the division could usually manage in retaliation was to arrange a day's intermittent fire programme for machine guns and rifles, supplemented by a few trench mortar shells.

During May, when the wind blew from the north troops sometimes complained of sore eyes. The German use of gas at Ypres caused intense activity within the South Midland Division and resulted in lectures and demonstrations during May and June about how to reduce its impact. Orderlies of the field ambulances (in addition to some hired civilians) made and soaked thousands of anti-gas face pads from flannel, gauze and converted cap comforters; 800 empty wine bottles were collected for trench storage of bicarbonate of soda and vermel sprayers obtained when possible. There are no reports of gas actually being used in the division's sector but the inequality between the British and German field batteries remained distinct. One battery commander noted that for every shell he fired, the Germans retaliated with five. Batteries did on occasions attempt some counter-battery work by firing in the direction of German muzzle flashes and were also allowed one or two shells to disperse working parties attempting to repair wire destroyed by mine detonations. In early May, the division was ordered "to pin the enemy to his ground" by means of a demonstration in support of the Festubert attack but, although the infantry fired their weapons and even managed the odd rifle grenade and trench mortar shell, the combined effect made

31 C.R.Cruttwell, *The War Service of the 1/4th Royal Berkshire Regiment*, p. 12.
32 The 'tower' was soon rebuilt but the battalion under whose gaze its sentries fell was refused permission to fire mortars or rifle grenades at it because the Germans fired back 'at least four for every one of ours.' G.Greenwell, *An Infant in Arms: War Letters of a Company Officer 1914–1919* (London: Allen & Lane, 1972), p. 19.

"little impression…on the enemy." The Germans were equally unimpressed when the Warwickshire Brigade was ordered to reveal "obviously concealed" trench bridges in the hope of distracting the enemy's attention from the French attack at Souchez.[33] In similar disconsolate vein, one RFA brigade noted the 12 rounds per gun allocation was also "too few [to make] any appreciable effect." Besides annoying the infantry by firing short and "destroying the wire we had been putting out for four days", the gunners spent most of their time improving and camouflaging their pits and shelters. The RFC cooperated by flying above the positions to assess how effectively they were disguised and aircraft also occasionally assisted in spotting the gunners' fall of shot. Unfortunately this was never entirely successful because 15 pdr shrapnel was reportedly "difficult to spot from the air."

In mid-May, the formation became known officially as 48th (South Midland) Division. The infantry brigades were also numbered, with the Warwickshire, Gloucestershire and Worcestershire and the South Midland Brigades becoming, respectively, 143, 144 and 145. Later in the month the length and method of holding the line was adjusted in order to allow one brigade to be out at rest as divisional reserve. With the prospect of a slightly less demanding routine, one battalion CO hoped to capitalize on the change by immediately and optimistically recommending that all men should be allowed at least 24 hours' rest between coming out of the line and being tasked for working parties. This was seldom possible. He also argued that bathing once a month was clearly inadequate to prevent scabies and the "violent" attacks by "plagues" of lice, and reported that his men were "over-fatigued" when they came out of the line. Despite the exhaustion, some of the non-working time had, of course, to be devoted to training. As troops were thought to have acquired bad habits from "snap shooting" over the parapet, whenever the opportunity presented itself they fired on hastily constructed ranges in the rear. They also practised company and battalion assaults as well as managing the odd game of football. Equipment permitting, specialists were able to practise some of their skills but what the men needed most of all was decent food, rest and comfortable billets. The sanitation section did crucial work in trying to keep the streets and accommodation in the rear free of civilian refuse and disease but there were limits to what the section could achieve. Farm middens and cesspits, generally swarming with flies, were treated with lime, agreements made with farmers about burning manure and measures agreed with local mayors over the disposal of civilian rubbish and the notification of infectious diseases. Thrush disinfectors began to make their appearance to help reduce the incidence of scabies and lice and, with the opening of divisional baths in late May, hygiene and personal cleanliness improved. 2/Field Ambulance alone, for example, was responsible for washing over 25,000 shirts and over 21,000 pairs of pants in May.

That the men were suffering from the effects of little rest and poor conditions was apparent in the numbers reporting sick and in the number of courts martial held for

33 Cruttwell, *War Service of 1/4th Berks*, p. 11.

men accused of sleeping at their post. 3/Field Ambulance dealt with 941 sick in May but did record with some satisfaction a drop in the following month to just over 700; 2/Field Ambulance admitted 10 officers and 824 other ranks to the divisional rest station in the same month. There was little that could have prevented the 313 cases of measles admitted by 2/Field Ambulance in June,[34] but improvements in hygiene and medical facilities meant that the incidence of other infectious diseases had fallen.

Although never an excessive number, and little different to the totals serving in regular divisions, there was concern at divisional HQ about the alleged lax discipline of troops in the trenches. Ten cases of sleeping at their post were heard in the five weeks before June, a crime which usually attracted a suspended sentence of five years' penal servitude. After its first two tours in the trenches 5/Gloucestershire reported the occurrence of "several" accidents while men were cleaning their weapons. It is possible that some of these were self-inflicted wounds as in the early months of active service unit war diaries were understandably often reluctant to record such events. It may have been concern about this practice which caused the divisional staff to issue instructions as to how self-inflicted wounds should be identified and recorded.

Accidents did take a steady if not particularly large toll of officers and men, with the most frequent being those which occurred during demonstrations of the unstable grenades then in use by the BEF. For example, and although the recorded number of fatalities was later reduced, Second Lieutenant Guise and six men of 5/Gloucestershire were reported killed during one such demonstration. Bad luck or simple carelessness could also prove deadly: five sappers of 1/Field Company were killed or died of wounds and six seriously wounded when a barrel of gunpowder they were handling exploded. 3/Field Company responded to the emergency by dispatching all of its available wagons to Nieppe to transport the wounded to hospital.

In addition to those killed and wounded in accidents, there was of course a steady trickle of casualties caused by the enemy. Furthermore, there was also the natural wastage through men going home for commissions, returning to munitions work, as underage for overseas service and for general sickness and incapacity. In addition to Lieutenant Colonel Schofield's departure, in the first three months of trench holding, several other senior commanders also departed for home. Major General Heath left suffering from angina and was replaced as GOC Division by Major General Robert Fanshawe. The new GSO1, Lieutenant Colonel Baumgartner took up post in late April, Lieutenant Colonel Sinnott, the TF CRE departed for Rouen and was replaced by the regular Lieutenant Colonel Marshall. Colonel Raywood, the ADMS left for the UK and the CRA, Brigadier General Butler, was replaced by Brigadier General Ross-Johnson. The practice of occasionally replacing TF COs with regulars begun during the post-mobilization training period continued in the first months of overseas service. There appears to have been no deliberate policy of removing existing

34 Men of 4/Ox&Bucks were thought to be offering about two days' pay to sleep next to a man who looked like he was contracting measles. Greenwell, *Infant in Arms*, p. 17.

COs but when the opportunity arose, pragmatism did sometimes, but not always, prevail. When Lieutenant Colonel Martineau of 6/Warwickshire returned to the UK he was succeeded by Lieutenant Colonel F Wethered TD, a former CO of the Bucks Battalion rather than by a regular.[35] The move caused both envy and annoyance in 7/Warwickshire. When Elton, a regular who had been posted into 7/Warwickshire before embarkation went home, he was replaced first by Price of the Royal Fusiliers and then soon after by Hanbury, another regular. The A&Q's war diary noted that divisional HQ wanted another regular to be appointed but the battalion itself clearly hoped for promotion from within. With icy pithiness, its war diary commented, "There are several Lieutenant Colonels of 7/Royal Warwicks, yet a stranger has been appointed." 5/Warwickshire was probably pleased when Major Franklin of the Newfoundland Regiment, who had been attached to the battalion since March, was appointed temporary CO, but was possibly equally as happy when he was succeeded a few weeks later by 5/Warwick's long-serving adjutant, Captain Sladen of the Rifle Brigade. This is a good example of how the War Office could take advantage of an opportunity which satisfied both officialdom and the TF unit. By the time of his appointment to 5/Warwickshire, Sladen had been with the Royal Warwickshire Regiment for 24 months. He had known it both in peace and war and was thus reasonably familiar with its traditions, its officers and men as well as its TF idiosyncrasies.

Major-General Sir Robert Fanshawe. (Soldiers of Oxfordshire Museum)

Although the division's number of officer fatalities was low, a total of three captains, five lieutenants and four second lieutenants, there was a steady number of officers who were wounded or found the demands of active service too much: Majors Pauli of 5/Warwickshire and Baker of 4/Gloucestershire were invalided home and Dore of 7/Worcestershire was wounded and evacuated all within the first two months. 6/Warwickshire had three of its company commanders invalided home in July and 4/Gloucestershire had one captain, one lieutenant and two second lieutenants

35 Wethered relinquished command of 1/Bucks in January 1915. He had been replaced by Lt. Col. C.P. Doig, a regular of the Seaforth Highlanders. When Wethered recovered from sickness he was posted to 6/Warwickshire but was quickly invalided home.

severely wounded in June. All battalions seem to have received a small number of second lieutenants as replacements, usually from their 2nd Line. These were needed to replenish those subalterns who were wounded whether accidentally, such as Owen, or by the enemy such as Plaistowe. Others were injured behind the line: Watson was thrown from his horse and Riddlell went to hospital for a routine operation. Officers were also often away on courses and in July at least one per battalion left to join their respective brigade grenade company. Others were simply struck off strength without any reason being recorded. The comings and goings between April and July meant that 6/Gloucestershire, with only 23 of its establishment of 30 officers, was probably fairly typical of the 12 battalions.

Two of the three RFA brigades retained their TF GOCs during this early period abroad. Lieutenant Colonel Cossart, a regular, was brought in to command III South Midland Brigade, but most of the TF officers who left with their brigades and batteries remained until at least the division moved south in July. One brigade major, Murray-Smith of I South Midland, a very rare example of an artillery brigade major with a background in the Volunteers and the TF, was replaced by a "younger and more experienced" regular, officer at the request of the CRA. Murray-Smith went to become OC of another formation's divisional ammunition column (DAC) at about the same time as the medical officer (MO) of 48th Division's DAC exchanged places with the increasingly rheumatic MO of 5/Gloucestershire. The field companies and field ambulances during this period retained their existing OCs and very largely those officers who had embarked in March.

Like their officers, the other ranks (ORs) of infantry battalions had suffered relatively few fatalities in the first three months. The total was probably 218. 145 Brigade lost 49 ORs killed or died of wounds in total by mid-July; 143 Brigade suffered 21 during June alone; 144 Brigade recorded the highest number of 65 fatalities between April and July. When the number of wounded, invalided and returned home for other reasons is taken into account, it is clear there had been a steady but less than substantial drain on brigades' strength. At the end of June, 143 Brigade had a fighting strength of 101 officers and 3350 ORs, while 145 Brigade was in rather a better position with 114 officers and 3677. GOC brigades and battalion COs were anxious to maintain strengths but had quickly begun to realize that War Office policy was to reduce TF battalions from their mobilization strength of about 1,000 to around 800. The division had enquired in early May about the availability of drafts from home but had been told in reply that none were likely to be received in the foreseeable future. What particularly frustrated the commanders was the knowledge that numbers of 2nd Line men had landed in France but, as 8/Worcestershire's war diary noted, "apparently there is no prospect of the draft…which arrived on 26 June being sent to join the battalion." Hopes were raised, however, when at the start of July officers were sent to Le Havre to collect "large numbers" of reinforcements. It seems likely that most battalions received about 100 men, with the field ambulances, artillery and field companies also accepting proportionate numbers of replacements.

The drafts arrived at their new units while the division was resting and training in the mining villages close to Houchin. The landscape was not attractive but the area allowed the troops some opportunity to relax and recuperate. Various divisional schools were established and specialists were able to receive instruction in newly-available equipment. All units worked to schedules prepared by their brigade staffs and occasionally undertook all-arms exercises. Although there remained a degree of flexibility, it was becoming more usual for particular field companies, RFA brigades and field ambulances to be associated with a particular infantry brigade. This allowed coordination and cooperation to develop more easily between the supported and supporting arms and also for the officers of the different units to fraternize and even socialize with each other. There were occasional night schemes, staff rides and tactical exercises for COs and OC companies, but there was also the inevitable digging. The division had been warned it would take over the extreme right of the British line from its fellow territorials in 47th (2nd London) Division near Notre Dame de Lorette but it was informed unexpectedly in mid-July it was to head further south to relieve French troops in the Hébuterne sector. To what were later described as "great rejoicings", *en route* the RFA brigades exchanged their worn out 15 pdrs for new 18 pdr pieces and between 19 and 23 July the division assembled in the villages close to Sailly-au-Bois, Authie, Bus-les-Artois and Coigneux. With only fairly local adjustments in the sectors of line held, this region was to be the home of the division for the next 12 months.

3

Trench Warfare

In his post-war reflection, Henry Ogle, formerly an officer in 8/Warwickshire, decided that in 1915 it became clear "to us that we were not first class troops."[1] Other territorials in other units echoed this early lack of confidence as their roles in that year appeared to be merely to support the Regular Army or simply to hold the line. Indeed, line holding was to be the task of 48th (South Midland) Division for most of the next year. The reason behind the authorities' decision to use the division in that role is uncertain but GHQ clearly decided that the formation would be better utilized in instructing newly-arrived divisions in trench acclimatization than employing it in an offensive role. Rumours of deployment to Egypt or Gallipoli had been sweeping through the division for some weeks so its move to the Hébuterne area in July 1915 came as something of a surprise.[2] The shift to the south was in response to a French request for the British to take over more of the Allied front; French corps so released could then be used in new offensives. With New Army divisions beginning to arrive on the Western Front, the British were able to agree to the French request and opted to send the South Midland to this quiet area of the line where new formations could be taught the necessities of trench life in relative peace. Given General Sir Ian Hamilton's post-mobilization endorsements and the good reports submitted on its acclimatization period, it is probably unlikely the authorities genuinely believed the division to be unequal to the task of taking the offensive. Nevertheless, for the offensive at Loos in September they were to choose the two TF divisions which had been in France only marginally longer than 48th Division and several New Army divisions in preference to the South Midland.[3]

1 M.Glover (ed), *The Fateful Battle Line. The Great War Journal and Sketches of Captain Henry Ogle MC* (London: Leo Cooper, 1993) p. 5.
2 Compiled, *1/6th Royal Warwickshire*, p. 13.
3 47th (2nd London) and 46th (North Midland) Divisions were the two TF divisions used at Loos. 50th (Northumbrian), 49th (West Riding) and 51st (Highland), as well as 48th (South Midland) were also available. The Northumbrian, however, was still rebuilding

The South Midland gradually took over the French trenches, artillery pits and horse lines during late July. The trenches were typically French, with inadequate drainage and sanitation facilities but the departing French had thoughtfully left flowers in the dugouts.[4] As the French dead had been buried in the parapets or close to the trench lines any attempt at improvement by the South Midlanders usually resulted in the uncovering of corpses.[5] Trench hygiene had not been the highest priority and huge heaps of military and civilian refuge lay rotting in the villages behind the front.[6] Both sides in the sector had employed a 'live and let live' system with, according to an oft-told tale, both sides keeping a milking cow in the front lines.[7] The priority for the South Midland troops was to make the trenches habitable and rather more secure. Initial attempts were quickly hampered by some ferocious summer storms which caused flash floods to sweep through the trenches and villages. Somewhat ironically, the RE had been at the time heavily employed in sinking wells and conduiting streams in order to lessen the impact of a water shortage. Several of the local wells had been contaminated which resulted in water having to be transported by hand for a distance of up to two miles. This caused problems at the horse lines as well as at water points closer to the lines where battalion carts were filled. Among other measures issued by divisional HQ about countering the dangers of contaminated water was the one which suggested a German prisoner should be made to drink a pint of suspect water. He would then be observed closely for an hour in case of any adverse reaction. The storms swamped gun pits and collapsed many sections of trenches. With the French practices of digging only occasional sumps and of hollowing out unsupported funk holes many trenches were quickly awash with deep, filthy water and were without effective parapets and parados. Men of the sanitary section were fully employed beside the RE, infantry and even the divisional cyclists in digging out and draining the flooded sections and cleaning and disinfecting semi-immersed dugouts. Meanwhile, the carpenters of the field companies hammered together new trench boards and bridges while wood cutting parties foraged for timber. There was an acute shortage of timber for dugout

after its catastrophic losses at 2nd Ypres, and at the time the authorities thought the West Riding and Highland were somewhat suspect.

4 On first inspection, and during what was a period of dry weather, the CO of 4/Ox&Bucks thought they were 'the cleanest set of trenches we have yet seen.' Greenwell, *Infant in Arms*, p33. In January 1916, 8/Worcester blamed the 'faulty construction' of a French built dugout for the deaths of seven men and another eight wounded. A report concluded that if the dugout, which took two direct hits, had been built to British standards its roof would not have collapsed.

5 There had been fighting in the sector in the early months of the war but Carrington, *1/5th Royal Warwickshire*, p15, rather strangely asserts that French casualties between November 1914 and August 1915 amounted to 10.

6 Petrie, *R.Berkshire*, p128 described Bayencourt, one of the villages in the rear of the division's sector, as 'a stinking little village full of flies and harlots.' Cruttwell, *War Service of 1/4th Berkshire*, p26, changed 'harlots' to 'odours.'

7 See, for example, P.L.Wright, *The First Buckinghamshire*, p. 17.

construction and revetting, and requests to higher authority to be allowed to quarry flints were refused. Bricks and stone from destroyed farms and villages were, however, allowed to be plundered for roads and communication trenches.

The arrival of the territorials of 5/Sussex in late August as the division's pioneer battalion came as a welcome relief to the hard-pressed troops. With parties of gunners and orderlies having been taken from other jobs to help local farmers gather the harvest, the addition of another 900 men whose main task was to assist the three field companies in road and trench maintenance was appreciated.[8] The Cinque Ports Battalion had arrived in France a few weeks before 48th Division and had since been serving with 1st Division. Following very heavy losses whilst attached to regular divisions, 5/Sussex was one of the nine TF battalions converted to pioneers in 1915. War diaries are usually silent on how the conversion was accepted by the officers and men of those battalions but personal recollections suggest that it was generally considered to have been something of a betrayal. These units had agreed to be detached from their divisions to be sent early to France, had fought alongside the regulars and earned the Old Army's admiration only to be rewarded with what to many of the men was relegation to a support service. The diarist of 5/Sussex made no comment on what the battalion thought of the conversion but its companies were immediately put to work maintaining their allocation of 12 miles of trenches.

Two of the busiest men in the division during the first few weeks of arriving in the sector were the CRE, Lieutenant Colonel Marshall, and his adjutant, Major Brandon. Either together or singularly, these men were constantly touring the trenches, consulting with the infantry and artillery COs, delegating work to the OCs of the field companies and the CO of 5/Sussex. Their time was spent in trying to buy or obtain raw materials, selecting sites for wells and water troughs, securing authority to begin laying tramways, meeting with camouflage experts to discuss screening roads and constructing observation posts, organizing the sites and construction of huts as winter billets and conferring with division and corps staff officers about defensive positions and strong points in their sector. Pressure on the RE was intense along the British front, with the result that corps issued directives declaring that if the field companies continued to be used to the same extent there would soon be no RE left.[9] Consequently, divisions were instructed to use infantry for all digging and the RE only as supervisors or advisors. Even with the arrival of 5/Sussex, however, there remained a severe shortage of labour in the South Midland Division. 1/Field Company recorded its "disappointment" at the number of working parties that had to be cancelled because, it believed, the infantry were so depleted it could not provide the men. Furthermore, it

8 2/1st South Midland Field Company, a war time raised unit, arrived at the division in mid-June.

9 See, for example, TNA: WO95.2727: WD of 140 Bde., 47th Division. Hand written note by brigade major, 9 Jul.1915.

considered the system of trench reliefs then in operation compounded the manpower difficulties both for them and for the battalions themselves.

The shortage of labour remained a constant complaint of the RE but the demand for infantry working parties disrupted the possibility of purposeful training when battalions were out of the line. In reality, however, there was little alternative. By November, the hard work had resulted in a much improved trench system and the construction of several alternative routes to the front in case shelling prevented the use of particular tracks and communication trenches. Much work had also been done on completing battalion and company HQ dugouts, bomb stores and shrapnel proof shelters had been built in the second and third lines. In addition, several newly-constructed keeps behind the front lines now housed garrisons in case of a German break through. Stores and raw materials remained, however, in short supply. 1/Field Company could do little to repair a series of burst pipes until it retrieved its tools from a field company of another division which had asked to borrow them. Flints and stones for road repairs and timber for telegraph poles were still frequently unobtainable, as was, perhaps less surprisingly, a diving suit required to help repair a broken pump in the depths of a well. The onset of winter with its successive frosts, snows and thaws brought additional flooding and trench collapses. Those which had been properly drained and graded survived the worst of the weather, but those which had remained unrevetted, especially in the sector in front of Foncquevillers, frequently could not cope. Constantly harassed by salvos of *minenwerfer* shells, day and night the infantry and pioneers struggled to repair the broken parapets and drain the trenches. Some, including one of the keeps known as Fort Grosvenor, had to be temporarily abandoned. One battalion recorded that "from a military point of view" the simultaneous snow and thaw made 4 March "an uninteresting day, both sides fighting the elements."

The unrelenting work of the field companies over the winter was drawn to the attention of the corps commander. He wired his congratulations and gratitude, expressions which were later echoed by Major General Fanshawe, the GOC Division. Although it had taken two drafts amounting to 90 men, 5/Sussex complained in February 1916 that another 250 men were "urgently needed" if it was to fulfil its work. Despite its reduced numbers the battalion had provided two platoons as a garrison for one of the Hébuterne keeps throughout the winter and in March it was allocated its own stretch of front line to hold. It had relinquished its Maxims in January and received four Lewis guns as replacements but the opportunity again to act as genuine infantry was appreciated by the men. It was only when the better weather arrived and the infantry battalions were being brought closer to strength that the work began to ease off. The pioneers could then undergo some "very useful training" with the RE who were also able to have a break from their usual work. The two original field companies both had almost three weeks out for training during the spring but it is unclear how close to the approximately 218 other ranks establishment the companies actually were. A draft of 33 had arrived at 2/Field Company in August 1915 "without any warning, smoke helmets or rations." In addition to the lack of provisions, the new arrivals included a

A view well-known to troops of 48th Division during their Hébuterne sojourn. The photo looks across no man's land towards the German positions in Gommecourt Park. Z Hedge lay in the field to the left of the photo. (Author)

mounted corporal and three drivers, all supernumerary to establishment who were "not required or asked for." This example of a "lack of organization" was laid firmly at the door of OC No.1 TF Base at Rouen. Whatever their actual strength, the field companies trained in various types of bridging, demolition, route marching, signalling and musketry but were soon back in the line.

The terrible weather of the winter resulted in increased work for the orderlies and staff in the field ambulances. The three OCs were constantly travelling between their several aid stations to check on how they were functioning and assessing whether they were adequately staffed, supplied and protected from enemy shellfire. Among its other responsibilities 3/Field Ambulance was tasked with operating the divisional rest station (DRS). Bell tents were erected as wards in an orchard at Vauchelles and gradually expanded to include barns, a former school room and five huts. The OC bought[10] bricks from demolished houses to use as roads and paths and boilers for a bath house were acquired from Amiens. Brick ovens were built and the Red Cross offered a number of vehicles as the DRS's transport. The function of the station was to admit a maximum of 200 patients suffering from minor septic diseases, 'flu, trench fever and

10 As the war diary (Dec.1915) does not mention from whom the bricks were 'bought' this may be a case of the diarist's misuse of 'bought' rather than 'brought'.

rheumatism and treat them for up to a maximum of 10 days.[11] Further forward, the advanced dressing stations (ADS) were continually improved by working parties from the ambulances themselves, with floors being lowered and bricked, bursting layers built up on the roofs and sandbags piled around the walls. The ADS at Hébuterne had a small extension added as an emergency operating theatre but a continuing problem, and one which took a considerable time to resolve, was the inadequate provision of heating and lighting in the ambulances' barns, tented wards and messes.

The numbers of wounded admitted to the field ambulances were "comparatively few", with an average of only about 50 per ambulance between November and January. There were the occasional busy nights such as 9-10 April when 26 casualties were sustained during the digging of an advanced trench in no man's land, and on 16 May when the consequences of an intense bombardment on 145 Brigade's front almost overwhelmed the ADS in Hébuterne. This incident resulted in nearly 50 of the most severe casualties being evacuated to the casualty clearing station (CCS). January saw the highest total number of wounded during the winter period, with one ambulance alone admitting 53; 20 of those were returned to duty within a week, with 28 being sufficiently serious to be sent down the line to a CCS. The same month also saw the largest number of sick admitted to the DRS, a total of 557. Sixty-five percent of those were returned to duty within seven days, with 31 percent having been sent to a CCS. Despite the wet trenches and what was recorded by some units as an alleged shortage of thigh length gum boots there seems to have been remarkably few recorded cases of trench foot. For its part, 8/Worcestershire recorded a "plentiful supply" of gum boots which, together with a regular supply of clean socks and attentive care when men came out of the trenches, apparently resulted in substantial success against frostbite and not one recorded case of trench foot in January 1916.[12]

In January a dental department had been established at Bertrancourt and in February a 'sick station' was opened to deal specifically with the division's growing number of scabies cases. The ADMS frequently commented on the number of officers with neurasthenia and nervous disability and also on the numbers suffering from piles, German measles and bronchitis. He also noted the substantial number of men with dental problems, a complaint which today is often linked to stress and general physical debility. The facility at Betrancourt, with another soon to be housed in the chateau of Souastre, "greatly helped" to check the number of men sent to the base for minor repairs. There is no evidence to suggest that stress or tension within the division was any worse or any better than in other formations living and working under similar conditions but there are comments in several war diaries that the frequent

11 One of the DRS's most prestigious patients was Brigadier General McClintock, GOC 145 Bde. He did, however, prove too ill to return to command and was invalided home to the UK in December 1915.

12 Together with 6/Gloucestershire, 8/Worcestershire with 33 admissions, had the lowest number of men in the division sent to the field ambulances during January 1916.

visits of Major General Fanshawe and his staff to the front lines, to the aid stations and the ambulances, in addition to his regular messages of thanks to working parties and patrols, did much to sustain morale at this difficult time.

Another reason for the low number of sick cases was the thorough and relentless work performed by Captain Dale and his sanitary section. Dales' brief was extensive and his observations meticulous. He noted a rise in diarrhoea cases and on investigation concluded it was owing to the men eating green apples and drinking the local spirits. He ordered regular testing of water quality in the estaminets because it was used to dilute the various local 'syrops' the troops found so appealing, and he was an inveterate hunter of lice.[13] He agitated constantly for separate, raised bunks and disinfected palliases, for more disinfectors to cleanse blankets and underclothes and for better latrine provision. He noticed most scabies cases were affected on the buttocks, which he blamed on poor hygiene of latrine seats and campaigned endlessly for better laundry facilities. He complained about the lack of sulphur, soap and other preventatives and organized the conversion of oil drums into washing bowls. He criticized the lack of heating in men's billets, especially because it meant the men were unable to dry their clothing or wash adequately, and regularly checked the health of the local civilian population. When typhoid broke out in the villages of Coigneux and Authie he organized the inoculation of 100 civilians, engaged the local gendarme to force the evacuation of one positive case and bought barrels to supply the civilians with chlorinated water. He managed to secure the services of men classified as 'Permanent Base' to clear manure heaps dating back to the French occupation and eventually decided it was probably not worth the effort to check an outbreak of German measles in March because most of the sufferers were back at duty within two days. In May, when his battle against the fly population was moving into top gear, he was visited by the sanitation officer of Fourth Army. Dale noted dryly that this visit was the great man's "first… in 14 months."

Equally as dynamic as Dale in his quest for a healthy division, although perpetually mournful and disconsolate, was the redoubtable ADVS, Lieutenant Colonel Harris. Still constantly complaining about the quality of stable management and of the difficulties his lack of staff and transport caused him, Harris was always on the move. He held at least one meeting a month for the division's veterinary and transport officers, travelled extensively between the horsed units inspecting and advising, railed against the incompetence of one of his sergeants and condemned the inefficiency of the Divisional Train for losing the veterinary stores. He went frequently to railhead to examine the often nearly 200 monthly remounts and even found time to watch his officers and men fire their five compulsory rounds across no man's land from Foncqevillers. In February 1916, Harris left for eight day's leave but such was his

13 Soon after moving into the area, the River Authie was found to be littered with dead fish. On investigation, it was discovered that an estimated one ton of lime had been emptied into the river by 'person or persons unknown.' TNA: WO95.2747: 15 Aug.1915.

exhaustion, he did not return to work for another three weeks. Once back he again threw himself into an endless round of visits and equine emergencies.

One of Harris's major concerns and responsibilities was overseeing the care of the artillery's horses and mules. An outbreak of glanders in III (Warwicks) Brigade, for example, led to the destruction of 24 beasts in that brigade and the time-consuming testing of animals in the other brigades. Throughout the winter many of the horse lines and even the few available hard standings were hock-deep in mud; these conditions, of course, caused additional problems for animal welfare and management. As the batteries were reasonably static during this period the horses were not over worked but there was a shortage of oats and hay consumption was only about half the amount advocated by the vets. The batteries, with their newly acquired 18 pdr pieces, were handicapped in their firing routines by the ongoing shell shortage but, despite the problems, in April a new battery was formed in each brigade.[14] In the following month the old familiar names of the batteries and brigades were changed to numbers and the newly-created D Battery of each brigade was transferred to the 'new' 243 Brigade. Previously this had been the heavy howitzer brigade but the former 4/Warwicks (H) and 5/Warwicks (H) batteries, together with a heavy battery which had joined earlier from 37th Division, were distributed across the three 18 pdr brigades. The remaining antiquated 5 inch howitzers had been replaced by the new 4.5 inch guns in January which meant that by mid-May 1916, three of the four brigades comprised three 18 pdr and one heavy battery, with the remaining brigade being armed with only three batteries of 18 pdrs.[15]

This alteration in divisional structure involved the transfer of considerable numbers of men from one artillery brigade to another, in addition to the absorption of drafts from England.[16] One brigade commander complained about the "colossal" amount of office work the expansion process and ordinary administration necessitated but did wax lyrical about the new 18 pdr guns. "It is such a treat" he recorded because they were "shooting splendidly and the fuses are quite good." Furthermore, he added, "The infantry are also very pleased with us." Experiments undertaken by the brigades to develop air-land cooperation, however, proved largely futile because each brigade was restricted to 185 rounds each week and the aircrafts' wirelesses were almost completely unreliable. When during the poor weather the breeches of two guns in one battery were reported to be under water, reserve and alternative positions were ordered to be dug in various places. About once every two months the CRA adjusted the batteries' zones and arcs of fire, a decision which also often resulted in the digging of new pits. Finding the timber and bricks to give a degree of protection to these new sites remained, however, continually

14 This was D Battery.
15 Effectively: I SM (Gloucs) Bde became 240 Bde RFA; II SM (Worcs) Bde became 241 Bde RFA; III SM. (War) Bde became 242 Bde RFA and IV SM (War.H) became 243 Bde RFA.
16 An indication of the complexity the cross-postings and restructuring involved can be gauged from the nominal rolls included in 241 Brigade's WD, May 1916.

problematic. Personnel were frequently occupied in scrounging for additional materials to improve the protection of casements and observation posts, baling out their pits and dugouts and repairing wires cut by wagons. The relentless work, especially the necessity of burying new telephone wires when positions were altered, added to the general exhaustion of the men. All gunners had to fire a musketry course from the trenches and were, at times, even allowed to fire a shell or two at unusual targets. One battery sought and achieved permission to fire at a lone German cyclist who, in his surprise at being targetted, was seen to fall of his bike and into a ditch.

Additional restrictions were placed on the guns in September. Orders came down that "until further notice" they were to fire only if the Germans actually attacked. The enemy, who engaged from time to time in what was described as "promiscuous shelling", were curious to know why the division had ceased firing and dropped about 150 shells in the false hope of prompting some retaliation. All the South Midland batteries could do for almost two weeks was to observe how "cheeky" German working parties were becoming, sit it out and hope the enemy shelling would be ineffective. When 8/Warwickshire requested severe retaliation on the German *minenwerfer* battery which had sent over 14 canisters, one of which managed to block the entrance to the battalion's HQ dugout, it was dismayed to discover that all that could be despatched in revenge was a mere eight 18 pdr shells. War diaries are, however, generally derisory in their comments about the worth of German shelling. They frequently record the number of shells fired at an area by the enemy, such as the 200 which landed on 242 Brigade's positions on one day in March 1916, but usually claim that little or no damage was done. Later that month the same brigade's pits were repeatedly straddled by 4.2 inch and 5.9 inch howitzers, with several direct hits on the positions. Again, the war diary recorded "no damage." Only rarely do the diaries acknowledge a gun being disabled or a dugout destroyed.

There is certainly a degree of frustration in the records when commanders complained the shell shortage prevented them from deterring German working parties repairing lanes cut in the wire by the 18 pdrs, but the difficulties of cutting the wire with faulty shells and inadequate fuses were often minimized. For example, 240 Brigade recorded one of its batteries fired 150 rounds at belts of wire 25 yards deep. The guns managed to cut a lane up to 15 yards wide, seemingly without difficulty. The reality in 1915 was, however, usually different. Similarly, there is frequent mention of batteries firing a few shells quickly and efficiently to destroy machine gun and rifle grenade posts, and others which record the swift silencing of enemy guns by counter-battery fire. When compared to the recorded lack of success the Germans allegedly managed to inflict on the British trenches and guns, it seems strange that the South Midlanders were apparently able to wreak so much more destruction. There are instances of brutal honesty, such as, "Our 9.2 inch hows fired 35 rounds at Point K23b – many blinds, enemy took no notice," and "one of our shells peppered our infantry," but the more common comments are: "fired successfully at a TM position"; "many direct hits on enemy trenches"; "fired with excellent observed effect."

The artillery was, of course, learning new skills and adapting existing ones to the changed operating environment. This process would take time, especially as the Germans continued to hold a significant advantage in the number of shells they could fire in reply to any British bombardment. Nevertheless, experiments and trials were made to discover the optimum methods of maximizing the impact of the rationed shell allocations. Results and observations of the trials were distributed and discussed at regular conferences between brigade and battery commanders. Two of the conclusions reached by these meetings and which were then adopted by the division's brigades were to deploy one 18 pdr periodically roving between several positions in order to confuse the enemy and to have another positioned to hit the German wire in enfilade from 2,500 yards. This was well within effective range for the weapon but the gun was eventually actually sited in dead ground only 800 yards from the enemy trenches.

The numbers of killed and wounded in the infantry brigades during these periods of intermittent shelling were low, with probably only a maximum of 30 fatalities between August 1915 and May 1916. The forward brigades where subjected to two days of particularly intense shelling in October from the so-called "Bavarian Circus", an itinerant group of 5.9 inch and heavier calibre guns which stayed for a few days in a sector before moving on.[17] Some months later, 4/Ox&Bucks described 3 May as a "most unlucky day" when it was strafed by heavy howitzers, scores of rifle grenades and machine guns for several hours. This was an exceptional day because the battalion lost two officers killed and one wounded. The numbers reporting sick vary according to the time of year but there was a significant spike in the numbers of one brigade being admitted to hospital in the second half of April 1916. These may have been late victims of the German measles outbreak but the 35 men admitted to hospital in two weeks was greater than the number admitted during a four week period in December 1915 and January 1916.

Despite the appalling state of the trenches in December, and the collapse of dugouts which on one occasion killed four men, the diary of 4/Ox&Bucks considered the men's "cheerfulness" to be "wonderful."[18] The almost incessant shelling of February which then continued into March and a longer than usual tour in the trenches did, however, "begin to tell" on the men. The sick list "grows longer every day" but the men were still considered to be "sticking it well." That morale was tested in such conditions is not surprising, and there is some evidence to suggest that the staff were again becoming concerned about the incidence of what were either self-inflicted or accidental wounds. In December 1915, divisional HQ reiterated its order of May which had insisted that owing to "the excessive wastage arising from accidental injuries", units were to report

17 In a long but essentially cheery letter home describing its activities, Greenwell explained the purpose of the 'travelling circus' as simply to 'simply cheer the Germans up a bit.' Greenwell, *Infant in Arms*, p. 64.

18 In contrast, the OC of one of the field ambulances apparently decided that if they did not get rest, 'The Oxfords would all go sick if they went on much longer.' Ibid, p. 80.

Many of the division's men killed in the Hébuterne sector were buried in the village's military cemetery. The men are buried in what are largely regimental or battalion rows. (Author)

on how each of the incidents occurred. In order to maintain a check on the frequency of the incidents, divisional HQ recorded for several weeks the numbers reported to it by unit adjutants. It also recorded the number of courts martial held to hear cases ranging from sleeping at a post to striking a NCO. The number of cases was not excessive in comparison to other divisions but did included, for example: two privates in 5/ Gloucestershire given two months Field Punishment No.1 for drunkenness; Private Hullis of 4/Ox&Bucks three months hard labour for possessing a camera; Private Weston of 4/Gloucestershire had his punishment for sleeping at his post reduced from five years penal servitude to three months Field Punishment No.1, and Private Dawson of 4/Ox&Bucks was also given a term of Field Punishment No.1 for an offence involving the abuse of a green envelope. Among others which were investigated in case they had been self-inflicted rather than accidental was that of Sergeant Heavens of 5/Gloucestershire; he was deemed not to have deliberately injured himself with a Very pistol.

In 1915 and 1916 the local identity and ethos enjoyed by territorial units helped to ensure there were very few serious disciplinary cases. The disciplinary record of 48th Division was typical amongst the TF divisions already in theatre but in a formation of over 18,000 men it is unsurprising that a few of these civilians in uniform found the strain or environment too challenging. Although the number of deaths and injured was in comparison to other divisions small, the three infantry brigades did spend a larger proportion of their time than most other brigades in the line. Hébuterne was a quiet sector but the men remained exposed often to intensive German shelling and sniper fire and had fewer opportunities to escape to the relative safety of the rear and training areas. When the division first moved into the sector, inter-battalion reliefs took place every 16 days but this was extended to 32 days in late September.[19] Training did take place on those occasions when a battalion was withdrawn for a few days but it was usually interrupted by poor weather or the inevitable demand for working parties. Lessons were quickly learned about how to lessen the impact of enemy shelling by, for example, thinning the numbers in the front trenches and, with the arrival of more British divisions and the with the divisional mounted troops and cyclists undertaking trench tours, it was decided the divisional front could be held by two rather than three brigades. When battalions of 143 Brigade were out of the line they were often sent on route marches, sometimes accompanied by the cookers, to harden the men's feet after the swamps of the trenches; 144 Brigade realistically drew up a less than comprehensive training programme in August 1915 for its units. Noting that it 'was hoped' only two or three days of its period in divisional reserve would be spent digging, the brigade major instructed all battalions to practise company attacks and as much "steady drill and handling of arms" as possible. Even these modest proposals were disrupted by the almost incessant demand for working parties. The troops' exhaustion was becoming so acute that by December one unit in 143 Brigade allowed what was probably the euphemism of "individual training" for some of its men.[20]

When 8/Worcestershire was fortunate enough to be allowed four days training in January 1916, only one of the days was taken for working parties. The diarist recorded that the benefits of this period of training, cleaning and inspections were "very apparent in the men, who had been showing slight signs of staleness." In contrast, the three days spent in reserve by 8/Warwickshire in theory allowed two days for company and one for a full battalion practice attack but the usefulness of the period was limited because on all of the three days working parties had also to be found. Having attended and studied a practice attack undertaken by 6/Warwickshire while it was out of the line, the GOC Brigade distributed his conclusions to all battalions within his brigade. They concerned the need to detail sufficient personnel for laying telephone lines, bombing the flanks and carrying ammunition across to captured trenches as well as some thoughts on the role of stretcher bearers during an attack. These were all very obvious conclusions but their dissemination did demonstrate that the brigades were learning and thinking about how best to instruct and deploy their men. In addition, from early 1916 there is a marked recorded increase in the number

19 On the 16 day *roulement*, a battalion would spend four days in brigade reserve in a village just to the rear, eight in the forward trenches and four in support just behind the front before moving forward again for eight days.

20 Recreation facilities did gradually improve in the rear areas, assisted by, for example, a cinema presented to 143 Brigade by the Birmingham Small Arms Company and two concert parties formed by units within the division.

of divisional and brigade conferences and lectures attended by the division's officers. Yet, despite the improved opportunities for training, even in May 1916 4/Ox&Bucks complained all it could do when out of the line was to practise "elementary musketry." This was because, its CO claimed, "The training areas allotted are ludicrously small and makes anything like field work for anything more than a section impossible." This shortage was largely the result of farmers refusing to allow their pasture land to be used by troops for training purposes. More opportunities had, however, gradually become available in the early months of 1916, by which time divisional schools for officers and NCOs had been established.

The establishment of these schools was a vital development as it meant that with the appearance of the growing number of new and unfamiliar weapons NCOs could instruct their platoons or sections in their use. In the early stages of the war German weaponry was, in general, of better quality than that of the British. By 1916, this was beginning to change. The 48th Division had recorded its envy of German light trench mortars, *minenwerfers* and rifle grenades and had suffered casualties, such as Captain Tomkinson and six other ranks of 7/Worcestershire, whilst trying to examine unexploded ordnance in order to determine why the enemy's were so much better than the British. Improvisation on the part of the British had also resulted in casualties. Lieutenant Schwalm, 144 Brigade's Grenade Officer, was killed when the released arm of the West bomb thrower hit the back of his head. Schwalm was not the first to be struck by this "cumbrous weapon, the results obtained from which are by no means commensurate with the danger incurred by the user and the difficulty in manoeuvring it." With the appearance of the Lewis gun and then in May and June the rearming of the battalions with the Short Lee Enfield rifle, the fire power and efficiency of the division was substantially improved. In addition, a modified and more effective version of the Bangalore torpedo was demonstrated in April; in May, 145 Brigade "much enjoyed" a demonstration of the new 3 inch mortar. Nonetheless, accidents did still happen. The diarist of 7/Worcestershire appears to have written with some relief that "no one was gassed" during a lecture and demonstration of anti-gas measures, but five men were killed and seven wounded when an "unfortunate accident" occurred during a trench mortar demonstration held in conjunction with a practice attack by two battalions of Warwicks.

The division grew increasingly concerned about the possible use of gas in the sector by the enemy. There may have been a small number of actual releases by the Germans but the frequency of false alarms became tiresome. Some of the alarms were a result of nervousness amongst the largely inexperienced troops who could on occasions mistake the smell of chloride of lime in their own trenches for German chlorine gas. Smoke hoods were tested regularly and there was criticism of relying on the alleged inadequacy of the noise generated by clanging an 18 pdr shell case. By January 1916,"'everybody was very fed up with false gas alarms." During the preparations for the first British use of gas, at Loos on 25 September 1915, the division had been ordered to prepare itself for an advance in its sector. The divisional artillery began a programme of wire cutting which, to the observing infantry, was less than convincing.

To the diarist of 4/Ox&Bucks the fire was "without very much effect" and decided that as there would be no way through the German wire, they would "hope for the best." If the offensive at Loos had proved successful, 144 Brigade was tasked to lead an assault against the enemy lines near Gommecourt but instead of charging across no man's land in the wake of a defeated enemy the brigade spent 25 September in its billets waiting for orders to advance which never arrived. With news that First Army had failed to make any substantial gains the brigade reverted to a conventional trench holding role the following day.[21]

In daylight hours there was little visual evidence of the Germans in the trenches opposite. Working parties were seen occasionally to the rear of the support and reserve trenches but, like any inadvertent opportunity offered by the South Midlanders, to be seen was to invite a reaction. Snipers on both sides were active, with the Germans managing to kill Lieutenant Serjeant, the sniping officer of 8/Warwickshire, whilst he was observing for a rifleman. In an attempt to gain revenge the battalion set off an explosion in a sump in the hope that curious Germans would pop up their heads to see what was going on. The ruse worked and one German was claimed as killed. In October, one particular sniper was causing so much trouble that a patrol was sent out by 4/Ox&Bucks to capture him. To the frustration of the patrol the sniper very sensibly "ran away" when he realized what was afoot. There was the occasional German deserter who successfully gave himself up to the division and the enemy were sometimes heard calling out to the Warwickshire battalions asking whether they were from Coventry or Birmingham. The Germans were also sometimes heard singing heartily. On one such occasion in May 1916, 8/Warwickshire became convinced the enemy was indulging in a "drunken debauch" as "ribald songs" were heard for several hours coming from their Gommecourt billets. German aircraft were also a fairly common sight above the trenches. Their presence usually heralded a barrage or flurry of trench mortar shells but in December the troops of 145 Brigade watched in fascination as one aircraft attempting to fly over the British trenches into a strong head wind appeared to remain virtually motionless for five minutes. The aircraft was beyond the range of small arms fire and the anti aircraft guns also fired short. The lesson to be learned, thought one officer, was to have anti-aircraft observers closer to the front lines so that they could correct their batteries' fire.

In addition to learning how to adapt to living as comfortably and safely in trench conditions as possible, troops of the division were used to instruct newly arrived formations of the New Armies in trench acclimatization. Among those which received instruction from the South Midlanders during the winter of 1915-16 were battalions and units of the 36th (Ulster) and 30th Divisions. The learning programme for the novice divisions was comprehensive and involved two infantry companies of each new

21 Owing to the configuration of the sector's trenches 'thousands' of spent bullets fired by 37th Division to the north as part of their demonstration in support of the Loos attack landed in 48th Division's trenches. Cruttwell, *War Service of 1/4th Berks*, p. 42.

division being in the trenches with one battalion of 48th Division. The training was intended to build upon the schemes the new divisions had been working to in the UK but with emphasis on the fundamentals of trench warfare. These included, for example, sentry duties, patrolling beyond the wire, erecting wire obstacles, sniping, orderly room procedure, distribution of rations and the care and evacuation of the wounded. The supporting arms were, as those of 48th Division had been in their early weeks, attached to similar units of the division for a period of about 10 days. When they were not actually under instruction in the trenches the infantry of the newly-arrived divisions were employed in digging, drainage and carrying parties. There is no suggestion in the war diaries that the instruction was regarded as an unwelcome chore as it did to some extent relieve the South Midlanders of some tiresome and dangerous work. The inexperience of the New Army units did, however, become apparent in several ways and did occasionally present unnecessary dangers to their tutors. Troops were prone to peer, sometimes fatally, over the parapet and to make too much noise when in the trenches. This often invited an aggressive response from the enemy's artillery. Unsurprisingly, the officers and NCOs lacked knowledge and thus confidence in trench routines and there was an innocent naivety among many men with regard to the dangers of German shelling. The unfortunate battalions of the Manchester and Liverpool Pals of 30th Division received their instruction in November and December 1915 when the trenches were at their worst. The Manchesters' chosen method of disposing of the liquid mud was to cut through the front trenches and push the mud through with boards nailed to long handles. According to an historian of 21/Manchester, as far as trench routine was concerned the course instruction resolved itself into "Push the mud, push the mud."[22] As there was no spare accommodation in the cellars of Foncquevillers and other neighbouring villages, when the Manchesters returned from their tour of instruction they were housed in unheated tents. 21/Manchester was reported as losing a "large number of men through sickness and exhaustion" owing, it was recorded rather unnecessarily, to them "not appearing to be sufficiently acclimatized to the conditions presently prevailing." Even when in the rear areas, the new arrivals could lose men through freak accidents. Lieutenant Johnston of 17/Manchester was apparently hit and killed by a shell case from a British anti-aircraft gun.

In preparation for the forthcoming offensive on the Somme the usual routine of trench maintenance was for several nights in April supplemented by a major new initiative. It was decided that as no man's land in the division's sector was in places up to almost 400 yards wide a new front trench should be dug closer to the German line and used as the jumping off point for assaulting battalions. 145 Brigade was tasked to do the digging on a front of about 850 yards. The actual distance the new line was dug in advance of the existing front lines varies in two battalion war diaries. The

22 Compiled, *The 21st Battalion Manchester Regiment. A History*. (Manchester: Fleur de Lys Publishing, 1994).

brigade diary simply gives the map reference points, which suggests it was roughly 340 yards in front, while 4/Ox&Bucks record it as 380 yards and 5/Gloucestershire at a meagre 180 yards. Whatever the precise distance, the construction of the new trench was a remarkable piece of staff work. Wire, tools, revetting hurdles and sand bags were readied in preparation, the digging parties from 5/Gloucestershire and 4/Ox&Bucks rested during the day of 9 April and the artillery was warned to be ready to fire on the enemy trenches and battery positions should the work be detected. 1/Bucks and 4/Berkshire provided covering parties for the digging and wiring teams which comprised most of the rifle strength of the brigade's other two battalions. The work began under a cloudy and dark sky at about 2100 and finished at about 0430. The Germans, appearing either not to have been sufficiently bothered to interfere with the work or simply did not hear it proceeding, fired only occasional shells in the general direction. By the time dawn was about to break, knife rests protected the new trench which was dug to an initial depth of roughly four and a half feet. Consolidation work and connections with the original line continued during the next few nights. By this time the Germans had spotted the new line and shelled it with the intent of gaining, it was recorded, "their revenge" for its construction. At a cost of two killed and about 20 wounded from the approximately 1,500 men involved, the new trench greatly reduced the distance any attacking battalions would have to advance across open ground.

Very soon after the division arrived in the new sector it instituted a policy of active patrolling of no man's land. The purpose was to gather intelligence and endeavour to secure a degree of moral supremacy over the enemy. With the exception of October, when the division's patrols laid up without success almost every night in the hope of catching enemy patrols, the Germans appeared anxious to contest this strategy. Rival patrols consequently regularly bumped into each other in the dark and confused exchanges of fire followed. A patrol sent out on 3 August by 4/Ox&Bucks of one officer and four men was probably the first undertaken by the division but inexperience and confusion in the darkness resulted in one of the men attacking and nearly killing his own officer.[23] One conducted the following night by 5/Gloucestershire was more successful and resulted in the award of two Distinguished Conduct Medals. A later one undertaken by 1/Bucks went out with the intention of holding what was known as Z Hedge in no man's land.[24] Carrying a telephone and armed with rifles and a Lewis gun the patrol opened fire in the December dark at a number of Germans seen to be approaching the hedge. The Germans turned and fled just as the cocking lever flew off the Lewis. A desperate search in the mud failed to retrieve the essential part and the Germans escaped. One of the Bucks was killed and then to add more misfortune and

23 Greenwell, *Infant in arms*, pp. 37-8

24 'Z Hedge' was to become a much contested feature in the sector. Pickford, *The War Record of the 1/4th Ox&Bucks* p. 13, records that 'one night in March 1916, every single man of one of the companies patrolled with his platoon to the famous hedge.' The hedge lay about half way across no man's land close to the lane linking Hébuterne to Gommecourt.

confusion to the enterprise a telephone call from battalion HQ was mistakenly interpreted as an order to withdraw. When it was realized the withdrawal had not actually been ordered a bombing patrol scurried out and discovered some enemy ammunition as well as a working watch and chain. The Germans also evidently quickly recovered their composure as by daylight they had a patrol in the hedge which had perhaps been despatched to search for the officer's watch. Another equipment malfunction occurred when a patrol from 6/Gloucestershire ran into a German party. The Gloucesters' hand grenades failed to ignite with the result that the enemy managed to escape with the loss of only one man. Until the more efficient Mills bombs began to appear in increasing numbers later in 1916 the British, and much to their oft-recorded chagrin, were at a permanent disadvantage in such encounters. Deaths on patrols were not infrequent. Lieutenant Doyne of 4/Ox&Bucks was killed in December by a burst of machine-gun fire and his body later recovered but when Lieutenant Moore and Lance Corporal Rodway of 5/Gloucestershire were killed during a patrol encounter, a group which went out to recover their bodies was driven away by German fire.[25] The other four members of Second Lieutenant Piper's patrol also made "every effort" to bring the wounded officer back to his own trench, with one NCO being reported killed in the attempt, but had to abandon him to his fate.[26]

A fairly major encounter came in early April when 1/Bucks sent out a patrol of 25 other ranks under Captain Combs and Lieutenant Aitkin. Its purpose was to lie low until a German patrol approached and then to try to capture as many of the enemy as possible. The enemy appear to have quickly assessed the situation and despatched a force double the size of the Bucks. A bombing exchange ensued and the Bucks gradually withdrew behind their own wire. Four were killed and two wounded but in order to prevent the Germans from discovering their identity, Combs, Lance Corporal Vincent and Private Bloomfield, who fired salvoes of rifle grenades in the direction of the Germans, provided a covering party while others carried the casualties back to the British trenches. Although badly wounded, Sergeant Baldwin brought in one body and then went forward again to assist the covering party. He was eventually helped back by another officer who had gone out to see what was happening. In the post-action report the men were praised for their calmness in recovering the bodies, for the "slow and deliberate" withdrawal and the fact the officers had the men "well in hand." The patrol had clearly performed well against odds of at least two to one, with all ranks demonstrating courage, resourcefulness, commitment and, on the part of the officers and NCOs, leadership and initiative.[27]

While these casualties were the direct result of enemy action, accidental deaths and injuries did sometimes occur in listening posts: Private Sampson of 5/Gloucestershire

25 The Germans later retrieved the two dead and buried them in Puisieux churchyard.
26 2Lt Piper of 6/Warwickshire, died of wounds in German hands. Sgt Cotten, who was reported killed, appears to have survived.
27 Combs was awarded the MC, Baldwin the DCM and Vincent and Bloomfield the MM.

was shot dead by a colleague when mistaken for a German and, when out in a sap, Private Midwinter of the same battalion was wounded by a shot fired from the main trench. Excluding those killed and maimed by random or targeted shelling in this still relatively quiet sector, most casualties were the result of the recently instituted concept of raids on enemy lines.

In the second winter of the war, raiding enemy trenches, as opposed to patrol encounters in no man's land, was still both novel and experimental. Probably the earliest raid done by the division was conducted by C Company of 6/Gloucestershire on the night of 25-26 November. Its stated objectives were to take prisoners and assess the strength of the German trenches in what was known to be the fortified positions in the south-east corner of Gommecourt Park. A series of patrols had previously gathered sufficient intelligence about the extent of the German wire and the strength of their trenches to allow practice to be done over a similar system dug behind the British lines. A covering party of three officers and 50 other ranks was to wait at Z Hedge in no man's land from where two parties, each comprising a subaltern and 20 men, would assault the German lines. The men were armed with rifles, cudgels, bayonets and bombs.[28] To prevent the Germans from occupying Z Hedge the artillery fired on the enemy wire for most of the afternoon and soon after dark a platoon preceded the raiders out to the hedge. It was hoped the afternoon shelling would cause a nocturnal working party to be sent out to repair the wire and it was from this group the Gloucesters expected to capture prisoners. The main group of raiders was scheduled to join Lieutenant Nott and his covering platoon at the hedge just before midnight. Captain Young, the OC Company who would command the raid from the hedge, was accompanied by an artillery officer and two signallers who were in telephone communication with the batteries of III (SM) Brigade.

Owing to the bright moonlight, Second Lieutenants Badgeley (left group) and Pryce (right group) made slow and deliberate progress across no man's land and when 70 yards in front of the German trenches telephoned Captain Young to ask that the Number 1 barrage be fired. Young waited until cloud obscured the moon before passing the message down to the batteries. The barrage was intended to force the German sentries to take cover and to prevent the arrival of reinforcements from the support line. It commenced at 0103 with an initial 30 seconds of intensive fire on the flanks of the two points where the raiders would enter the German trench. It was then to reduce to a slightly slower rate. The two assaulting parties rushed forward, with the left group encountering some unexpectedly thick wire. Badgeley and 10 men hacked their way through and into the trench where they killed two Germans and bombed a dugout as other enemy troops withdrew down a communication trench. Touch was gained with Pryce's party just before Badgeley was wounded when, on his command, his party withdrew The right group did not encounter as much wire and surprised the Germans in their dugouts. Pryce and his men made their way down the trench, bombing dugouts as

28 The bayonets were to be used as daggers.

they went, before being confronted by a large group of Germans who were assumed to have made their way along deep underground passages. Bombs were exchanged before Pryce, who had been slightly wounded, ordered a withdrawal. There had evidently been an unrecorded problem with one of the groups because immediately the request for the Number 2 barrage was made to the batteries, the command 'Stop' was received and the Number 1 barrage was restarted. Presumably enemy reinforcements were advancing from the support line and either Pryce or Badgeley wanted the artillery to thwart the Germans' progress. The batteries fired for a further nine minutes but whatever the precise unexplained problem was, the two parties continued their withdrawal. They were pursued for a small distance but the Germans were quickly dissuaded from following too far by a flurry of bombs thrown by the raiders and a fusillade of rifle grenades fired by a covering party under Lieutenant Hartog.

One raider was killed by what was described as a "chance" bullet, one man was missing and in addition to the two officers, 18 other ranks were also wounded. One prisoner was brought back to the Gloucesters' trench; he later proffered information on unit identity and approximate numbers of the trench garrison. Eight dead Germans were counted in the trenches and it was assumed a larger number were killed by bombs thrown down the shelters' steps. This was the first major attempt by the battalion to penetrate the enemy's line and it was considered a success. The design and state of the German trenches were reported with clarity, their depth, general construction and drainage were usefully described and there were deductions made about the extent of the shelter system and connecting tunnels. The success was ascribed to the appropriate use of gathered intelligence, the determination of all ranks to see the scheme through and the repeated rehearsals over the replica system of trenches. Of the 25 men in each party, only eight carried No.5 grenades. Between them they possessed 96 bombs, a total which in subsequent raids when greater numbers of Mills bombs became available would be substantially increased. Technically the No.5 grenades worked well but the raiders reported difficulties in throwing them successfully to the bottom of the steps in the German dugouts. They suggested that had the grenades contained gas they might have prevented the enemy from reinforcing the front trenches by means of the underground tunnels. Communications throughout the raid were well maintained but the enemy was possibly remiss in not laying a barrage on no man's land which would very probably have cut the telephone cables; artillery in support of the raiders might not then have been so prompt. The infantry considered the barrage, which comprised over three hundred 18 pdr shrapnel shells, to have been effective and the fact that the Number 1 barrage could be almost instantly recalled is testament to the efficiency of the cooperation between the supported and supporting arms. The enemy artillery response, which fell largely on the Gloucesters' front and support trenches, was described as "slight and rather dilatory." This might suggest the Germans had been shaken by the size and swiftness of a raid which had temporarily disrupted communications between infantry and artillery.

There appears to have been no significant raids by the division during December, regular patrolling being instead the normal night time practice. The Germans, however, maintained their offensive spirit and made "so many little night attacks… that we are getting a bit jumpy."[29] In late January they launched a small raid but one preceded by a particularly vicious bombardment. It began at 0200 and in the course of the next 35 minutes, trenches, communication trenches and buildings in Foncquevillers were hit by an estimated 2000 *minenwerfer*, 5.9 inch, 4.2 inch and 77mm shells. One observer reported it was "quite impossible" to offer an accurate assessment but the bulk fell on the front of 143 Brigade, with the heaviest concentration on Trench 17. Such was the ferocity that all sentries sought shelter and 36 yards of front trench were completely destroyed. A party of what was later described as four Germans, although as none of the badly dazed British soldiers actually saw them the number is certainly a guess, entered the British front line using ladders carried for the purpose. They took a Lewis gun and three rifles and without "stopping to make further trouble" escaped unnoticed after what was thought to be only a few seconds. Such was their desire to get away quickly, one report later speculated, they left behind a small collection of bombs and cudgels. Casualties in 143 Brigade were remarkably light, with two killed and three wounded by shelling in the rear of the support line.

In retaliation, the South Midland Division organized an undertaking five nights later involving battalions from both 143 and 144 Brigades. The main thrust in the Warwickshire Brigade was to be done by 5/Warwickshire and in 144 Brigade by 6/Gloucestershire. The other three battalions in 144 Brigade were to make demonstrations while 6/Warwickshire was to support its sister battalion in a special mission should gas cylinders be discovered in the enemy trenches. Combined conferences between the two brigades' commanders, their brigade majors, the CRA, artillery brigade and battery commanders, the DA&QMG and battalion COs were held to discuss the scheme, request the provision of certain stores and to coordinate practice. Patrols went out nightly to find suitable places for the raiders to enter or harass enemy positions, with one patrol in 144 Brigade lying out all day within 150 yards of the German front trench. This allowed the officer to sketch the enemy wire and select a likely spot to penetrate. The divisional artillery fired at regular times during the preceding nights to lull the Germans into thinking all was as usual, 1/Field Ambulance was instructed to establish an ADS in Foncquevillers and troops practised their assaults over similar trenches and posts in the rear. An alarm was sounded in the evening of 27 January when it was thought the Germans had released gas but having spent over an hour in uncomfortable smoke helmets the 'gas' was discovered to be no more than yet another "excessive application of a common disinfectant." A final conference between the two brigade commanders was held in the morning of 29 January. The meeting agreed all was ready and reaffirmed zero for the raids and diversions to be 0400 that night.

The artillery had been briefed to provide what was by now becoming the norm for such raids. The first barrage would hit the German second line and communication

29 Greenwell, *Infant in Arms*, p. 88.

trenches to hamper the arrival of reinforcements and cover the noise of the raiders' approach; a second barrage would then fall on the enemy front line once the order for withdrawal had been signalled by the raiders. The continuing shell shortage meant, however, that the barrage would be laid only by 18 pdrs using shrapnel. The artillery would be supplemented by a machine-gun barrage firing over the heads of the assaulting troops into Gommecourt Park. It is not clear how many of 5/Warwickshire were tasked for the raid but support battalions in 144 Brigade were to use two or three parties averaging about one officer and 25 men. The brigade's main assault by 6/Gloucestershire was to be made by one company. The objectives of 143 Brigade's support battalions were either saps in advance of the German front line or a short section of the line itself. Their presence was intended to draw fire, create confusion and generally divert attention away from the main raid going in by 5/Warwickshire. The raiders were to carry the usual weapons of bayonet, bludgeons and bombs, were equipped with wire cutters and wore, for the division's first time in such circumstances, steel helmets. Their covering parties were to remain about 150 yards away from the German trench and supervise the removal of prisoners, reinforce the assault parties if required and protect the withdrawal.

Everything appeared to be in order and the night sky was lit by a brilliant display of stars when, at 2100, Major General Fanshawe visited 143 Brigade's HQ to reiterate the order that 5/Warwickshire was to make a special search for gas cylinders in the enemy trenches. If any were found word was to be sent back immediately and the raiders were to hold the trench until two companies of 6/Warwickshire arrived. C and D Companies, with five additional Lewis guns, were awarded "the honour" of going across no man's land and defending the trench until the gas cylinders could be neutralized or destroyed. The men were to carry picks or shovels and issued with 10 bombs and 170 rounds. The other two companies were to act in support by carrying another 30,000 rounds, 2,000 sandbags and 2,000 grenades.

By a little after 2300 hours, the formerly bright sky was covered in deep fog. A patrol on 5/Warwickshire's front reported in at 0200 with confirmation that the fog in no man's land was too dense for the officer to locate the place where the battalion was to pass through the German wire. On receiving the report the CO decided the raid should be postponed that night but when given the option, the GOC 144 Brigade decided his battalions would go ahead with their enterprises. While 5/Warwickshire's assault parties settled down for the remainder of the night and 6/Warwickshire returned to billets, the raiding groups of 144 Brigade slipped over their parapets, made their way through their own wire and lay out in front of the German belts to wait for the signal gun. At 0359 the lone gun signalled the start of the first barrage and groups from the three support battalions of 144 Brigade made for the enemy lines. An enemy wiring party in front of 7/Worcestershire ran back to their own front line leaving the Worcesters to cut through some hanging wire before next coming up against concertina only 10 yards from the enemy trench. Deciding it would be impossible to cut their way through, the attackers hurled several volleys of No.5 bombs before withdrawing to the covering party and in due course to their own trenches. The first party of 8/Worcestershire threw their bombs and then the second fired 18 rifle grenades at their objective and withdrew with the help of the ground and darkness to their own lines. 4/Gloucestershire had a similar experience but 6/Gloucestershire, for who these other battalions were effectively undertaking these small scale assaults, lost direction in the smoke and fog and returned to their own trenches without having thrown a bomb or firing a shot.

The night was clearly a disappointment in that the two principal attacking parties either failed even to start their raid or to reach their objective. The weather was certainly against them and perhaps Lieutenant Colonel Sladen, the CO of 5/Warwickshire was prudent to have cancelled his battalion's attack. He was evidently not condemned by his superiors for being over cautious because he not only remained in command but would subsequently become brigade commander. Nonetheless, parties from three other battalions did reach their objectives, the two artillery barrages worked well and the signalling, which involved not only telephone links but also lamps which did manage to penetrate the fog, between the assault groups worked well. Similarly, the covering parties and the batteries were reported to have operated "without a hitch." Casualties were minimal, with a few men receiving slight wounds, and useful experience was certainly gathered in undertaking such enterprises. They probably did kill and wound a number of Germans, especially in the crowded trench to which the enemy wiring party withdrew, and the German response to the assaults was "very feeble." With perhaps a hint of criticism, the diarist of 7/Worcestershire made the point that having to wait for the attack by 6/Gloucestershire which never materialized meant that his men had to lay out for more than an hour in the bitter cold. The result of the discomfort, reported the diarist, was that his men found it difficult with frozen fingers to pull the split pin from their grenades. The raiders did fail to achieve their primary objective of taking a German prisoner, but the brigadier was reported to have been pleased with the results.

Two nights later 6/Gloucestershire tried to make amends for is failure. Supported by a meagre barrage provided by one trench mortar, which fired a paltry 20 bombs, one battery of III South Midland Brigade, which fired a mere 30 shrapnel shells, and three machine guns loosing off bursts at two minute intervals, one officer and 12 other ranks attempted to capture a prisoner from a sap running towards the enemy wire in the familiar area near the south-east corner of Gommecourt Park. The raiders were thwarted by the thickness of the German wire and had to content themselves with throwing a few bombs towards the sap. Just over two weeks after this failure the Germans again demonstrated how such a quick snatch and grab raid should be conducted. At 0130 on 18 February, an intense bombardment erupted on the British front, support and communication trenches close to Foncquevillers. Sentries in the front trenches were forced to seek shelter in dugouts as a "rain" of what was later estimated as at least 2,000 shells of all types and calibres poured down for about 35 minutes. In Trench 55, which had been completely isolated as a result of the atrocious weather, two sentry posts were spaced about 30 yards apart. Unfortunately, the sentries were not in mutual view. In one post, a sentry of 8/Worcestershire was wounded before he reached the comparative safety of a nearby dugout but managed to crawl inside to join a group of six men who were "ready to rush out" when the shelling stopped. While the British troops were unaware that the shelling had lifted monetarily from their stretch of trench, about 30 Germans entered the line by means of a disused sap. Two surprised sentries at the north end of Trench 55 saw six Germans advancing towards them and offered some resistance from inside their dugout until they were both wounded. Another sentry half way along the trench saw a second group and shouted the alarm into a dug out before he, too, was wounded. Lying on the duckboards he saw Germans throw several bombs into the dugout, some of which were promptly thrown back by Sergeant Webb, before the occupants surrendered. Leaving the wounded sentry for dead, a few rifles and some wire cutters (which were considered to be far superior to any in use by the British) the Germans disappeared with what transpired to be 12 prisoners, one rifle and a Lewis gun under the still intense box barrage. Troops in nearby posts did apparently witness the Germans approaching Trench 55 but the configuration of the ground as well as the smoke and night's gloom hid the raiders' departure. A lack of common and effective procedure between brigades of the same division meant that communications between the British infantry and the batteries, which were not those of its usual supporting brigade, were poor. When it came, the British artillery response was described by Lieutenant Colonel Peake, the CO of the unfortunate victims of this extremely well coordinated and executed raid, as "very late and weak." In defence of his gunners, the CRA's report on the operation claimed the guns had reacted as quickly and efficiently as they were supposed to do. He did acknowledge, however, short comings in communication between forward observation officers at infantry HQ and a bad error of judgement by one brigade commander. Battery commanders, he insisted, had shown initiative and once the requests for barrages on the SOS lines had been received the guns went swiftly into action. Nearly 600 shells, he wrote, had been fired in response. Nonetheless, when compared to the reported effects achieved by the artillery of the adjacent division the following night when it was raided, the results of the South Midland guns do seem to have been rather less than convincing. Improved communication procedures were instituted but for 8/Worcestershire the experience had been a disturbing realization that the enemy, with his seemingly bottomless reserves of *minenwerfer* and artillery shells, was a very capable opponent in the dark art of trench raiding.

A handful of men from 143 Brigade had also suffered from the German barrage. Divisional HQ decided the Warwickshire Brigade should reassert the South Midlanders' moral ascendancy in no man's land by conducting a major enterprise consisting of a two battalion raid at the end of February. As far as the division was concerned this was raiding on an unprecedented scale and, as such, required additional planning and organization. The scheme proposed that 5/ and 8/Warwickshire would be supported by batteries of trench mortars, much of the divisional artillery, 143 Brigade's machine-gun company and a section of 2/Field Company. An advanced dressing station was to be established by 3/Field Ambulance in Foncquevillers and there were specific instructions about what should and should not be done with prisoners. In the event, these comprehensive plans came temporarily to nothing because the ground on the night of the raid was determined to be too frosty and white for the operation to go ahead. Important and useful thinking had, however, been expended during the planning process, the outcomes of which were to be put to use during the following month.

The GOC 143 Brigade and his brigade major went up to the brigade's trenches on 16 March to study the enemy's wire and determine whether a cutting party would be able to hack its way through. Intelligence had already been gathered from patrol reports, aerial photography and telescopic observation and, having seen it all with his own eyes, Brigadier James decided the operation was feasible. He ordered 5/ and 8/ Warwickshire to dust off the earlier plans and be prepared to make a major raid later that month. The weather had taken a slight turn for the better but a rude reminder of how clinically the enemy could execute raids occurred three nights later. Under a barrage of shells, smoke and gas, a German cutting out party stormed three posts held by 6/Gloucestershire. The divisional batteries put up a "magnificent" barrage and the Gloucesters "fought magnificently" but they failed to stop the Germans from capturing three men, killing 10 and wounding three of the posts' 24 man garrison. They did manage to leave one of the raiding party in the Gloucesters' trenches but the whole thing was over in 40 minutes from start to finish. Whether this prompted the GOC to bring forward his proposed raid is unknown but the planning does show a degree of depth not previously seen in the division's schemes. For the first time in surviving documents, "security" warranted a section on its own. The men were warned, for example, not to discuss the operation in estaminets or other locations where civilians might be present and the proposed points of entry were made known only to a very few. Men were to be "carefully" checked to ensure they carried no identification or regimental badges. In addition to the two main assaults by 5/ and 8/ Warwickshire, which were to be about 700 yards apart, there was also a diversionary raid against a demolished *sucrerie* by another party from 8/Warwickshire. Smaller raids by 5/Gloucestershire of 145 Brigade and 8/Worcestershire of 144 Brigade were also to take place to the south. The latter battalion had been told on 19 March that it was to conduct an enterprise with four officers and 80 men against a strong point known as the Quadrilateral, an instruction which had apparently come as a "great relief" to the men chosen. Practices had been undertaken on a replica of the enemy post but a somewhat cryptic entry of 22 March in the war diary suggests a degree of unease amongst senior battalion officers. Major General Fanshawe visited the front line trenches on the day preceding the night attack. On witnessing the condition of the ground and trenches, "and realizing for the first time the impossibility of making sufficient reconnaissance in the short time given, forbade the battalion to make the raid." Why Fanshawe became cognizant of the appalling state of the ground only a matter of hours before the raid was supposed to be underway is unknown but, with 8/ Worcestershire prohibited from taking part, 144 Brigade's role in the larger scheme was now that of spectator.

With the restricted supply of shells from the UK easing, the barrage was a considerable improvement on earlier ones. It was arranged in three phases and was to employ two brigades of field artillery, one of 4.5 inch howitzers and also a counter-battery group. This latter group was to be restricted to a maximum of only 30 rounds but over the three phases, the 18 pdrs had a total of 1,526 shrapnel and 266 high explosive shells available; the howitzers enjoyed a ration of 239. This concentration of force, with the possible exception of the counter-battery group, might seem impressive, but because the artillery was ordered to spread its fire along the entire brigade front it was still far from overwhelming. It was, however, much closer to the sort of fire power the Germans had been using to support their raids. The assaulting parties were equipped with the by now usual telephones link to the batteries and would also have the supporting fire of trench mortar barrels and the brigade machine-gun company firing an overhead barrage. One section of 2/Field Company was standing by, regimental aid posts were equipped and staffed and an advanced brigade HQ was established in a dugout on the Foncquevillers-Hébuterne road. Patrols went out in advance of the assault parties to lay tapes to within 150 yards of the enemy first line; when the raiders reached this point they would signal the artillery and wait for the barrage to fall before rushing forward to begin cutting the wire. The signal gun was due to fire for the parties of both participating brigades at 0030 on 23 March.

The diversion by 5/Gloucestershire of two officers and 64 men, which included a quaintly named group of eight known as the Souvenir Collectors, were in position in good time. Fifteen minutes after the signal gun was due to have been fired, however, the Gloucesters received a message that 143 Brigade would be late. Hearing nothing more for another 20 minutes, either nerves got the better of Captain Sumner or he decided to use initiative and called for the barrage to begin. His wire cutters made slow progress against aprons of concertina wire and when rifle grenades began landing amongst his men, Sumner ordered the withdrawal. The diarist of 4/Ox&Bucks, which manned the line between 5/Warwickshire to its left and 5/Gloucestershire on its right, was not surprised because a "quite insufficient time had been allotted for this prearranged scheme." A similar fate befell the party of 5/Warwickshire when it came up against the German wire. It managed to get through the first belt in three minutes, came under machine-gun fire whilst clearing the second and had to give up and return to its own trenches when it was discovered the third line was covered by a bomb screen made of wire netting. The Warwicks threw bombs towards the German trench but when they repeatedly bounced back off the screen the officer decided it was prudent to withdraw.

The small group of 8/Warwickshire tasked to penetrate the abandoned *sucrerie* and draw fire from the main body found no Germans occupying the ruins. This was probably fortunate because Second Lieutenant Fish, the officer in charge of the party, had managed to lose the lighter needed to ignite the fumite bombs and he carried no matches. His party withdrew in good order but a similar problem with igniters also bedevilled the main assault group 400 yards to the north. With blackened faces, covered steel helmets and wearing white arm bands for identification, the wire cutting group rushed forward under the barrage and laid the first Bangalore torpedo under a belt of wire. Owing to damp igniters it took four frustrating attempts to light the weapon before it exploded. A second weapon was then pushed under the next belt but nothing could persuade it to explode; when the third was brought forward it broke in half and was abandoned. The wire cutters were then called forward to begin their work while the barrage on the front line continued to keep the Germans' heads down. The first Bangalore was ignited with a "remarkable report and flash" which "may" a later report suggested "have had considerable moral effect" on the defenders. This may indeed have been the case, but a sufficiently wide gap about 10 yards wide was blown through which the bombers were able to rush. Once in the trench the three parties, which comprised men specifically tasked to capture prisoners, collect materiel, block the adjoining communication trench, escort prisoners to the control centre and provide flank protection in case of counter-attack, struggled to maintain any practical cohesion and organization. Congestion and some confusion reigned as men collected the required booty, established the trench block and drew and noted the dimensions, style and construction of the front trench. When the signal to withdraw was given, the raiders piled out of the entry point and succeeded in regaining their own trenches together with one lone prisoner, Gustav Appel.

Musketier Appel may have felt himself to have been unfortunate in now being held within British lines but he was possibly rather luckier than some of his comrades. The South Midland Division was clearly determined to discover what had gone right and what had gone wrong with the raids. Seven officers of 8/Warwickshire submitted reports on what they believed had occurred during the hectic 40-odd minute period. One report suggested that more prisoners might have been taken had all of the men been under the direct control of officers during the raid. The suggestion was that rather than escort them back to the British lines some men simply disposed of their prisoners. Another officer was a little more circumspect when he explained that three prisoners were killed whilst on the way back because they offered resistance. Nevertheless, gaining at least one prisoner and killing others was one of the objectives of the raid; several others were also achieved. Smoke helmets, rifles and other accoutrements were secured, although not a machine gun which was one of the items on the 'wanted' list, and detailed descriptions of the trenches were delivered to the intelligence gatherers. A final objective was "to maintain the fighting spirit of our troops." Given the low casualty list of only two officers and 15 other ranks wounded, and most of them slightly, in 8/Warwickshire at least that objective of developing the morale component may well have been secured. But, there were certainly aspects of the operation that had not been satisfactory. Apart from one officer, who believed the shrapnel barrage was "irregular" because one section of the German line was "not searched thoroughly", the artillery and trench mortars appeared to have done what was expected. The fire of the heavies was thought to have been particularly effective but a point made several times in the reports concerned the physical component of fighting power: the Bangalores were universally condemned as unreliable. When they worked, they were extremely useful in blowing gaps in wire but their fuses were far too unpredictable. There were also demands that considerably more revolvers and electric torches should be made available. For the close combat in constricted space which such raids involved, rifles and bayonets were often too cumbersome. Although 18 revolvers had been carried, one report suggested three times that number would have been nearer the mark. Aspects of the conceptual component were also criticized. With the exception of two officers who believed they were unnecessary, the other reports emphasized the need for flanking parties. There was, however, unanimity in the belief that trying to put three large assaulting parties, which in this case amounted to nearly 140 men, through one gap in the German wire caused unnecessary confusion and congestion. The parties themselves were also considered to have been too large; smaller groups using the advantage of surprise were thought likely to achieve more. To avoid prisoners being killed it was suggested certain NCOs should be told off to escort them back and know that they were responsible for their safe arrival. There needed to be an improved method of signalling the withdrawal (one officer suggested a bugler running along the parapet blowing for all he was worth into post horn would be better than the klaxon used)) and also more training to develop command, initiative and leadership skills so that situations where raiders had entered a trench at the wrong point could be effectively and swiftly redeemed.

After the excitement of February and March, April was a relatively quiet month in terms of raiding activity. Patrolling continued but there were no significant raids along the South Midland front. A German attempt against 144 Brigade had limited success but in mid-May the enemy made a more determined and effective effort. The objective of the raid were the trenches occupied by 4/Berkshire. Under the cover of what the nearby 4/Ox&Bucks thought was "the heaviest bombardment to date", the Germans created mayhem in the Berkshires' positions. They succeeded in killing at least 18, wounding more than 50 and driving back across no man's land an estimated 29 prisoners. This was a severe blow not only to the battalion but to the division as a whole and came as yet another reminder that while the enemy enjoyed superiority in guns and munitions they held the distinct advantage. The British were very much on a general learning curve, raiding being just one of the elements of trench warfare that was attracting considerable thought and development in terms of weapon capability and training. With increasing practical experience being used to improve conceptual and tactical skills, the British were demonstrating they were capable of learning. Yet some units, or their brigade commanders, appear to have been rather more reluctant than others to undertake raids: 145 Brigade, for example, did significantly fewer raids than those conducted by the division's other two brigades. Why this was the case is unclear but within brigades some battalions did more than others. In 143 Brigade, which was the most active of the three, 5/ and 8/Warwickshire did not do one until a year after they had landed in France; by that time 7/Warwickshire had already attempted three.

Furthermore, although the division had probably established the record for an unbroken length of service in the line, the 14 months spent in the trenches had in comparison with some of the other Territorial Force divisions been fairly unremarkable: 46th

(North Midland) had seen two of its brigades all but destroyed at the Hohenzollern in October 1915; 47th (2nd London) had been used at Loos and was currently experiencing action on Vimy ridge; 49th (West Riding) had also been reasonably underused but had been in the Ypres Salient for months; 50th (Northumbrian) had sustained huge casualties at 2nd Ypres and 51st (Highland) had suffered at Festubert. 42nd (East Lancashire), 52nd (Lowland), 53rd (Welsh) and 54th (East Anglian) had all served between five and seven months on Gallipoli. Although it had spent long winter months in the wettest of trenches, 48th (South Midland) had been fortunate. Its total of other rank infantry fatalities during its 15 month period in France until the opening of the Somme offensive was approximately 567. Several TF divisions had lost almost that number in single days. With the build up to the offensive gathering momentum, however, the division was to increase its patrol activity and spend more time training. It may have been fortunate so far but the division was soon to experience the same sort of severe casualties suffered by other TF formations.

4

The Battle of the Somme: June-August 1916

In June 1916, the Anglo-French Somme sector witnessed a further intensification of the concentration of materiel and manpower which had begun some weeks earlier. At the Chantilly Conference in December 1915 the Allies had decided that a coordinated offensive on the Western and Eastern Fronts should be launched in the early summer of 1916. The German assault on Verdun, which began in February, led to ever more incessant French demands that the British should be ready to attack in Picardy by May. The contribution to be made by the French to the forthcoming offensive diminished with every passing week; the consequence being that the British assumed a greater share and responsibility for the assault. When the offensive began, the recently arrived Kitchener divisions were to be supported by several regular divisions and a smattering of TF formations. It was hoped the apparent enthusiasm and perhaps even naivety of Kitchener's Army would, in the opening period of the campaign, allow them to punch their way through the formidable German defences and restore the war of movement and manoeuvre. The expanding number of British divisions moving into the sector also meant that others could be relieved from line holding work for rest and training.

In early June, both 144 and 145 Brigades of 48th Division had almost a fortnight in the rear to practise tactical exercises and specialist skills. There were of course at the same time the inevitable working parties, with groups of over 200 regularly despatched to railheads for unloading fatigues. Other groups were found to dig cable trenches, carry rations and engineering stores to the front, fell trees for timber, sap into no man's land to create yet more advanced trenches and for the painful and awkward task of carrying almost 500 uncompromising gas cylinders to the front trenches. Nearly 1,000 boxes of smoke bombs and unstable phosphorous grenades had also to be carried and dumped, while parties working for the artillery helped to transport forward over a 1,000 rounds for each 18 pdr field gun and 800 for the 4.5 inch howitzers. The CRE was everywhere inspecting sites under construction and liaising with his counterparts in the artillery and medical branches as to where observation posts and ADS should be sited. The field companies responsible for carrying out his orders worked in sections around the clock. In June, for example, 2/Field Company, completed 12 observation posts, dug, maintained or supervised the digging of an unknown yardage of new trenches, improved the water supply and storage facilities at various horse lines, screened roads, fitted anti-gas blankets, marked new transport routes from Sailly to Hébuterne and continued hut construction in the rear areas. On one night alone 400 sappers and attached infantry dug a dummy trench of almost 2,000 yards in two hours. The work was harassed by German shelling and also by a fire which broke out by the spontaneous combustion of sandbags in one of its stores. Over 80,000 sandbags and 300 rolls of felt burned for seven hours and attracted a considerable amount of German interest. The pioneers of 5/Sussex were also labouring hard. They worked shifts of up to 14 hours a day, most of the time wet through and with little opportunity to dry out, frequently under fire and using men from the signal section, Lewis gunners and even officers' batmen to swell the size of fatigue parties. Infantry were also often attached but 1/Field Company was not entirely content with the way the press ganged troops behaved. A change of brigade in the front sector meant "eight hours of infantry working parties lost", groups often turned up late, their work was "irregular" or lethargic and even when they were not actually working under RE supervision, occupied dugout or cellars on which the engineers themselves needed to work.

The ADMS, Lieutenant Colonel Young, was equally active. In addition to his usual duties of inspecting cookhouses, baths, latrines, writing and circulating pamphlets on sanitation and deciding whether 'unfit' men sent to the ambulances were actually 'unfit', he was also deeply involved in ensuring the medical provision for the forthcoming offensive was sufficient. He liaised with a nearby French battery which was attached to the corps but which had no medical facilities of its own, detailed parties from his three ambulances for attachment to 29th CCS at Gezaincourt and another section to 88 Brigade as bearers, arranged with the sanitary officer and DDMS about where and when lectures could best be delivered to the orderlies and medical staff and dealt with requests from the ambulance OCs for increased supplies of dressings. This involved trips by the OCs to an advanced depot run by the Red Cross to obtain extra fittings and equipment for the new officers' ward. With a few exceptions all existing cases held in the field ambulances were to be transferred to a CCS at least five days before the start of the offensive. This move was to leave, for example, only 11 patients in 3/Field Ambulance; these were presumably reasonably fit because they were instructed in how to load ambulance wagons by the unit's sergeant-major. Owing to a re-arrangement of the line this ambulance was also involved in the construction of a new ADS in the cellars of Hébuterne's ruined houses. After treatment there, doctors and orderlies were to pass the wounded on to the existing ADS and ambulance in Sailly. Other cellars close to the new ADS were requisitioned and converted into accommodation for the section's personnel. A new evacuation trench was dug by parties of the already over-worked infantry to link the ADS with the open fields on the western edge of the village.

A visit from Major General Fanshawe and several from the DDMS and ADMS to check on the how the arrangements were progressing allowed the OC 3/Field Ambulance to confirm he would be able to accommodate a total of 400 lying cases, with room for another 120 if needed in additional huts. The new ADS, although incomplete, could house another 80 lying and 60 sitting cases. A violent thunder storm flooded the OC's HQ site on 23 June but he was also able to establish advanced posts manned by orderlies sited between the RAPs and the ADS. Abdominal cases and what was described as "other seriously" wounded were to be taken first to 2/Field Ambulance and thence to the corps operating hospital at Authie. The lightly wounded were to be treated at the MDSs and then taken by light railway to 1st CCS at Acheux. Finally, 2/ and 3/Field Ambulances were each ordered to have one section fully equipped and ready to march by 0800 hours on 1 July. It was anticipated these apparently thorough and extensive preparations would resolve the difficulties and chaos in the medical arrangements which had so blighted the evacuation of wounded from the Loos battlefield. Unfortunately, as in September 1915, the huge number of casualties suffered on 1 July was to completely overwhelm the medical facilities of Fourth Army.

The increasing concentration of formations in the sector could hardly be disguised from the Germans; it was also a constant reminder to the British troops that what was being termed the 'Big Push' would soon be under way. Having been in the sector for almost a year already the men of 48th Division could reasonably have assumed they would be in the forefront of the battle. It was possibly with some surprise and perhaps even disappointment that the division learned only two of its battalions would be used for the initial assault. What was probably an even more surprising blow was the arrival of an order on 13 June which announced the two battalions, 6/ and 8/Warwickshire, were to come under orders of 11 Brigade, 4th Division. The remainder of the division's infantry was to continue to hold the line or act as corps reserve. The decision to launch what was only a 'Chinese' attack on the division's front also meant that the artillery could be loaned to other formations. In the meantime, early June gave the entire 240 Brigade RFA the opportunity to be fully assembled for the first time in 11 months. Those few days in the rear allowed the brigade to train, clean and service their weapons as well as to watch the infantry practising their assault methods. Infantry officers were also at times attached to the batteries to liaise and discuss tactical coordination. Two batteries were later either attached or loaned to 4th Division and another four to 29th Division. Another fired in support of a raid by 31st Division but the remainder of the batteries began their fire plan for the preliminary bombardment on 24 June. The principal targets were the wire fields in front of the German forward and reserve positions, suspected OPs, machine-gun posts and junctions of forward and communication trenches. The 18 pdr batteries fired an average of about 125 rounds per gun per day and the 4.5 inch about 120. There were "frequent bursts of fire" during the hours of darkness together with, when the wind permitted, discharges of smoke and gas. Reports on the effectiveness of the fire programme varied. On 27 June, one battery of 240 Brigade decided it had cut the wire sufficiently on its target to be able to shift fire onto a new position in front of 31st Division. Revealing rather less confidence in its own abilities, 242 Brigade reported it had cut about 100 yards of German wire at one point, but declared that at the same range it was "difficult to guarantee" to fulfil requests from the infantry to cut additional gaps. Similarly, reports from patrols suggested there were great swathes of wire that had barely been touched. Divisional HQ noted pithily on 28 June that the bombardment "is apparently not being effective in cutting wire."

The British bombardment clearly did fail to cut the wire and to destroy a significant number of enemy dugouts but there is evidence to suggest that a creeping barrage of sorts was fired on 143 Brigade's front at zero. The creeping barrage had made its cautious appearance at Loos but it was not until the Somme was under way that it became increasingly commonplace. Divisional HQ not only recorded several times that although the enemy's artillery response tended to be "feeble" it did manage to do "material damage" to British trenches (143 Brigade described a section of its front line as having been "flattened") but also issued orders about the procedure when the assault began of how the infantry should follow the barrage. The published orders talk of artillery "lifts" but also of the "creeping method" to be employed. They stressed how "success or otherwise…largely depended on the infantry thoroughly understanding" and conforming to the method which involved a 100 yard lift from the enemy's front trenches at the start of the infantry assault. It would then "continue lifting at the rate of 50 yards per minute to the objective firing three rounds per gun at each step." The rate of advance, although not the rate of fire, was similar to what developed into a fairly standard feature of a creeping barrage. The orders also directed certain batteries to concentrate on counter-battery work, a practice which owing to the lack of reliable intelligence and to the shortage of gun and ammunition was considerably neglected during the opening stage of the campaign.

The period spent by the infantry in company, battalion and brigade training was disrupted not only by the constant demands for working parties but also by the rain and the need for groups to train separately for raids. The weather also frustrated several attempts to practise contact procedures with aircraft. After a number of sessions had eventually been completed there was some disagreement about their actual utility: 143 Brigade considered them to have been only "fairly successful" whereas the diarist of 7/Warwickshire thought them to have been both "very interesting and successful." Brigade route marches were accompanied by two ambulance wagons but despite the time they had spent in the trenches few of the infantry actually fell out of the column. The progress of a brigade could be disrupted by such mundane events such as a long train dawdling interminably over a level crossing, but the marches were also useful for experimenting in the best way to carry items of newly-issued equipment. Daily sessions of PT, bayonet fighting and doubling in the new fighting order apparently allowed 8/Worcestershire to produce a "quickness of movement in what first appeared to be impossible equipment."

When in the line, the infantry was very active during the month, with frequent nocturnal patrols studying the state of the German wire and raids attempting capture a prisoner or two. The patrols brought back depressing reports about the few gaps being blown in the wire and the raids evidently failed to secure a single prisoner. It was discovered a scattering of garrisoned enemy rifle pits lay in front of the German wire and that the front line itself was strongly held by an alert enemy. When the sentries heard activity to their front they quickly sent up flares and opened fire. Patrols reported the 2 inch trench mortars were having "practically no effect" on breaching the wire and when 6/Warwickshire was about to send a bombing party down the German front line to capture a prisoner, it swiftly abandoned the scheme because a sudden bombardment killed five and wounded 17 of the raiding party. 7/Worcestershire sent over two groups of nine raiders accompanied by RE sappers and protected by a covering party on the night of 15-16 June. The raid had earlier been postponed but went ahead that night because it was believed a relief was taking place in the trenches opposite. 242 Brigade RFA maintained what was called "sniping fire" while the sappers tried to explode six Bangalore torpedoes; after they had failed to ignite and six sappers wounded by their own weapons, the parties withdrew. 242 Brigade cooperated by bringing the centre of its barrage down onto to the German front line and by quickening the rate of fire to cover the withdrawal. Battalion HQ next requested the howitzers also to open fire to protect the covering party which had still to regain the British lines; by 0200, after the howitzers had fired 83 rounds and the 18 pdrs more than 1,000, the 'Stop' was ordered. The raiders had nothing to show for their efforts but the six wounded sappers; 242 Brigade had already had seven killed by a direct hit on a gun pit the previous day. 7/Worcestershire tried again with four officers and 75 men on 28 June but failed owing to "lack of time for reconnaissance and preparation" and, at 1000 on the following day, 4/Ox&Bucks was ordered to conduct one that night. Tasked with capturing a prisoner and having been assured the artillery would have successfully cut the wire, a party of 52 left their own trench at 0015. The first belt of German wire was found to be cut but the raiders next came across eight rows of completely undamaged concertina wire. Attempts to cut through the first row attracted a great deal of German fire and the group withdrew. The omens for the coming major attack were, thus, poor. The fact that such an impenetrable and, despite the regular patrolling and air observation, previously undiscovered field of wire still lay in tact in front of the enemy trenches only 28 hours before the infantry were due to assault was hardly encouraging.

The low number of casualties sustained by 48th Division since its arrival in France and a steady dribble of reinforcements since April meant that the infantry brigades were up, or very close to establishment. In June, 145 Brigade, for example, recorded a strength of 146 officers and 4039 ORs which was, in fact, a little over official establishment; 6/Gloucestershire, however, did note that it was nine officers and 60 other ranks under strength. Fatalities among the infantry brigades in June amounted to 43, but a disproportionate 29 of these were incurred by 6/ and 7/Warwickshire. Seven second lieutenants are known to have been wounded but because all three brigades spent some part of the month out of the line, the overall number of wounded and sick was probably low: 2/Field Ambulance treated only 52 wounded during the month although it did also admit over 650 sick. The majority of the sick returned to duty fairly quickly and there were also a few drafts in the month to help to maintain unit strengths. Several units appear to have received about 30 men, with the largest group to join any one infantry battalion being the 60 who arrived at the transport lines of

4/Gloucestershire. These men were reported to have come from the regiment's 10th Battalion and were considered to be "a good type of man." A series of drafts took the total number received by 5/Sussex during the month to 193. There is no suggestion in the pioneer battalion's war diary that these were men of anything other than of the highest medical category.[1]

By late June, 48th Division filled the gap between 31st Division to its south and 56th (1st London) to its north. It also constituted the left flank of not only VIII Corps but also of Rawlinson's Fourth Army. With 56th (London) and 46th (North Midland) of Allenby's Third Army to its left, both of which were in the process of openly and brazenly making their preparations for a supposedly diversionary attack against the Gommecourt salient, it meant there were three TF divisions together in the line. 144 and 145 Brigades were ordered to hold themselves ready to relieve 10 and 12 Brigades of 4th Division, probably during the second night of operations and probably on the Grandcourt-Puisieux Ridge; the two non-assaulting battalions of 143 Brigade were to be prepared to follow up any success of 11 Brigade. 6/ and 8/Warwickshire were to operate on the left of the regular 4th Division and on the right of 31st Division, a formation of Fourth New Army. In terms of the length of time it had served overseas, the South Midland Division was among the most experienced divisions in the area. It had lost only 37 officers killed, died of wounds or died of other causes since its arrival, the GOC had been in post for over a year, the CRE a little longer and the GSO1 and CRA between two and four months. Two of the brigadiers had been in command since 1915 but the GOC whose brigade was to be in the attacking waves on 1 July 1916 had only taken command in May. Although at least 75 percent of the August 1914 COs of the division's 13 battalions[2] had been replaced by early 1916, and many other officers had been invalided to the UK, there remained considerable numbers of pre-war officers, NCOs and other ranks in the units of all brigades. These men and the drafts which had arrived from their 2nd Line units maintained the battalions' sense of local cohesion and identity and also the units' TF ethos and traditions. As the two Warwicks battalions tasked for the assault moved into the front line and the other two battalions waited in reserve, 143 Brigade was virtually at full strength. It contained only a small proportion of men who had not been born or lived in Warwickshire and who, in Sir Ian Hamilton's assessment of nearly two years earlier, served in one of the best divisions in the TF. Other than in its patrols, its stoic endurance in the worst of the winter weather, its low recorded level of crime and its trench initiation duties for others, the division had had little opportunity to confirm that assessment. When the CO of 8/Worcestershire, Lieutenant Colonel Peake, addressed his battalion on 24 June about the coming operation, he reminded the men of the "high importance of a

1 There is some evidence to suggest that men of a lower medical category were being sent to pioneer battalions as drafts once the Somme campaign was under way. The real surge in non-A1 Category men to such battalions did not, however, begin in earnest until 1917.

2 Including 5/Sussex.

sense of individual discipline and of devotion to duty." Even allowing for a degree of bias and perhaps cognizance on the part of the diarist of what his CO might want to read, the entry in the war diary was probably typical of what others might also have written: "The men's response to this was clearly indicated in a redoubled keenness over the daily training showing that after 15 months' of trench warfare they were more rather than less ready to meet the enemy in the open."

The companies of 6/ and 8/Warwickshire moved into their advanced positions during the night of 30 June-1 July. The two leading companies of the latter battalion reported themselves to be in their jumping off trenches by 0200 hours. Over their heads the British bombardment continued to roar and burst but, although for the time being it was nowhere near as intense as that of the British batteries, German retaliation was also falling on the front and rear areas. The two remaining battalions of 143 Brigade manned the front lines in the gap of over a mile between 31st and 56th Divisions. Smoke was released before zero but as the wire in front of the British trenches had not been cleared and the artillery bombardment was not as heavy as elsewhere, it was fairly obvious to any observing German that there was unlikely to be an attack in this sector. Behind the lines as corps reserve 144 and 145 Brigades assembled in the villages around Bus, with both brigade HQs located in Mailly-Maillet. The divisional artillery was active in support largely of 31st Division but did also commit some batteries to firing on the trenches opposite the divisional front. Between 0730 and noon on 1 July, the 4.5 inch howitzers fired about 1,500 rounds per battery onto the enemy third and fourth lines; the division's 18 pdrs batteries each fired about 2,000 shells in the same period. The corps' plan of attack was to have one section of RE per brigade available to go forward to help with consolidation once the objectives had been taken; meanwhile, the rest of the field company personnel were generally to continue with their routine but essential duties. None of 48th Division's RE had been attached to an assaulting brigade so, with an advanced HQ established at Couin, the bridging trestles were left with the transport at Rossignol when 1/Field Company moved to Mailly-Maillet in the early hours of 1 July. There they were joined by the pioneers of 5/Sussex, whose diarist noted that this was the first time the battalion had been together for almost 11 months. To join the gathering throng in the village, one section of 2/Field Ambulance also went into bivvies at Mailly-Maillet and was attached to 144 Brigade. 2/Field Company remained in Sailly and was soon to be split into sections for dispersed work.

At 0720, as the howitzers shifted their fire from the forward German positions, the leading companies of 8/Warwickshire climbed from their trenches to form up and lie down in no man's land until zero. Enemy machine-gun fire and artillery had been hitting the Warwicks' positions for some time but once the British howitzers' fire moved eastwards, a storm of small arms fire began to lash the Warwicks' parapet. At 0730, hit initially by frontal fire and also by enfilade from the right, the companies headed for the *Heidenkopf*; on their right, 1/Rifle Brigade began its advance towards the Redan ridge. Ten minutes after 8/Warwickshire left its trenches, 6/Warwickshire followed behind but lost about 80 men even before they crossed the British front trench. 8/Warwickshire penetrated the *Heidenkopf*, with some sections even reaching as far as the German fourth line, but was hampered by the German defenders who had been ordered to blow up the strong point and withdraw just before any enemy infantry reached the front line. The *Heidenkopf* was a marked salient in the German line and the defensive plan was for it to be evacuated soon after any attack began in order to straighten the line. One lone machine gun, a few riflemen and some engineers were tasked to defend it briefly and then blow it up. Several German pioneers disappeared in the blast when the mines were either accidently blown sooner than intended or, more courageously, because some of the garrison deliberately delayed their escape. Despite the falling debris 8/Warwickshire managed to get in and through the strong point but as the now two very mixed Warwicks battalions continued to advance towards their final objectives another 5-600 yards further on, they were swept by machine-gun fire from the front and from both flanks. The failure of 31st Division on the left to reach Serre village allowed German machine guns thought to be hidden in burnt hay ricks to concentrate on the left of the Warwicks. Opposite the stalled central zone of 4th Division, machine guns and riflemen in the Redan Redoubt, supplemented by artillery which brought down a constant and heavy barrage on no man's land and the British front line, continued to pour fire across the open ground from the south. This torrent of bullets and shrapnel prevented carrying parties from replenishing the bombs and small arms ammunition of the forward troops. Despite all these obstacles, within about 40 minutes of zero 8/Warwickshire had successfully reached its objective. As the battalion was now so few in number, however, 6/Warwickshire decided not to pass through towards the final objective near Pendant Copse but to stay instead with 8/Warwickshire and consolidate the gains. At about 1100 the one remaining unwounded officer of 6/Warwickshire carried a message back to brigade HQ explaining the situation. Meanwhile, the Germans repeatedly bombed towards the Warwicks from both north and south and twice forced them to withdraw to the German third line. Having scavenging for more German and British bombs, on both occasions the Warwicks counter-attacked and regained their lost ground. On the third time of being forced back, having exhausted just about all of their ammunition and with no fresh troops coming across to relieve them, the survivors were eventually compelled to withdraw to the former British front line. Just before midnight on 1 July, the shaken remnants of both Warwicks battalions slumped into billets in Mailly-Maillet.

Losses among the two Warwicks battalions had been enormous. Of the 24 officers and 626 ORs of 6/Warwickshire who actually took part in the attack, 10 and 148, respectively, were dead by the end of the day. Fatalities in 8/Warwickshire had been even more severe: 12 officers, including Lieutenant Colonel Innes, and 223 ORs were killed.[3] Both battalions suffered further substantial losses in the next few days as men collected by the stretcher bearers and infantry during periods of tacit truce died of

3 The fighting strengths of the two battalions were recorded on 30 June 1916 as 32 officers and 754 ORs, and 35 officers and 1035 ORs.

wounds in ambulances and casualty clearing stations. The battalions and several of the other units of 11 Brigade had performed very well during the day but it had all, in the end, brought no success. The barrage had broken some of the wire in front of the *Heidenkopf* but the lack of heavy guns meant that the more substantial defences remained intact. The physical component of British fighting power was clearly inadequate: insufficient artillery fire power, the limited availability of light mobile infantry fire support and inadequate training, especially the failure of the advancing troops to mop up Germans left in dugouts as they moved forward, were crucial factors. These elements, together with the effectiveness of the enemy barrage on no man's land and the enfilade machine-gun fire from the flanks where other formations had not managed to get forward, condemned 11 Brigade to failure. The GOC VIII Corps, Hunter-Weston, wanted to renew the attack later in the day with 48th Division and the reserve brigades of 4th and 29th Division, but such was the chaos and congestion in the trenches, the uncertainty of how far some of the attacking British troops had actually reached and the mix of Clausewitz's 'frictions' and 'fog of war', that the decision was made to halt and reorganize. 144 and 145 Brigades in Mailly-Maillet no doubt breathed a collective sigh of relief. Elements of the division returned to Couin that night but divisional HQ was almost immediately warned that it would make an attack in the early hours of 3 July. Corps had decided that in view of the failure to capture Serre, a defensive flank should be formed on the heights north of the Ancre between Y Ravine and Station Road (Beaumont Hamel). At 2000 on 2 July, 144 Brigade, less its battle surpluses and 8/Worcestershire which was to remain as divisional reserve, moved off. Such was the confusion that at Knightsbridge, 7/Worcestershire converged with 6/Gloucestershire and "owing to non-existent or totally inadequate traffic control" neither battalion could move for the press of ration parties and returning wounded of other units. The brigade was then further blocked by a company of 1/Essex trudging back from the front. At 0200 on 3 July, verbal messages were passed down the column of 6/Gloucestershire that the proposed attack had been cancelled and that the battalion was to about face. It did so and then collided with 7/Worcestershire. The two battalions tried to make their way back down the communication trench but ran into 4/Gloucestershire and the pioneers of 2/Monmouth who were struggling to make their way up to the forward sector. "Progress was further impeded by constant passing of unauthentic and contradictory messages" until the battalions "finally dribbled out of the end of the trench at about 0245." Having lost one man somewhere *en route*, the brigade was back in Mailly-Maillet by 0400. By that time, 145 Brigade had relieved what was left of the ill-fated 31st Division and within four days 144 Brigade was also in the line.

There remained a huge amount of salvage work to be done in the trenches and numerous wounded still to be recovered from no man's land. The former task was made more difficult and exhausting because two companies of 5/Sussex had been loaned to the stricken 29th Division. Two platoon-sized reconnaissance patrols of Warwicks went out in the early hours of 6 July but failed to get into the enemy trenches because the Germans were alert and prepared. Tension in the sector was sustained by occasional discharges of smoke and salvoes of phosphorous bombs; in response the enemy shelled and fired gas onto battery positions. The RE wanted empty gas cylinders removed from the front line but when 4/Ox&B was ordered to carry them away only 20 were taken during the course of one night. The battalion blamed the wet and collapsing trenches as well as the lack of expert assistance for the tardy progress and when six parties each of over 80 men from 5/Gloucestershire and 4/Ox&B were tasked another night, misunderstandings and confusion were again blamed for preventing completion of the job. With the rain, salvage, shelling and gas, troops remained busy, uncomfortable and possibly lethargic. On 13 July, 143 Brigade moved from corps reserve to come under orders of 25th Division and the following day staff officers of 115 and 36 Brigades arrived to reconnoitre the line in preparation to relieving 48th Division. The South Midland moved to Bouzincourt but 143 and 144 Brigades were swiftly back in the trenches either side of the ruined village of Ovillers. During the night relief, and intrigued by the devastation through which the battalion stumbled and cursed, the diarist of 7/Worcestershire noted passing the "alleged position" of the village's former church. To avoid congestion in the trenches, three platoons of 7/Warwickshire were ordered to advance across the open; they managed only to cover 70 yards before losing about one third of their 120 men. The CO ordered the other companies to make their way up by way of the trenches but they were shallow and already crowded with 3/Worcestershire. German artillery hit them hard but amidst the subsequent confusion the brigade major and CO of 3/Worcestershire seem to have made decisions which allowed the Warwicks to gather their wounded, which included Lieutenant Colonel Knox, and withdraw to the reserve trenches. That night 5/Warwickshire, still under orders of 25th Division, was ordered to make an attack on Ovillers alongside other battalions of its adopted division. According to brigade HQ the battalion failed to get to the jumping off trench in time for zero. The battalion war diary contradicts this assertion and recorded that at a cost of over 40 dead it took the trenches against little opposition and then held them against several counter-attacks. 8/Warwickshire moved up on the night of 16-17 July to relieve 3/Worcestershire and in a short tour of line holding lost nearly 70 men. The several attacks by the South Midland units attached to 25th Division had certainly helped to hasten the fall of Ovillers and during the morning of 17 July, 144 Brigade pushed a little further north and consolidated its gains.

While 8/Worcestershire had waited at Coigneux in the days immediately after the initial Allied assault, its diarist had written of the disappointment of VIII Corps' failure to take Serre; he also wrote of the pride 48th Division felt in the work done by the two Warwickshire battalions. He noted how the corps' attack had "greatly lightened the task" of the British and French troops to the south and decided, "The spirit and moral of the battalion were therefore in no way impaired by what at first seemed a failure." The battalion spent a few days in the line, the lack of gum boots adding to the general discomfort, and took no part in the demonstrations made by the division on the night of 14 July to distract the enemy's attention from the major night assault by XIII Corps at Bazentin. Having moved forward again to Bouzincourt the diarist noted with some relief and joy that 16 July was to be "the first day of 48th Division's share in the great offensive." He went on, however, to decide that, "Even now it could hardly be called 'field fighting' or 'open warfare' [because] it chiefly consisted of 'nibbling' trenches 'bit by bit'". Yet, he thought, "All ranks looked eagerly to the day when their turn should come to meet the enemy in fair fight after the comparatively tame and wearying monotony" of 16 months of trench warfare.

The battalion's first taste of the offensive was recorded as a "disappointment" but its sister Worcestershire battalion was hurled into the chaos of an assault when it was ordered to support an attack by 75 Brigade on 16 July. In an unfamiliar maze of trenches, and in pitch darkness, the battalion was supposed to negotiate first the tricky operation of pivoting in order to gain touch with units on its left and right and then to cooperate with an attack by 4/Gloucestershire. Communications with brigade HQ were tenuous and when battalion HQ decided it was "almost impossible" to offer any cooperation, it suggested the use of flamethrowers, Stokes mortars and machine guns to mark the position which the Gloucesters were supposed to be assaulting. It also offered to create a diversion which might draw fire away from the Gloucesters' front. The Gloucestershire battalion, meanwhile, had delayed its attack until patrols reported on the state of the German wire. The trench and area to be assaulted could not be seen from the British line and although the trench itself was reported to be strongly held, the wire was thought to be patchy. Battalion HQ decided that a short 10 minute bombardment should be sufficient to secure surprise and to allow penetration by the two attacking companies. Although they could not get into contact with the Worcesters to their right, bombing parties of the two companies eventually made contact with each other and secured the trench. Meanwhile, a series of desperate messages such as "Get in touch with 4/Gloucester" and "Hang on to Point 24" were exchanged between brigade and battalion HQ of 7/Worcestershire during the following day, all of which highlighted the confusion and lack of accurate information being received. The Worcesters only lost one killed and over 20 wounded but, unlike the Gloucesters, achieved little in the way of progress. Had they known of their supposed availability, the troops in the network of closely confined trenches and saps might have wondered what use it was that vehicles of 8th Light Armoured Car Battery had been placed at the disposal of 48th Division.

The two battalions were to attack again during the night of 18-19 July. This was to be made under the cover of a Stokes and machine-gun barrage and a bombardment which would lift from the German front line to their communication and reserve trenches at the same time as the infantry jumped off. 145 Brigade was also to attack in cooperation but brigade HQ was informed that its units would not be "involved in a heavy engagement." Instead, patrols were to be pushed forward and if the enemy trenches were empty to occupy and consolidate them. The Bucks Battalion carried out this task and gathered "much valuable information" but met with no great success as far as the capture of enemy territory was concerned. 4/Ox&Bucks tried the following night but lost direction and made little headway when the companies bumped into some strongly-held posts. A second attack was ordered but cancelled when it was realized it could not be adequately organized before dawn broke. 5/Gloucestershires did make some progress and managed to advance its bomb stops before also coming up against strong wire and a determined enemy. In 144 Brigade, 4/Gloucestershire on the left had very hurriedly to organize two companies for an attack at 0130 on 19 July. They met "stubborn resistance" which included a machine gun firing along a trench and the deliberate burning of dugouts to hamper their advance. Over to its right, but with which it had no contact for more than 24 hours, 7/Worcestershire was experiencing similar problems. Its two companies had been unable to advance more than a few yards before running into strong resistance. One platoon was reported to have been "very shaken" by enemy shell fire and another which did seize a German post was forced to withdraw as it had no support. Such was the lack of accurate and up to date intelligence and coordination that a report from C Company noted that it had come across "signs of a recent fight." By the end of the day the companies were all back in their original line. The next hours were spent, where and when possible, in burying their dead and improving their largely razed positions. To maintain pressure on the enemy Major General Fanshawe issued a special instruction ordering sniping to be conducted as frequently and regularly as circumstances permitted. The two days had cost the battalion 36 dead and over 100 wounded but respite seemed to be on the way. The CO was informed at 1030 on 20 July that the battalion was shortly to be relieved by 8/Worcestershire.

Just after midday that message was rescinded. The "disappointment" noted above by the scribe of 8/Worcestershire was to have unfortunate consequences for its sister battalion but although the 8th Battalion itself was to suffer, in the long term the 'disappointment' turned out to have been something of a blessing. While out on a digging party during the night of 19-20 July near the Albert-Bapaume road, about half the battalion had been subjected to an intense bombardment of gas. The full effects were not felt for between 10 and 12 hours when men started to vomit violently and collapse. They were taken to the field ambulance at Albert where about a dozen of the stretcher bearers who had carried them down also developed the symptoms. The ADMS visited the field ambulance and then 8/Worcestershire's camp and decided the men would be unfit for at least a week. He ordered complete rest as men who seemed to have recovered were liable to collapse again if they attempted any physical exercise. Within three days, over 100 men were evacuated to a CCS. The battalion was able to provide a carrying party of 150 men two nights later but when the rest of the brigade marched to a rest area at the end of the month buses were provided for the Worcesters.[4]

4 The gassing of 8/Worcestershire caused an unseemly row between what the battalion's historian called some of the 'Military Authorities' and the division's ADMS because they could not agree on the severity of the men's incapacity. The ADMS's view that the effects were far more serious than some of his superiors believed proved to be correct. Corbett, *1/8th Battalion The Worcestershire Regiment*, p. 39.

The inability of 8/Worcestershire to relieve its 7th Battalion meant that the unfortunate Kidderminster and Stourport Territorials would themselves have to undertake the next.bombing attack against the succession of enemy posts. Behind a brief two minute bombardment, five battalions from 144 and 145 Brigades were to assault at 0245 on 21 July. They were to be supported by machine gun and trench mortar barrages and, if the wind was favourable, a smoke screen. The attackers were to carry only essential equipment and ammunition, together with screens intended to show the artillery the depth of penetration they had attained. Troops were ordered to be in the German trenches immediately the barrage lifted onto the enemy's reserve positions and several cages of pigeons were provided to aid communications. In what might was possibly sardonic vein, the diarist of 1/Bucks thought everything went "like clockwork" until the assault actually began. The trench mortar barrage, which according to one report had begun 10 minutes before the infantry attacked, immediately attracted a German response. The British bombardment had "absolutely no effect" on the heavy machine gun and rifle fire lashing the Bucks' parapet. In marked contrast, a report from 5/Gloucestershire claimed the enemy's defensive fire was checked by the British artillery until it lifted to the Germans' rear positions and that the leading companies were within 100 yards of the German posts before they were spotted. Paradoxically, another report from the same battalion indicates the assaulting platoons were fired on even before they left their own trenches. When close to the posts they were hung up by wire, a "very thick barrage of bombs" and machine guns on the ridge behind firing over the heads of the posts' garrisons. The attacking companies were silhouetted against the rising moon and offered a "good target" but some did get into the enemy posts and drove out the garrisons. It did not take long for the Germans to organize counter-attacks which, in turn, forced most of the British troops back to their own start line. One platoon of 6/Gloucestershire reported it could hold the "particularly unhealthy" Post 28 unless ordered to give it up but the battalion's other two parties withdrew because they had run out of rifle grenades, the supporting Stokes had exhausted their bombs and 7/Worcestershire on their right had failed to get forward. For its part, 7/Worcestershire reported that it had to withdraw because its left flank was in the air owing to 6/Gloucestershire having been "badly held up." One company commander of the Worcesters even requested a platoon of 5/Sussex be sent forward to help consolidate his newly-won position but 50 minutes later what was left of his own company and the Sussex were struggling over the broken ground back to their own lines. A hand written note by an officer of 5/Gloucestershire declared his men were exhausted and almost out of ammunition after three hours of continuous fighting against "overwhelming odds."

These bombing attacks were to set the scene for the next five nights. It is extremely rare for the war diaries to record divisional or brigade conferences in preparation for the attacks but rather than division or brigade staffs simply issuing orders without any previous consultation, some meetings must have taken place. 145 Brigade recorded one such occasion involving infantry COs and artillery and RE commanders in preparation for the attacks in the early hours of 23 July. Verbal orders were issued immediately, followed some hours later by written ones which specified objectives and tactics. Divisional HQ wanted two new jumping off trenches each of 300 yards dug before the attack but orders as to who should do it were unclear. Originally 145 Brigade was told to organize the digging together with 5/Sussex, but this instruction was later contradicted. "Through various misunderstanding and other causes which were never cleared up but remained the subject of much correspondence, [this resulted in] little work [being] done." 144 Brigade's brigade major and company commanders of 6/Gloucestershire, which together with only two weak companies of 7/Worcestershire held almost the entire brigade's front, went forward on a reconnaissance to establish jumping off points. They were fired upon by both British and German artillery but regained their own lines. Under a barrage of high explosive and protected by flame throwers, three of the battalion's companies advanced at 0030 with a section of RE in support. They did so in the sobering knowledge of having been informed that if the attack failed they would be required to do it again at 0400. Contact aircraft were scheduled to fly above the battalion at specified times to look for identification flares but these were not required because the Gloucesters were met immediately by heavy machine-gun fire. Some men did manage to enter the enemy trench but the last waves and the consolidation parties did not even enter the zone swept by the machine guns. The reason, they later explained, was because they had seen the unit to their right (probably 5/Gloucestershire) falling back and decided to conform. Two of the companies lost all of their officers and only one officer of the third returned. Rather than have to try again a few hours later the battalion was ordered to assist with machine guns, rifle grenades and Stokes a new attempt by the other two brigades at 0630.

On the other (eastern) side of the destroyed light railway line which had in calmer times linked the villages of Ovillers and Pozières, and beyond the area attacked by 5/Gloucestershire, 4/Ox&Bucks did have some success. The brigade's objective was to make contact with 1st Australian Division which was assaulting Pozières from the south and south-east. The South Midlanders were approaching the ruined village from the west across the warren of trenches which covered the rising ground between it and Ovillers. The Oxfords found it heavy going, with at least one platoon getting too far forward and falling victim to its own barrage; others were disorganized and "suffered heavily" from German fire. The platoons became engaged in ferocious bombing exchanges but when the Berkshires brought forward a fresh supply of bombs the Oxfords succeeded in securing a stretch of enemy trenches south of the railway. To try to straighten the line, at 0630 1/Bucks attacked over the ground from which 5/Gloucestershire had earlier withdrawn. With one company "seriously impeded" by the barrage the remaining companies stormed into the German trenches almost at the same time as the barrage lifted. An astonished German officer later told his captors that he and his men were waiting for the barrage to move before emerging from their shelters.[5]

The success was, however, limited because touch had still not been made with the Australians. 143 Brigade relieved 145 Brigade and tried to extend its hold that night.[6] It was held up by several strong points, one of which proved impossible to take. The post was later evacuated by the garrison and when examined was found to have contained at least three machine guns and underground accommodation for possibly up to 300 riflemen. Bombing assaults and "minor enterprises" continued through the night of 24-25 July with what was described as "varying success." Staff work suffered from the lack of reliable information which resulted in "miscarriage of orders" and further confusion. Touch with the Australians was not eventually made until the early hours of 26 July. The process had been protracted and bloody and had involved, of course, more than just the infantry. It was to become almost standard practice for pioneer battalions and divisional artillery to remain in the line for an additional tour when their infantry were out at rest or training and the South Midland RFA brigades did not leave their positions when the division's infantry was relieved in mid-month. The gunners were eventually relieved later in July but in accordance with by now usual practice the guns were left in situ for the incoming division.[7] During major operations the brigades usually worked in groups, sometimes with the guns of other divisions attached for additional fire power. Half batteries or even individual 18 pdrs could be sent to forward positions if the situation or the infantry demanded close protection but the usual practice was for the field guns and howitzers to be in pits behind the lines and connected to the infantry brigades and their attached forward observation officer (FOO) by telephone. Enemy shelling, horsed transport and the encumbrances carried by infantry working parties could frequently disrupt the lines with the result that at times the response to infantry calls for fire support were not immediately met. Flares could sometimes be missed in the dust and smoke of battle and messages by runners often arrived too late to have an impact.

By the time of the Somme, cooperation between gunners and infantry was improving. In normal periods of trench holding the RFA brigade covering its allocated infantry brigade would be informed when patrols or raids were underway. During periods of intense fighting, artillery liaison officers were generally attached to infantry brigade HQ to secure rapid communications between the two arms. The fire

5 These actions marked the first attack by some of the battalions in 145 Brigade. 4/Berkshire was to spend six days in the line and lost six second lieutenants and 230 other ranks from a total engaged of 650. The battalion was subsequently praised by its CO, division and corps HQ. Cruttwell, *4/Berkshire*, p. 78.

6 One officer of the Oxfords, despite his returning company having lost almost 100 of those who took part in the action, described his men on relief as being 'in tremendous spirits.' Greenwell, *Infant in arms*, p. 118.

7 The usual practice was to leave the guns, artillery boards, Vermorel sprayers and trench maps for incoming units.

plan for the attacks during the night of 22-23 July was fairly typical of those devised for subsequent operations. The usual night time barrage of about 40 rounds per battery was to be fired but, from four hours before zero, every 15 minutes the batteries would fire salvoes of two or four guns at the enemy posts to be assaulted in order to mark them for the observing infantry. From dawn onwards one battery of 18 pdrs was told off for each of the attacking infantry brigades, with the battery commanders being themselves positioned at the infantry brigade HQ ready to pass on to the guns any calls for immediate assistance. Occasional shoots of up to about 30 rounds per battery were to be fired at almost random points behind the German front line in addition to the main barrage which had lifted from the front positions. The infantry were ordered to fire flares to mark their new positions both to the artillery and to contact aircraft at specified times. Batteries positioned sentries at those times with orders to observe for the flares.

In order to get some idea of who was actually where in and around Pozières during the bombing operations in the days before its capture, 242 Brigade RFA despatched two subalterns to the ruins. Their reports illustrate the chaos and uncertainty that existed in the area but these FOOs also managed to report when the batteries were firing short and were able to order fire in anticipation of German counter-attacks. On another occasion they called down fire on a single German waving a white flag and then dispersed a neighbouring group of about 50 enemy troops. The subaltern later reported he believed the party to be a legitimate target because, although one German waved the flag, the remainder were carrying rifles. A later wire noted with some satisfaction that when the FOO reported Germans attacking in waves, his call to the battery resulted in them being driven back in disorder. The number of situation reports despatched by the two officers demonstrates that despite the enemy shelling many messages did arrive safely at their intended destination. Nonetheless, accidents and mistakes could still happen because communication channels were not always as rational as might be wished. For example, three times on both 26 and 27 July, 143 Brigade received complaints from its battalion COs that British guns were shelling the brigade's trenches. On investigation, brigade HQ decided that it was either batteries of 25th Division which were also covering the division's front or batteries working directly under the CRA. Neither of the groups had a liaison officer attached to 143 Brigade HQ. By again firing short the British barrage had also "seriously impeded and somewhat disorganized" the support company of 1/Bucks as it moved forward to follow the assaulting companies on 23 July.

The German artillery was not, of course, a passive bystander during the bombing operations. British control of the air did sometimes limit the extent of the German ability to observe for their guns but the supply of replacement guns, shells and gas was sufficient to ensure most attacks by 48th Division were met with an immediate counter-barrage. The many German counter-attacks were also effectively covered by their own guns. The bombing enterprises undertaken by the division were, however, in such a confined space, with the distances between the opposing sides so limited, that the artillery of both sides had necessarily to restrict their fire on the enemy's front trenches and concentrate instead on the communication trenches and reserve lines. On 24 July, for example, such was the intensity of the shelling on the communication trenches that 7/Warwickshire did not get to its jumping off place in time for the scheduled attack. In another part of the line, of the approximately 100 prisoners taken by 1/Bucks and directed to the rear only about 30 managed to survive their own counter-barrage and reach the comparative safety of Crucifix Corner. Even 4/Gloucestershire's transport officer, Lieutenant Master, fell as a fatal victim to enemy shelling on battalion HQ on 25 July.

The activities of 48th (South Midland) and several other divisions to the west of Pozières during July were, in comparison to events undertaken further to the south-east, relatively small scale. The objectives in the three divisions were to capture Mouquet Farm, cut off Thiepval and gain observation over Courcelette and Grandcourt. Seizure of the Pozières Ridge was vital to achieving these aims but the operations engaged substantially fewer numbers of divisions than those involved by corps attacking Guillemont, Lonqueval and High and Delville Woods. By maintaining a "vigorous offensive", which comprised a relentless series of surprise bombing assaults usually referred to as "minor enterprises", the division would nibble away at the enemy's positions and morale. Larger, set piece assaults would only be undertaken if and when these smaller attacks failed. Divisional HQ, possibly on orders from corps HQ, organized the assaults as nocturnal attacks because if successful darkness would provide several hours of unobserved consolidation. Parties of RE and pioneers were usually standing by to supervise or help with this process but such was the German desire to win back lost ground that assaults and counter-attacks sometimes went on well into the daylight hours. The growing exhaustion of troops, the danger to which relief parties were exposed on their way up and the frequent uncertainty about who was actually holding which post, were likely to sap morale and effectiveness equally on both sides.[8]

In early July, and before the brigade was effectively reduced to three battalions owing to the gassing of 8/Worcestershire, an order from 144 Brigade HQ stated that battalions would not be required to work on the day of relief or the subsequent day. They were to take over schemes or projects then currently being undertaken in the rear but would first be allowed a period of rest. For operational purposes this order was swiftly ignored. It is clear that during the period of 14-28 July, the division's battalions spent very little time out of the line and that for the odd 24 hour period that they were supposedly 'at rest' they were frequently required for working parties. Neither were they beyond the range of German heavy guns during whatever short period of rest they might have been granted. This had significant implications not only for their

8 On the night of 26-27 July, for example, 4/Gloucestershire received information that the Germans in a post opposite had withdrawn. When patrols pushed forward they were met with a fusillade of enemy fire which proved the intelligence to have been entirely erroneous.

mental state but also their general physical condition. War diaries only occasionally mention that men were able to take a bath and draw clean underclothes, which probably suggests such opportunities were inconsistent or at least infrequent during this period. With the constant transit of troops, the divisional sanitary officer noted how difficult it was during operations to keep the rear areas free of flies and contaminated water. He recorded only three cases of infectious disease during the month but a "considerable amount" of trench fever and influenza. As it was "impossible" to obtain anti-flea ointment and powder the men were again infected with lice. Furthermore, the periods out of the line experienced by the division's units were too short to devote any purposeful time to training, to absorb new drafts or simply to rest both mind and body.

The BEF was in the process of learning from its brutal experiences at the start of the Somme offensive but these and later lessons would take time to be absorbed and disseminated to division and brigade level. Like many other formations, during July 48th Division enjoyed few opportunities to develop the conceptual component of fighting power.[9] Certain administrative and operational points had, however, already become obvious. 4/Ox&Bucks was one of several battalions which regularly noted the importance of battalion HQ being informed early of its commander's intent and allowed sufficient time to organize attacks. When comparing the battalion's assaults of 19 July and 23 July, battalion HQ concluded there had been little hope of success for the first attack because there was no time for officers to reconnoitre the objectives and because the troops had only reached their jumping off point 15 minutes before zero. In contrast, preparations for the action on 23 July had been considerably better paced: officers had time to study the front positions and to relay that knowledge to their platoon commanders and NCOs. There was also sufficient time between the issue of orders and the move forward for the troops to draw stores, eat and rest.

The often very narrow width of no man's land meant the division's gunners had little opportunity to practise the intricacies of the creeping barrage but, as was noted earlier, opinions varied within the division's units about the effectiveness of artillery support. While 1/Bucks could praise it for its accuracy, 6/Gloucestershire described its covering barrage as "quite useless" in keeping down German heads. There were, the diarist reported, "long periods" when no shells fell. The consequence of this was, "Having nothing to worry them [German machine gunners] were able to fire on the assaulting troops as they pleased." Divisional expertise in the laying of machine-gun barrages as a supplement and adjunct to the artillery was considered to be improving through the experience gained by its machine-gun company firing frequently in support of its own infantry and also that of neighbouring 1st Australian Division.

9 The Brigade Major of 143 Brigade took it upon himself to produce hand written tactical instructions to 7/Warwickshire on the best way to take a specific enemy strong point. Within a few weeks of its production the sort of detail included in his treatise was to be reproduced in centrally issued tactical pamphlets.

The infantry's physical component, such as the supply of effective grenades, Lewis guns and Stokes mortars, was certainly improving but they, too, required time to be assimilated into company and platoon tactical schemes. These close infantry support weapons were crucial to 48th Division in the sort of operation in which it was involved during July and August. Although it had had reasonably lengthy periods out of the line during its Hébuterne sojourn the division was almost as innocent as many of the New Army formations when it came to prolonged periods of fighting in a sustained offensive. Grenades were certainly more plentiful and essential when clearing trench barricades and dugouts but, like other units, 8/Warwickshire complained of being "out thrown" by the German model during bombing encounters and of being at a disadvantage when showered by enemy rifle grenades. If they were fortunate enough to discover stocks of German stick grenades in abandoned trenches, they were the preferred weapon for distance throwing of many British troops.

Lewis guns were also being absorbed into platoon tactical work. Useful as they were in helping to offer mobile covering fire and flank protection they could use substantial amounts of ammunition. Similarly, 2 inch Stokes trench mortars were being issued in increasing numbers but they, too, required a regular and heavy supply of ammunition. 145 Brigade recorded that an attack by 5/Gloucestershire failed because insufficient Stokes ammunition had been brought forward before daylight broke. The guns were therefore unable to cooperate with the infantry for as long as intended and, as a result, much of the enemy wire remained untouched. 143 Brigade also complained several times during July of the "unsatisfactory nature of the work" of the Stokes. One report condemned the mortar crews for taking too long to get into action and another for killing six and wounding 10 of the infantry when the guns fired short. This incident was thought to be the result of base plates shifting in the soft ground but if, as was suggested, they were to be adjusted every 10 rounds the rate of fire would drop substantially. The Warwicks troops on the receiving end of the shorts were described as having been "considerably shaken" and it was suggested that if two guns and crews were attached to each battalion, as indeed were the Lewis gun detachments, it would lead to greater control of their use and boost the infantry's confidence in them. The present system, the report concluded, worked against efficient communications (and thus effective fire) between the arms and added to confusion and "misunderstandings."

Although the division's July enterprises took place over a confined area and short distances, the difficulties of passing reliable reports back to battalion and brigade HQ remained acute. Reports suggest that in the face of "impassable" German fire the other ranks behaved well but also that if the officers and seniors NCOs were hit, the men went too quickly to ground. The *Official History* makes the point that when a German bombardment on 23 July cut 48th and 1st Australian Divisions' signal cables and prevented their repair both HQ had to rely on runners and pigeons. Visual signals could not be seen through the smoke and, furthermore, if messages were to be of any use to those in the rear they had to include accurate information of positions and the state of the men and equipment. A junior NCO or even a private had to have sufficient relevant knowledge, have the initiative to write it and then persuade a runner to carry it through the likely German barrage. Birds were, as we know, carried by certain of the assaulting troops but pigeons could be less than reliable.[10] It was also preferable to have men familiar with their handling close at hand because other than to eat it, most men in an average infantry platoon would have little idea of what to do with the bird. Several of the division's battalions had worked with aircraft contact patrols when out of the line so understood the principles of how to pass positional messages to pilots who then relayed them to brigade HQ. It seems likely that 143 Brigade did succeed in contacting low flying aircraft of 4 Squadron when the brigade's battalions came into the line on 26 July but the earlier doubts as to the utility of contact aircraft do seem to have persisted.

The brigade's tour was to be a short one and by the end of the month 48th Division was a long way from the trenches north of Ovillers. As the weary troops trudged towards the camps on the Bouzincourt Ridge, few would have given much thought to the changed landscape through which they passed. Had they been awake or enthused sufficiently to cast glances about them, and if illuminated by the glare of flares and the bursting of shells, those few may have noted the work done by the field companies and pioneers during the month. There was now an inner defence line consisting of keeps and lesser strong points in La Boisselle and Ovillers, new tramways had appeared, wells had been opened up and gun lines moved forward. Aspects of the work had been impeded by German shelling and the necessity of wearing gas masks for long periods but the main road through Ovillers had been substantially improved. Communication trenches had been cleared of debris and deepened, at least two new tunnels offered some protection to troops moving to and from the line and new wire was laid as part of a wider defensive scheme. When, however, 143 Brigade reached their camp and were allowed a few hours sleep they awoke to discover the army reasserting rest area discipline in preparation for a move. The troops were harangued for being too lax in the care of picks and shovels, warned of the dire consequences of looting from abandoned houses, reminded of the need to adhere strictly to traffic regulations and told to keep away from fields of growing crops. For those who had not already heard, they were informed that Private Arthur Earp of 5/Warwickshire had a few days earlier been shot at Bouzincourt for quitting his post during the offensive's preliminary bombardment. Other units might have heard that Driver Loder of 241 RFA Brigade had been sent to a military prison for two years and Private Rouse of 4/Ox&Bucks for ten.[11] They might also have learned that their army, corps and divisional commanders had all expressed satisfaction and pride in what the division had achieved and that on 23 July their success had "far exceeded our reasonable hopes." There was, however, also a veiled warning that victories easily gained were not as "really decisive" as those which

10 On 27 July the FOO of 242 RFA Bde despatched a message to Bde HQ by runner. He explained he could not send a pigeon because 'we cannot find the clips.'

11 Loder's crime is not specified in the war diary but Rouse was charged with refusing to go on patrol.

were won by "the determination to win no matter what the odds in numbers and difficulties against us."

With the known exception of 200 men of 6/Warwickshire who were forced to march with the brigade transport, most of the division's units seem to have been transported by motor vehicles. They were conveyed to several villages east of Abbeville which served as rest and training areas. Here, the men had the opportunity to bathe, draw clean underclothes, train and be again in the presence of civilians. Some of those civilians did, according to the diarist of 4/Ox&Bucks, regard the new arrivals with an initial degree of suspicion, and 7/Worcestershire reported its allotted village failed to provide the battalion with sufficient water and accommodation. In contrast, "much to our joy and the joy of the inhabitants who had not forgotten us for the excellent way the battalion had behaved" when it was last billeted in the village, 4/Berkshire looked forward to its stay. The time in this quiet and largely unspoilt area of France was to be brief but it was an important period for the units as they rebuilt their companies and platoons with new drafts.

In spite of the July fighting, when the division left the forward area its infantry brigades remained reasonably strong. The *Official History* gives the divisional casualties for the period 16-28 July as 124 officers and 2,720 other ranks. To these should be added the enormous losses suffered by the two Warwickshire battalions on 1 July and the lesser numbers sustained in the assaults made before 16 July. 143 Brigade recorded figures of 26 officers and 288 other ranks killed, 40 and 986 wounded and 12 and 292 missing respectively. This computes to an average of 390 other rank casualties per battalion. When the brigade left for Abbeville it took with it a fighting strength of 127 officers and 2,825 NCOs and men. This compares to the formation's fighting strength on 30 June of 127 officers and 3,595 other ranks and which thus represents an average reduction of fewer than 200 per battalion. Battalion strengths had been sustained by the arrival of large drafts during the course of the month: for example, 539 men joined 6/Warwickshire and 275 were taken by 8/Warwickshire.

Numbers collated after the war suggest the four Warwickshire battalions suffered a total of 550 other rank fatalities during the month in addition to probably 40 officer deaths. As far as can be determined, the drafts which arrived before the opening of the Somme had come from the 2nd or 3rd Line, but 8/Warwickshire did certainly receive a reasonably large draft posted from the Wiltshire Regiment. In July and early August, the brigade as a whole received a large draft of men from the Hunts Cyclist Battalion; these new arrivals were divided between the four battalions. 1/Bucks pointed out that these were the "first strangers sent to us"[12] but the men were trained and fit and the group sent to 5/Warwickshire was later described as "probably the finest draft" received by that battalion. In contrast, a large draft from the UK which arrived at the end of July was described as having had "very insufficient and superficial training", with "many of poor physique" and "quite unfit to serve with an

12 Wright, *First Bucks Battalion*, p36

infantry battalion." This last draft was spared the engagements of July but it is evident that with the exception of a few men from Wiltshire, the great majority of July deaths in 143 Brigade were of volunteer territorials from Warwickshire.

It is a similar mixed picture in the other two infantry brigades. 4/Berkshire recorded dissatisfaction with a draft which arrived towards the end of the month. During the march to the rear area 131 men fell out and the diarist noted that 102 of them were from this last draft. He recorded, "Some of these men should not have been sent out. They had not handled a rifle before, only broomsticks, they had not been taught to turn and had no knowledge of a bomb. Many of the elementary points of sanitation were unknown." The diarist did qualify his remarks by adding that they "referred only to a few" but the battalion ran special classes for those men who had not previously thrown at least two live grenades and for those whose rifle skills were clearing lacking. In May, 4/Ox&Bucks had received almost four dozen men, probably from its reserve battalion, who were thought to be "mostly very young and small" and, in July, took a substantial draft of Derby men from the Devonshire Regiment. Having observed the drafts, in a moment of reflection Greenwell, who had been with the battalion since October 1914, wrote to his parents that although "we shall never see such lads again [the mobilized men of 1914]...these fresh men have something of the same keenness."[13] 4/Gloucestershire also received in August 60 "of a good type of man" from 10/Gloucestershire and, soon afterwards, at least 20 from 14/Gloucester. 5/Gloucester of 145 Brigade had a draft of 54 from its regiment's regular and service battalions in early July and at the end of the month sent another 85 who had come from the reserve units of 4/ and 6/Gloucester to 144 Brigade's HQ for posting. Evidence of those who were to die in the battles of August suggests, however, there must also have been a number of men arriving at the division who did not come from the battalions' traditional recruitment areas. Nonetheless, when compared to several other divisions, the South Midland was certainly not swamped by an influx of men with little geographical association to the remaining original members. The history of the Worcestershire Regiment condemns the later posting in of non-Worcestershire men as "folly" but the history of its 8th Battalion went a stage further and wrote of the 'careless cruelty' of the posting staff at Rouen. Their policy, it recorded, "often led to very distressing results and showed how little they appreciated the meaning of the territorial system of recruiting and its enormous value of morale and discipline."[14]

For several reasons, not least to try to dilute the number of men from a particular area dying on the same day, the posting officers at the base camps had been instructed to adopt a policy of trying, when possible, to send men to units of the same *regiment* but not necessarily from the receiving unit's own reserve *battalion*. The introduction of conscription had meant territorials could now be sent to regular or Kitchener units

13 Greenwell, *Infant in Arms*, p. 122.
14 Stacke, *The Worcestershire Regiment 1914-1919*, p. 184; Corbett, *War History of 1/8th Worcester*, p. 5.

rather than just to battalions of their own corps or regiment. The War Office was attempting to create an 'Army' rather than individual Regular, New Army or TF 'spirit' but this policy was criticised by many who believed efficiency and ethos would suffer as a consequence. A few fortunate TF formations and units did continue to receive preferred treatment and remained able to draw drafts very largely from their own catchment areas. Although it did not fall into this special category, the South Midland as a whole does seem to have been fortunate during this period largely to have local men posted to it. Unlike some other TF divisions which did manage to retain a strong territorial character, in later months the division was to receive drafts of men from rather more widely dispersed areas.[15]

At the time the offensive opened, the division's hierarchy was well established. Major General Fanshawe had been with it for over one year, as had two of the three infantry brigade commanders. The CRA had been in post since February 1916 and the regular officers who had replaced the three original RFA brigade commanders had been in command for several months. Two of their TF second-in-commands had, however, been with their brigades in the pre-war era. The CRE had been appointed in April 1915 and the division's two original field companies were still commanded by August 1914 TF officers. The ADMS had been in command for over one year and although only one of his field ambulance commanders had sailed with the division, the other two were well established. The long-serving GSO1 was promoted away in April 1916, but his GSO2 and GSO3, as well as the infantry brigade majors, had all been in post or had held similar positions in other formations for several months. Lieutenant Colonel Langham, the TF pre-war CO of 5/Sussex remained in post, but only two of the 12 August 1914 TF infantry commanders, Innes of 8/Warwickshire and Peake of 8/Worcestershire, had survived until the offensive began.[16] Two regular officers who had been quickly posted to battalions within the division soon after the declaration of war had sailed with their adopted unit in March 1915 remained, and two other COs had served as adjutants to their battalion or another in the same brigade.[17] One CO was probably a formerly retired TF lieutenant colonel of a different battalion of the same brigade and another, R.J.Clarke, an August 1914 major in 4/Berkshire, had been promoted to CO from within his own unit. The remaining four seem to have been regulars posted in to replace COs invalided home during the Hébuterne period or as the result of wounds inflicted in July.[18]

15 For example, 55th (West Lancashire) Division.
16 Innes was killed on 1 July 1916.
17 Micklem was promoted from adjutant to CO in 6/Gloucestershire; Sladen, adjutant of 8/Warwickshire, was given command of 5/Warwickshire.
18 For example, Stewart, the replacement CO of 5/Warwickshire, was apparently invalided home in July 1915 with hay fever. (WD of ADMS). Typical of the type of man posted in was Lt.Col. Harman. He had retired from the Rifle Brigade in 1913 as a captain and was posted as CO to 7/Worcestershire in May 1915 aged 38 years. Dobbin, posted in as CO of 4/Gloucestershire in June 1916, was two years younger. He was commissioned into

Trench warfare in the months before July 1916 had taken its toll of majors and captains with the result that many of the surviving junior officers of August 1914 were now company commanders. Furthermore, many of the officers who had joined their battalions abroad had also been promoted to temporary captain. Compared to the total of all officers ranked from full lieutenant and above who were killed by the end of July 1916, the percentage of August 1914 officers was not in some battalions particularly large. They ranged from the 63 percent of 4/Ox&Bucks and 55 percent of 5/Warwickshire to the zero percent of 4/Gloucestershire and 7/Warwickshire. As might be expected, 6/ and 8/Warwickshire also had some August 1914 officers amongst its huge number of wounded of 1 July: both battalions lost a major who had sailed as a captain and a captain who sailed as a lieutenant. Many other 1916 company commanders, most of whom who had been posted into battalions as second lieutenants during the division's time in France, were also killed or wounded but a grievous blow to the original TF character of 5/Gloucestershire occurred on 24 July when not only was one of its pre-1914 officers killed but four captains, all of whom had been lieutenants on the outbreak of war, were wounded and evacuated. Several of the division's units original officers were to return on recovery of wounds but trench warfare and the division's first large scale encounters with the enemy meant that by August 1916 the great majority of the its pre-war TF officers were no longer with the formation.

Such had been the attrition and subsequent pace of replacement of junior officers that during July, 143 Brigade had suffered casualties among second lieutenants who had been posted from, for example, the Dorset, Northampton, East Surrey and South Staffordshire Regiments. It was not unusual for each battalion in the division to lose between four and six second lieutenants each month between January and June 1916. Not all of these, of course, were killed or wounded but could also have been invalided home or posted to other units for a variety of reasons. During July, 8/Worcestershire was fortunate in receiving eight subalterns from its own reserve battalion but 7/Warwickshire absorbed 13 from 3/Dorset and 6/Gloucestershire received 10 from the Devon Regiment. Many of the pre-offensive replacement platoon commanders were with their battalion for only a matter of weeks before the Somme campaign opened and may, consequently, have had only a fairly sketchy knowledge of the men they commanded. Those who joined as part of the flurry of replacements which arrived at battalion transport lines during July had even less time to acclimatize and get to know their men before they were hurled into battle.

the DCLI in 1899 and had been with the West African Frontier Force until 1913. An even younger regular, Lt. Col. Bartlett, only commissioned into the Ox&Bucks LI 1903 and former adjutant of the Bucks Battalion, was appointed CO of 4/Ox&Bucks in June 1916. His youth was thought to be 'a great thing; it prevents him fussing and worrying his company commanders when the time for action comes.' Greenwell, *Infant in arms*, p. 142.

Almost 20 officers were sent to the field ambulances with pyrexia during this period of company training and rest in the peace of a bucolic setting. Time spent in the ambulances was probably viewed as an opportunity for them to have an additional break from the stress of command rather than purely as a cure for the fever itself. The men were entertained by a mobile cinema, performances by the several *troupes* within the division and were allowed to bathe in rural pools. Those of 8/Worcestershire who were still suffering from the effects of the gas attack on 19 July were sent to the seaside and many NCOs were given passes to visit Abbeville. The period of rest was described by 3/Field Ambulance as "delightful but too short" because, by 10 August, the division was on the road marching back towards the front. Despite repeated warnings in battalion orders about the need for care in billets to avoid "accidental and unnecessary fires", the almost inevitable blaze broke out in a barn occupied by 8/Warwickshire. This delayed the battalion's departure which, together with the severe heat of the day and "mistakes" resulted in long detours because parties had not been sent forward to reconnoitre the prescribed route. In the confusion, the men "rapidly" became exhausted. To compound this further, when the infantry arrived at Bouzincourt the staff work again proved inadequate and there was some unseemly competition for billets. The problems continued when 4/Berkshire, with two companies of Bucks attached, moved up to Ovillers to relieve 37 Brigade. The six companies all of about 150 men were ordered to take over dugouts which had housed five companies of only roughly 100 men apiece. Brigade HQ was advised and the Bucks companies were sent back to their own battalion. After considerable disruption the division relieved 12th Division which, during the night of 12-13 August, had managed to capture the tactically important Skyline Trench.[19]

As they moved across the devastation to the forward area, some troops may have recalled the words of Sir Douglas Haig read to them a little earlier by their platoon commanders. Haig had issued a special order of the day which praised the work of the BEF and the Allied armies in the period up to the beginning of the campaign. Haig believed the Germans were now making "a desperate effort to save himself from utter defeat and from the punishment he has merited" and went on to assert that although the enemy would continue to fight, the growing numbers, experience and resources of the British meant "our worst difficulties have already been overcome." Troops of 4/Ox&Bucks in Skyline Trench about to experience the ferocity of a German counter-attack might have questioned the optimism so apparent in Haig's message. For many of those moving up this was their first experience in a front line trench. Their sympathetic company commander described them as "rather windy" but blamed the situation rather than "my poor men."[20] As Skyline Trench allowed observation over the strong point of Thiepval and, to a lesser extent land to the north and east, it

19 In some war diaries, Skyline and Ration Trench (which ran parallel to Skyline to its SE) are referred to as 6th and 5th Avenues respectively.

20 Greenwell, *Infant in arms*, p. 123.

The view from Skyline Trench looking across the eastern slopes of Nab Valley and the trees covering the position of the Leipzig Redoubt beyond. While 48th Division assaulted in an approximately northward direction, other divisions attacked up the Thiepval ridge from the west. (Author)

The view from Skyline Trench across to the Pozières ridge and the village. 48th Division made several attacks against the trench and the area beyond in cooperation with the Australian assaults on Pozières village. (Author)

was unsurprising the Germans regarded its loss with alarm. At 0800 on 13 August, the Germans (and it was thought several British guns) opened a heavy barrage on Skyline and Ration Trenches which increased in intensity at about 2100. The Oxfords despatched five messages noting the massing of enemy troops and the falling short of British shells but none managed to get through to the rear. At 2200 two German battalions attacked. The two platoons of Oxfords and their Lewis guns assisted by two Vickers and a Stokes crew repulsed the first attack but when the second wiped out one of the Vickers' teams the remainder of the garrison was driven back to Ration Trench. They rallied and attempted to bomb back up the communication trench connecting the two. Two platoons of 4/Berkshire carried up a fresh supply bombs but these were quickly exhausted. This, together with a dwindling number of men, resulted in no consolidated progress.

Two companies of Berkshire and two of 6/Gloucestershire were ordered to regain Skyline at 0300. In bright moonlight, over completely unfamiliar ground and "in the face of almost certain failure" they advanced into heavy machine-gun fire which inflicted over 140 casualties on the Berkshire and forced the survivors back to their own trench.[21] In preparation for another bombing attempt, during the next few hours the divisional artillery hit Skyline with everything it could bring to bear. At about 2200, two parties of 1/Bucks forced their way into Skyline and then began bombing outwards, eventually to make contact with Australian troops on the right. To the left, 6/Gloucestershire also attacked but failed to get into the group of trenches at the south-western end of Skyline. What was left of the already obliterated trench was then systematically pounded by a barrage of heavies, trench mortars and minnies fired from the direction of Mouquet Farm. Under this punishment the Bucks were forced to withdraw and held only the heads of the communication trenches leading into Skyline. Garrisons in adjoining trenches were also thinned out to avoid heavy losses from enfilade fire. The men were ordered to occupy shell holes parallel to the front and rear of the increasingly destroyed trenches in the hope of reducing casualties. During the very dark night of 15-16 August, 144 and 145 Brigades made further attempts against the trenches at the south-western end of Skyline. The Germans were clearly expecting an attack as the advancing troops were fired on from shell holes outside the trenches which had escaped the attentions of the barrage. Another attempt was made at 0500 on 16 August by two companies of 5/Gloucestershire supported by a bombing party of 1/Bucks. Preparations for the attack had not been helped by some confused staff work between 145 Brigade and the Australians to its right. This caused some unnecessary overcrowding and delays in the front trenches. Intense machine gun and rifle fire opened on the companies immediately the attack began which quickly resulted in five of the six Gloucesters' officers becoming casualties. This disorganized the attack and, with the Bucks exhausting their supply of bombs, once again no progress was made.

21 Cruttwell, *War Service of 1/4th Berkshire*, p. 80.

Another view from the commanding position of Skyline Trench. This looks across to Thiepval village and ridge, with the British Memorial to the Missing on the left. (Author)

Taken from the approximate position of Ration Trench, and to the north-west of the light railway track which in pre-war days had run up to Pozières, this photo looks down the upper reaches of Mash Valley towards the village of Ovillers. 8th Division had attacked up Mash Valley on 1 July but the village was not cleared by 25th and 48th Divisions until 16-17 July. (Author)

When the Germans attempted to regain Skyline Trench on 17 August the Oxfords spotted the enemy infantry assembling in preparation for the attack and called down a barrage which smashed the assault parties. The heavies were helped in their task by the timely repositioning of the twelve 18 pdrs of C/243 and C/242 which had just moved forward into Mash Valley in order to shorten their range. Later reports from captured prisoners confirmed this barrage had been decisive and had badly affected German morale. Momentum was maintained on 18 August when 143 and 145 Brigades were ordered to attack trenches on the slope dropping away from Skyline Trench towards the north-eastern end of Nab Valley. The artillery was tasked with obliterating a concentration of trenches known as the Quadrilateral and two companies of 5/Gloucestershire were in reserve ready to exploit any success and sweep the enemy off the south-western slopes of the valley. The waves of the assaulting companies were to leapfrog towards the objective; once in them troops of 4/Berkshire were to wave sandbags on the end of bayonets to indicate to 143 Brigade where they were. Smoke was to be released by 49th Division on the left provided it did not hinder artillery observation. When it was released, however, the smoke did obscure the FOOs' spotting but it had the beneficial effect of deceiving the Germans about the actual direction of the attack. While German guns shelled 49th Division in anticipation, to the right 5/ and 6/Warwickshire, supported by bombers of 7/Warwickshire, left their trenches early. There was some loss of direction in the smoke, and one company was held up by machine-gun fire, but the others were in the German lines almost under their own barrage. Nearly 400 prisoners were taken in return for "comparatively light" casualties.[22] Carrington later reflected that the greatest difficulty had been "to hold the men back".[23] Such, apparently had been their enthusiasm that some platoons of 5/Warwickshire had advanced too far and lost contact. When the Germans launched a counter-attack, rather than leave it to the artillery, 5/Warwickshire broke it up with Lewis gun and rifle fire. This success was recorded as "a great stimulant to the confidence of all."[24] To maintain pressure on the enemy, 143 Brigade continued to send bombing parties forward on the following two days but, generally, they met with little success. When one attack across the open petered out almost before it began, one frustrated officer in 7/Warwickshire blamed the failure on the men of the "last draft who would not get on." B Company of 4/Berkshire cooperated with the hesitant Warwicks and, with perhaps a degree of self-satisfaction, the Berkshires' diarist thought that the training given to his battalion's recent draft with dummy bombs had "proved of great value." Another attempt was made under the cover of a Stokes barrage which did enable 7/Warwickshire to capture one of their earlier objectives but overall the days' activities were once more disappointing.

22 6/Warwickshire suffered a little over 130 casualties.
23 Carrington, *War Record of 1/5th Royal Warwickshire*, p. 33.
24 Ibid.

Although these bombing attacks had taken on a somewhat formulaic hue there was the beginning of a noticeable improvement in the coordination of effort by adjoining divisions and corps. In preparation for the attacks of 18-19 August, Lieutenant General Jacob issued a memo which he ordered should be read to all officers and men of his corps. The missive insisted that all troops of 12th (Eastern), 49th (West Yorkshire) and 48th (South Midland) Divisions were required to understand their corps commander's intent for the coming attacks and emphasized the thoroughness of the preparations. He wanted the men to know that liaison officers acting to coordinate work between divisions, brigades, battalions and the artillery were all in place, that there was to be effective control over the supporting machine-gun teams, that sections of RE and pioneers were ready to open up new trenches and consolidate those captured, and that there were sufficient flares, signal screens and telephone wires to enable efficient communications from the front to the rear. Forward dumps had been established and filled, follow up troops had been well drilled in mopping up methods and salvage groups would concentrate on collecting and re-distributing discarded buckets of bombs and rifles. There was a good supply of phosphorous bombs to clear the deep dugouts but troops were told to use them sparingly so that the shelters could be readily occupied by the assaulting platoons. Jacob's memo was intended to encourage and reassure his men that all possible preparations were in place. It addressed both the physical and moral components of fighting power and was reinforced by another message which was similarly concerned to raise morale. The note explained the enemy positions had been heavily bombarded for over a week and that "no portion of our line has ever experienced such continuous and concentrated bombardment by such heavy shells." Jacobs thought it was unlikely the German garrisons had been relieved during that period and were therefore bound to be short of food and water. In addition, he explained, the enemy was also exhausted and demoralized from the bombardment and the nightly bombing attacks. In contrast, Jacobs stressed that his own men were fit, fed and healthy, were acknowledged to be superior in hand-to-hand fighting and "knew their business." The result, he thought, "was a foregone conclusion."

Unfortunately, Jacob's assumption about the inevitability of success was proved to be false. On 20 August, 144 Brigade, with 7/ and 8/Warwickshire attached, took over the entire divisional front. Corps wanted the attacks to continue and ordered that if specified posts were not captured by minor enterprises during the night a daylight assault by the brigade would have to be made on 21 August. The next three days were to witness some particularly ferocious fighting in the sector as both sides sought to gain and regain ground. During the night of 20-21 August, 6/Gloucestershire made some progress in the area north-east of the Nab and a major assault was launched at 1800 on 21 August. Officers and NCOs of 4/ and 6/Gloucestershire reconnoitred the approach to the German trenches on the south and south-east sides of the Leipzig Redoubt; good communication was established with 1/Wiltshire of 25th Division who would be attacking on their left. Additional bomb dumps had been created, the attacking companies were to advance in waves, leapfrogging through to the third objective and the Lewis guns of the pioneer battalion were to follow and cover the consolidating parties. Additional fire power was provided by four guns of No.4 Motor Machine Gun Battery and six Hotchkiss of the Yorkshire Dragoons. The almost constant bombardment by heavies and 18 pdrs of three divisions was to increase in intensity for five minutes before lifting. Meanwhile, guns not firing on the specific objectives were to continue to smother other targets either side of the area under assault. As was usual by this stage of the campaign, artillery brigade commanders were located within infantry brigade headquarters and in direct communication with their batteries. The smashed communication trenches caused the companies "great" difficulty in getting up to the front trenches but they were in position by 1715 and crawled out into no man's land at 1750. Under "an excellent" barrage the Gloucesters were quickly into the enemy trenches and, according to 144 Brigade HQ, "were able to walk about in the open without being shot at." To their left the Wiltshires and 3/Worcestershire successfully captured sections of Lemberg Trench. The lull was, however, to be short lived. At 2000, the artillery dispersed at least one battalion of Germans massing to counter-attack but other groups escaped the shells. Under the cover of their own counter-barrage these companies organized a succession of attacks against Hindenburg and Lemberg Trenches.[25] The engagements seesawed as posts were captured and recaptured, prisoners taken earlier were released and later recaptured, company commanders lost control of their platoons and platoon commanders of their sections. Enemy bomb stores were plundered as the hand-to-hand fighting swayed to and fro and the fire of Lewis and Stokes guns proved crucial on several occasions. Such was the intensity of the fighting that some of the companies which had advanced into no man's land before 1800 on 21 August were unable to be relieved until 0900 on 23 August.

The incoming troops were immediately tasked with continuing the offensive. The chaos of collapsed trenches and scores of corpses and wounded which greeted them had to be dealt with quickly so that a proposed attack could be made at 1500 on 23 August. 145 Brigade was to assault, supported by the machine guns of 143 Brigade firing on Thiepval and 144 Brigade providing working parties. Known enemy strong points were to be targeted by the heavy artillery in preparation and, as usual, RE sections under strict orders not to get involved in the actual fighting were on stand-by to move forward and help with consolidation. Other troops were ready to exploit any significant success. An intelligence report described the "knocked about" condition of the objectives but also highlighted the number and depth of some of the dugouts in, for example, Lemberg Trench. Some were of two storeys and 40 feet in depth and most had at least four entrances. The Wonderwork, which had caused so many of 32nd Division's losses on 1 July, and Konigstrasse Trench were similarly described as considerable obstacles. It was the failure of the heavy artillery accurately to locate and smash these defences that was to doom the next South Midland attack to failure.

25 These trenches lay on the spur running up from the Leipzig Redoubt to Thiepval.

There was certainly confusion as to the precise positions held by some British troops. For examples, one set of orders stipulated that "if" 7/Worcestershire was actually in possession of a position known as Point 79, it was to withdraw from it during the bombardment. Whether this message actually reached the garrison is unclear but at 1500, companies of the Bucks and Oxfords crossed no man's land behind what was described as an "excellent" barrage. They discovered the enemy front trenches to be empty but came under close range field gun shelling and withering machine-gun fire from trenches onto which the British barrage was actually falling. Some Germans were allegedly seen to be standing on their parapets to fire on the attackers and others were reported to be wearing British uniforms. A number of bomb stops was eventually established on the eastern slopes of Nab Valley but the ground gained was negligible and the Bucks Battalion reported a casualty list of more than 100 from the two companies involved.

Brigadier General Done, GOC 145 Brigade, immediately submitted a report explaining the failure of his brigade to gain any significant ground and suggesting means by which future attacks could be improved. The principal causes of the reverse were the failure of the heavy artillery to hit the main enemy trench, owing largely to the lack of good observation positions, and its apparent failure to demoralize the enemy. Done also believed 145 Brigade's assembly trench was too shallow, there had been no time to deepen it and that because the enemy had witnessed the relief and the preparations, they were fully expecting an attack. Knowing this, the Germans put down explosive and shrapnel along the front of their line at zero. Despite the British barrage being reported as "very good" the Germans were still able to man the parapet and bring down fire on the attackers. Done suggested that future success depended on adequate time being accorded to the heavies to smash the enemy dugouts and rather more imagination and innovation with regard to the barrage. The heavies, for example, could cease firing perhaps a day before the assault and 18 pdrs should be tasked to fire several intense but bogus barrages before the one which heralded the actual assault. Sufficient time also had to be given to deepen the jumping off trenches and their approaches. Finally, the hour of attacks had become, Done thought, a little too predictable.

Done's report was typical of those currently being written by GOC brigades and divisions based upon those submitted to them by their own battalion commanders. 1/Bucks thought it had been "greatly handicapped" by a shortage of trained Lewis gunners and bombers, noting that eight sections of bombers had been used up in a few hours. It believed fully supplied advanced stores of rifle and hand grenades had to be established and permanent parties, rather than already fatigued platoons just out of the line, should be tasked to re-supply them. Although the artillery had clearly failed to silence the enemy positions, the Bucks thought the divisional gunners were "the best" and had "won the entire trust and confidence" of the infantry. Divisional unity could be maintained, despite the artillery's inability to smash the deep dugouts, by implying that it was the corps' heavies rather than the division's own artillery brigades which had failed. Lessons were certainly being absorbed but there was still only a limited variety of ways as to how these slogging attacks of attrition could actually be delivered. On 24 August there was something of a temporary lull in 48th Division's relentless assaults; the day was devoted to consolidation, sniping, laying down harassing fire from Lewis guns and restocking dumps. Paradoxically, 8/Warwickshire was fortunate to have been out on a working party when its camp close to Aveluy Bridge was heavily shelled. Two large bomb dumps near the Warwicks' camp were destroyed by the German shells. While the troops laboured, senior officers conferred about when the next attack should take place and who should make it. Several local bombing enterprises were timed to coincide with II Corps' next main attack which was undertaken by 25th Division on 25 August against the trenches on the Thiepval spur. 48th Division's artillery was used to support the operation and to break up a subsequent enemy counter-attack; 25th Division's artillery repaid the complement on 27 August by assisting the South Midland's guns fire the preliminary bombardment for an attack by 143 and 145 Brigades. Rather than the usual late afternoon, and after several bogus barrages had already been fired, the attack was timed for early evening. Care was taken to ensure all watches of the infantry and artillery brigades had been synchronized and that the FOOs and artillery liaison officers were in position. There was confusion when a party of 8/Warwickshire discovered the ladders it had been ordered to carry forward were not where they were supposed to be. After an initial fruitless search, brigade HQ informed the party of their correct location but, by the time the ladders were in place, the party had only 30 minutes back in camp before it moved up again to be in place for the actual assault. Their objective was Constance Trench which lay on the slope beneath Skyline. In the absence of any land marks the right company lost direction and wandered too far to the right. The platoons entered what was left of the virtually obliterated Constance Trench but when attacked from both flanks withdrew to their start line. The left company lost its commander immediately it went forward and, over-running the flattened objective, ran into its own barrage and intense machine-gun fire. When it fell, the night was extremely dark. Brigade HQ had little idea of what was happening until about 0400 when an officer of the right company managed to struggle back with a situation report. Other reports subsequently suggested all surviving troops were back in their own original front lines by dawn. Although the war diary praises the men's behaviour, the evidence suggests that perhaps once the officers had been knocked out, NCOs were unable or unwilling to assert authority. Rather than organize resistance and hold on to what they had gained they probably decided to withdraw to the relatively safety of their own lines. Contact was eventually made with 4/Berkshire on the left, which had also found it difficult to locate their precise objective. With the help of 40 pioneers of 5/Sussex they established several strong points and made touch with 5/Gloucestershire which had run into some severe resistance from Germans in dugouts unaffected by the barrage. Lewis guns were turned on the defenders and an estimated 200 were killed as they withdrew across the open ground. For the next 12 hours the Germans then proceeded to bombard with high explosive the captured lines and their associated communication trenches. One company of 4/Ox&B acted as carrying parties during the remainder of the night but, unlike 8/Warwickshire to their right, the Gloucesters and Berkshires were not only able to hold onto their gains but also by means of telephone and runner maintained communications with their respective battalion headquarters throughout the night.

With the exception of a feint attack in support of 39th Division on 30 August, the attack against Constance Trench and the complex of trenches to its south-west marked the start of a very short interlude of peace for 48th Division. The battalions were relieved and made their way back to the rear. The Oxfords were unfortunate to arrive at their allocated bivvies near Bouzincourt only to find a battalion of 7 Brigade already in occupancy and a billeting party from 25th Division also laying claim to the site. A compromise was reached but when the Oxfords moved into huts near Bus Wood they discovered all the furniture had been carried off or burnt by the last occupants. Incidents such as these did little to raise morale among exhausted troops. Nonetheless, the infantry made their way back to the peace of the rear and were able to look forward to a few days of rest, bathing and recuperation. Despite the trauma of the month, the men of 4/Berkshire were reported to be "in great spirits" because they had defeated the Prussian Guard who, they were told, had been specifically sent by the Kaiser to defend Thiepval. Messages from General Gough, GOC Reserve Army, Lieutenant General Jacob, the Corps Commander and Major General Fanshawe were read to the battalions thanking and congratulating them for their efforts. They were joined in the quiet villages by the RE field companies who had a break from their work of maintaining tramways, constructing deep dugouts in Ovillers and supporting the infantry in consolidating captured positions.[26] Tasked to fire in support of 49th Division's ill-fated attack on Thiepval on 3 September, the artillery brigades were to remain in the line for several more days.

One of the division's field ambulances was also to remain working for an additional few days before it joined the other two in the rear. The ambulances had, of course, been extremely active during the month coping with the wounded and dying. The *Official History* noted that the division's casualties for 13-28 August amounted to 92 officers and 2,562 other ranks. 145 Brigade reported a total of 45 officers and 1,139 other ranks, of who two and 167 respectively were missing.[27] The number of the brigade's other ranks dead was noted as 150; with many of the missing later confirmed as dead, post-war records take the total to 281. Drafts had clearly arrived during the month because fighting strengths on 12 and 25 August were 123 and 95 officers, and 3,965 and 3,228 other ranks respectively. None of the battalion commanders had been killed, although two did have a short time away from the front. The casualty list had,

26 One of the new communication trenches dug under the supervision of the field companies between Skyline and Ration Trenches was the aptly named Brimstone Trench.

27 1/Bucks' historian believed that the battalion's 20 missing of 15-16 August had been killed, '... and so killed that no trace could be found of them.' Wright, *First Buckinghamshire Battalion*, p. 40.

however, certainly taken more of the pre-war originals.[28] Perhaps the most significant 'casualty' was, however, Brigadier General Dent of 143 Brigade. Dent had only joined the brigade in May 1916 and was replaced on 2 September by Lieutenant Colonel Sladen who, it will be remembered had begun the war as adjutant of 8/Warwickshire. Neither the divisional nor the A&Q war diaries make any mention of Dent's departure and it is possible he was sacked. Two of his battalions had been attached to 4th Division on 1 July so he bore no direct responsibility for the failures of that day and, overall in July and August, 143 Brigade seems to have done no better or worse than the other two brigades. He was only 44 years of age in 1916 so, if he was degummed, it may have been the disappointing performance of 8/Warwickshire on 27 August which sealed his fate. Nevertheless, he did go on to command two battalions before again becoming a brigade commander in April 1918. Whatever the reason, his replacement, Brigadier General Sladen, was known to possess a reliable pair of hands and was a recognizable figure throughout the brigade. He took command as his brigade and division enjoyed their period of rest in the villages around Varennes and Bus.

28 *Soldiers Died in the Great War* records a total of about 617 amongst the 12 infantry battalions.

5

The Battle of the Somme: September 1916-January 1917

As the Somme campaign ground on, a steady but a comparatively insignificant flow of men suffering from pyrexia and other similar maladies sought treatment in the field ambulances.[1] Unsurprisingly, however, these men were considerably out-numbered by the dying and wounded who arrived daily at the units. The division had two collecting posts, one at Crucifix Corner east of Aveluy and the other at North Chimney, Albert. These were in addition to six subsidiary aid posts scattered closer to the front. From the collecting posts the wounded were evacuated to a triage centre at Bouzincourt where the ambulances sorted them into three categories. According to the type and seriousness of the wound, they were next either retained at the field ambulances, despatched to II Corps Operating Station at Warloy, or other ambulance sections based at Varennes. The division's ambulances did not only treat the wounded of 48th Division but the majority of the cases were certainly from the division. The numbers admitted daily varied, of course, according to the degree of activity going on further forward: on 19 August the total amounted to only 45 whereas it was 263 and 337 on 17 and 20 August respectively. 2/Field Ambulance alone recorded treating 165 sick and 2,163 wounded during the month, of who 23 died. No doubt many of the 1,759 evacuated to a CCS died further down the line but the ambulance was clearly proud of the fact that 14 percent of its admissions were almost immediately returned to duty.

Several battalions returned to the forward sector after only two days at rest. 145 Brigade was concentrated on and around the White City and Bowery sectors; 144 Brigade was a little further east near Mary Redan. Because it had not immediately been withdrawn for an extended rest there appears to have been a belief that the division had been "ill-used"[2] during July. Unlike the gunners, however, the battalions were relieved fairly quickly and enjoyed a considerable period of recuperation and

1 For example, the ADMS reported a total of 194 'sick' admissions for the week ending 13 August. The sanitary section noted that the 'many' cases of pyrexia and diarrhoea recovered quickly.

2 Wright, *First Buckinghamshire Battalion*, p. 45.

training. The artillery brigades had been divided into two groups and fell under the tactical control of 25th and 49th Divisions. One group assisted in those divisions' attacks on 3 September and at least one battery also supported 39th Division's "half hearted" attacks north of the Ancre. 242 Brigade's diarist reported 39th Division's howitzers had failed to soften up the enemy defences sufficiently before the attack and that its 18 pdrs had not achieved the rate of fire ordered during the creeping barrage. With an obvious degree of self-satisfaction, he recorded that his own guns had fired as instructed.[3] In the middle of the month 240 and 243 Brigades moved to Usna Valley and fired in support of the Canadian attack north-west of Courcelette. At the end of September, several of the division's batteries assisted 11th (Northern) Division in its attack on the Zollern and Stuff Redoubts and 18th (Eastern) Division when it assaulted the Schwaben Redoubt. Registration was hampered by unstable firing platforms and by mist which prevented any successful observation from the air. To add to the difficulties, enemy retaliation was severe and communications with the infantry were frequently severed. Some guns were withdrawn during the month for overhaul or replacement but it was not until the night of 29-30 September that the personnel were relieved by 25th Division. Leaving behind the guns, but without dial sights and small stores, the men made their way back to the wagon lines and rest. Three officers, including the CO of 241 Brigade, Lieutenant Colonel West, are known to have been killed during the month but the number of dead and wounded other ranks is difficult to determine.[4]

Like the artillery, the pioneers of 5/Sussex were also loaned to other divisions before they, too, were eventually withdrawn to rest. Detachments worked on tramways and spent some time clearing debris from their old haunt of Ration Trench. The field companies had arrived in the rear a little before the pioneers and were already into a routine of sports, drills, bayonet practice, route marching and engineering training. Together with the sanitary section, they had also been busy erecting or improving bathing facilities in the villages where the division's units were to be accommodated. With the cooperation of quartermasters they ensured an adequate supply of replacement clothing and established a disinfecting unit at Souastre capable of dealing with about 500 blankets per day. Men of the salvage company were trained as sanitation orderlies but the sanitation officer continued to complain there were still no anti-lice powders or ointments. As a consequence, and at the behest of the medical personnel, battalions ordered their men to improve sanitation discipline and food hygiene to help reduce the prevalence of flies in the rest villages.

The mixed weather during September resulted in lectures often being delivered to troops in their billets. The total number of meetings held is unknown but Major General Fanshawe hosted at least one conference attended by all officers and several

3 242 Brigade RFA, hand written account attached to August 1916 war diary.

4 One of the few ORs mentioned in the war diaries is Gunner Williams. He had his leg blown off when standing in front of No.6 gun of 242 Brigade.

for brigade and battalion commanders. These gatherings usually preceded brigade schemes, some of which were postponed owing to the inclement weather, but most training appears to have been conducted by company and platoon commanders. Fanshawe toured the several camps and in a speech delivered to at least one brigade praised the men for their courage in the recent fighting. This, he said, had proved their superiority over the enemy and stressed that they would now be training for open warfare. Additional responsibilities would fall on the officers and NCOs who must, he emphasized, be ready to accept this and show command and leadership. Initially training was, however, restricted not only by the weather but also by the lack of suitable areas. This was rectified after the brigades marched to Candas where the harvest was in and fields subsequently become available. It is likely divisional HQ instructed battalion COs on what should be taught but then left it to the battalions to decide how time should actually be allocated. As it was a little too early for the publication of what was soon to become a steady flow of training pamphlets, Lieutenant Colonel Hanbury of 7/Warwickshire ordered all company officers to read Chapters V-IX of *Field Service Regulations* in preparation for delivering their scheme of work. The expected trips to the musketry and bombing ranges were interspersed with route marches, PT and bayonet training. Specialists improved their particular skills while transport sections were able to spend considerable time with their animals and overhauled their vehicles. In the evenings there were concerts and the occasional cinema film. Baths were allocated to companies at a rate of 40 men per hour and inoculations were brought up to date. Forty of 4/Berkshire witnessed the execution at Beauval of Private Depper, a member of their battalion who had been convicted of desertion. To emphasize the point being made, the battalion paraded the following day to hear the promulgation of the sentence. Private Mann, of 5/Gloucestershire, was rather more fortunate than Depper. He was found guilty of cowardice but owing to his youth the death sentence was commuted to five years' penal servitude.

That the men needed time to rest and recover was not in doubt. When it was relieved from having provided supporting fire for 39th Division's failed attack, 144 Brigade recorded that after 10 days in wet trenches its men were "quite unfit" to march back to Bus. By the end of the month, such had been the rate of recovery that battalions were marching at the standard rate of three miles per hour. Battalion strengths had also improved during the training period but heavy criticism continued to be directed at the base authorities for the methods by which drafts were sent up the line to divisions.[5] Major General Fanshawe and the AA&QMG journeyed to Rouen "to see about drafts" during September but it is unclear as to what the trip actually achieved. Twenty-five "undesirables" examined in 5/Warwickshire were deemed to be unfit for service and more than 100 others were at least temporarily medically or physically unfit for front line work. There was a fairly steady flow back to the bases of boys discovered

5 For the controversy surrounding the issue of TF drafts during the Somme, see Mitchinson, *The Territorial Force at War*.

to be under age but, given the numbers in which men were being despatched from the UK, there were bound to be some who escaped the net. The drafts came in varying numbers and from several sources. 6/Warwickshire, for example, received 278 men during the month from various regiments; in contrast, 5/Gloucestershire was fortunate to receive 74 from its own 3rd Battalion in one draft alone. Similarly, 4/Ox&Bucks welcomed back nearly two dozen "old hands" and another 59 who had originally been intended for its 5th Battalion. Soon after they arrived, COs usually inspected and then addressed new troops on the traditions and expectations of their (often) adopted regiment. Although after one such parade, Lieutenant Colonel Clarke of 4/Berkshire thought the men were "a good lot, well turned out and well set up," he bemoaned the fact that with "two or three exceptions, no one had more than three months' service." It was perhaps for reasons such as this that battalions were instructed to read to their men at least once a month the means of safely cleaning a rifle.

The arrival of drafts gradually brought the battalions closer to establishment: 5/Gloucestershire, for example, added 201 other ranks during the month to bring strength to 806 by the end of September. In total, its brigade had received 57 officers and 684 other ranks during the training period. The officers were particularly badly needed as sickness, wounds and deaths had significantly reduced their numbers in all battalions. With a mere 15 officers, 4/Berkshire had probably the lowest number of all. In order to help address this shortage, survivors of the pre-war battalions noticed the odd familiar face re-appearing at the transport lines. Among those returning was Major Pauli of 5/Warwickshire. He had held the same rank on the outbreak of war but had been posted home soon after arriving in France. Pauli rejoined his old battalions but, overall, it appears a greater number of long-serving members were leaving rather than rejoining their units. Among them was the last of the August 1914 infantry COs: Lieutenant Colonel W.K.Peake went home sick and was not to return. In 1916, Peake was 47 years old and had retired as a captain from the Regular Army in 1900. He joined the Volunteers before transferring to the TF in 1908 and had been CO of 8/Worcestershire since 1911. Perhaps the strain and hardships of command had finally proved too onerous. He was temporarily succeeded in turn by two of the battalion's August 1914 captains but they, too, were both soon posted elsewhere.[6] They were succeeded by Lieutenant Colonel H.A.Carr who, although a regular was at least from the Worcestershire Regiment. Lieutenant Colonel Barling of 2/Field Ambulance, who had sailed with his ambulance, also left for other duties as did a number of other well known individuals who had spent their territorial career in one particular unit. 7/Warwickshire, for example, lost Major Hake, who had been

6 Rather than being made permanent CO of his own battalion, Major Kerwood was given command of 13/Cheshire in 25th Division. The division had served alongside 48th Division in II Corps in July and August. When Lt. Col. Carr arrived in October, the second temporary CO, Major S.H.Clarke, a captain in the battalion in August 1914, returned to his job as 48th Division's Claims Officer. Captain H.J. Clarke, also a captain in the battalion in August 1914, was appointed Carr's second-in-command.

with it since the Volunteer days, to become a permanent town major; he took with him the long-serving Sergeant Burgess as his QM. Major Aldworth, a captain in 4/Berkshire at the start of the war was to leave in early October for a commanding officers' course in the UK but did later return. The only Warwicks listed officer fatality of the battalion during the August fighting was Captain Godfrey-Payton. He had sailed with the 7th Battalion as a lieutenant; news of his death in a CCS arrived at battalion HQ in early September.

The considerable numbers of subalterns (as well as the occasional captain) posted to battalions during the recuperation and training period arrived from a variety of regiments. Rather than wait until battalions of their own regiment needing reinforcement, the base was concerned to send any available officers to battalions which required them. To add to the survivors of those who had joined 48th Division in July from, for example, the Devonshire and East Surrey Regiments, 10 officers from the Royal Welsh Fusiliers and five from the Royal Scots Fusiliers joined 7/Warwickshire; seven from the Scottish Rifles joined 4/Ox&Bucks. Twenty-one subalterns from a variety of regiments, including seven from the HLI, were taken on by 5/Gloucestershire and the arrival of 13 second lieutenants from the Essex Regiment at the HQ of 1/Bucks was recorded as "something of a shock" to the battalion.[7] In the same way as the other rank volunteers, Derby men and conscripts posted into the division from other regiments and other parts of the country had been told on enlistment what was expected of them in their training regiment, the young officers would have been lectured on the traditions and achievements of their own original regiments. Some of those particular preconceptions had now to be abandoned in favour of adopting the ethos of their new battalions. The time spent in the villages behind the lines in August allowed the new officers to get to know their platoons and the men to know each other. The tactical training, evening concerts and local passes allowed a new but not necessarily territorial cohesion to be formed. This was to be of crucial importance in the months to come when the division spent weeks doing little except endure the depths of a Somme winter.

In October, the division moved back to the sector where it had served its long trench apprenticeship. With a few exceptions the front trenches around Hébuterne were still in the same positions as they had been when the division had first taken possession of them in August 1915. Since the repulse of 56th (1st London) Division in the sector on 1 July 1916, little had changed. The trenches were wet and very knocked about and no man's land remained littered with the detritus of the attack and of the decomposing bodies of the Londoners. Compared to areas to the south, however, this initial return to the trenches was relatively comfortable. A warning order for an attack around the middle of the month caused a flurry of conferences for GOC division, brigade, artillery and infantry COs but after prolonged periods of wire cutting the attack was first postponed and then cancelled. The prospect of attacking what was

7 Wright, *First Buckinghamshire Battalion*, p. 46.

still such a formidable position must surely have been daunting, yet Carrington noted his disappointment at the authorities' decision. He thought that in 5/Warwickshire, "Never had morale been so high, never had all ranks felt so confident before a very stiff fight."[8]

There was again time for training, lectures on the use of tanks, staff rides, brigade schemes and a blood thirsty talk by the renowned bayonet enthusiast Lieutenant Colonel Campbell. PT, drills, inspection and working parties of up to 500 for tunnelling companies occupied the time of those units out on rest. When in the line and in what seems to have been a new procedure, infantry officers watched how well wire cutting was progressing from artillery OPs in order to ascertain the routes where night time patrols should creep. Wire cutting was not progressing particularly well, partly because there were difficulties with the heavy 9.45 inch mortars tasked to assist the artillery in the programme. The mortars were apparently "not shooting well" owing, it was claimed, to "faulty ammunition." Furthermore, the 18 pdr batteries were also having problems because it was discovered a number of the field pieces taken over from 18th Division were excessively worn and cracked. Several were replaced and others overhauled but high winds, the seemingly ever-present enemy aircraft overhead and what were considered to be ill-sited pits for the newly allocated fire zones added to the difficulties. To emphasize the lack of Allied progress, D/242 occupied the same positions it had built in 1915. Others pits were dug and some existing ones modified to allow a widened arc of fire but frustration reached a new high point when in October an ammunition column driving across the plain west of Hébuterne at night lost its way and managed to severe the telephone network of lines linking brigade, battery and battalion HQ. There was the occasional need to respond to an infantry SOS, which on one occasion prompted a jubilant diarist of 4/Berkshire to record "shells fairly rained in." Much of the month was, however, generally very quiet. The artillery brigades were reorganized into two six-gun 18 pdr batteries and one 4.5 inch howitzer battery. To add further weight a new heavy battery, 531 (H), joined 242 Brigade from the UK.

The arrival of the additional artillery personnel added to the already pressing accommodation shortage. When out of the line most units in the Hébuterne sector were allocated huts around Souastre but the pre-fabs were described as better suited to summer rather than winter conditions. Failures in staff work, such as when 145 Brigade set off on a march to the rear with what turned out to be contradictory orders and then arrived at its supposed billeting site to find another division already ensconced, were wearing for the men. Field companies and pioneers were put to work building additional huts as well as performing their usual duties of drainage, maintaining roads, tramways, bath houses and dumps. Some sections were sent further forward to the ruins of Martinpuich and Bazentin-le-Grand to work under rather more sustained shell fire where they were joined from time to time by 8/Warwickshire

8 Carrington, *War History of 1/5th Royal Warwickshire*, p. 36.

and 7/Worcestershire. These two battalions were temporarily attached to other brigades to provide working parties.

Although not in the same numbers as those arriving in August and September, drafts did still dribble in to replace those reporting sick during the month. Even in quiet times, 8/Warwickshire, for example, lost four second lieutenants to hospital and 5/Gloucestershire was so under strength that it received a total of nine subalterns and a new second-in-command. The battalion would have been pleased to discover that five of the second lieutenants were posted from the regiment's own 4th Reserve Battalion and 4/Berkshire recorded its delight at receiving permission to commission six of its own sergeants. One of the month's larger drafts of other ranks was the 150 men posted from 2/1st Worcestershire Yeomanry to 8/ Worcestershire. It was a fairly typical draft of men from a number of 2nd Line yeomanry units which were in the process of being transformed into infantry. The majority of these men were volunteers of late 1914 and early 1915 but, as the battalion diarist explained, although the men were of "good physique" and had been in the army for as long as two years many of them had only "a fortnight's training as infantry."[9] The arrival of such a large number of reinforcements was unusual in October but this exception was because 8/ Worcestershire was still in the process of rebuilding following the gas attack of 19 July. During September, more than 420 men of the battalion remained so incapacitated that they were sent to a convalescent camp on the coast to be "gradually brought to fitness." Once they had regained their strength and able to take their place in an active battalion, it was insensitively deemed they should be used as drafts rather than be returned to their old battalion. The battalion's fighting strength at the beginning of October was 24 officers and 470 men and by the end of the month it had risen only to 22 and 613. Nevertheless, and no doubt to the relief of the division as a whole and especially to its own brigade, in October 8/Worcestershire again became a functioning element of 144 Brigade.

The actual number of deaths in the infantry during September and October was a comparatively low 668. The places of birth or residence of the fatalities reveals that although the personnel no longer reflected the battalions' original territorial identity, the brigades were still largely composed of men who came from a reasonably compact geographical area. Troops might not be from the original catchment area of their battalion but did come from areas in close proximity to them. For example, of the 61 fatalities in 5/Gloucestershire, 26 percent of them came from outside the county. The majority of these, however, came from adjoining counties and those which had traditionally recruited men for other units of the South Midland Division. Besides the men posted from the Hunts Cyclist Battalion and the Wiltshire Regiment mentioned earlier, there had clearly also been a substantial posting of men from Somerset, Devon

9 Drafts continued to arrive from various yeomanry regiments in batches until January 1917. Most did come from 'local' regiments such as the Warwickshire, Oxfordshire and Buckinghamshire Yeomanry.

and Cornwall. Nonetheless, of the 148 fatalities in three battalions of 144 Brigade,[10] only 20 percent had not been born or lived in Worcestershire and Gloucestershire at the time of enlistment. Most of those 20 percent hailed from areas reasonably close to those two counties. Yet, although the number of *fatalities* may have been mercifully low in comparison to other divisions, the wet weather of October continued to take its toll. During the month, 2/Field Ambulance admitted 23 officers and 719 ORs sick and two and 74 wounded. Despite 36 percent and 30 percent of these totals being returned to duty fairly quickly, the absence of the equivalent strength of about one battalion in a brigade meant increased workloads for those who were still in the line.

The growing shortage of available doctors and the expansion of facilities in casualty clearing stations forced the authorities to reduce the establishment of all field ambulances by one officer. In October, several of the medical officers who had been temporarily transferred from 48th Division's three field ambulances to CCS or regimental duties during the summer fighting returned to their original unit. Those who rejoined 3/Field Ambulance, however, faced an additional challenge. It is unclear why the unit was chosen in October to supervise the improvement and expansion of III Corps Rest Station on Becourt Hill but it was ordered to accept responsibility for developing the camp's meagre facilities. At the time, those facilities largely amounted to several marquees and a collection of smaller tents virtually floating in an ocean of mud. The physical conditions hampered any attempt at rapid improvement but the first necessity was to bring some sort of order to the chaos of tents. Rations often did not arrive and the supply of hot water and feeding accommodation needed swift development. The DDMS, a frequent and anxious visitor to the site, was often the recipient of OC 3/Field Ambulance's strident ire. Lieutenant Colonel Green's principal complaint was that trying to run a large corps' rest station with its continually changing field medical units was impossible unless it could be administered in the same way as a CCS. Permanent personnel were, he argued, essential if care was to be consistently delivered and if record keeping was to be efficiently conducted. To simplify management he divided the camp into sections of one per division of the formations within the corps and another solely for corps troops. Cases "poured in at all hours" and because medical officers were frequently on duty day and night they remained utterly exhausted. The situation was made worse by the opening of an outpatients' clinic which regularly attracted 100 men every night. Green organized salvage parties of convalescent patients to sweep mud from the 'roads' and pathways into trenches and to dig pits into which faeces were dumped because the incinerator could not cope. As the weather continued to deteriorate these parties seemed to be fighting a losing battle and then, in a storm on 31 October, eight of the large marquees were blown down. Conditions did gradually improve, especially when the RE finished a log road from the entrance to the central area of the camp but, with patients arriving in large

10 8/Worcestershire has been discounted because most of its men saw little action during August and September owing to the continuing effect of the gas attack on 19 July.

batches, compiling accurate nominal rolls continued to pose problems. With stoves gradually being fitted into the larger marquees and with the sanitation officer of 50th Division's acceptance of responsibility for the drainage and sanitation provision, order and reasonable hygiene were eventually established. Just when, however, Lieutenant Colonel Green believed the camp was running close to efficiency, he was instructed to begin reducing the number of patients to 500 in preparation for an eventual closure of the facility. Somewhat ironically amidst the mud and flooding, the water supply at Becourt Hill remained problematic and it was decided the rest station should be transferred to a site near Millencourt The new facility was to be managed by 1st Division and from the middle of November 3/Field Ambulance began to transfer equipment and patients to Millencourt.

If 48th Division had been fortunate to have had the Gommecourt operation scheduled for early October cancelled, it was even more fortunate to have had two plans for attacks in November similarly abandoned. The division moved into the wilderness astride the main Albert-Bapaume road and, on 4 November, received orders to be prepared to attack the Little Wood area on or around 7 November. The shell-smashed area concerned lay to the north of the main road, a little beyond the ruins of Le Sars. 144 Brigade, using 4/Gloucestershire and 7/Worcestershire, with 8/Worcestershire in support, was to be on the right and 145 Brigade on the left. The plan of attack generally followed what was by now a familiar pattern. Battalions were to advance in four waves, with the first and third waves pressing on to the objectives while the second and fourth consolidated. Sections of RE and pioneers were to follow the assaulting battalions to decide on where strong points suitable for about 10 men and a Lewis gun should be constructed. They would then supervise the infantry as they consolidated the positions. One less than usual element of the operation was the decision to send out patrols of about 20 men before zero to enter Warlencourt village and report back on the strength of its defences. Why or how these patrols were expected to penetrate the enemy lines and then succeed in despatching situation reports in the November darkness to the waiting assault companies is unknown, particularly as runners ran the risk of having to get through their own as well as any German shelling. The corps' heavies were tasked with shelling enemy trenches both on and behind the objectives, while the divisional artillery was to begin its barrage 150 yards in front of the assault companies assembling in Scotland Trench. It would then lift to begin a creeping barrage advancing at 50 yards per minute. At zero plus 65 minutes a box barrage was to fall isolating the areas which should have been captured. The by now usual provisions for a machine-gun barrage, inter-battalion liaison officers located with units on either flank and the establishment of collecting posts for the wounded were also put in place.

It is likely that had the planned attack gone ahead, the result would have been similar to many others which took place in the same area and month. The condition of the trenches and the ground of no man's land precluded the likely success of any attack. Nonetheless, on 16 November, 144 Brigade was warned to prepare another attack to take place on 18 November. Its implementation was to depend on whether 50th Division succeeded in taking The Hook but, in preparation, Lieutenant Colonel Clarke of 4/Berkshire ordered four patrols to reconnoitre the ground in front of the Butte de Warlencourt. Clarke proposed that the left attacking company, with its left on the main road, would attack in an easterly direction and meet up with the right company which would assault the Butte almost frontally. Clarke himself spent two hours in the front trenches looking at the ground to be crossed which lay under constant observation from the enemy on the Butte. There were no shelters or dugouts for the two unfortunate front companies in the British trenches but as 50th Division failed to take The Hook a few hours before the South Midlanders' attack was scheduled, 48th Division's assault was cancelled. The companies sought what little shelter they could from the almost continuous German shelling. Uncomfortable as the flooded trenches were, unlike the Australians to their right and the Canadians to their left, the South Midlanders at least did not have to advance across the flooded landscape into a hail of machine-gun bullets and exploding steel.

After the long-suffering 50th Division had made another futile and costly attempt on the Butte and its nearby quarry, 48th Division was again warned that it would be its turn in December. Divisional HQ decided 144 Brigade should undertake the effort with the support of 1st Division on its right.[11] The usual barrage plan and arrangements for support from the RE and Special Brigade were in place but frequent snow falls caused the attack to be postponed and then subsequently cancelled. Instead, patrols continued to be despatched to observe the German wire and capture the occasional prisoner. Preferring to create a trained group for such tasks, 4/Berkshire organized a special permanent raiding party of one officer and 20 men based in Destrement Farm. On one occasion the group claimed to have killed about 30 Germans of a working party at no cost to itself but when 8/Worcestershire tried a combined raid with 7/Worcestershire the raiders were not so fortunate. The British barrage fell short and landed on the Worcesters rather than the trench they were raiding. A little later, another of 8/Worcestershire's patrols failed to return and although Lieutenant Potter went out twice to search for it, no trace of the men was discovered.

Patrol activity such as this was meant to boost the moral component of fighting power by providing the psychological boost of dominating no man's land. There are few references to morale in the war diaries of the period but great emphasis was placed on ensuring cases of trench foot were kept to a minimum. III Corps issued a memo detailing the precautions to be made and of the consequences for men who ignored the strictures. 4/Berkshire recorded its surprise at having only five cases during a three day tour, especially as it was the first time in the forward zone for a recent draft of yeomanry,[12] but 7/Warwickshire was probably not alone in believing its men were "very weak" and that trench foot was "prevalent." Providing a spare pair of dry socks

11 1st Division was to assist by making another raid on the notorious Hook.
12 Cruttwell, *War Service of 1/4th Berkshire*, p. 96.

every day for men during their six day tour in the front and reserve trenches[13] was not always possible but at least the men who were in theory out on rest sometimes had the opportunity to wash and grease their feet before applying dry socks.[14] The appalling condition of the routes up to the front further helped to reduce the number of men in carrying parties who did eventually reach their intended destination. With usually only one brigade holding the line, the other two provided half battalions at a time to carry up rations, water and engineering equipment, bury cables and clear blocked trenches. To add to the physical difficulties, guides regularly lost their way and RE officers or NCOs failed to appear at what the infantry thought were the correct rendezvous.[15] The diarist of 4/Berkshire described November as a series of "wretched days" while that of 7/Worcestershire thought it a "hard working month." The brigade's support battalion's position was usually in Martinpuich, described by 6/Warwickshire as "perhaps the abomination of desolation"[16] while further back, and despite the work done on trying to improve them, the camps at Shelter Wood and Fricourt similarly offered little in the way of comfort to those allowed a few hours rest. The accommodation was largely in tents without floor boards or heating. Rations were believed still to be being issued on the summer basis so Expeditionary Force Canteens at the camps where men could buy additional food to supplement their inadequate rations became even more vital. The difficult conditions meant that in late October an average of about 50 men per battalion reported sick each week. These casualties were in addition to those killed, wounded, on leave or returned to the UK for work in munitions. As the winter dragged on the worsening physical conditions were reflected in the numbers recorded as admissions: the sick treated by 2/Field Ambulance soared from 201 in November to 587 in December. Of that total, however, 304 were returned to duty, although probably still exhausted and somewhat undernourished, within a few days.

The ADMS daily visited at least one camp to inspect conditions and facilities and frequently to order the digging of more latrines and the removal of refuse. His field ambulances were handicapped by the fatigue and sickness of their orderlies and officers and also by the regular return to the UK of medical officers who had completed their period of service. There was, consequently, a regular turnover of personnel who had gained practical experience but who on the expiration of their contract might not

13 The division's three infantry brigades slightly varied the length of time their men spent in particular sections of the front. The *roulement* applied depended largely on the local conditions but the normal period for a battalion in the forward area was six days.

14 Juniors officers were ordered to inspect their men's feet daily and were instructed how to identify the onset of trench foot. Men's hands were also inspected and when bathing, medical officers were supposed to examine the troops' bodies for excessive scratches and boils.

15 At least four battalions of the division, and probably more, maintained a permanent working party of 80 men drawn from all four companies. It is unclear whether these men were excused duty in the line.

16 Compiled, *History of 1/6th Warwickshire*, p. 30.

reappear to put that experience to good use for another term. Furthermore, the sanitary section had been removed from divisional and transferred to corps control. There does not seem, however, to have been any disadvantage to the division with the new arrangement. Captain Dale, the sanitary officer, believed the altered system was more efficient because, rather than moving with the division, personnel remained in the same sector and came to know it well. There was a predictable increase in the number of cases of infectious disease as the winter wore on, especially in the severe enteric group, but these diseases were almost insignificant when compared to the numbers of men laid low by the weather and general debility.

To help compensate for those lost to illness drafts of sometimes well over 200 at a time, often from convalescent camps, continued to arrive. Battalions remained, nonetheless, well under strength: 6/Gloucestershire reported it was 260 under establishment in December while 5/Gloucestershire had a fighting strength of 651 in November. These low strengths were by no means remarkable but 4/Berkshire, for example, claimed that out of its current strength of 650, only about 300 were actually fit enough to be part of a working party. In the six weeks spent in Le Sars salient the infantry strength of the division as a whole fell from about 9,000 to 6,000 rifles. The quality of drafts continued to vary in their physical condition and in the extent of their training. 8/Worcestershire thought the draft arriving in November was "of poorer physique" than earlier ones but 4/Ox&Bucks was rather more content with its new arrivals. Its draft from the Buckingham Hussars were "mainly of good physique" and although the 154 men from the Oxfordshire Hussars "knew very little of infantry training" the diarist thought "they will turn out well with a little training."[17]

The RE did what they could to improve conditions in the camps and in the approaches to the front. They built huts and drying rooms, laid tramways across the devastated ground and made stoves for tents from old oil drums. The companies were split into sections but their efforts were constrained by the shortage of metal for roads. Plank roads were laid but many routes were improved by spreading debris of brick and timber plundered from the ruins of the local villages. The pioneers of 5/Sussex dug latrines, built soup kitchens and cleared roads and reported that with breaks from continuous night work and careful nurturing of their feet the battalion's health and morale actually improved. Morale amongst the artillery may have suffered as the men struggled to bring up and clean ammunition to feed the guns which continued on occasions to assist the batteries of other divisions.[18] They fired false barrages as well as wire cutting programmes and suffered from premature bursts as well as counter-battery fire: C/241 was shelled by 5.9 inch guns guided by an air observer for over two hours losing one gun in the process, while C/242 laid a light railway across the sea of

17 Greenwell, *Infant in Arms*, p. 156, was delighted with the draft. The yeoman were, 'As keen as mustard, very cheery, and have thoroughly brought back the old spirit.'

18 For example, the artillery fired in the programme which assisted 51st Division's capture the ruins of Beaumont Hamel.

mud to extricate one of its damaged guns and to bring in its replacement. The daily allotment in December varied but at one stage it was 230 shells for 18 pdr and 200 for 4.5 inch batteries. Bringing up even these limited amounts sapped the energy of men and pack animals. Some pits were flooded and the sandbags of others collapsed as the weather alternated between frost, snow and rain. In the same way as the infantry was short of men, one of the division's RFA brigades also reported that it had too few men to work the guns efficiently.

The animals, too, suffered in the conditions. The long-serving ADVS, Lieutenant Colonel Harris, travelled around the division's units inspecting the horses and ordering improvements in head cover and hard standings. In September he reported that preparations for winter needed to be put in train and, amongst other things, complained about the lax attitude units had about collecting their remounts and the habit of 'borrowing' additional animals from neighbouring units. He condemned the water arrangements and drinking troughs at Bouzincourt and, as he had believed since his arrival in France in1915, felt he was hugely unappreciated. On this occasion he cited as evidence the fact that the authorities refused even to provide him with an office. Between delivering lectures on horse management he dealt with outbreaks of mange, contagious 'flu and glanders, supervised the disinfecting of stables and, when two of its men proved positive with German measles, placed the entire MVS into quarantine.

Amidst the squalor, disease and death, the highlight for many in 48th Division would have been the Christmas dinner. Those units fortunate enough to be at rest and in a reasonable camp on 25 December enjoyed either pork or goose, generally paid for from canteen funds.[19] Those who were in the line may have had their meal on a later day but for the division as a whole relief was on the way. In January the division, with the initial exception of the artillery brigades, began to withdraw to the rear and then entrain for the hamlets around Warloy.[20] For much of the month the weather was awful, with snowfalls interrupting the training schedule, but there were frequent meetings of senior officers and staffs, staff rides and tactical exercises without troops (TEWTs). Battalion specialists practised their particular skills, men performed drills, bathed at a rate of 50 per hour, suffered inspections and engaged in the first rounds of the inter-unit Fanshawe Football Cup. About half of 145 Brigade crowded into a barn to watch boxing matches, steeple chases were organized and cross-country races held. The weather sometimes drove the men indoors for lectures but scouts had to brave the conditions to conduct exercises while officers and senior NCOs attended bombing and trench mortar demonstrations. If visibility allowed, contact exercises were carried out with aircraft and officers followed the instruction to practise firing

19 A little over a week before Christmas the last batch of men who had not had UK leave since arriving in France in March 1915 left for home. As they made their way towards the rear and the leave train a shell fell amongst them causing several casualties.

20 The Warloy region had been designated No.5 Training Area.

their revolvers. They and NCOs were lectured by COs on leadership and command, at least one CO gave a talk on 'The Defence of Gommecourt' from a captured German document, and one NCO per company was sent on a course of gym instruction. The divisional concert party, *The Curios,* was reconstituted and the well-known entertainer Lena Ashwell gave a performance to the division in which units appeared to attend in the rather less than balanced proportion of one officer to eight other ranks.

What is apparent in the war diaries is that the way in which training was actually conducted was adapting to the experience gained on the Somme. 48th Division had been witness to several of the scores of attacks made during the latter part of the Somme which produced little or no territorial gains. Tactically and operationally these assaults were a disaster and did little to aid the maintenance of the moral component of fighting power. The cost in dead and wounded was invariably high and, to the troops in the morass of mud and flooded trenches, appeared futile. Many of them were, of course, simply that. Nonetheless, from the chaos, mud, blood and disappointment several important points on how future operations might be framed emerged and new doctrine formulated. The *Memorandum on Trench to Trench Attack* appeared in October 1916 and an increasing number of post-battle reports were analysed by staffs and their conclusions passed down the chain of command. By December it was tacitly recognized that the platoon had replaced the company as the principal tactical unit and pamphlet *SS. 135: Instructions for the Training of Divisions for Offensive Action* appeared soon afterwards. This gave guidance on the tactical coordination of infantry weapons. Instead of the usual practice of simply listing some of the types of training undertaken, several of the division's war diaries state "training as per the divisional training scheme." That of 4/Berkshire, however, goes even further. It mentions the elements commonly expected in any training scheme before next explaining that the training area provided good fields for platoon training which is "to be considered the unit for all future training, the idea [being] to make each platoon a separate unit complete with its Lewis gun, bombing and rifle sections." This entry is a rare mention in a unit diary of the specific aspects around which the conceptual component of fighting power was to be built. Rather than allow COs and adjutants a relatively free hand in how they conducted training, the experience of the Somme convinced many of the more progressive faction within the army's hierarchy of the need to establish uniformity in the means of delivering tactical instruction across the BEF and training battalions in the UK. Codification of battle drills was to proceed apace and by emphasizing the platoon's increased fire power in trench and open warfare a succession of pamphlets signalled a return to pre-war doctrine of fire and movement. They also helped to build small unit cohesion and partly addressed the growing problem of ill-trained troops going quickly to ground when coming under fire. It had been long recognized that mutual confidence in each others' abilities and the fear of opprobrium and shame built understanding and unity in small, compact groups. The new drafts arriving at battalions' HQ may not have enlisted specifically as territorials and may not have had the earlier cohesion based on immediate locality but the new training schemes were partly designed to replace those earlier cohesive bonds. The new emphasis was now to be based on confidence and faith in the physical as well as moral and conceptual components of fighting power.

There were also significant changes taking place in the BEF and 48th Division's hierarchy. With the appointment of Lieutenant Colonel Skinner of the Indian Cavalry to command 5/Gloucestershire, by the end of January 1917 only seven of the division's 13 battalions[21] were commanded by men holding commissions in the TF. There remained a reasonable sprinkling of August 1914 TF officers within units but with six COs from the Regular Army, 48th Division was taking on a similar hue to those of the Regular and New Army divisions. Since August 1916, the division had also seen a new GSO1 and AA&QMG and was also about to appoint a new CRE.[22] Another significant change was the replacement in November 1916 of Brigadier General H.R.Done, GOC 145 Brigade. Done left for the UK to command a reserve brigade with the declared intention of returning to 145 Brigade after three months but, like the departure of Brigadier General Dent in September, the circumstances of Done's return to the UK are unclear. Only one divisional commander had been sacked for his part in the disappointment of 1 July but in the following weeks many brigade and battalion commanders were replaced by men with trench experience and with growing reputations as commanders and leaders. Increasingly, men were being promoted on merit into positions where they could influence the handling of future battles. Unit war diaries rarely mention the departure of brigadiers let alone the reasons surrounding them, but there is an intriguing account of Done's replacement in the diary of 4/Berkshire. Its scribe goes to some length to explain, "There was complete understanding between him (Done) and the Commanding Officers; all work ran smoothly and it was a pleasure to work with him in any way. No Brigadier could have been more trusted by the Commanding Officers, and all ranks under him." While this sounds like a ringing endorsement of Done's merits, it follows a sentence which explains, "During his command he had completely eliminated the feeling that had existed between the Brigade and the various units under the command." This ambiguous statement suggests that either Done had inherited a brigade staff which did not endear itself to its COs, a situation which Done had then rectified, or that Done's own style and attitude at the start of his command had been the cause of the friction. He had been GOC for nearly 12 months, which would have given him time to heal any rifts, but the words of 4/Berkshire's diarist are so mellifluous as perhaps to contain an element of sarcasm. Whatever the reason, Done did not return to the division and was replaced by Brigadier General D.M.Watt of the Gordon Highlanders. As Watt was promoted from command of a territorial battalion of the West Yorkshire Regiment he had at least some knowledge of the territorial ethos.

21 This included the pioneer battalion.
22 H.R. Cumming, the GSO1, was given a brigade; G.N. Smyth-Osbourn was promoted to AQMG; H.J. Marshall, the CRE, appears to have gone back to the UK and retirement.

During January, the artillery underwent a fairly minor reorganization and remained in the line supporting other divisions for much of the month. On 25 January, Lieutenant Colonel Colville of 241 Brigade and his battery commanders visited what was to be their new area of operations. Colville decided this new sector offered "the best OP positions since we left Flanders" and proceeded to begin making arrangements with the current occupants of the gun pits. Colville followed in the footsteps of several infantry COs and brigade staffs who had already visited the area they were to take over from the French. The CRE undertook a survey of the existing roads, camps, trenches and accommodation and his field companies were soon at work improving and extending. The ADMS reported the general sanitation of the area as "very unsatisfactory", a view confirmed by the sanitation officer who condemned the lack of incinerators and suitable latrines. The field ambulances occupied sites vacated by their French counterparts, with one section of 2/Field Ambulance opening a 150 bed hospital near Le Hamel; tented sections operated as usual nearer the line. Divisional HQ was established initially at Mericourt, with the infantry brigades centred about Eclusier, Herbecourt and Flaucourt. The immediate concern of their staffs was to organize the relief of the French 152nd Division. With an average length of frontage about typical for a division, and with no man's land in the new divisional sector varying from 100-300 yards in width, 48th Division decided to hold the line in what was generally accepted as a quiet area[23] with two brigades. The brigades were to have two battalions in the front zone with each deploying three companies forward and the fourth used for working parties. One officer and NCO from each of the South Midland companies was to spend a day or two with the French company to be relieved and to learn the French SOS and barrage signals which were to be used until the South Midland artillery moved in. All relief moves were to be done in silence because it was hoped to keep the secret of the exchange for as long as possible. Incoming battalions were ordered to adopt the same attitude as the French, which meant there was to be no increase in sniping or artillery activity and no telephones were to be used east of Flaucourt. The French telephone network, which was to be left intact, was considered to be good; the trenches and wiring were assessed as adequate. After consultations with senior officers the CRE decided divisional policy should be to maintain a permanent party of 50 pioneers as caretakers of the three main communication trenches serving the front lines.

The divisional artillery took responsibility for the defence of the sector on 5 February; within only a few days the infantry was reported to be "utterly worn out." Despite the mud and cold they were, however, thought to be in "good spirits." Additional drafts had arrived during the training period but all battalions seem to have been below

23 The division was informed that the daily casualty rate for the French had been between zero and 10. According to one battalion, during the first few weeks of the relief, 'There was a glamour of peace and quiet about.' Complied, *History of 1/6th Warwickshire*, p. 32.

800 rifles. They quickly organized a system of nocturnal patrolling across the flooded and difficult land while divisional HQ began to devise larger enterprises for when the weather improved. Meanwhile the division was concerned to maintain morale, prevent a serious outbreak of trench foot and, when possible, continue with training for what it expected in the spring would see a return to open warfare.

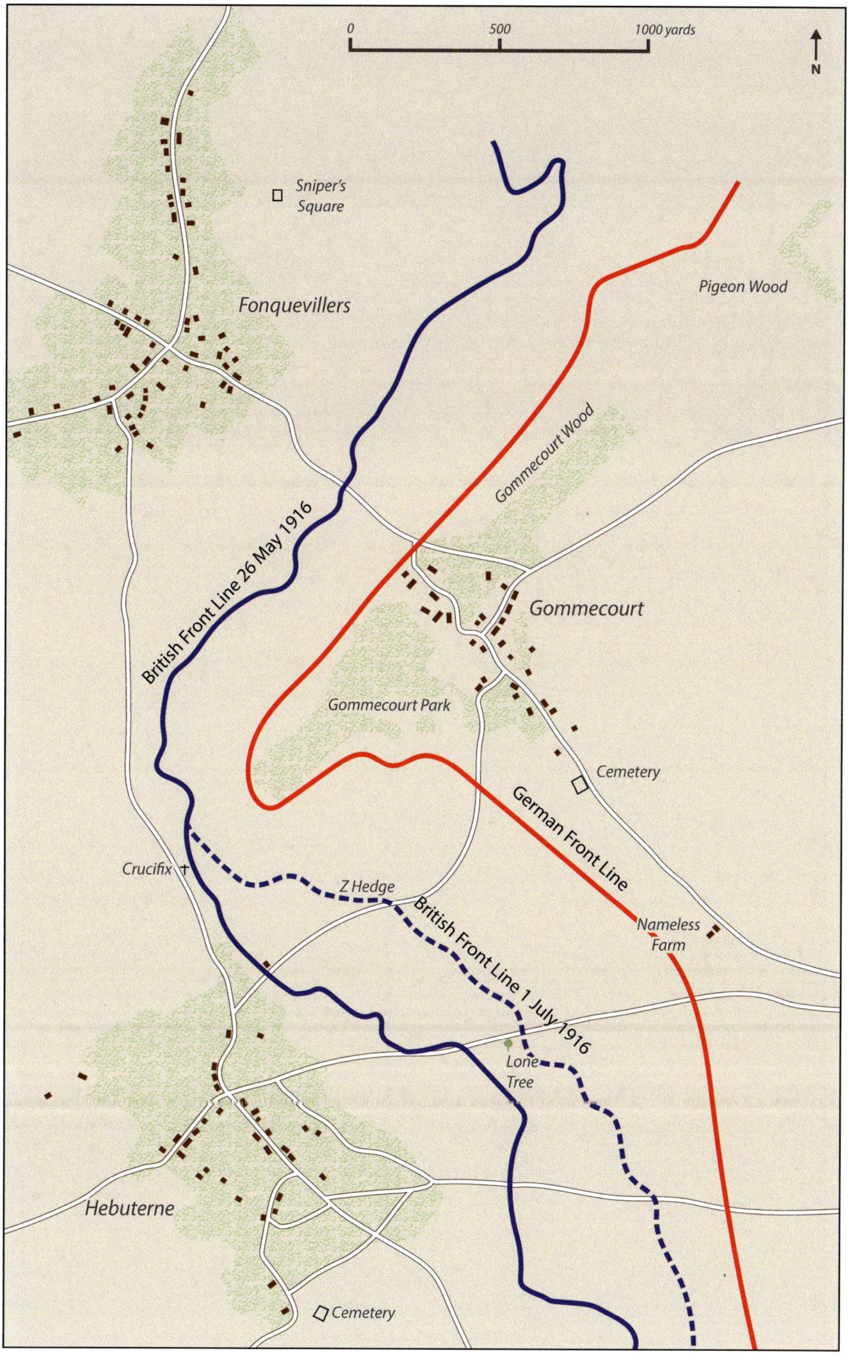

Map 1 The Hébuterne Sector, spring 1916.

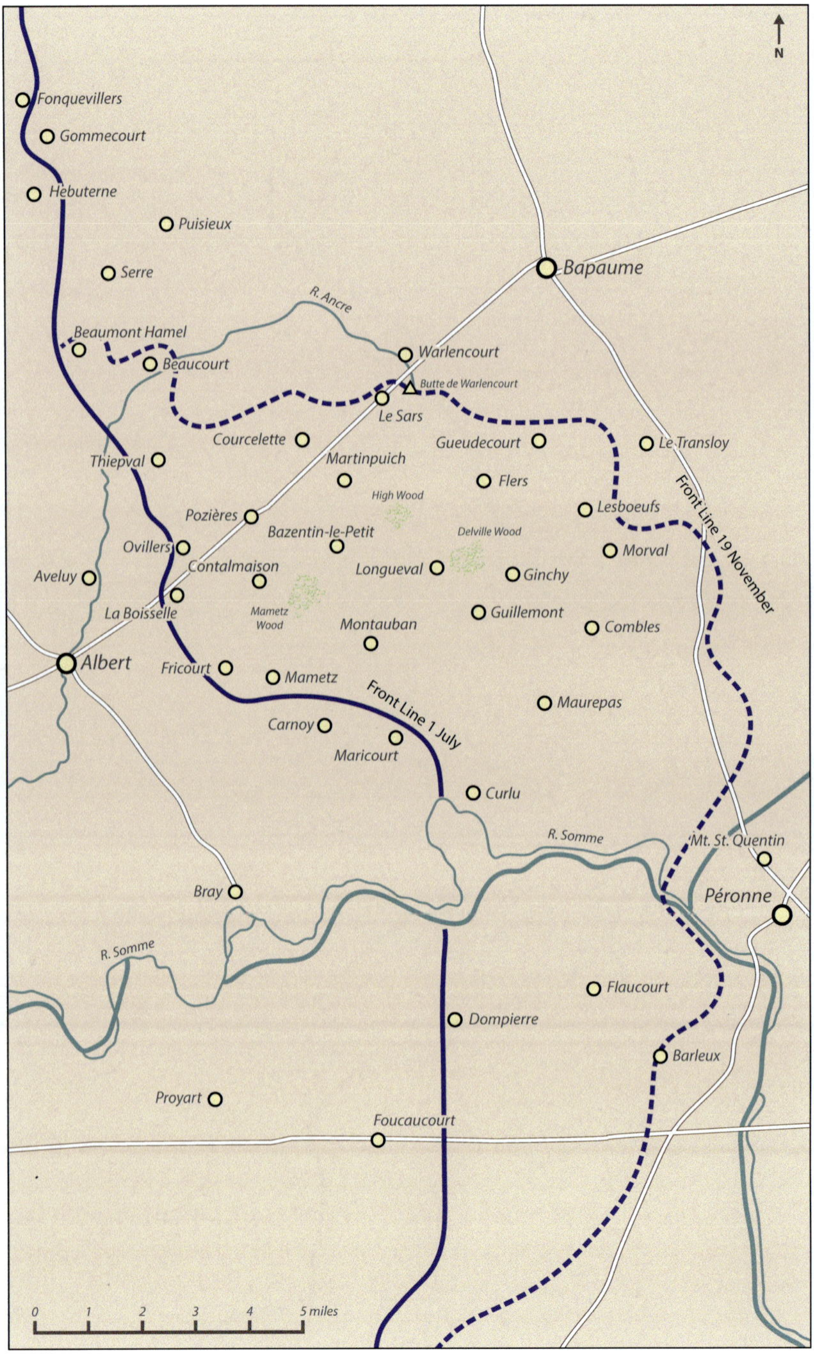

Map 2 Battle of the Somme, July-November 1916.

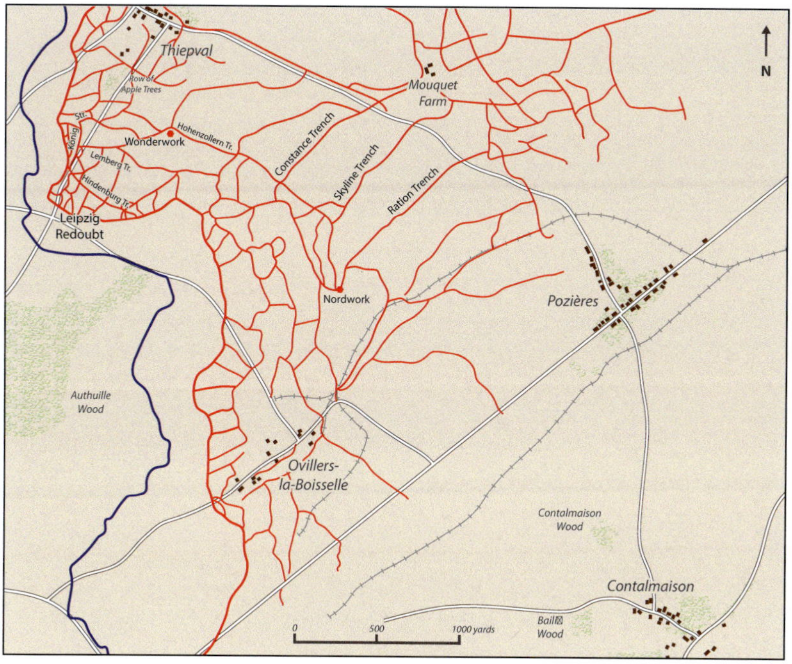

Map 3 48th Division Area of Operations, August 1916.

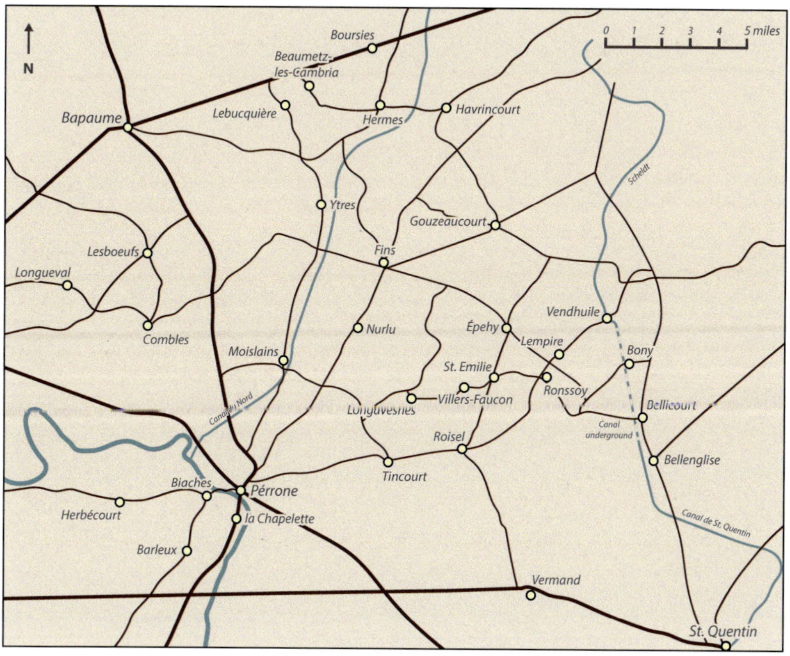

Map 4 The Advance to the Hindenburg Line, spring 1917.

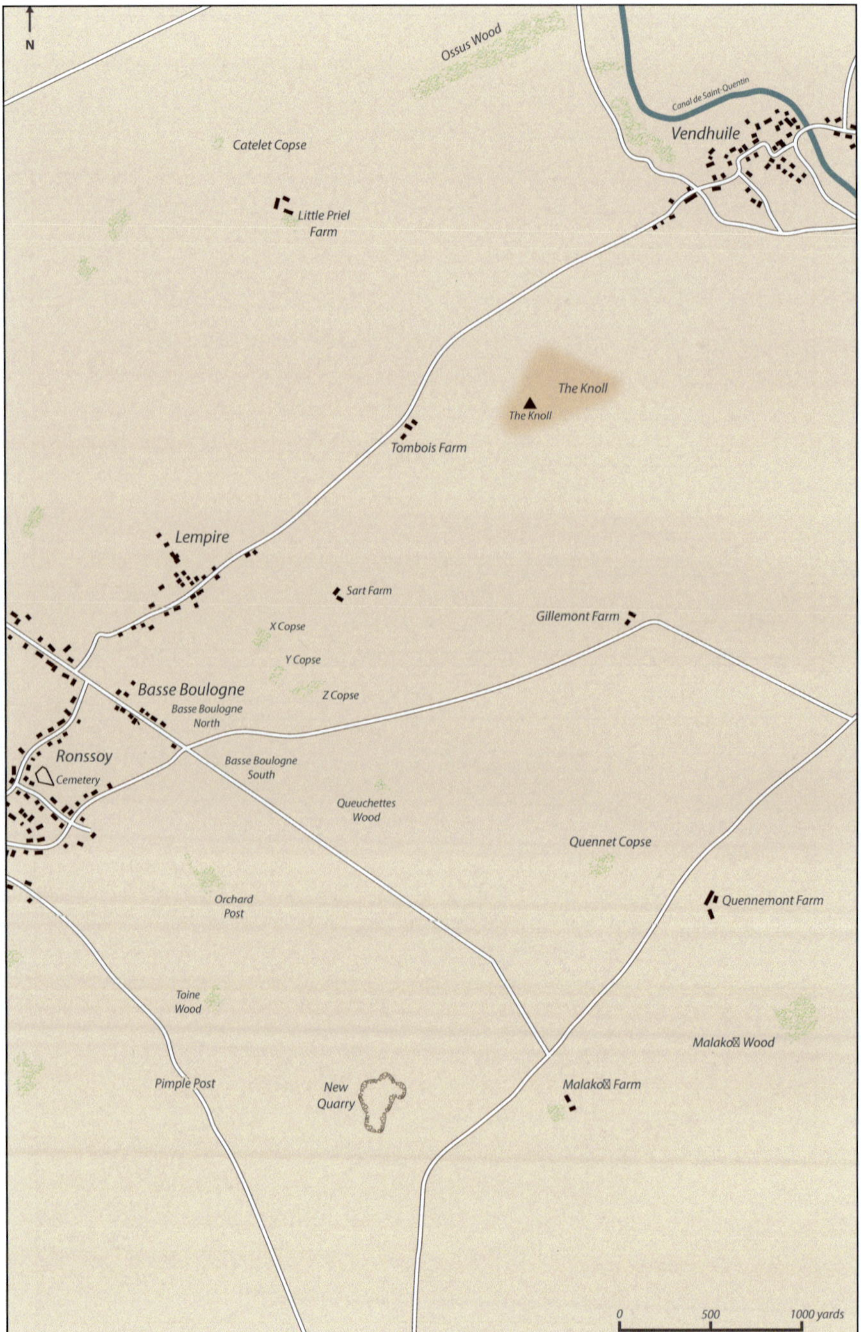

Map 5 48th Division Area of Operations, April–June 1917.

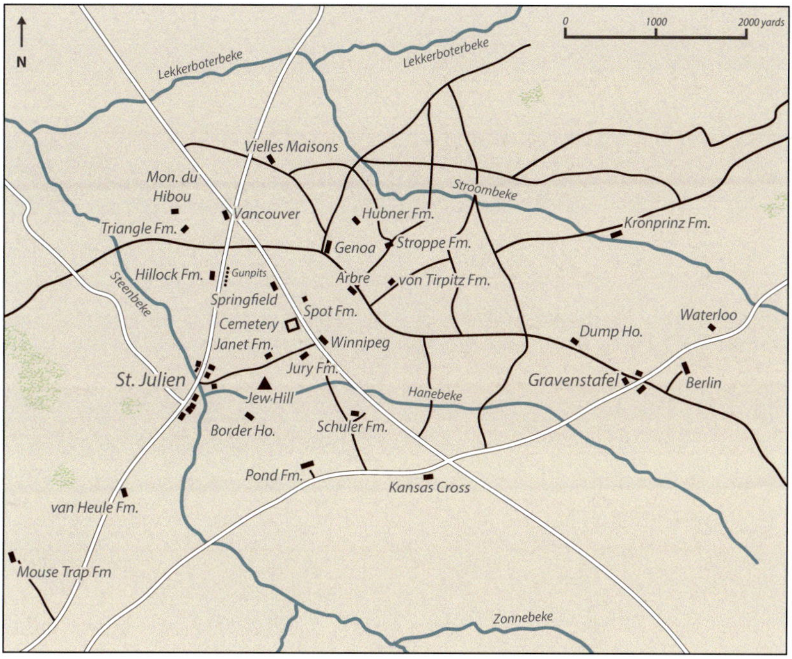

Map 6 48th Division Operations, August 1917.

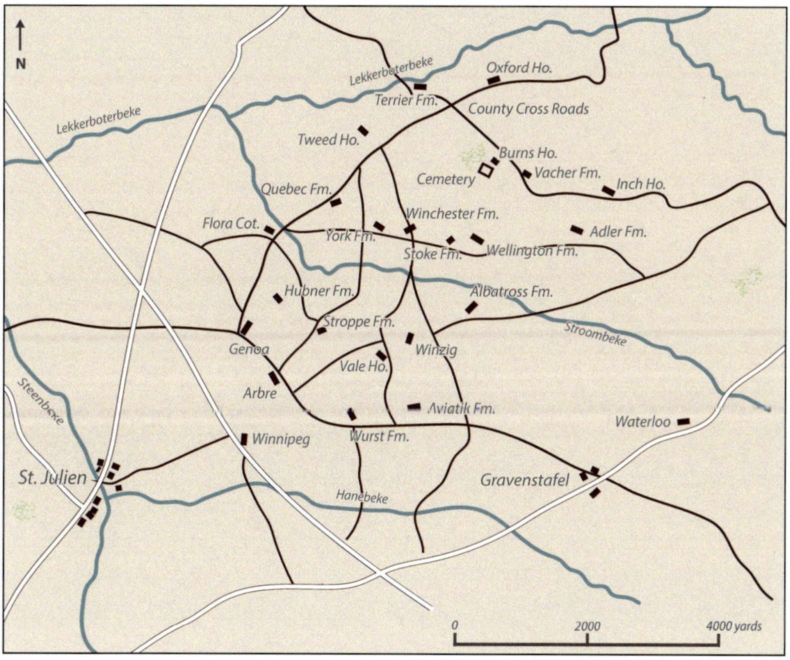

Map 7 48th Division Operations, October 1917.

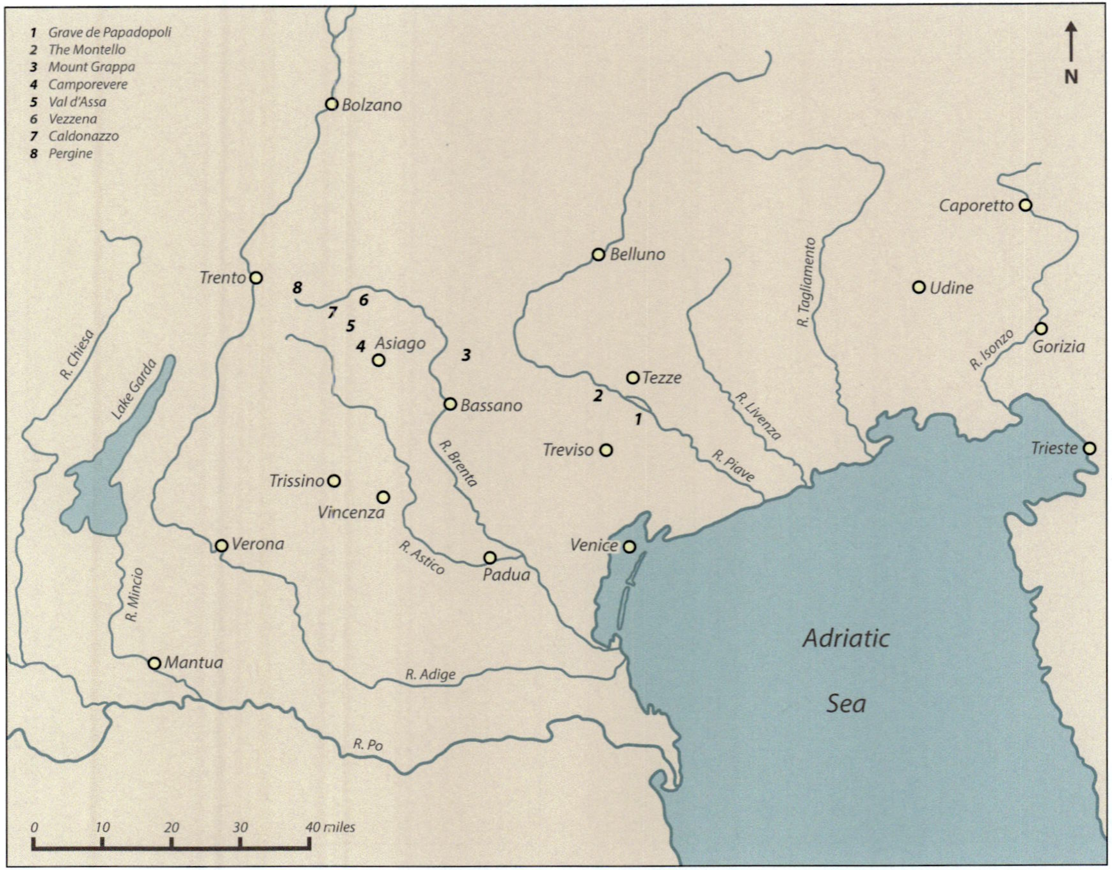

Map 8 North-eastern Italy 1917-18.

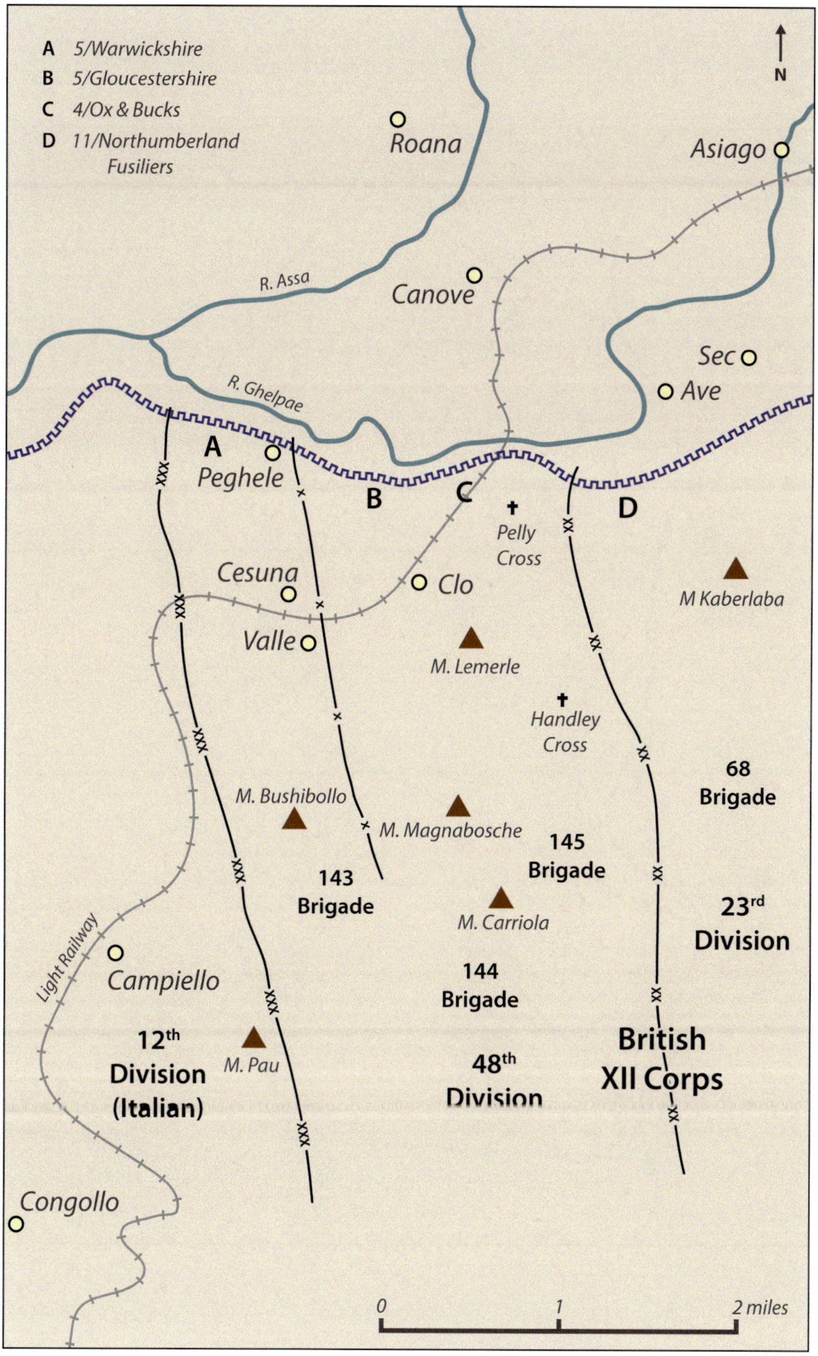

Map 9 48th Division Area, 15 June 1918.

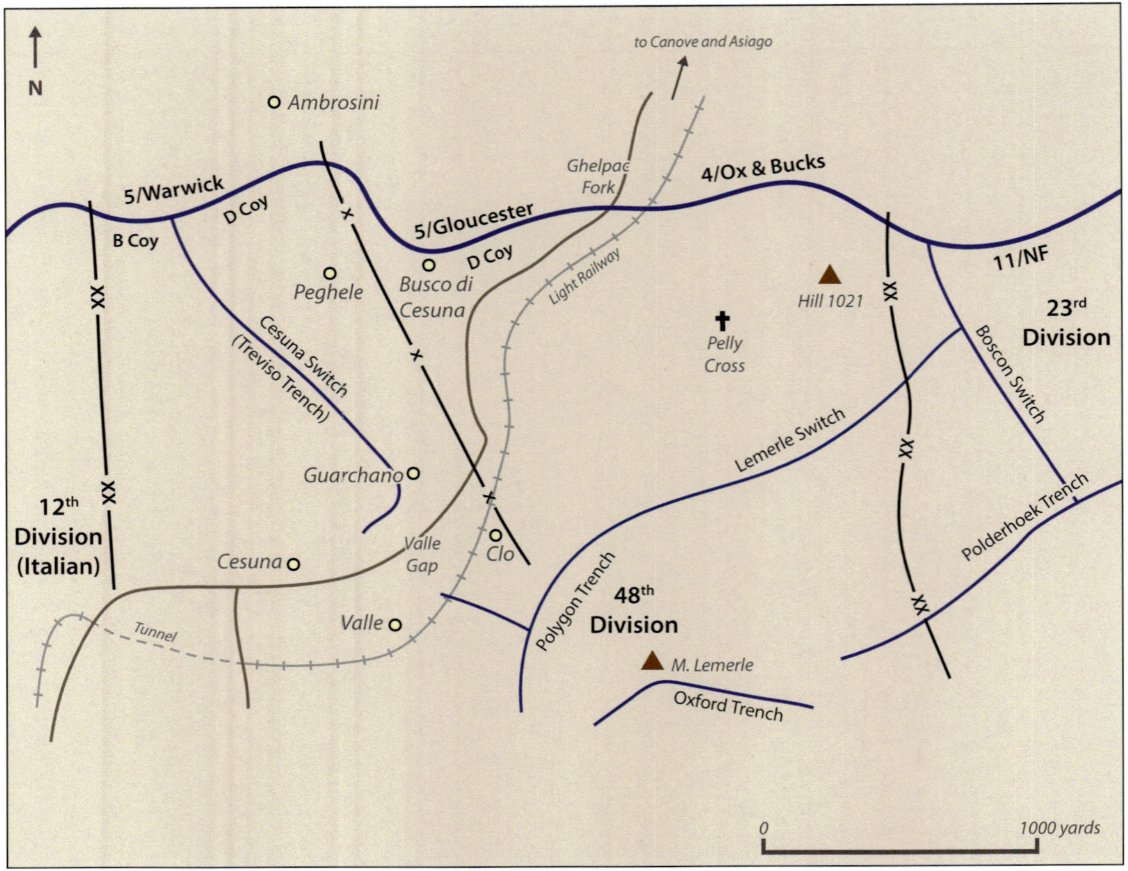

Map 10 Principal Trenches on 48th Division Front, 15 June 1918.

6

A War of Restricted Movement

The weather at the start of February was cold and frosty with occasional falls of snow. The billets were basic and very short of fuel; this might explain the fire in one occupied by a company of 7/Worcestershire which resulted in the loss the building and some equipment. Water in the carts and petrol tins brought from the rear was often frozen by the time it reached the front zone and work attempted on improving the trenches was hindered by the rock-hard earth. Mid-way through the month a rapid thaw set in which collapsed the trenches and when combined with the darkness of the nights made reliefs and working parties exceptionally difficult. Communication trenches became impassable and the men were reported to have been "floundering" in four feet of mud and ooze. Reliefs which should have taken two hours took four or five. In desperation, brigade reliefs were staggered over a much longer period in order to allow the "very exhausted" men some rest.

In such "deplorable conditions", as the diarist of 5/Warwickshire noted, outbreaks of trench foot were almost inevitable. There seems to have been sufficient gum boots for the companies in the front trenches and the signallers, but those at rest and on working parties were denied them. When entering the front area, the men dumped their ankle boots in exchange for the gum boots but were issued with dire warnings about penalties if they failed to mark clearly their own pair. In true Regular Army fashion an additional administrative system was devised to ensure the correct numbers of boots were signed for and receipts issued in triplicate provided. The ADMS travelled around the various camps ordering foot washing facilities be constructed and that buckets and stoves should be available in the trenches for washing feet. When in the trenches feet had to be rubbed with whale oil every 12 hours and on relief the men were instructed to wash and powder their feet under the supervision of an officer before applying clean socks and turning in. The senior commanders were "yelling themselves hoarse with bloodthirsty threats" about what would happen to those who succumbed to trench foot with the result that in at least one company men were paired off to be responsible for the other's feet. If one man developed the disability and went off to hospital, his partner was 'crimed'.[1] Despite the precautions, the number of cases grew from 43 on 23 February to 67 the following day. 3/Field Ambulance recorded that 4/ and 6/Gloucestershire were the worst affected battalions but it is unclear whether it was their procedures that were at fault or the peculiarities of that part of the line held by the two units.

The CRE's adjutant spent much of the month discussing with the French about which properties and facilities in the division's new area the units would be able to use; his boss meanwhile visited the front lines and ordered the construction of observation posts, trench mortar emplacements and a new divisional HQ of seven Nissen huts. The field companies also attempted to improve the camps inherited from the French in which, according to the sanitation officer, the general sanitation was "unsatisfactory." The construction of ablution blocks and drying rooms, the provision of soup kitchens at strategic positions and the removal of accumulated waste were all put in train. Town majors were questioned about how they were intending to improve their facilities and there was also the endless routine of trying to make the trenches more habitable. Stone was carted from nearby quarries to be laid on roads, wood cutting parties were despatched to nearby copses and duckboards were made by the hundred. The pioneers of 5/Sussex described it all as "very heavy work" but, as ever, working parties from the infantry not in the front zone were detailed almost nightly to assist them and the engineers. Training was interrupted by such demands but interspersed with the fatigue parties there was time for the occasional NCOs' class, PT and company training. Due to return to the trenches the following day, one CO disobeyed an order and refused to send his men on a nocturnal working party. Deciding his troops were already exhausted he kept them in camp and allowed them a few hours more precious rest.

The war diaries continue occasionally to make mention of some of the new doctrinal and training pamphlets then being issued as a result of the experience of the Somme. Detail is scarce but *SS. 135: Instructions for the Training of Divisions for Offensive Action* was clearly being put to use by the divisional staff and it is likely that *SS. 143: Instructions for the Training of Platoons for Offensive Action* and *SS. 144: Normal Formation for the Attack* were also being studied and applied. Fanshawe convened at least one divisional meeting of brigade commanders and staffs do discuss training methods in early March and GOC brigades then cascaded the conclusions to their COs. While the staffs planned future offensives and how they should be conducted the troops were kept occupied with trench routine and, when the weather and ground conditions allowed, nocturnal patrols and raids. These tended to be small scale and, like those attempted by 144 and 145 Brigades towards the end of February, frequently failed when they came up against uncut wire or lost direction in the absolute darkness. Before the thaw set in, however, the Germans undertook a substantial raid on a scale which for a time clearly shook the division. The various war diaries give several different dates for the raid but during daylight on 4 February German artillery fire

1 Greenwell, *Infant in Arms*, p. 157.

gradually increased before reaching its greatest intensity at 1650 hours. Only some of the division's batteries were in the line at the time and these were drenched with gas; meanwhile, trench mortars concentrated on destroying the British wire. Sections of the front trenches had by that time been almost flattened or blocked by large lumps of frozen earth. The "drumfire barrage" as the diarist of 6/Gloucestershire described it, had necessitated linesmen going out at least 15 times to repair cables between battalion HQ and the French batteries. French artillery officers posted to the division's battalion HQ were able to order a counter-barrage onto the enemy front positions just before the lines were cut again but failed to prevent the raiders leaving their trenches. Under the close cover of light trench mortars, showers of rifle grenades and the fire of light machine guns the Germans came over in two waves. They managed to get into the trenches of 6/Warwickshire and 6/Gloucestershire but after some 45 minutes of severe hand-to-hand fighting the Germans were finally expelled. During their withdrawal several Lewis guns were deployed into no man's land to catch the raiders in the flank, but the damage had been done. In the reports which followed, the Germans were thought to have "suffered heavily" but, for example, 6/Warwickshire recorded 35 dead, four who later died from wounds, another 66 wounded and 14 missing. Divisional HQ thought the total figure of dead was 52, with at least another 150 wounded. 3/Field Ambulance alone treated about 130 casualties in the 24 hour period and noted the "unusually large proportion of dangerously and seriously wounded." German casualties were unknown, although 6/Gloucestershire had nine dead raiders, "all big men", in their trench and enemy stretcher bearers were out for much of the night in no man's land collecting their dead and wounded.[2]

Corps and division HQ soon turned their attention towards revenge. Small raiding was both encouraged and expected but a more ambitious plan took shape during February. Rather than rush blindly and headlong into an immediate and possibly ill-fated response, an objective initial assessment of what was needed before a general advance on the corps front could take place was undertaken. It conclusions were, however, pessimistic and gloomy. It was originally intended that a major operation should be carried out before the end of the month but as the poor weather and conditions continued to prevail the possible date was pushed further back. This allowed time for further consideration and planning. The operation could not be mounted, so the staff believed, before the front trenches had been substantially improved and the ground had had a minimum of between three and five days of good drying weather. Three days of clear skies were necessary to allow for good aerial observation of German battery positions and substantial intelligence had to be collected on the enemy's trenches by constant night patrolling. There was also the need for the artillery to have registered accurately on the enemy's front lines, batteries and dead

2 Somewhat puzzlingly, and without any explanation as to what they were doing there, 6/Gloucestershire reported that three French soldiers who had previously been captured by the Germans were discovered and sent to the rear.

ground and have forward observation posts connected to prepared and well-stocked camouflaged gun positions. In addition, and this is the element which caused the planners most anxiety, was that the infantry had to be "fit and fresh." Two brigades were tasked to lead the operation with the third being sufficiently capable of holding the old British front line and any captured ones for at least 24 hours after the assault. Platoon strengths had to be as strong as the new pamphlets were suggesting, which would mean those other ranks who were currently detached to railway operating and construction companies and other units had to be returned. Furthermore, it was stressed that the assaulting infantry should not be used for working parties before the attack. To ease their burden, but simply to place it elsewhere, the field companies, pioneers, the salvage company and even the divisional band, would have to ensure the communication and assembly trenches were as well maintained as conditions allowed. The planners concluded, however, that as the "weather is the deciding factor in nearly all these points" unless spring suddenly began in earnest the operation was unlikely to be carried out in the near future.

The object of all this attention as to how the planning should be conducted was a collection of ruined farm buildings on high ground known as La Maisonette; these, it was thought, held the key to an advance to the Somme near Péronne. As the belief grew that the Germans were likely to begin a withdrawal to their prepared positions known to the Allies as the Hindenburg Line, it became imperative in the minds of divisional staff that these ruins should be taken. The neighbouring 50th Division and XV Corps were also planning to attack and, as part of the wider scheme, 48th Division was promised additional brigades of artillery, trench mortar batteries and machine-gun companies in support. No.2 Special Company RE would discharge smoke and gas, 34 Squadron would fly contact patrols and brigade boundaries were in the process of being adjusted to suit better an advance. In accordance with training pamphlet *SS. 135*, the existing front line was to be thinly held and it was stressed that "vigour and speed" must be infused into the work of consolidation. 145 Brigade would attack the farm buildings and the surrounding area on a three battalion front, with 143 Brigade using two battalions to clear the village of Biaches. As it was thought the cellars of La Maisonette were capable of sheltering 300 troops, special clearing parties were detailed and trained and there was a significant amount of tactical deception built into the scheme. Frequent artillery shoots and regular raids were designed to fool the Germans into believing no major operation was planned. New batteries and trench mortars were to concentrate on registering enemy gun positions but this was to be done carefully and under the pretext of covering raiding parties or retaliation for German "strafes". Coordination between infantry brigades and their field artillery group was by this stage of the war reasonably commonplace so existing procedures were to be employed to ensure that 18 pdrs would provide sniping and harassing fire to prevent working parties repairing holes in the enemy wire.

The detailed planning demonstrated the doctrinal sophistication now becoming apparent in British procedures yet the preparation work, for the time being, came to nothing. The weather remained uncooperative and all that could be conducted were

The present day hamlet of la Maisonette and the land to its immediate west. The division drew up extensive plans to raid the well protected collection of farm buildings but the staged German withdrawal to the Hindenburg Line meant that when companies of 5/Gloucester and 4/Ox&Bucks eventually entered the strong point on 16 March 1917, they met little resistance. The front German trench ran away from the camera across the ploughed field. (Author)

small scale enterprises which varied in their achievements. A proposed patrol by 7/Warwickshire was abandoned when the supposed protecting barrage fell short and landed on the British front trenches before the patrol had left and another enterprise by 6/Gloucestershire was so hurriedly ordered there was insufficient time for the patrol to organize itself efficiently. The battalion was just relieving another in an unfamiliar sector and orders were slow in delivery largely because the runners were already exhausted and did not know the trench system. Unsurprisingly amidst the confusion the patrol achieved little. By contrast, others were executed with what was later recognized as commendable efficiency. 6/Warwickshire sent out a patrol of 20 men under one officer in four groups and a covering Lewis gun party. Two prisoners were brought back and an estimated 30 Germans were killed for the loss of 12 wounded. A FOO went with the patrol, the Bangalore torpedoes worked perfectly, Stokes bombs were rolled down dugout steps which, when used in conjunction with Mills and phosphorous grenades, were "highly satisfactory"; "nothing could have been better" than the cooperation of the heavy and field artillery with the infantry. Major General Fanshawe and Lieutenant General Pulteney, the Corps Commander, were both effusive in their praise. 4/Berkshire was similarly praised when a small party scrambled into a deserted German trench and then went to look for two prisoners who were successfully taken back to the battalion's trenches. The post-action report noted that the artillery support was "so good [the raiders] walked up to within yards" of the German trench. As an added sophistication, a Lewis gun was tasked to fire occasionally in the darkness to guide the returning raiders to their own front.

The purpose of the patrols during early March was to gather intelligence on the strength by which the Germans were holding their trenches. To the north, the enemy had begun his deliberate withdrawal to the east but on 12 March the diarist of 5/Gloucestershire noted "still no sign of an enemy retreat." He added rather hopefully, "It cannot be long delayed now" and the following day reported, "Péronne would appear to be in flames." On 15 March a deserter declared his battalion was withdrawing east of the Somme, save one machine gun and 20 men of each company. Divisional HQ decided that the oft-postponed attack on La Maisonette should now be executed but with a clearly changing operational environment the assault was reduced in scale to that of only two companies of two battalions of 145 Brigade. The companies, two from 5/Gloucestershire and two from 4/Ox&Bucks, had trained in conjunction with each other and had made arrangements to ensure good communications could be maintained during the raid. Faces were blackened in preparation, wire cutting by the artillery continued, a liberal issue of hand cutters and mats to throw across uncut wire was made and the attackers were instructed to shoot promptly anyone who uttered the word "retire". Reconnaissance by the RFC had discovered the existence of a dummy trench in front of the main German lines and by the evening of 16 March, the wire was reported as being well cut. The raid was expected to last 30 minutes but the men were told that if circumstances permitted they should extend the time but to be wary of German ruses left behind in dugouts and trenches. Units of 143 Brigade were ready to offer support if required but when 5/Gloucestershire and 4/Ox&Bucks entered the farm area and neighbouring trenches they found them almost deserted. The few remaining Germans were quickly dispersed and according to a report from 4/Ox&Bucks their own wire caused more of an inconvenience to the attackers than did the German. Despite the thought that had gone into the earlier planning, the preparatory work proved not to have been flawless; traffic congestion and a lack of suitable duckboard tracks had delayed the start by one hour.[3] This meant that not only did the Oxfords have to use the single track allocated to them by the staff but also had to share it with the two companies of Gloucesters and a large carrying party of Berkshires. As the ruins were explored reports were despatched to the rear confirming the Germans evacuation and patrols were immediately sent out by the attacking battalions and some from 143 Brigade to locate the new German position. 5/Warwickshire reached as far as the banks of the river Somme and one from 4/Gloucestershire of 144 Brigade halted on the canal bank at La Chapelette.

Patrols from 7/Warwickshire advanced through the deserted desolation of Biaches and also reached La Chapelette, where one ran into some Germans; these continued

3 Greenwell, *Infant in Arms*, p. 162, describes it as 'a ghastly muddle.'

to snipe at the Warwicks from ruined houses for a reported seven hours at a distance of only 30 yards. At about 2100 hours on 17 March, one company of 8/Warwickshire crossed the river Somme near Bazincourt Farm and occupied the hamlet of Halle. It then sent out patrols which reported Mount St Quentin and Péronne itself to be empty. The Somme canal had also been crossed, albeit with 'great difficulty' in several places and, by 20 March, corps' mounted troops were operating in front of the infantry. They established a series of outposts and waited for the infantry to relieve them before moving on. Divisional RFA batteries were also across both river and canal by 19 March and, by a series of leap-frog movements, a succession of outpost lines and lines of resistance were pushed eastwards. The three main obstacles to a swift rather than a more measured and deliberate pursuit were the state of the terrain, booby traps and the determined resistance of small rearguards. The booby traps came in varying shapes, sizes and types, from delayed action explosives buried in crossroads and ruined houses to an infantry footbridge which exploded when first stepped on and bundles of grenades hidden in branches of felled trees. Many wells had been poisoned by the dumping of dead animals and most bridges had been made impassable. Rebuilding or replacing those which had crossed the Somme river and canal presented particular problems to the engineers. They and the pioneers of 5/Sussex had spent many months carrying out basic trench construction and maintenance, road repairs and other routine work. Much of this was to continue, although the infantry were to take on a yet larger role in the care of roads, but the field companies and pioneers now had to rediscover or acquire the skills of rather more complicated civil engineering.

On 18 March the CRE noted, 'preparations were begun' for crossing the Somme. Rafts were constructed in the rear but taking them up to the river and canal was a long and tiresome business. In places the alert enemy was only 200 yards from the river bank and in the darkness of the night the cumbersome rafts became snagged on unseen obstacles. It took four hours to transport the first raft one mile but, remarkably, it reached the water at 0300 on 17 March; within hours the engineers began ferrying the infantry across. Constructing bridges was an even more difficult task. Trestles were built in the rear and carried forward with the pontoons sometimes being rowed up the river. But so thorough had been the German destruction of the existing bridges and their approaches, and the river and canal had themselves been deliberately blocked by felled trees and other detritus, that securing the trestle legs to the bottoms proved exceptionally difficult. One underwater booby trap exploded killing an officer of 2/Field Company and the work of spanning the waterways was frequently interrupted by hostile shelling. One heavy trestle bridge over the canal was abandoned because it was impossible to drive the piles through the wreckage on the canal bottom. On other occasions, improvisation was required to build a heavy pontoon bridge with rails because no baulks were available when a truss broke under the weight of a 60 pdr gun. Iron bands to strengthen its replacement were scrounged and adapted and traffic over the bridge was disrupted for only five hours while repairs were completed. Between 18–30 March, the divisional engineers and pioneers built at least six bridges in and around Péronne capable of taking light wagons and guns, and one able to carry heavy traffic up to a weight of 12 tons.[4] In addition they built an unknown number of foot bridges, light pontoons and rafts. Once constructed, the bridges then had to be maintained, repaired and often strengthened by the addition of further wooden and eventually metal girders. Sappers were also engaged in supervising the construction of the outpost line and the successive lines of resistance. This frequently involved digging cruciform posts and breaking down German wire and repositioning it around the new defences. There was also a multitude of other routine tasks such as testing well water and digging new ones, establishing water troughs and arranging the early construction of what would develop into camps. In the same way as sections of the three field companies worked in autonomous groups, the pioneer companies were split and worked in often widely separated zones. Principally to them fell the task of building a light railway from Flaucourt eastwards and to supervising infantry working parties attempting to make the roads passable. In III Corps, which was a typical three division corps, one division in rotation was primarily involved in road maintenance and improving accommodation.

The wanton and wilful destruction of Péronne shocked many of the troops. The Germans had deliberately blown away the front walls of houses and the town hall and railway station had been so utterly destroyed as to be almost unrecognizable. It was not only the men of 42nd Division recently arrived from Gallipoli and Egypt,[5] but also the seasoned troops of the South Midland Division who were amazed at the scorched earth policy of the Germans. Not all villages had been completely destroyed, partly because the Germans had continued to use them for accommodating their own troops until the final stage of the withdrawal, but also because there remained a considerable number of civilians in the area. The Germans had removed to Germany all boys and girls aged between about 16 and 30 and had concentrated the remaining civilians from several villages into one. In Vraignes, for example, 5/Gloucestershire found about 1,400 civilians and another 400 in Bouvincourt. Tincourt, a reasonable sized and not entirely destroyed village which also still housed inhabitants was quickly transformed into a large rest area and dump for divisional units. One section of 1/Field Ambulance was quickly sent forward to the village to examine the refugees before they were evacuated to the rear. The diarist of 4/Berkshire was clearly affected by the destruction and by "the piteous spectacle" of the inhabitants, whose faces 'showed what misery and unhappiness they had been living in.'

4 When the advance began the ADVS used the bridges as vantage points. He controlled the traffic as it crossed in order to get a good view of the condition of the division's horses.

5 See, K.W.Mitchinson, *Amateur Soldiers: A History of Oldham's Volunteers and Territorials, 1859-1938,* (Jade, 1999) pp. 92-93 for the impact of the destruction on an officer of 10/ Manchester. The 4/Berkshire diarist believed 'a more organized system of destruction was hardly possible.' This included even the breaking of children's toys. Similarly, Compiled, *History of 1/6th Warwickshire,* p. 37 tells of the 'horror' of Péronne.

In order to stay in touch with the withdrawing enemy, two mobile columns were formed. Ward's Column, named after the CRA of 48th Division, comprised two batteries of 240 Brigade, two battalions of (initially) 145 Brigade, a section of RE and a section of 3/Field Ambulance. Mounted troops also operated alongside the column and on occasions there were several armoured cars available for support. The tactics employed by these columns were largely novel and improvised but during some of the meagre training time in February companies had practised advanced guards and different means of deploying over open ground. How much practice had been devoted to cooperation between batteries and infantry on the move is unknown, but it is clear that on occasions communications were problematic. On 28 March, for example, 1/Bucks reported, "Telephone lines were out for several hours, and communications forward entirely broke down." It probably tended to be more coincidental than planned if an armoured car arrived fortuitously but two did appear at the right moment and assisted 4/Ox&Bucks when it attacked Roisel on 26 March. Although a relatively small operation, the attack showed how the infantry was adapting to the more mobile and all-arms style of warfare. Under a 30 minute barrage fired by 18 pdrs, a section of 4.5 inch howitzers and two 60 pdrs, two companies of Oxfords set off towards the town. One platoon was almost immediately held up by a machine gun but another platoon rapidly shook out into an alternative formation and quickly brought suppressing fire to bear on the troublesome gun. It soon gained fire supremacy over the German rearguard, a task aided by its platoon commander who enterprisingly borrowed a dismounted Hotchkiss from one of the armoured cars. A contact aircraft circled above and troops of cavalry patrolled both flanks to ward off or warn of any counter-attacks. At a reported cost of four dead and 14 wounded, the small town of Roisel was occupied.

In recognition of it having been the first battalion to enter Péronne, at the end of the month 8/Warwickshire provided a company to act as guard of honour for the French Premier when he visited the benighted town. The division as a whole, however, spent most of the final days of March either following up the German rearguards, working on the roads or trying to gain what little rest they could in the squalor of the devastated terrain. The weather was changeable and the facilities behind the forward area offered little in the way of comfort. The threat of delayed action mines meant billeting in the cellars of ruined buildings was dangerous and there was a hugely inadequate supply of tents. Baths and disinfectors had yet to be organized so there were no opportunities to change underclothes or clean off the accumulated mud and grime.[6]

6 On 5 March 4/Berkshire noted the incinerator would be available for two hours each day for use by the battalion when it was out at rest. This, the diarist recorded was 'very badly needed.' It is conceivable that when the pursuit began and the battalion moved frequently, there was no opportunity to issue another new supply for at least three weeks. The seemingly indefatigable Captain Dale, Divisional Sanitary Officer, was promoted to Fourth Army HQ during the month, but both he and his successor travelled extensively lecturing unit officers on the need for appropriate sanitation as they moved eastwards and organizing parties in Péronne to clear the 'enormous accumulation of refuse.'

The further east the outpost line reached the further rations and comforts had to be carried across the devastated zone. The two mobile columns were disbanded before the end of the month, by which time villages such as Villers-Faucon and Saulcourt had been reached. The Germans continued to slow the pursuit on ground of their own choosing but by 30 March the division had a line of observation over the large village of Épehy and the smaller adjacent ones of Ronssoy and Lempire. To the east of these lay the outpost system of the Hindenburg Line.

Casualties during the month had been remarkably few; so, too, had been the numbers arriving as drafts. Just over 120 other ranks were killed during the month, with 1/Bucks suffering by far the greatest number. A gas attack on one of its company HQ on 10 March killed three officers and 14 men in the space of a few minutes. The total wounded for the month was approximately 340, with more than 50 of those belonging to 4/Gloucestershire who also had five officers wounded on 31 March. On 19 March, during the first tentative stages of the pursuit, 3/Field Ambulance made a point of reporting no wounded had passed through its sections for 24 hours. Yet, although there were relatively few wounded, the field ambulances continued to treat a substantial number of sick. For example, while 2/Field Ambulance dealt with a small number of wounded during the month, 521 men sought treatment for various ailments, with 86 of these still retained in the tents at the end of the month. According to the figures available, it seems unlikely that any of the battalions had more than a rifle strength of about 700: 6/Gloucestershire, for example, reported it was 368 other ranks below establishment and 1/Bucks finished the month with 17 officers and 645 other ranks. Two Warwicks battalions noted they had received drafts amounting to only 13 and 23 respectively. These two battalions made no mention of the quality of the drafts but after the war the historian of 4/Berkshire considered that the quality and physique of a draft which arrived in April 'was not beyond criticism.' Of the 35 men, "five wore trusses and three suffered from malformations of the foot." Although the advance itself might have raised morale, the troops of the under strength battalions were clearly exhausted. The weather remained poor and the next series of attacks against the villages close to the enemy outpost line, all of which had been precisely registered by the German artillery, were to be made in snow, mist and rain. The enemy had no intention of holding on to the villages while they settled into their prepared positions further behind, but were determined to exact a heavy toll and to make the lives of the new would-be occupants as miserable and as uncomfortable as possible.

The division's first operation against these final positions was not entirely auspicious. The small hamlet of Ste Emilie was to be taken by 4/Gloucestershire but it was a rushed affair and one which cost more casualties than it should have done. Corps, eager to maintain momentum to disrupt the German withdrawal, ordered the attack to be undertaken swiftly. Because, however, the Germans were never actually off balance or capable of being significantly disrupted it was almost impossible for the pursuers to seize anything other than occasional local tactical initiative. There were few opportunities to employ deception or genuine surprise but corps and divisional GOC knew their army commander's intent was to maintain pressure and take ground.

The German withdrawal was executed to a steady, deliberate and coordinated timetable which involved halting for a time on ground which suited defence and by means of small rearguards of a couple of machine guns and a company or even a platoon of riflemen covered by 77mm fire, to delay the advancing infantry. Furthermore, until the British railhead could be brought beyond Péronne and the condition of the roads made good for a heavy flow of continuous traffic, any attack was likely to be difficult logistically to sustain.

The attack on Ste Emilie by two companies of 4/Gloucestershire was to begin at 1600 on 30 March. One company was to make a frontal assault while the other, covered by a troop of cavalry, approached from the north. Two further platoons were to attack Pleasant House, a neighbouring farm on an adjoining spur. The companies were ordered to advance "widely extended and in considerable depth." The divisional artillery was to have registered on the hamlet during the day and at 1600 to fire a two minute burst as the signal for the infantry to advance. The company attacking from the west was immediately repulsed but that approaching from the north managed to get into the German trenches and, following some hand-to-hand fighting, took the ruins. Two hundred Germans evacuated the position in reasonable order; the Gloucesters lost five officers and 75 men. 144 Brigade's war diary tried to make the best of it and noted, "Considering this was the first time they had attacked in open warfare the attack was well carried out." Nevertheless, the diary also noted that rather than remain widely separated the sections had tended to bunch and thus became an easier target for the German riflemen. The real fault, however, lay with the inadequate artillery barrage. While a short burst of two minutes might have caught the defenders by surprise, the one fired was not of sufficient intensity to intimidate or destroy the defences; furthermore it fell well beyond the intended trenches whose defensive fire had to be suppressed if success was to be achieved. Pleasant House had also been captured but the unfortunate company tasked to hold and consolidate Ste Emilie during the night was on the receiving end of intermittent and precisely registered German shelling. Had the entry in the divisional war diary of, "4/Gloucestershire assisted by artillery fire captured Ste Emilie" been known to the troops involved, it may have raised a hollow laugh.

The planning for the successive operations to take the larger villages of Épehy and Lempire was allowed greater time and greater resources. At 1700 on 31 March, four widely separated platoons in artillery formation, two each from 6/Gloucestershire and 7/Worcestershire, advanced under a barrage to establish a jumping off line to the west of Épehy. To the left of 6/Gloucestershire, 6/Warwickshire conducted a similar move. As instructed, when German shrapnel began bursting above them the platoons halted and dug in on a forward slope. The German retaliation spread as far back as 144 Brigade HQ which, it was noted, "put the brigadier and brigade major in considerable danger." During the night the forward positions were reinforced and orders issued at 2200 warning the divisional cyclists and two reserve battalions to be ready to move up, consolidate and report once Pezieres, Épehy and Malassise Farm had been taken. The attacking battalions were ordered to make as much use of the ground as possible and to avoid what were deemed "regular formations." Sections were not to extend until they were within 50 yards of the enemy or were receiving fire. This suggests they may have advanced in 'worms', a formation which had only fairly recently been introduced. There was to be no covering artillery fire but if the infantry did send up a SOS, it was to fire for five minutes on the objectives. The only scheduled bombardment was to fall on Malassise Farm for 40 minutes from 0630.

The advance began at 0500 in complete darkness and with a snow storm blowing onto the backs of the attackers. There was some initial confusion when one company of Gloucesters advanced at right angles into one of the Worcesters but order was restored and the attackers reached to within 50 yards of the enemy positions before being spotted. With the defenders caught by surprise and protected by only patchy wire, the Warwicks, Gloucesters and Worcesters swarmed into the villages with little resistance. The defenders steadied themselves for a time but a weak enemy counter-barrage fell largely on empty positions and failed to interrupt the passage of the supporting companies. So quick had been the progress that 6/Gloucestershire was at the railway bank before 0630, the scheduled time for the artillery to open up on it and Malassise Farm. The foremost company thought it prudent to withdraw from the advanced position; when the barrage moved on the company followed behind. It was anticipated the farm might house a considerable strong point but it also fell swiftly to the infantry. So rapid had been the success that as early as 0830 the brigadier went up to the new front positions to assess the situation for himself. Enemy fire on the captured positions grew in intensity during the day but, as ordered, German wire was recycled and consolidation work "vigorously pushed through." The German dead were buried and elementary sanitary precautions put into place. Patrols went out regularly but were hampered by two German searchlights which were switched on intermittently and also by loss of direction. One group of 4/Ox&Bucks, for example, had wandered directionless in the dark for so long that when daylight began to break the NCO decided to shelter in a shell hole for 10 hours until night again cloaked its movement. For the next few days positions in the northern sector of the divisional front were enlarged and extended and the remaining brigades of the divisional artillery arrived to offer their support.

The artillery had traversed the waste lands east of the Péronne river and canal crossings. It deployed into pits and positions which, it was estimated, by 8 April would allow all component brigades to fire on the Hindenburg Line. Until concentration was complete those batteries which had arrived provided what support they could. Two batteries of 18 pdrs were kept as a mobile reserve to support the outposts but 240 Brigade made an honest admission that its fire had failed adequately to support early patrol activity towards Ronssoy. The 6 inch howitzers and 60 pdrs were sufficiently forward by 4 April, however, to support the next large attack on that village and the two neighbouring ones of Lempire and Basse Boulogne. All three of these villages lay a little to the south-east of Épehy. Three battalions of 145 Brigade were tasked to attack and there was sufficient time for the brigadier to go forward to observe the objectives and give a detailed brief to COs. On a very dark and misty night, with snow squalls adding to the misery, the battalions moved up to their jumping off positions on congested and heavy roads. At 0430 they were to advance about 1,600 yards on company frontages of 200 yards to the first objectives and then another 1,100 yards to the final ones. The German response to the attack was immediate. Fortunately, the enemy barrage fell behind the attacking troops and by 0600 4/Ox&Bucks, 5/Gloucestershire and 4/Berkshire had reached their objectives. The British barrage had fallen short on the right and caused about 30 casualties to the Berkshire but about 50 retreating Germans were killed by Lewis gun fire of the Gloucesters as they waited for their own barrage to lift. Despite the enemy clearly having expected the attack, for the return of a casualty list of just under 300 it had been a "brilliant success" and earned the praise of both the corps and army commanders.[7] One battalion history was jubilant in its praise for such a deep advance over unfamiliar ground which involved some complicated manoeuvring both outside and inside the village. The men "were wonderfully excited and delighted at their achievement…it was the best fight they have ever had in France."[8] Similarly, a company commander was delighted with the performance of the yeomanry who had been drafted in earlier 'to replace the old Derbyites' who had arrived the previous August. This was their first chance to use the bayonet and was, so their officer thought, "simply glorious."[9] The successful attack had been supported on its right by an assault on Templeux-le-Guerard and its nearby quarries, known as the Mound, by 8/Worcestershire. Disconcertingly, the Worcesters discovered the information supplied to them by 59th Division on their right was far from accurate, as were the maps with which they had been issued. Despite 59th Division's claims to the contrary, it did not hold the village and the Mound proved to be far larger than portrayed on maps. Furthermore, its surface was riven by spoil tips and ravines which made it an exceptionally difficult physical obstacle to capture. By a series of well executed flanking movements, the Worcesters took the enemy posts one by one.

To allow the division's infantry to have what was hoped would be genuine rest, brigades of 42nd (East Lancashire) Division, which had about completed their trench acclimatization, were attached to the South Midland Division. This attachment was not, however, always a particularly happy arrangement because the Lancastrians' lack of Western Front experience showed up in several unfortunate ways. For example, the South Midland Division's 241 RFA Brigade was tasked to fire in support of 125 Brigade's attack on a copse but 7/Lancashire Fusiliers neglected to carry any telephones or other communications with it when the assault began. It was over five hours before 241 Brigade received any news from the Fusiliers and had in the meantime fired "a large expenditure of ammunition uselessly." Vaughan recounts the story of a fist fight between his battalion and the Oldham Territorials of 10/Manchester. According to Vaughan, the Warwicks had again been ordered to retake the evil Gillemont Farm

7 As the troops looted abandoned German packs, they were particularly pleased to discover each contained spare underclothes and three pairs of socks.

8 Cruttwell, *War Service of 1/4th Berkshire*, pp. 109-10

9 Greenwell, *Infant in Arms*, pp. 172-3

The German strong point of Gillemont Farm to the east of Basse Boulogne. The Knoll is the rising ground to the left. These positions were part of the Hindenburg Outpost Line and were the scenes of particularly bitter fighting by the division in April and May 1917. (Author)

because the Manchesters had not fought hard enough to hold.[10] Towards the end of the month, when two platoons of 126 Brigade had been forced out of Canal Wood, Major General Fanshawe investigated and reported that communications had been "ineffective" and implied that organization within the Manchester Brigade needed to be considerably improved.

For the days following the capture of the final line of villages, during which the weather continued to alternate between showers of rain and snow, the infantry were to push on to establish an outpost line almost 3,000 yards to the east. As protection the artillery fired demonstrations of 'curtain' 'dropping' and 'drenching' fire towards the Hindenburg Line. The line wanted by corps lay on the areas of high ground which, if occupied, would allow observation over the outpost positions of the Hindenburg Line itself. This made the ground essential to the enemy and for this reason they resisted any further advance. The relatively easy progress of III Corps was now over and the area occupied was to witness some of the most bitter fighting seen in 1917 in any supposedly 'quiet area'. The operations were managed at inter-corps level which in theory, although not always in practice, prevented one corps from launching an unsupported

10 Vaughan makes several references to 42nd Division as a whole being 'frightfully windy', pp. 89, 91

attack. Liaison officers became increasingly frequent visitors to neighbouring corps, divisional and brigade headquarters in order to coordinate simultaneous action and support. The system did, however, fail when 4/Gloucestershire and 7/Worcestershire were ordered to advance their outpost positions onto the Tombois Farm – Malakoff Farm ridge on 13 April. 144 Brigade was told that 59th Division on its right would cooperate but when Lieutenant Colonel Tomkinson despatched a message to 2/5th Lincoln on his right asking what the Lincolns were intending to do by way of attack, the reply stated that they had not been ordered to make any advance. 'This message was rather a surprise' and, according to Tomkinson, was also "very upsetting" because his right would be exposed and against the snow covered ground on such a bright night his men would be visible to the enemy. Nonetheless, and on ground which was unfamiliar, the attack went ahead. The Germans' response was immediate yet despite the handicaps the objectives were taken and Tomkinson reported "There are seven dead Germans in view and I hope many more." He concluded enemy morale must have been bad because, protected by good wire and in the bright moonlight, he believed a half company of determined men and three machine guns "could have held up a brigade."

The morale of 48th Division's battalions was to be severely tested a few nights later when 143 and 145 Brigades again tried to advance their posts to gain observation over the Hindenburg Line. The objectives were Gillemont, Tombois and Little Priel Farms, the Knoll and Catelet Copse. If successfully taken the three farms were to be incorporated into what was known as the Outpost Line of Resistance. Other posts just to the west of the German wire were also to be taken *en route t*o the farms and the enemy wire retained as part of their defences. Gillemont Farm, perched above two important valleys both of which allowed the Germans to reinforce the position in reasonable safety, overlooked the canal tunnel which formed part of the main German line. Once the farm was captured it was to become an advanced outpost with a small garrison. Parties of sappers and pioneers were to follow the advancing companies and quickly consolidate the captured positions. In the southern sector 4/Berkshire was allotted the task of capturing Gillemont Farm while 1/Bucks went for Tombois Farm a few hundred yards to its north-west; to the north of 145 Brigade and supported by 241 Brigade RFA, two Warwick battalions were to make for Catelet Copse. Men from 144 Brigade were sent forward to act as additional stretcher bearers and the field ambulances increased the number of orderlies at the ADS.

The weather on the night of 16-17 April was severe. Storms of rain and snow had raged all day and continued as the companies began their march to the front. The two companies of 4/Berkshire had a two mile march in the pitch black night across saturated ground. Zero was scheduled for 2330 but just as they formed up, a party of Germans attacked their right flank. A platoon was sent out successfully to ward off the attack but zero was delayed for five minutes. Just as they were about to struggle forward, a heavy barrage fell on them. By this time they were wet through, chilled and numbed and with many whose fingers were so frozen they could not fire their weapons. Deciding any advance was impossible the company commanders ordered the men back to some scrapes a few yards to the rear. The weather grew even wilder and at 0130 brigade HQ sent a message informing the companies, which had already lost nine dead and over 20 wounded, not to try again. The attack should clearly not have been attempted in such conditions. Army and corps HQ subsequently realized the mistake and sent messages congratulating the battalion for having managed even to reach the start line. Their efforts were "worthy of all praise" with "no blame" being attached to the officers or men. No doubt as an attempt to reconcile the men to what had been an error of judgement on the part of the staff, Major General Fanshawe addressed the battalion a few days later to offer his congratulations and to praise the men for the reputation earned and their stalwart efforts. "Everything" he said, "had been against them." 241 Brigade's diarist summed up the night by recording, "Heavy casualties for the infantry for a minor operation."

There had been some success, however, as the two Warwicks battalions had taken Catelet Copse and Pigeon Ravine and 1/Bucks had secured Tombois Farm. The attack on Gillemont Farm and the Knoll, 400 yards to its north, was to herald the start of a series of attempted assaults, some by mere platoons and others by almost complete battalions, which were eventually to result in stalemate. 4/Ox&Bucks tried to take the farm on 18 April but this failed, as did similar attempts against the Knoll. After the war the historian of 4/Ox&Bucks claimed that the failure to take the farm was a consequence of the battalion being allowed to use only one company: "As previous operations had been successful with comparative ease, we were forbidden to employ any further troops except to exploit success."[11] If this assertion is true, it suggests a grave misjudgement on the part of the brigade or divisional staff. The staff may have considered earlier failures in the sector to have been purely the result of the weather but they should certainly have realized that the dominant position of the farm meant the Germans were bound determinedly to resist attempts to take it. Given the state of the ground and the known strength of the German defences it does seem to have been an error.[12] The failure meant that a better planned, organized and larger attack by 144 Brigade and 126 Brigade, which was still attached to 48th Division, was undertaken on 23 April and continued the following day.

In view of these successive failures the staff decided the objectives for the attack should be altered. Rather than attempt to take both farm and Knoll themselves by frontal attack, by advancing either side of them they could be denied to the enemy by persistent flanking fire. 8/Worcestershire later claimed that 10 minutes after their zero of 0345, intense German fire swept the ground to be covered which prompted the men to charge the farm. The Germans apparently fled but because 6/Gloucestershire had not reached their objective, the Worcesters were compelled to withdraw in the

11 Pickford, *War Record of 1/4th Battalion Ox&Bucks*, p. 30.

12 Vaughan, who is not always accurate in the dates given in his memoir, *Some Desperate Glory* (Macmillan, 1981) p. 93, claims there was an estimated 700 dead around the farm buildings as early as 15 April 1917.

face of ferocious counter-attacks. 6/Gloucestershire later reported that its first wave had reached the objective but that German fire disrupted the second and the first was then compelled to withdraw. The same report, however, noted that battalion fatalities amounted to two officers and two men. If the attack was launched with the determination expected, this would seem a particularly low total, especially as 7/Worcestershire immediately reported four officers and 15 men killed.[13] The other two battalions of 144 Brigade were then ordered to repeat the attack. The CO of 4/Gloucestershire, Lieutenant Colonel Parkinson, was killed while orders were still being issued and 7/Worcestershire's companies were very scattered and needed time to assemble. Despite 4/Gloucestershire's later accusation that 126 Brigade on its left "failed to attack" both features were taken and lost twice but a foothold was retained on the farm's western enclosure. Two companies of 4/Berkshire had made a march of over seven miles, after a night spent providing working parties, to protect the right flank of 7/Worcestershire while it attacked the farm. The companies assembled on time and were ordered to advance but as the right of the Worcesters could not get forward, and with daylight breaking, the exhausted Berkshires were fortunately told to stand fast. A report written after the attack by 144 Brigade mentioned a number of British shells falling short but one infantry CO wanted the artillery to know that the work of the guns "was magnificent and thoroughly appreciated by us." Three German counter-attacks had been broken up by the artillery and then several 18 pdrs did some "very fine sniping" when the main fighting had died down. Lieutenant Colonel Tomlinson wanted to appease the gunners who, he thought, had been "distressed" by his earlier accusations of shorts. On investigation, Major General Fanshawe concluded the short firing had been done by guns of a division other than the 48th.[14]

There was a slight pause in front of the farm for two days while 145 Brigade supported an attack to its south by 59th Division but the brigade was warned that it would again assault the Knoll in conjunction with 126 Brigade in the early hours of 28 April. Two brigades were to be used to push on to the two valleys behind the Knoll and farm, clear Canal and Ossus Woods and force the Germans back across the canal. There was some local success for the left brigade but, overall, the attacks again failed to secure the intended observation over the defences above the canal tunnel. Nevertheless, Fourth Army and corps HQ despatched their "warmest thanks" to the division for its 'brilliant success.' At least for the infantry of 48th Division the worst was for the time being over. 42nd Division began relieving the South Midlanders on 29 April, although the field companies, pioneers and two batteries of 240 Brigade RFA had to wait a little longer for their reliefs.

13 After the war Wyrall, *Gloucesters,* p. 212 reported a more realistic total of 95 casualties. He also asserts the Gloucesters failed because just before zero the left of 126 Bde, 42nd Division had been attacked. This meant its battalions were unable to cooperate.

14 Such was the confusion on and around the Knoll that 241 Brigade RFA simply noted, 'Situation obscure for three days.'

At times the fighting had been severe and prolonged. One of the field ambulances noted the number of "serious" cases was greater than might have been expected and that 50 percent of the casualties were stretcher cases. This put an added strain on the evacuation process because there was a particularly long carry from the area around Gillemont Farm and the Knoll to the nearest point where they could be put onto horse or lorried ambulances. Almost 200 wounded passed through 3/Field Ambulance's two ADS in two days on their way through to the MDS at Péronne. Additional horse ambulances had to be borrowed from other units to cope with the flow and because the fighting was over a fairly compact area when barrages came down, there were few places which could offer sanctuary. The frequency of the engagements within this small area also made any collection of wounded laying out in the often fluid boundaries of no man's land difficult. Neither was it the sort of fighting which offered the opportunity for any real subtleties in the tactics employed. The essential physical components of fighting power were available in numbers but there was little room to manoeuvre or put into effect the evolving tactics specified in the recent training pamphlets. The Berkshire's historian frankly admitted that on at least one occasion the work of the battalion was "not wholly satisfactory" but does make the point that the new platoon organization and its greater degree of specialization did "throw a greater strain upon the intelligence of the average soldier and upon the responsibilities of platoon and section commanders." This was indeed the case, and when Fanshawe

Graves in Villers-Faucon Communal Cemetery of three of the officers of 6/Gloucester killed in the battalion HQ by a booby trap on 18 April 1917. Right to left, Lieutenant Colonel T.W. Nott, DSO, Major R.E.Gerrard, and Captain Nott, MC. (Author)

addressed the battalion after the misery of its aborted attack on the night of 16-17 April, he stressed the importance of leadership at all levels. Such was the demand for labour during the pursuit towards the Hindenburg Line, however, there had been few opportunities for the men to be trained in the new tactics. Given the consistently appalling weather, the state of the terrain and the strength, extent and depth of the German defences it is difficult to image any division being successful without an overwhelming preponderance of fire power. This was unavailable to the division because the fighting was only a side show to what was going on further north. Third Army's offensive at Arras was absorbing any available additional manpower and heavy guns. All III Corps was able to do was to attempt to prevent the enemy sending reinforcements from its front to Arras and by maintaining pressure in the sector to try to secure suitable jumping off positions which could be used if and when the Hindenburg Line itself could be assaulted.

During the course of April conditions behind the lines gradually improved. German prisoners were used to help the RE and pioneers develop accommodation; drying huts were established and baths opened at Tincourt and Villers-Faucon, the latter of which could cope with 500 men per day. The engineers worked continuously on clearing wells and sinking new ones; soup kitchens were established at several strategic points close to the line but a major and continuing obstacle to progress was the danger of undiscovered German booby traps. A mine in the HQ of 6/Gloucestershire killed Lieutenant Colonel Nott, his brother the Adjutant, the second-in-command Major Gerrard,[15] the MO and two other officers. One day earlier two men and eight animals of 7/Worcestershire had been killed by a mine left in their transport lines and six men of 144 Machine Gun Company were killed in a cellar in Villers-Faucon. The ADMS ordered the ADS in that village to move from ruined buildings into tents and 4/Berkshire moved its battalion HQ from cellars in Hamel. Under a divisional order mid-way through the month all buildings and ruins had to be evacuated but bricks and garden walls could be used to build shelters. Railway cuttings and banks were also permitted as refuges. The RE searched suspect locations and discovered explosives behind walls, under floors and roof timbers and removed, for example, a charge of 150 kilos from under a road in Templeux-la-Fosse.

Initial returns recorded a total loss to the infantry battalions during April of 23 officers and 181 other ranks killed, 46 and 902 wounded and two officers and 71 men missing. Figures produced after the war suggest the total of other ranks' deaths came closer to 300. At the start of the month only three battalions had a fighting strength of lower than 600 rifles but by the end of the month only four had a figure higher than 600; one battalion was below 400 and the division as a whole was described as "absurdly weak."[16] Two battalions, 7/and 8/Warwickshire, had been particularly

15 Major R.E. Gerrard was a TF officer posted to 6/ Gloucestershire from 4/Royal Scots, Edinburgh Rifles.

16 Greenwell, *Infant in Arms*, p. 180.

fortunate to miss any of the engagements in the quieter northern divisional sector and returned a remarkable total of only seven other rank fatalities between them. It is unclear why these two battalions, which were both up to about the average strength within the division, were not selected to take part in any of the larger engagements.

The infantry received 49 new officers during the month and a little below 700 other ranks as drafts. It is known that several of the officers posted to 5/Warwickshire came from the regiment's 3/8th Battalion but the majority of other officers seem to have come from a range of regiments including the Highland Light Infantry and the Hampshire. Similarly, little is known about the origins of the other ranks except that 8/Worcestershire noted one of its drafts "consisted mainly of regulars." Whatever their origins, those who arrived just as the division was being relieved, as well as the survivors of the battles during the month and before, were shortly to undertake a move northwards. They were to go to another relatively quiet area before next being able to enjoy several weeks to learn and polish the new skills which the infantry were now expected to acquire.

The first few days out of the front area were spent in and around Péronne. Working parties were needed for unloading coal at railhead, but there was time for general cleaning, disinfecting blankets, bathing, drawing fresh clothing and inter-platoon football tournaments. Inoculations were given, officers were ordered to practise the use of their revolvers and because at least one CO had been "working up a 'hate' for a considerable time against those unlucky individuals"[17] who could not ride, officers were required to attend a riding school. A conference for all brigade commanders and their staffs convened by Fanshawe was followed by three days of brigade training and tactical schemes for commanding officers. The scenario posed was very similar to that which had faced the division on 18 March as it was about to enter Péronne. The three infantry brigade commanders, their battalion COs, OCs field companies and at least one battery commander had to plan the staff work for a two brigade advance into the town. Unfortunately, and just as the division as a whole was beginning to think it was about to enjoy a prolonged period out of the line, training was suspended when it was ordered at short notice to relieve 11th Division.[18] The first brigade and its attached units was ordered to leave the following morning at 0600, with the other two brigades following quickly afterwards. It was hoped 'it may be possible' to give the artillery and field companies, who had only just come out of their attachment to 42nd and 59th Divisions, "a short rest before moving."[19] Major General Fanshawe had just left on leave so command for the move devolved upon the temporary divisional commander, Brigadier General Watt. The march northwards was a testing one for units which had

17 Wright, *First Buckinghamshire Battalion*, p63

18 Falls, *Official History 1917 Vol. I*, footnote citation p. 475 states that 48th Division was chosen to relieve 11th Division, which was under orders for Flanders, to save 1st Australian Division moving from Bullecourt.

19 Two of the field companies remained with 42nd Division until 12 May and left with other elements of 48th Division only two days later.

spent so long in the mud of the trenches. In broiling heat and laden with packs and other equipment, 275 men of 145 Brigade fell out with exhaustion. Lessons had been learnt, however, and the following day's march from Combles to Bancourt was easier because it was led by the band and the pace was kept deliberately slow.

When they it reached the new divisional area, which stretched from Havrincourt Wood, over the Bapaume – Cambrai road towards Lagnicourt, one officer at least thought it "depressing country…with the litter of war" but the troops were surprised and pleased with the accommodation available. The area had been devastated during the German withdrawal but the diarist of 4/Ox&Bucks noted this was the best supplied area since "we crossed the Somme" and 241 Brigade RFA recorded it was the first time since it landed that it had been accommodated in a standing camp. There were still some undiscovered booby traps which did occasionally cause problems and the broken and scarred land with its confusing trench layout temporarily bewildered new arrivals. Furthermore, most of it lay uncomfortably under the gaze of the German system. The Germans did, initially however, seem compliant. One scribe believed any aggressive activity by the division was "sternly discouraged" because it was being preserved for the Flanders offensive but another, more belligerent individual, thought that the Germans, "soon showed by their unpardonable neglect to come, that they would have to be fetched out."[20] On his return from the UK, Major General Fanshawe adopted the latter policy. He immediately ordered the division to initiate a policy of frequent active patrolling to reconnoitre and discover the location of enemy posts. He wanted particular attention paid to those close to the Spoil Heap[21] which lay to the north of the Hermes-Havrincourt road on the canal bank. As early as 20 May, strong patrols from 5/Gloucestershire and 4/Ox&Bucks were sent out to examine the Spoil Heap and to take and hold two enemy posts on the west side of the canal.

On 21 May, Fanshawe laid out his intent in a document defining divisional policy. In addition to the constant reconnaissance of no man's land by night and close observation through telescopes by day, small local tactical actions would be undertaken to take enemy posts in their outpost line and eventually to capture the Spoil Heap. This would improve the division's jumping off position should any attempt to cross the canal be made in the coming months. Fanshawe considered the division would probably eventually become involved in the capture of Havrincourt village and the Flesquieres ridge beyond but for the moment acknowledged divisional strength was insufficient to man all existing advanced British posts. To rationalize the sector he ordered a reduction in the number of posts sufficiently large to retain a small garrison of about two sections and a Lewis gun. What were called "combat patrols" were tasked nightly to enter the abandoned posts and stay there for a few minutes in case German patrols approached. If a patrol found the enemy already in occupation, a reserve force in the British front trenches would immediately be called to retake the position. This,

20 Stacke, *Worcester Regiment*, p. 264; Compiled, *History of 1/6th Warwickshire*, p. 40.
21 In some war diaries this is also referred to as the 'Slag Heap' and also as 'Spoil Bank'.

in other words, was to be a deliberately aggressive policy aimed at dominating no man's land, demoralizing the enemy and, it was assumed, maintain morale in the division's own units. Fanshawe was a commander who had always valued the importance of training but, given the length of line to be held in addition to the incessant demands for working parties, was forced to concede that training would be done when "opportunities offered."

Fanshawe also pointed out that active patrolling would warn of possible future German operations. He speculated the enemy might attempt to penetrate the division's defences in order to stage a major counter-attack north and south of Bapaume. Alternatively, he thought a possible thrust through Lagnicourt would threaten the British forces to the north. He insisted, therefore, on careful reconnaissance to discover whether gaps in the German wire were being made, a "bold" use of Lewis guns, a lamp alarm system and allotted fire zones for every battery. Further measures included A/241 being harnessed and ready to move one hour before daylight in case tanks approached through the half light; the reserve battery was to provide "roving guns" by day and night; pioneers of 5/Sussex were to man alarm positions alongside the brigade currently in divisional reserve and Fanshawe insisted every man in a HQ position should be able to fire his weapon and be capable of acting as a nucleus garrison.

Frequent patrolling did swiftly become a standard feature of life in the division's trenches. 4/Gloucestershire used a full company in May but when it came across an even larger German party trying to work around its flanks it quickly withdrew. 6/Warwickshire abandoned another company-sized attempt when conditions were already "unfavourable" and during its withdrawal subsequently ran into a strong German post and patrol. One platoon of 7/Worcestershire decided to lie doggo when it observed an enemy patrol creeping across its path only for the same Germans to successfully raid and bomb a post further up the line. 6/Warwickshire did rather better in mid-June when two companies, with another from 5/Warwickshire available if required, went out under the cover of a V-shaped box barrage and a creeping barrage fired by 241 Brigade. The raiders brought back one officer and seven men and went out the next night to look for their own missing. Two platoons from 4/Gloucestershire had the misfortune to run into two German patrols and a few nights later found themselves the victims of a well-laid ambush. In early June, one company of 1/Bucks supported by a RE officer and a platoon of 5/Sussex managed successfully to capture and hold a German post west of the canal and took 11 prisoners. Later in June an unsuccessful raid by 8/Warwickshire covered by 241 Brigade resulted in accusations of short shooting and consequent casualties. An "exhaustive enquiry" by the artillery brigade's own commander apparently proved the shelling to have been German, "Thus," the brigade's diarist jubilantly recorded, "triumphantly vindicating the character of the Brigade."

It seems probable that German activity increased in response to the division's policy of aggressive and frequent patrolling. Patrols often came into contact in no man's land and several battalions reported enemy patrols throwing bombs from outside the division's wire. 4/Berkshire repulsed a raid by 70 Germans who were then chased over no man's land by the Berkshire's own support platoon until it lost them in the dark. The Berkshire also recorded over two hundred 5.9 inch shells landing in a short period on two platoons of its support company and having had two of its guns knocked out in June, 241 Brigade RFA decided it was expedient to split up its sections to avoid further losses. Troops away from the front and out at rest were still liable to come under fire from the longer range German guns and enemy aircraft were another consistent threat. In Havrincourt Wood, Corporal Goburne of 8/Worcestershire managed to shoot down a German aircraft with his Lewis gun but 2/Field Ambulance suffered three bombs on its tents which fortunately did no harm to patients but destroyed several officers' tents and kits.

In the summer months, and in the absence of set piece attacks, there was a steady but never significant flow of wounded and sick through the division's field ambulances. There were occasional spurts of activity when, for example, three officers and 35 men arrived at 2/Field Ambulance following the big raid by 6/Warwickshire in June but most of the work was fairly routine. A platoon of 5/Sussex built the ambulance, which for a time also doubled as the corps' scabies station, and a new ADS at Doignes, while 3/Field Ambulance continued with its work of running the corps' rest station. This had the usual facilities of baths, laundry, defumigation plant and recreation rooms and was capable of ministering to 350 patients. The ambulance was also very proud of another service it was providing. Dentists from nearby CCS attended the rest station on certain days but what was unusual was the establishment of a dental workshop paid for by the citizens of Birmingham and manned by four technicians who were already in service with the division. The facility they provided was considered to be far more satisfactory and efficient than the normal procedure of sending men who required dental work, on the rare occasions they could be spared, to the base. The division's ADMS was clearly happy with the plaudits he and his men received for the initiative but was probably less pleased with another issue that took his time during May, June and July. Captain MacKay, former MO of 4/Berkshire was court martialled for "absence from his post and neglect of duty." Similarly, Lieutenant Baylor was accused and quickly convicted of drunkenness, reprimanded and despatched elsewhere with the recommendation that he should be found duty in 'another sphere.' Both men had been commissioned into the Territorial Force RAMC and while Baylor's case was dealt with swiftly, MacKay's took rather longer. He was eventually found guilty of the second charge and dismissed the service. By the time sentence had been passed, Colonel Young, the division's ADMS since May 1915, had been promoted to DDMS I Corps. The only other non-routine incident was the arrival of a torrential storm in late June which destroyed 14 marquees of the rest station and caused significant flooding and loss of equipment.

Besides the regular patrolling, the bursts of German shelling and the continual working parties,[22] some of which involved the less dangerous task of haymaking, there

22 At least one battalion designated one of its companies as a permanent working party.

was little other activity.[23] A scheme was already in place, however, for a substantial gas attack on the German positions between Queant and Havrincourt; this had been scheduled for the night after the division took over responsibility for the line. On the division's front one thousand gas projectors, supported by 4 inch trench mortars, heavy artillery and smaller calibre guns, were to concentrate their fire on the area around the Spoil Heap. The attack was delayed several times owing to adverse winds but it did eventually take place almost two weeks after originally planned. The divisional RE and pioneers had been involved in some of the later preparatory work for the operation but most of their time was spent working on roads, maintaining bridges, improving the corps' defence line, digging wells and generally developing camp accommodation and facilities. When not working, the field companies did have rare opportunities to practise other skills such as the two day bombing course undertaken by sappers of 1/Field Company. 240 Brigade RFA hoped that it might find the opportunity to give its 'backward drivers and gunners special instruction' and the GOC 145 Brigade found time to inspect his officers' uniforms, boots, their proficiency in saluting and their compass and rapid wiring skills. Throughout the two months there were fairly frequent divisional conferences for brigadier commanders and brigade conferences for COs and adjutants. Brigade schemes, such as practising how to retake the divisional support line should it suddenly be captured during an enemy offensive, were undertaken but perhaps the most significant development was the several demonstrations to other battalions given by 6/Warwickshire towards the end of June. These exercises were entitled *The Platoon in Attack*. It seems likely that the demonstrations were partly a consequence of an earlier divisional instruction which, because of the poor weather, had caused the staff to order a reduction in the number of patrols. Another instruction had already ordered reserve battalions to use the increased time now available to practise platoon, company and battalion attacks as well as devoting more time to musketry. The artillery brigades were ordered to build dummy positions and to move 18 pdrs up to disused trenches closer to the front to give nocturnal harassing fire and the RE were to practise bridging the Canal du Nord in case the Germans withdrew as they had in March. But, two-thirds of the way through June, the worsening weather meant more time was needed to maintain the trenches and their approaches, screening roads and improving the defence lines. As evidence, however, that the pamphlets published by the Training Directorate were being studied and put into instructional programmes by corps and divisions, Major General Fanshawe stressed increased concentration on individual and collective musketry practice, the training of the four specified sections into which platoons were now split and TEWTs for officers and senior NCOs. The objective was, "To get the individual and minor units" collective training progressing and ready for "combined training in the larger units when opportunity offers." It is

23 A divisional order of 20 June instructed those units with horses to include hay making or hay cutting as part of their daily work. 5/Warwickshire noted the issue of scythes and sickles.

unknown whether 6/Warwickshire had mastered the new platoon skills more successfully or quickly than other units but during July the recent tactical developments were to be addressed over a longer and more concentrated period of training.

The South Midland was relieved by 3rd Division early in July. In scorching heat the division marched away from the front zone and quickly felt the effects of having been so long in the trenches. 144 Brigade reported "many" as having fallen out on the first day and 6/Gloucestershire alone sent 30 men to the field ambulance. In comparison, 4/Berkshire claimed only one many fell out. The further they marched from the front the brighter the mood. The selection of 145 Brigade's first night's bivouac position was "not a happy one" but after that "the men marched splendidly [and were] highly delighted to find civilians and undamaged houses." 4/Ox&Bucks noted the "great enthusiasm aroused at the sight of an estaminet" and on arrival at the training area troops were allowed a day to "enjoy themselves." 143 Brigade was able to hold what it thought was its first full church parade and a memorial service for the fallen of 1 July 1916 yet, as the training programme of six hours a day began in earnest on 7 July, time was still found for sports, cinema and the concert party. The divisional area was around Adinfer, Fremicourt and Pommiers, much of which had been devastated during the Somme fighting and the subsequent withdrawal. 4/Berkshire thought it an ideal area whilst 144 Brigade HQ complained of a lack of suitable ground. TEWTs were conducted for senior commanders and their staffs, divisional schemes were held over old trenches near Morchies while brigade exercises were organized nearer to the specific brigade camps. In the afternoons and evenings regular conferences for COs and above pored over and analyzed the outcomes of the various schemes. There were battalion practices with and without transport, the artillery overhauled its guns while the field ambulances practised map reading and route marching as well as medical skills. It was obvious to all that a major attack was about to take place. War diaries record lecturers to officers and NCOs on "the coming offensive" and how the training, which often specified the use of pamphlet *SS. 143*, "was along the lines the battalion may have to work with in the big attack in Belgium."[24]

Units were also brought significantly closer to establishment during this period. There had been very few drafts been May and June so the rifle strength of most battalions was probably 550-600. Despite the presence of some physical deformities, 4/Berkshire recorded the arrival of a "good lot" of just over 30 in May and in July, 5/Warwickshire received 206 from a Training Reserve Battalion, 6/Warwickshire took 232 and 4/Gloucestershire seven officers and 280 other ranks. Most of the 145 men

24 Following an embarrassing occurrence the officers' riding school established in May was revived for the benefit of junior officers. A second lieutenant was ordered to take a company out on a route march but he returned after a short while leading his horse and complaining he 'couldn't make it go.' Junior officers were then ordered to learn to ride but the school was abandoned when the horse belonging to the instructing major decided to take himself off to the stables. The other horses followed with desperate 'purple-faced young officers clinging to their saddles.' Vaughan, *Some Desperate Glory*, p. 178.

who arrived in one draft to 8/Worcestershire were from the Norfolk Regiment and were considered to be of "good physique and well trained" while a group of 58 who arrived at battalion HQ a few days later were assessed as "poorly trained." 4/Berkshire received one draft of 92, all of who had been out before either with the battalion or 6/Berkshire, another of 65,[25] all from London and with three months' training, and one of 43 which came from the Norfolk and Bedfordshire Regiments. This raised its establishment to 930, the highest it had been since it arrived in France. The ADMS inspected a draft to 6/Worcestershire which, he thought, "were up to the average of the reinforcements now arriving." The arrival of theses reinforcements during the month meant battalion strengths were raised to between 870– 930 other ranks.

After nearly three weeks of training and recreation the infantry moved north. One officer remembered being "restless and unhappy at the termination of our jolly holiday" but at least the infantry had had a good rest and a welcome change of scenery.[26] In comparison, the three field companies, the pioneers and the machine-gun companies had enjoyed only a fraction of the infantry's time out of the line. They were to have only another five days rest at Poperinghe before beginning work in the forward area under 39th Division. They maintained roads, improved shelters along Canal Bank, cut new tracks through the bank towards Irish Farm, were shelled out of their first camp and suffered from the effects of mustard gas. 5/Sussex had 100 gas casualties during the month and 1/Field Company almost 60 in a nine-day period. When the infantry left the training area they were considered to be in "splendid physical condition", sang lustily on the march and were delighted when arriving at Houtkerque because "every house appeared to be an estaminet." Unfortunately, the GOC 145 Brigade was not happy with the length of the men's hair. The diarist of 4/Ox&Bucks recorded the great man's fury in light vein. The brigadier apparently stormed away from a battalion inspection "in disgust" having seen the length of one individual's hair. There followed "a great strafe" and the subsequent note of, "Barbers collapsing through overwork. Curly locks go by the board. The camp resembles a prisoner of war cage." One day after his outburst, the brigadier re-inspected the battalion and expressed satisfaction. Divisional HQ opened at Border Camp west of Ypres on 22 July, with the infantry brigades close by. There were losses of men and animals almost immediately from bombs and long range shells and parties of all three field ambulances went further forward to assist 39th Division's ambulances and a nearby CCS.

Conferences of senior officers were held to detail what was expected of the division in the days to come. 48th Division was now part of XVIII Corps, which consisted of itself, 11th (Northern), 39th and 51st (Highland) Divisions. Orders for future operations had begun arriving at divisional HQ during the training period and gradually the essential information was disseminated down to brigade and eventually battalion

25 There was also a draft of about 150 sappers which seems to have been approximately equally divided between the three field companies.

26 Ibid, p. 181.

level. This process was done largely by second-in-commands after they had attended corps' school. The build up of troops and resources in the Salient was difficult if not impossible to hide and Ypres was, of course, the obvious place to attempt any exploitation of the success at Messines. Apart from the precise time and day of the assault, the element of surprise was probably unachievable so, as one scribe optimistically decided, "secrecy was to a great extent sacrificed with the hope of gaining greater efficiency."[27] Battalion officers were informed that XVIII Corps was to attack with 51st on the left and 39th Division on the right; 11th and 48th Divisions were in reserve respectively to those leading formations. Two brigades of 39th Division were to advance to the line of the Steenbeke and the village of St Julien where the third brigade would pass through and push out patrols to von Tirpitz and Genoa Farms and Mon (Maison) du Hibou. Fanshawe told his senior commanders that 48th Division would probably relieve 39th Division between two and six days after Z Day but that they must be ready to move up earlier if severe fighting demanded it. The expected jumping off point for the division, which would advance on an as yet undecided one or two brigade front, would be from around Triangle Farm to a junction with 11th Division to the north-west. The divisional front would thus be about 1,750 yards. Having taken Winchester and Wellington Farms, the final objectives were farms and houses lying south-east of Poelcappelle. The capture of these would entail an advance of about 3,800 yards.

As events were later to prove, these were outrageously ambitious targets. For the time being, however, planning went ahead on the assumption that the enormous concentration of heavy and field artillery, the huge dumps of ammunition, the deployment of tanks and with the infantry now trained in more efficient tactics a way would be smashed through the German defences. Divisions were instructed to be prepared to pursue and to ensure their supporting arms were capable of following swiftly and efficiently behind the cavalry and infantry. Medical officers were ordered to be sure they chose suitable points close to an extending evacuation chain for their RAPs; ambulances were to have runners, orderlies and additional stretcher bearers ready to move forward to establish new ADS; the means of providing a water supply to an advancing army were laid down in detail; staff captains busied themselves with ensuring there would be adequate ammunition and rations brought forward while brigade majors rushed to and fro between battalions and artillery brigades passing on orders from their brigadiers and the divisional staff. Several officers were designated to act as liaison with neighbouring brigades and divisions as well as with the artillery units. 48th Division's artillery fired in support of 39th Division on 31 July, as did the division's three machine-gun companies. The sappers and pioneers continued to work under corps' orders but most sections and platoons were effectively employed alongside those of 39th Division. A section of 48th Division Signal Company was in a forward report centre in Canal Bank. Often under shell fire, one sapper wrote: "Noise terrible. Have had no good night's rest since I left Adinfer. Suffering terrible

27 Wright, *First Buckingham Battalion*, p. 67.

hardships but must stick it bravely … No one can realize what I am going through."[28] Further to the rear, there was little for the infantry to do in their camps around St Jan as they waited for Z Day. The shells of the heavies roared over their heads, battalion officers, confident of the training and of their men, passed among their platoons checking equipment and speaking words of encouragement, and men scribbled letters or postcards home. According to at least one infantry captain, "Every arrangement appeared to be so thoroughly thought out that it seemed impossible that the attack could be anything but a complete success."[29] All would depend on the effectiveness of the barrage in destroying the enemy defences and silencing his batteries. And then, of course, it started to rain.

28 R. Bishop, 'A Signaller's Diary'. This unpublished source was discovered on-line but offered no reference or origin other than Bishop served in the divisional signal company.
29 Wright, *First Buckinghamshire Battalion*, p. 67.

7

The Third Battle of Ypres

During the months between the end of the Somme campaign and the division's arrival in the area to the rear of the Ypres salient, there had been several important changes in the composition of the South Midland's senior positions. Together with the new training regime, the arrival and departure of a handful of senior commanders, some of which had been forced by wounds and ill health, were designed to make 48th Division a leaner and more efficient formation. The divisional commander, Major General Fanshawe, remained in post, as did two of his three infantry brigade commanders, but the division had a new GSO1, AA&QMG, CRA and CRE. There were also several changes in battalion and battery commanders. The longer serving members of the division's hierarchy and units may well have had memories of Ypres from the time they had spent in the Ploegsteert sector in 1915 but the area to which they were again moving was by 1917 a much grimmer place. Most divisions of the BEF were to spend at least some time in the region between July and November 1917, with a good number being rotated through the campaign several times. 48th Division was reasonably fortunate in that it was to take a major part in really only two of the set piece battles which ultimately comprised the Third Battle of Ypres. The experience, however, was to be a shattering one, and one from which it would emerge as a much altered formation.

On 31 July, the division's three infantry brigades waited in their 'positions of readiness.' They had practised how to advance towards their known objectives, watches had been synchronized, stores drawn and all they could do now was to wait for the order to move east and pass through 39th Division. The troops waited and watched, initially with expectation, but anticipation was later replaced by growing indifference to the comings and goings of red-tabbed staff officers. At 0800 on 1 August, 143 Brigade was placed on one hour's notice to advance to the Old British Line and to come under the orders of 39th Division. At 1130 this was extended to two and a half hours' notice and soon afterwards the GSO1 visited all brigades with the news that there was likely to be a change of plans. The following day, and still with no news of any real gains having been made, one company of 145 Brigade was sent forward to act as stretcher bearers for 39th Division. The uncertainty came to a temporary end on 3 August when divisional HQ received orders for the infantry to relieve the troops of 39th Division during the night of 5-6 August. 145 Brigade moved forward to Dambre Camp and by 0315 on 6 August, it had completed the relief of the tired 39th Division. A patrol ventured east of the Steenbeke, a previously placid stream which the rain and shattered banks were causing rapidly to develop into a fetid lake, and captured two German soldiers. When the brigade again reached the relatively safety of Dambre Camp in the early hours of 9 August, the diarist of 4/Berkshire reflected on what had been the battalion's first salutary experience of the Salient. He offered a physical description of the terrain and the accommodation available at the front and recorded the continuous shelling had been "most trying to all ranks." The battalion had suffered 11 dead and over 30 wounded, totals, he thought, which would have been worse had it not been for "the successful leading and handling of their commands by the company officers and NCOs who were well backed up by all their men."

By 9 August, Brigadier General Sladen, GOC 143 Brigade, had command of the divisional front which was held by a composite brigade of two battalions, one from each of 143 and 144 Brigades. Further to the rear, army and corps staffs had been busily preparing new plans to reignite the campaign after the disappointment of the first few days. In consequence of these new schemes a divisional order announced that at a date still to be announced, 145 Brigade would attack the German position known as the Langemarck Line. In preparation for the offensive, which was later scheduled for 12 August, and with 4/ and 6/Gloucestershire holding the line alternately, 144 Brigade assumed responsibility for the entire divisional sector.

Once it had been withdrawn from the front positions 143 Brigade resumed training, but heavy rain and the constant demands for working parties interfered with the scheduled programme. This, in reality however, amounted to little more than continuing to hone the already practised skills of PT, range finding, route marches and platoon formations. The CO of 8/Warwickshire led his junior officers on a compass test and Lieutenant General Maxse, GOC XVIII Corps, lectured staffs and unit and company commanders on their leadership and command roles and his expectations of them. To disseminate information and to reiterate what the responsibilities of the different units and their officers were, there were frequent divisional and brigade conferences for senior commanders. A selection of officers and sergeants attended a lecture about capabilities and liaison given by the CRA, and others visited a replica model of the ground they were to attack. Staff, meanwhile, dealt and assimilated the growing number of orders arriving from corps HQ. The divisional role was for 145 Brigade to take the Green Line which ran close or through farms, houses or features known as Winnipeg, Spot Farm, Springfield and Vancouver, and then to advance to a section of the Gheluvelt – Langemarck Line. Outposts were to be established at Clifton House and von Tirpitz Farm and a general line was to be secured connecting Stroppe, Genoa and Hubner Farms with Flora Cot. Once taken, sappers and pioneers would build strong points at Jew Hill, Winnipeg, Springfield and Mon du Hibou. The other two infantry brigades were to be deployed in depth behind 145

Taken from the northern end of St Julien this photo looks north-east across the fields to the position of Springfield. Behind the farm, which is close to its original position, the rebuilt *Totenmuhle* can be seen near to the site of Genoa Farm. (Author)

ready to confront any major counter-attack. To protect the attacking battalions of 145 Brigade there was to be a machine-gun barrage and a creeping artillery barrage moving 100 yards every five minutes. Smoke would be used to cover the scheduled pause on the Green Line. The brigade would work with tanks from G Battalion, have one battery of 18 pdrs at immediate call for any target which appeared and a further two batteries to follow behind 143 and 144 Brigades if they were called forward to resist a counter-attack.

The influence and impact of the ever-growing number of training pamphlets can be seen in the schemes devised to overcome the perennial problem of communications. Divisional orders stated the general system to be employed was based on *SS. 148 Forward Intercommunications in Battle*. The pamphlet's strictures would, it was stressed, be "strictly adhered to." This meant 145 Brigade was to have two wireless sets, one for the brigade HQ at van Heule Farm and the other for the brigade forward station which would open on its capture at Hillock Farm. At least two metallic circuits were to be laid from the cable station near Mouse Trap Farm to brigade HQ and from there to Hillock Farm. These were to be supplemented by visual stations using Lucas lamps at the same sites. The brigade would also have two power buzzers for the attacking battalions in addition to the usual quota of runners, 20 birds from the pigeon loft at Vlamertinghe and a contact aircraft which would be signalled as prescribed by *SS. 148* and *SS. 135*.[1] When the attacking battalions were at their jumping off point on Y/Z night they were instructed to send the unlikely coded message of "Socks arrived at Transport Lines complete", or alternatively, "…pairs short."[2]

Comprehensive as the preparations seemed, they were not without difficulties. Captain Steward, brigade major for 143 Brigade, for example, questioned the time allowed for the brigade to concentrate, feed and march to its assembly area behind 145 Brigade. Similarly, the ADMS had briefed his OC field ambulances about how the evacuation chain was to operate, and they in turn organized their staff and teams accordingly. On the night before the attack, however, a spanner was thrown into the carefully completed works when Captain Soutter, in charge of the bearer teams for 3/Field Ambulance, reported sick with acute tonsillitis. Two companies of 8/Worcestershire had been detailed as additional stretcher bearers to the ambulances and were also providing squads to man stragglers' posts and guards for any prisoners taken.[3] All three field companies were already either close to or working in the forward zone and the artillery had been firing in support of 11th Division for several days. On 15 August, as the division's units moved up to their assembly positions in showers and strong wind, it fired practice barrages over the designated corps and divisional boundaries. Having satisfactorily registered on those targets it then developed into the more usual form of preparatory bombardment.

At 0445 on 16 August, 145 Brigade began its advance. On its left was 11th (Northern) Division and to its right, 36th (Ulster) Division.[4] 5/Gloucestershire was on the division's right, with the Bucks to its left and the Oxfords on the left flank. In brigade reserve was 4/Berkshire. Waiting in divisional reserve on the right was 8/Warwickshire of 143 Brigade and behind to the left was 7/Worcestershire of 144 Brigade. The attack was roughly north-eastwards towards the German defences of the Gheluvelt – Langemarck Line on the Gravenstafel ridge. The brigade's jumping off positions lay east of the flooded Steenbeke, with the three battalions advancing on a two company front. Random enemy shelling and the occasional British short caused several casualties as the battalions formed up but only a weak counter-barrage fell behind the forward positions. Within minutes, however, it developed into a more solid and organized effort with a particularly heavy concentration of shells on Kitchener Wood and St Julien, and shrapnel falling on the line of the Steenbeke. Within an hour of the start such was the intensity of the German barrage it was reported to be impossible to get into St Julien; all communications from the village forward were also quickly severed. When reports did begin to filter back, some by runner and pigeon,

1 The tanks of 20th Company G Battalion were also to have 22 birds and the FOOs four.
2 The number of 'pairs short' would represent the number of casualties known to have been suffered on the way up.
3 The other two companies went to Canal Bank as support to 145 Brigade.
4 Eight tanks had been allocated to assist 48th and 11th Divisions. They had been told not to utilise the roads in case of traffic congestion but as their commanders decided cross country routes were impossible, they abandoned their effort.

others from wounded officers and NCOs, it appeared progress was being made. It was known the leading waves had run into severe frontal and flanking fire as they began the gentle climb towards the ridge, but Border House and even Springfield were reported to have been secured. It was suggested approximately 25 Bucks had managed to fight their way into Springfield and establish a Lewis gun post. The leading wave of the right company had been all but annihilated from the frontal fire but the second and third waves had closed up and then fought a hand-to-hand encounter in the ruined farm. By the time the German garrison was dead or captured, the British barrage was far ahead and the surviving Bucks too few in number to attempt to follow. Machine gun and rifle fire fell upon them from three directions and they withdrew to a little south of Hillock Farm. To their left the Oxfords were held up in front of Triangle Farm from where at about 1000 hours a German counter-attack threatened to sweep away the gains of both battalions. Three Vickers had been brought forward and the German threat was contained.

At 0745, Brigadier General Watt, GOC 145 Brigade, signalled to divisional HQ that he wanted to use his brigade reserve (4/Berkshire) to reinforce the Bucks and to exploit what he believed to be their success. He pointed out, however, that because one half company of the Berkshire had already been knocked out by the barrage, he wanted to send another full company to help 5/Gloucestershire on the right to advance beyond Border House and Janet Farm. As the battalion's other platoons were occupied

Triangle Farm is on the right and the position of the concrete blockhouse of Mon du Hibou lay in the field to the left. (Author)

elsewhere, Watt wanted Major General Fanshawe to release the leading battalion of 143 Brigade. He was told by the GSO1 that the divisional general was not yet ready to release any of the divisional reserve and that Watt must deploy what was left of his own brigade reserve as he thought appropriate. Two hours later Fanshawe did order all companies of 7/Worcestershire, the lead battalion in 144 Brigade, to cross the Steenbeke and for 8/Worcestershire to move forward to replace it on Admiral's Road.[5] This order was probably in response to a message from corps HQ stressing that the capture of Winnipeg and Jew Hill were of "the first importance." 5/Gloucestershire was thought to be holding Jew Hill and another message timed at 0945 claimed the battalion had also taken Winnipeg. This was followed less than an hour later by one which rebutted the previous assertion and stated the battalion was held up by machine-gun fire from Winnipeg and from gun pits close by.

Things were not going well for the Oxfords on the brigade's other flank. The two tanks allocated had never arrived and within 200 yards of the Steenbeke the companies had been held up by "deadly" machine-gun fire. The Oxfords went to ground 100 yards south of the blockhouse at Mon du Hibou and Triangle Farm. Most officers were already casualties and all communications to the rear were down; neither were they were in touch with the Bucks to their right or 11/Manchester to their left.[6] The companies sought what little shelter they could from the fire and waited. At brigade HQ Brigadier General Watt had little precise idea of what was going on. By 1100 he was sure his brigade had not taken Springfield, Hillock Farm or Winnipeg but later in the morning, and then again in the afternoon, there were reports that troops had entered and taken stretches of the Langemarck Line. The Bucks were known to be using about 100 prisoners to dig strong points for them near Springfield and the OC of a company of 5/Sussex reported he hoped to have the St Julien – van Heule road open for field guns by 1800. To add to the general uncertainty, even when messages were received at brigade HQ, whether from poor handwriting or a liberal covering of mud, Watt and his brigade major had difficulty reading them. Soon after midday Watt spoke to Fanshawe and gave him a report of progress as he understood it to be. He proposed to use two of his reserve companies of Berkshire in the evening to support the Oxfords and the Bucks and requested divisional HQ make more runners available. He was denied these reinforcements and Fanshawe remained reluctant to bring back the barrage from the Langemarck Line because it was unclear as to where there might be pockets of 145 Brigade forward of the known positions. Watt was told to make use of the trench mortars attached to each of his four battalions, but their effectiveness was already limited by the few men available to carry forward ammunition. He was

5 7/Worcestershire had been instructed to have one company on the Steenbeke by Zero+3 hours and the remaining three by Zero+5.

6 The right of 11th Division had managed to advance rather further than 145 Brigade but was held up in front of the Cockcroft. 11th Division's left had also gained its final objective but the failure of 143 Brigade to keep abreast to the right of 11th Division handicapped 34 Brigade's effort to get beyond the strong point.

also told, however, that the leading battalions of 143 and 144 Brigades would be ready by dusk to assault the strong points holding up the advance. Fanshawe had already issued orders to these brigades instructing them to send patrols to "stalk" and capture certain positions which would then establish a line roughly Wurst Farm-Winnipeg for 143 Brigade and Vancouver-Triangle Farm-Mon du Hibou for 144. If these objectives could not be achieved by dusk, the operation was to be continued into the night. Once they had secured these lines, 143 and 144 Brigades would relieve 145 Brigade.

Immediately Brigadier General Sladen, GOC 143 Brigade, was informed that his brigade was to fight its way through to Springfield, which an erroneous message timed at 1600 had informed him was back in British hands, he telephoned divisional HQ. He told the GSO1 he would use one battalion on a two company front, one either side of the road, to get to Springfield. The GSO1 immediately responded that this was not the tactic prescribed by Major General Fanshawe. The divisional commander, and as Sladen was informed also the corps commander, wanted the operation executed by "stalking" and by the use of rifle grenades and light trench mortars. 8/Warwickshire was to attempt to push on towards Winnipeg on a three company front while one company of 7/Worcestershire was tasked to go for Mon du Hibou, Triangle Farm and Vancouver. The fact that just one company was detailed for this ambitious task suggests Brigadier General Done considered the project to be impossible. To further increase the likelihood of failure there was to be no barrage because British troops were believed to be sheltering in shell holes close to the objectives. At 1930, C Company of 7/Worcestershire began to advance; about 350 yards east of the Steenbeke it was brought to a halt by withering fire from Mon du Hibou. The troops dug in 200 yards short of the blockhouse[7] and then, to add to their misery, began receiving shorts from British heavy guns. Brigadier General Done informed divisional HQ that he did not intend to send another company to reinforce the failure but to wait for an organized barrage. This was duly ordered and at around 0230 on 17 August, B Company made its attempt. One report suggested some men did get into Mon du Hibou but were bombed out while others believed the attack reached no further than about 100 yards from the blockhouse. The survivors dug in where they could and were to remain under shell fire in these exposed positions until relieved by 8/Worcestershire almost 24 hours later. Based on the ultimately "unsuccessful" attempt by several Germans to surrender, the battalion later reported the enemy "appeared to have low moral."[8] In marked contrast, Lieutenant Colonel Clarke's post-battle report thought German morale was "good". Yet, despite the ground, the strength and morale of the German defenders and the overall failure to take its objectives, Clarke believed the fighting spirit and morale of his own battalion, and of 145 Brigade in general, was "excellent".

7 The battalion diarist later described the blockhouse as 'an extraordinary building.'

8 Another report from 144 Brigade wrote of Germans 'vigorously' shooting their comrades who tried to surrender.

The diarist of 1/Bucks also thought his men were "wonderfully cheerful" when in the early hours of 18 August they collapsed into Dambre Camp.

It was a long relief for 145 Brigade during the night of 17-18 August. The relieving companies had first to locate the brigade's dispersed outposts and were instructed immediately to relay those positions to their respective brigades' HQ. Contact aircraft had reported flares further east than divisional HQ believed to be possible but it was decided that should any isolated posts be discovered forward of where they might be expected to exist, they were to be brought in. Any posts, however, which were found near to Springfield and which were thought to be viable were ordered to be maintained and reinforced. Apart from some irregular shelling and intermittent sniping by machine guns and riflemen, the hours of daylight were largely uneventful. One battalion later recorded that rations had not always arrived but that men were coping by eating iron rations and plundering from the nearby dead. The stress and tensions of the days were, however, evident to witness. The diarist of 7/Worcestershire, whose own battalion had itself suffered badly, observed the men of 145 Brigade trudging back towards the canal and noted they had had "a very hard time." Fanshawe was, of course, acutely aware of how demanding the two days had been and was concerned that there were still posts of 145 Brigade as yet unrelieved and even undiscovered. He wanted to get those men, who were probably holding their positions because they had not been told to do otherwise, to the rear. He proposed an attack on a two brigade front that same evening, to be followed the next day by another push beyond the original Green Line.

The corps commander demurred and stated that even with the assistance of tanks such an attack ran too many risks and could not be justified as a means of extracting what was an unknown number of men. Rather paradoxically Fanshawe argued, "it would be worth 1,000 casualties to get even 100 men out" but the corps commander retorted by saying that because the division was likely to have to stay and fight for "some considerable time" it could not afford to sustain that many casualties for such a dubious operation. He explained his staff was working on a plan by which tanks would get up to St Julien that evening (17 August) leaguer there in the ruins all next day and attack the following morning. He wanted the infantry to act as what he called "adjuncts" to the tanks for mopping up strong points from the rear while the tanks attacked frontally. He instructed Fanshawe to select two companies from 144 Brigade to work with the tanks but did concur with Fanshawe's compromise plan to use two companies of 143 Brigade that night to try to get in touch with any posts in the area around Springfield. Patrols from 144 Brigade also went out and discovered a strong enemy post 40 yards west of Hillock Farm and a substantial out post line south of Mon du Hibou. By dawn on 18 August, patrols from 143 Brigade were convinced there were no isolated posts containing troops of 145 Brigade close to Springfield. With a better idea now of who was where, Fanshawe agreed that the barrage could be brought back onto the Red Line in preparation for the next attack.

Major General Fanshawe wanted his troops to know that the division was likely to have to hold and extend the same sector of line for the next 10 to 14 days. He despatched messages of appreciation to the men of 145 Brigade for the effort they had made and others addressing the division as a whole. He wanted the troops to understand that by continual sniping and frequent bursts of machine-gun fire, the division would "establish moral superiority" over the enemy. The result, he predicted, would be "no German [would] dare move by day in sight of our lines." By regularly advancing small tactical posts towards the Langemarck Line, he continued, pressure would be maintained on the Germans and better jumping off points secured for future attacks. It was not just about taking enemy positions, Fanshawe insisted, "but the determination of the fighting despite all the difficulties that shows the enemy he is beaten and must give in." The brigades, he continued, were to be taken out of the line in turn for periods of about six days in order to refit, bath and rest. 145 Brigade was to be the first to experience this new *roulement*.[9]

Preparations for the corps commander's next attack began late on 17 August and continued into the next day with a conference between tank, company and platoon commanders. It was agreed the tanks, seven of which were already in St Julien and camouflaged to hide from prying aerial eyes, would advance under a smoke barrage. Once they had silenced hostile fire from the objectives the infantry would rush in and secure the ruins. 144 Brigade's company was taken from 8/Worcestershire, with the objectives of Mon du Hibou and Triangle Farm, while a company of 5/Warwickshire made for Hillock Farm. A practice smoke barrage was fired in the afternoon and the lines of both 143 and 144 Brigades were substantially thinned during the evening. At 0445 on 19 August, the barrage poured smoke and shrapnel onto the St Julien – Langemarck road and the tanks of G Battalion and supporting infantry made their way towards the objectives. 5/Warwickshire found Hillock Farm and the gun pits just to its east unoccupied and proceeded with consolidation;[10] 8/Worcestershire reported its operation a "complete success" with the blockhouse at Mon du Hibou stormed and the garrison of Triangle Farm apparently fleeing at the approach of a tank.[11] As far as demonstrating divisional fighting power was concerned, these were small but important tactical advances. Furthermore, what was considered to be another satisfactory feature of the division's first four days of real fighting in the Salient, and one which materially affected morale, was the manner in which its casualty evacuation procedure had worked.

9 Fanshawe also reaffirmed that when battalions went back into the line a battle surplus of at least 10 percent of its strength would remain in camp.

10 A message from the company HQ sent at 1300 reported the platoon sent to capture the gun pits had disappeared and that there was considerable sniping coming from Springfield. Whether the platoon turned up later or its members taken prisoner is open to some conjecture.

11 The tanks did not risk leaving the road but their presence does seem to have had a psychological effect on the German garrisons. Stacke, *Worcestershire Regiment*, p. 282, called it a 'brilliant little success.'

For the initial three battalion attack, the regimental aid posts had been located at Alberta, St Julien and van Heule Farm. Depending on the condition of the roads, bearers either carried or wheeled the stretchers to the divisional collecting post (DCP) via a system of relay posts. The DCP consisted of a trench covered by sections of elephant iron and was housed in the former German trench known to the British as California Trench. Elements of 2/Field Ambulance were responsible for this section of the operation and for despatching the wounded, again usually by carried stretcher, to the ADS at Duhallow on the canal bank. On 16 August, 264 lying cases were treated at the DCP but by the following afternoon the number of new cases "fell considerably." The ADS was managed by 1/Field Ambulance which then passed the wounded further down the line to the MDS where sections of 3/Field Ambulance were working. About 100 infantry were sent to help the RAMC and regimental bearers in their work. These groups were changed daily but by 18 August all infantry bearers had been replaced by RAMC personnel.

The relief at the success of the minor operations to take Mon du Hibou and Triangle Farm with tanks was reflected in the haste that new orders were issued for another, similar attack. During the evening of 19 August, divisional HQ announced 48th Division would be part of a larger operation undertaken by its own XVIII and the adjoining XIX Corps. The first objectives were to be the same familiar strong points in front of the Langemarck Line. These were to be taken on 22 August with the help of 12 tanks, followed three or four days later by an assault with 20 tanks on the Blue Line. Both attacks would be on a two brigade front. When the initial orders were issued it was still undecided whether the attack would be executed in the same way as the operation earlier in the day, with special parties detailed to assist the tanks, or whether the tanks should help the infantry if *they* were held up by strong points. It was tentatively assumed both attacks would take place at dawn. The reason for the caution was concern over whether the tanks would be able to get up the St Julien-Winnipeg road. The decision that the assault should be a tank attack, supported by infantry for the mopping up process, was made the following day; the tanks' objectives were Winnipeg, the village cemetery just north of the cross roads near Winnipeg, Spot Farm, Springfield and Vancouver. Six tanks were to move from positions north of Hillock Farm with 144 Brigade in support, while another six working with 143 Brigade would advance from Jew Hill. A covering barrage would start creeping at the rate of 100 yards every eight minutes from Zero+10 and smoke would be kept on the Winnipeg – Springfield road until Zero+20. The infantry would follow the barrage to a line about 150 yards from the Green Line and then "definite and complete" parties were to work closely with a particular tank to take a designated site. One brigade of field artillery was to be ready to break up German counter-attacks and 16 guns from the brigades' MGC were to assist with consolidation and provide a defensive barrage.

Sappers of 225th Tunnelling Company had managed to repair the road bridge in St Julien sufficiently for it to bear the tanks and engineers from the division's field companies had removed fallen trees from the road out of the village. The assaulting battalions (5/Warwickshire on the right and 7/Warwickshire on the left of 143 Brigade, and 6/Gloucestershire of 144 to their left) moved forward during the night 21-22 August.[12] As always, finding their allotted position was problematic, made worse on this occasion by Major Pryor's assertion that he did not have "enough intelligent fellows" in his battalion to act as guides. 6/Gloucestershire and the two Warwicks battalions did, however, reach their jumping off points and several tanks also seem to have left their start points on time at 0455.[13] The first reports were encouraging. At 0630, 6/Gloucestershire reported it was within 50 yards of its objective and in touch with 143 Brigade which had taken Springfield; one tank was reported to be "dealing" with Vancouver. Reports then became less optimistic. At 0840, 144 Brigade said 6/ Gloucestershire's right had not got up which was causing the left to fall back, the tank "dealing" with Vancouver was not, in fact, "dealing" with it at all, and the Warwicks were seen to be withdrawing from Springfield. This was confirmed a few minutes later when 7/Warwickshire claimed its right company was held up in front of Spot Farm because a tank had failed to silence its defenders, that its left company and its accompanying tank were indeed withdrawing from Springfield and that the village cemetery remained in German hands. At 1021, 143 Brigade wired the tanks had failed even to pass Janet Farm (which was incorrect) and although the leading wave of infantry had reached to within 150 yards of the Winnipeg-Springfield road, the second wave had not passed through because the tanks "had failed". To add to the disappointment, 11th Division was reported to have again advanced further than 48th Division and was now having to throw out a defensive flank on its right to cover the South Midlanders' lack of progress.

When it had become clear the attack had failed, the GSO1 asked both brigade commanders whether they could make another attempt at the same objectives that night. Both replied their troops were exhausted and that fresh ones could not be brought up in daylight. While these wires were being considered at divisional HQ, a dramatic message from the OC of the tank company arrived. Apparently he had received a message from one of his tank commanders stating that one machine was in Springfield but was surrounded by Germans. The GSO1 wired Brigadier General Sladen to order his men immediately to "rush" Springfield and join the tank. Sladen again sensibly replied that no troops could move in daylight and that even if the tank were in Springfield, the enemy would still be capable of firing on his infantry. Despite the clear advice and assessment from the commanders on the spot, both brigades received a wire at 1300 ordering another attack either before or after dark. 143 Brigade was to take the ground around Winnipeg, the cemetery and Springfield in order to secure the

12 6/Warwickshire was relieved after a five day tour on 20 August. There had been no attack and no movement above ground, with the battalion having spent the time 'simply flattened in the slime.' It had lost three officers and 80 other ranks. Compiled, *History of 1/6th Warwickshire*, p. 45

13 There is some confusion about the action of the tanks. Several war diaries mention they made it to the start line but Falls, *Official History 1917 Vol. 1*, footnote citation p. 202, notes six were hit or ditched before they even reach their starting points.

left flank of 61st Division, while 144 Brigade should also advance and get in touch with 143 at Springfield. A message from 143 Brigade's brigade major quickly followed indicating that he had no idea whether his men or Germans were in occupation of the much contested gun pits and that in his view the cemetery was probably the best defended area on his brigade's front. Fortunately, divisional HQ seems finally to have appreciated the chaos confronting both brigades and the impossibility of bring another couple of battalions forward. It issued an order at 1710 declaring there was to be no further attack that night and that the Warwicks and Gloucesters should dig in and wait. The existing order that no ground gained was to be given up remained in force.

The day had again been one of failure. The infantry certainly believed the main reason for the lack of success was the inability of the tanks to work off the road.[14] This had not mattered on 19 August because the German defenders had shown less determination to hold their positions than did their comrades three days later. The ground in front of Springfield and the village cemetery was almost impassable for infantry and certainly so for tanks. It was a forlorn hope to expect the tanks to take ground when they could ditch so easily; they then become sitting targets for German gunners. Tanks need close infantry support and even on good ground, let alone the morass near Springfield, this is not always possible. While the tanks were confined to roads, the infantry generally had to deploy across the broken ground in artillery formation or in 'worms'. Laden with equipment and handicapped by the mud, they could not keep up with the tanks' even very low speed. The new attack formations and tactics espoused in the doctrinal pamphlets were capable of achieving success on good ground but to expect the notoriously unreliable tanks and the hopelessly bogged infantry to capture concrete islands in a sea of mud held by resolute defenders was expecting too much. When darkness fell on 22 August, Jury Farm and Springfield had been taken and lost, 7/Warwickshire was thought to be in possession of the gun pits but Vancouver, Spot Farm and Pond Farm remained in German hands. 4/Gloucestershire came up during the night to relieve its sister battalion but the two Warwicks battalions remained in the line. At its furthest point, this 'line' of scattered posts was about 200 yards forward from where the attack had begun.

There was relative quiet on 23 August. The Warwicks battalions were relieved and the artillery fired a programme of short but intense bursts on the Langemarck Line. On 24 August, Germans with flamethrowers retook the gun pits but when a company of 8/Warwickshire working with 5/Warwickshire attacked them the following day the pits were again discovered to be empty. To take advantage of the relative lull, 4/Gloucestershire and 8/Warwickshire were each ordered to dig and camouflage sufficient assembly positions for two battalions. When, however, the trenches had been dug the troops were told shell fire on the dump in van Heule Farm had destroyed the camouflage material to shield them. There were more reliefs on 25 August and, on 26

14 The two Warwick battalions were succinct in their reports. They both thought the tanks had 'failed'.

August, battalions of 143 and 144 Brigades resting at Reigersburg Camp were ordered to move immediately to Dambre Camp.[15] As if that was not warning enough of a new operation, later in the day three companies from the two brigades were ordered to report next morning to the ADS on the canal bank. If any further confirmation were needed, as battalions of 143 and 144 collected equipment, drew battle stores and trudged east during the night of 26-27 August, No.2 Special Company RE was discharging gas on the division's front.

Fifth Army headquarters had ordered another attempt to be made on a reasonably broad front. Once again, 11th Division was to be on 48th Division's left, with 61st Division on the right.[16] 48th Division was to use 144 Brigade on the left to take the Gheluvelt-Langemarck Line as far south as Genoa and 143 on the right to go for Winnipeg and Springfield. The brigade would then pause for 30 minutes before advancing to attack the southern portion of the Gheluvelt – Langemarck Line. 145 Brigade, which would be in the other two brigades' assembly and jumping off positions by Zero+4 hours, would pass through the two forward brigades to take the further objectives of von Tirpitz, Stroppe and Hubner Farms. There was to be the usual creeping barrage moving at a rate of 100 yards every eight minutes, a machine-gun barrage firing over the attackers' heads, and smoke, gas and shrapnel targeted on the enemy positions for about three hours. Liaison officers for the adjoining brigades were told off, contact aircraft were to fly overhead and an 'infantry protection machine' was provided to spot and report any build up of counter-attack forces. The division was allocated four tanks, all of which would pass through Triangle Farm before splitting up and heading for individual targets. The infantry, however, were informed, "It must be clearly understood that these tanks are entirely subsidiary to the operation and in no case are infantry to await their arrival." A troop of King's Edward's Horse was detailed to maintain communications between brigade and battalion HQ after the capture of the Red Line and one section of RE and a pioneer company were to go forward as soon as the objectives were taken.[17] They were to assist with consolidation, lay duck boards and roads for pack and wheeled transport and provide signage for routes and the site of former farms. The ADMS decided his arrangements for the wounded had worked well a few days before and opted to maintain the existing system.

During the night of 26-27 August, 8/Worcestershire moved into the assembly trenches between Hillock Farm and Triangle Farm dug earlier by the infantry and 477th Field Company. Close by on their left was 7/Worcestershire. Both battalions had been told at 2000 hours they were to attack the next day but the actual time of

15 Both camps were a little to the rear of Canal Bank.

16 61st Division was 48th Division's 2nd Line formation. This was the first occasion the two divisions had fought side by side.

17 It was left to the discretion of the troop commander as to whether his men should be mounted or dismounted.

zero was not revealed until later that night. In addition to their rations for two days, brigade had provided sections with tins of *Auto-Bouillante*[18] and an extra issue of rum. The men had to sit or crouch in the partially camouflaged, breast high and flooded trenches for over 12 hours during which time they were warned not to make a noise and to remain motionless.[19] Tins were thoughtfully provided in which to urinate. It rained almost continuously during that long night, cleared up a little in the morning and then rain again fell from about midday. Zero was timed for 1355. When it came, many men had to be helped out of the trenches partly because they struggled to gain a footing in the mud and partly because their muscles had severely cramped.

The opening barrage seems to have caught the Germans by surprise, with one report noting that several "were killed without their boots on." Some showed an early disposition to surrender but, when they saw the Worcesters struggling through the mud, changed their minds and opened fire. Another party tried to surrender but when a machine gun opened up on 7/Worcestershire from its right, the Worcesters shot several of the would-be captives to their front where upon the survivors "adopted a different attitude." 8/Worcestershire was soon held up by fire from Springfield because, as the report rather dourly noted "it had not been taken by others", and also by concrete emplacements to its north. The left was also halted by concrete bunkers about 250 yards in advance of the Langemarck Line. 7/Worcestershire advanced quite well before it ran into fire from Vieilles Maisons, one of 11th Division's objectives. The OC of the leading company decided to withdraw his men about 100 yards to where there was an element of cover and wait for 11th Division to come up.

To the right of 8/Worcestershire the two Warwicks battalions made little progress. In his brigade HQ at Cheddar Villa, Brigadier General Sladen received almost no news for the first two hours of the attack. Incorrect reports suggested Springfield had fallen and that 144 Brigade had taken all of its objectives but the reality was that the ground in front of 6/ and 8/Warwickshire was almost impossible to cross. Winnipeg was protected by a swamp and the approach to Springfield was little better. Sladen remained in virtual ignorance of events but received a message via divisional HQ from corps HQ at 1825 repeating the corps commander's wish that Springfield, Spot Farm and the buildings south-west of Genoa should be taken. Fanshawe had assured Lieutenant General Maxse that the division would try to secure the Langemarck Line as far as south as Arbre, thereby threatening Winnipeg from the rear. Sladen replied that his right was still at its start line and that Springfield probably remained in German possession. Disappointed at this news, Fanshawe wired both brigades

18 These were French-produced 1.5lb tins of stew. When water was poured into them a chemical reaction brought them to the boil in about 20 minutes. They were well liked by the troops but were bulky to carry and expensive to buy. Vaughan recalled how that night the 'troops blessed Fanny' for the gift. See Vaughan, *Some Desperate Glory*, p. 219.

19 The men were warned that as the camouflage material was highly inflammable they had to be particularly careful when smoking. Given the rain which had fallen steadily on the fabric, it seems unlikely it would have combusted.

again stressing how imperative it was that Springfield should be taken but, unknown to anyone other than a company of 8/Worcestershire, the strong point had already fallen. On his own initiative a subaltern of 8/Worcestershire led his men across the morass to attack Springfield from the north. After a struggle in the mud and ruins, the garrison surrendered. The Worcesters then quickly handed possession of the site to the left company of 8/Warwickshire which had also managed to struggle up. This had occurred at about 1845 but word of its capture did not reach divisional HQ until well over an hour later. Mon du Hibou, in which both Worcestershire battalions had established their HQ, spent most of the day under considerable shell fire and although the staffs inside the concrete building were safe, runners found it increasingly difficult to make their way to and from the blockhouse. Brigadier General Done was informed of Springfield's capture when a runner from Mon du Hibou staggered into his brigade HQ near Mouse Trap Farm. Still ignorant of its capture, however, at 1935 divisional HQ issued an order instructing the Oxfords, with the Bucks in support, to clear the Langemarck Line and Stroppe Farm from the north. 5/Gloucestershire was to assemble east of Mon du Hibou and 4/Berkshire was to follow behind.

145 Brigade had crossed the Steenbeke on schedule under "wonderfully slight" shelling but then soon ran into difficulties. The companies were only at about half strength, the men were "gloomy and dispirited…and the officers were not optimistic."[20] Night had fallen and platoons and companies became detached and lost their way. The HQ of 4/Oxford made its way to a bunker about 100 yards west of Mon du Hibou but advanced no further. Lieutenant Colonel Tomkinson of 7/Worcestershire urged the CO of the Oxfords, Lieutenant Colonel Bartlett, to relieve his worn out troops but Bartlett said he had no orders to do so. Instructions did eventually arrive at about 2330 and Bartlett moved his HQ forward into Mon du Hibou together with that of the Bucks. In the darkness and rain it took time to find and relieve many of the Worcesters' forward posts, with one undiscovered company of the 7th Battalion having to remain in position until the following night. The remainder of the two battalions made their slow and difficult way back over the Steenbeke to the canal. Companies of 4/Berkshire were at about the same time moving up to relieve all four battalions of 143 Brigade. Although two Berkshire companies disappeared on the way forward (they were found in the daylight of the following morning) battalion HQ reported the relief of 143 Brigade complete by 0250 (28 August). It did, however, later discover three isolated platoons of 8/Warwickshire on their right, the existence of which had apparently been unknown even to the Warwicks' own HQ.

Divisional HQ ordered Brigadier General Watt to continue to push his men forward and maintain pressure on the enemy defenders. No one seemed to know whether Vancouver had been taken and Fanshawe wanted Watt to ascertain whether, as one report suggested, it was held by an unidentified platoon of 144 Brigade. Watt was also told to hold all ground already taken in the Langemarck Line and

20 Greenwell, *Infant in Arms*, p. 192.

to press on towards Spot Farm, the village cemetery and Winnipeg. Patrols were sent out during the night but it was obvious nothing significant could be gained by ordering another company or battalion attack on one of the strong points. 145 Brigade settled down to seek what shelter it could, reported mud around Springfield to be waist deep and noted rifles and Lewis guns to be so clogged as to be useless. The brigade's time in the line was, however, to be fortunately short because after dark on 28 August elements of 58th (2/1st London) Division began to relieve it. The men of the London Division apparently arrived in full marching order, a sight which the bewildered diarist of 7/Worcestershire described as '"a most astonishing thing." "Astonishing" or not, 145 Brigade made its way over the Steenbeke and next by waiting lorries joined the other two brigades at Dambre Camp. There was time to rest and clean up before again moving yet further to the rear. For the time being, 48th Division was clear of the mud.

The infantry was shortly to be joined at least for a time by the field companies and most of the artillery brigades. The engineers and pioneers had spent much of the month working in the forward area with little respite, the majority of their time having been taken in laying and maintaining tracks and roads. In his evident frustration at the tasks undertaken, one OC explained the "extreme rarity" of successfully laying two successive trench boards in the same direction. Such was the nature of the broken ground he estimated it took three times the number of boards than had the track been able to be laid in a straight line. A store of German timber was used to make infantry bridges over the flooded Steenbeke but the engineers were often unable to camouflage assembly trenches and gun pits because wagons carrying the material could not get far enough forward. Like most engineers they were critical of work done by others: 2/Field Company, for example, complained about the state of dugouts at Hill Top Farm which had flooded "owing to slackness on the part of previous owners." Its OC also criticised the "zeal" of the tanks for using a road already improved by the pioneers as a "parade ground". Sappers and pioneers went up to erect blast walls on the east side of captured blockhouses and to drain them of their "indescribably filthy" water. 2/Field Company recorded only two deaths in the month but the four weeks it spent working in the appalling conditions took their toll of sickness and injury.

When the infantry brigades reached Dambre and then Brake Camp they bathed, drew clean clothing and were issued passes into Poperinghe. By 1 September, divisional HQ had opened at Wormhoudt and for the next three weeks the companies were able to train, rest and even enjoy outings to the coast. Before the brigades moved on to a new area near Recques, enemy aircraft bombed the horse lines of the divisional ammunition column, killing and wounding several officers and other ranks, By the middle of the month the field companies and most of the artillery had returned to the front area but the infantry continued to train. There were frequent brigade schemes with post mortems and conferences where officers were encouraged to suggest alternative ways of managing a battle. Practice assaults against concrete mebus using various attack formations were tried and battalion intelligence officers were invited to make suggestions as to how information gleaned from aerial reconnaissance could be better utilized. Officers were also repeatedly reminded to despatch patrols after the capture of positions and of the essential need to and report back regularly to battalion HQ. The importance of initiative among officers and NCOs was frequently stressed, as was the need to inform all platoon members of their objectives. Officers and men attended the various divisional specialist schools, and eight selected officers were despatched to the corps school for a course on 'The Flanders Offensive.' There was time, too, for brigade church, medal and 'thanks' parades.

Drafts arrived to fill the depleted ranks and companies were often reorganized to ensure a reasonable sprinkling of seasoned men within all four of the units. Losses during August had been heavy but not as severe as some other formations. 144 Brigade recorded a total of eight officers and 135 other ranks dead, 24 and 613 wounded and 17 missing. Post-war statistics were to show the brigade had been fortunate in that its two Gloucestershire battalions had suffered the remarkably small totals of 16 and 39 dead. Three battalions of 145 Brigade had suffered more than 100 fatalities, with 1/Bucks recording the largest total of 121. Excluding 4/ and 6/Gloucestershire, the average total per battalion for the month was 81, with perhaps about 400 wounded. The more than 300 dead of 145 Brigade reflected the changing composition of its battalions. It was noted earlier that the historian of 4/Berkshire believed the battalion had lost its Berkshire exclusivity during the Somme. Although this was clearly the case, the men who died in its ranks in August 1917 were still very largely from areas close to Berkshire. The brigade had received a draft of men from Cornwall and Devon but most of the men who served with the brigade at Ypres were from the south of England and from regiments whose traditional catchment areas were geographically close to Berkshire, Oxfordshire, Buckinghamshire and Gloucestershire. The numbers arriving during September was not recorded by most battalions but, for example, 6/Warwickshire received in total about 150 men in addition to returning wounded. It seems likely that when the battalion moved back towards the front fighting strength was probably around 700. There had been, however, a surprising number of new subalterns join the units: 8/Warwickshire certainly took an unknown number from its own Reserve Battalion; the Oxfords received 14 and 5/Gloucestershire 13. The Bucks Battalion accepted 12 new second lieutenants, all of who came from the Essex and West Kent Regiments or the Artists Rifles.

The time at in the training area was soon to end. At the front, the battles of September had been fought largely under the local command of General Plumer, GOC Second Army, and had made slow but geographical progress. 48th Division was about to be thrown again into the sloughs and mud of the Salient and, as the initial step in the evening of 28 September, 145 Brigade began to relieve 175 Brigade of 58th Division at the canal; the division assumed command of the sector in the morning. During the following night the first batches of what was eventually to become a total of 200 gas cylinders were carried up to the front line.

As part of the preparations for what was to come, after darkness on 30 September two battalions of 145 Brigade took advantage of the fog and night to straighten some sections of the line by moving it forward 50 to 100 yards. There was no response from the enemy and on 2 October orders were issued for the coming attack. This was to be conducted on a three battalion front by 143 Brigade, with 8/Warwickshire acting as brigade reserve. Two battalions from 145 Brigade were to be forward divisional reserve. The area to be assaulted was a few hundred yards further on towards the Passchendaele ridge than the area of the division's August battles. The tactical orders issued followed the now common practice of instructing "definite and distinct parties" to deal specifically with known and suspected strong points. 5/Warwickshire for example, was to have a special party detailed to assist in the capture of Stoke Farm and 7/Warwickshire was to have one ready to work through a civilian cemetery[21] and help take Burns House. One hundred and fifty of the gas drums now in place would be fired on Winchester and the other 50 on Albatross at 2145 on 3 October; an artillery and machine gun barrage was also to be simultaneously unleashed onto those targets for 20 minutes. To cover the infantry assault at 0600 on 4 October, a creeping barrage would lift 50 yards every two or three minutes in addition to a box barrage falling on Winchester, Wellington, Burns House and some concrete emplacements nearby. Liaison officers were appointed to coordinate actions with 1/Auckland Battalion on the right and 9/Lancashire Fusiliers on the left. Sappers, pioneers, machine guns and trench mortars were, as usual, to go forward to help with consolidation. Companies were to keep in touch with battalion and brigade HQs by runners, dogs, pigeons, power buzzers and, if possible, telephone.

Two officers from each attacking company made an initial reconnaissance of the area to be assaulted and to take compass bearings; platoon sergeants were then taken up the route to the assembly positions. Even in this preliminary period 6/Warwickshire had three officers and three sergeants wounded on the way up and had to call up one officer from the reinforcement camp and borrow two from 7/Warwickshire. The march up to the line on the night of 3-4 October was achieved, however, with few additional casualties and all three battalions were in the correct position by 0130. Reports vary as to whether any sleep was possible but rum was issued at 0500 and a German barrage began to fall 30 minutes later. 5/ and 6/Warwickshire seem to have borne the brunt of the shelling, with the latter's two leading companies losing two Lewis guns and most of their teams. Those wounded in this early exchange of fire were passed through one of the RAPs at Mon du Hibou or Janet Farm and then by RAMC bearers to aid posts in St Julien or van Heule Farm. The DCP was once again located in California Trench and from there lying cases could be taken by motor lorry to the ADS at Duhallow on the canal bank; less serious cases were to be evacuated from the light railway which had been extended to the DCP. Five of 3/Field Ambulance's medical officers were to work in the forward zone, 1/Field Ambulance manned the ADS and 2/Field Ambulance's personnel were deployed at the corps, MDS. The ADMS remained at

21 This was a different village cemetery from the one which caused the division such trouble the previous August. This one was on the west side of the small road running south-east from County Crossroads past Burns House to Vacher Farm.

From a position just south of the Stroombeke, the shot shows the ground of the division's approach to Winchester Farm (centre) and Wellington (extreme right). This was the area of extensive swamp across which the South Midlanders struggled in October 1917. (Author)

Duhallow to coordinate the arrival or road and rail traffic and to keep in touch with the CCSs further back.

At 0600, and "under an excellent barrage which could not have been improved," the three Warwicks battalions advanced. Using the formations practised during September – the two lead companies in extended order and sections following behind – platoons of 7/Warwickshire on the left made good progress over the cratered ground and reached the cemetery before they realized precisely where they were. As their own barrage was still falling on the site they withdrew about 100 yards.[22] Its left company took Tweed House and was in touch with 9/Lancashire Fusiliers. To avoid becoming embroiled in fighting for the first objectives, the two supporting companies kept at a distance of about 200 yards from the front platoons. Once the barrage lifted they moved forward and took Terrier Farm and the cemetery but with both flanks exposed they withdrew through County Crossroads and consolidated in depth. To their right, 6/Warwickshire had made a good start and quickly overran the posts west of the Stroombeke but after about 200 yards fire from York Farm drove D Company, its left company, to the right.

22 Private Arthur Hutt of the battalion was awarded the Victoria Cross for his work in the cemetery. When his platoon officer and NCOs were knocked out, Hutt captured up to 50 Germans, collected several wounded and covered the withdrawal of his platoon.

This opened a gap of some 200 yards with its 7th Battalion. On the right, A Company captured the higher ground west of Winchester and pushed on towards the farm itself which was already under attack by the displaced D Company. The ruined farm was discovered to be empty but as the company was now reduced to about 30 men, it was decided to halt and dig in 20 yards east of the site. C Company, which had also initially lost direction, waited until the protective barrage in front of Wellington lifted before moving onto its objective. As at least one company was completely without officers, leadership devolved to surviving NCOs. A post-battle report blamed the failure to secure all objectives on a number of factors. Primarily the CO thought it was the disorganized state of the companies, their reduced personnel and resistance from the many small posts which had to be overcome on the way to their principal objectives. He emphatically believed that it was not any lack of initiative on the part of his officers and men which prevented the battalion from taking Burns House and Vacher Farm. Incapable of doing more, his surviving troops established a series of posts with Lewis and Vickers guns some 300 yards west of Vacher Farm. They were able to communicate with battalion HQ which asked brigade to send forward two companies of 8/ Warwickshire in order to continue the attack towards Vacher Farm.

The brigade's right battalion, 5/Warwickshire had also made a good start and had taken Vale House by about 0640. Winzig and Albatross fell soon afterwards but a nest of machine guns to the north of Vale House cost all but about 30 men of the left company before that position, too, was taken.[23] The right company lost direction, which was partly thought to be the result of the Auckland Battalion straying over to its left. Nevertheless, Wellington was occupied only for its new garrison to be knocked out in the subsequent violence of the counter-barrage. In an attempt to regain momentum, Brigadier General Sladen was told he could use the two battalions of 145 Brigade in support and which were already east of the canal. They were ordered to move forward and by 1700 to have assembled behind Arbre (5/Gloucestershire) and east of Springfield (4/Ox&Bucks). The two companies of 8/Warwickshire requested by 6/Warwickshire attacked Vacher Farm and Burns House in the early afternoon with no success. The battalion's remaining two companies were then ordered to collect all available men from 6th and 7th Battalions as well as those from its other two companies and try again. 5/Gloucestershire had meanwhile managed to get up to its assembly position near Arbre but the Oxfords were still a long way from Springfield. Nonetheless, the Gloucesters were ordered immediately to attack Adler and Inch House at the same time as the Warwicks units went for Vacher Farm. They reached the supposed jumping off positions just as the barrage started but they had little idea of precisely where they were and headed too far north. The result of the two-pronged

23 In, *A Subaltern's War*, p. 143, Edmonds of 5/Warwickshire recalled pouring rifle and Lewis gun fire into a group of what he believed to be counter-attacking Germans. He then noticed 'they were running with their hands held up. Laughing, we emptied our magazines at them in spite of this.'

Once the site of Winchester had been captured, the division advanced across the cratered and flooded ground towards the civilian cemetery which lay south of County Cross roads. The photo is taken from the German positions on the site of the former cemetery. Winchester is the farm in the centre with *Totenmuhle* just visible behind. (Author)

attack over wet and deeply broken ground was predictable. Scattered men had to be assembled, given instructions and objectives and organized into makeshift units. The supporting barrage fell beyond the objectives, the garrisons were untouched, a rainstorm blew up and pitch darkness fell. There had been no opportunity to reconnoitre the ground, surprise was out of the question and there had been little effective concentration of force. The operation had been rushed and ill-conceived but at least the men were sufficiently prepared to disperse with rifle and Lewis gun fire a counter-attack which followed their own failure.

Divisional HQ remained unsure about what was going on for most of the day. Runners, dogs and pigeons had been used to carry messages because all lamps had seemingly been smashed during the operation and visual shutters were useless in such conditions. Major General Fanshawe received a message from 143 Brigade at 1730 reporting all objectives except Vacher Farm and Burns House secured. This was probably about as accurate a report as could be delivered at the time. Divisional HQ noted at 2210 that the picture was still "obscure" but was already planning operations for the following days. An artillery plan which involved periodic "crashes" interspersed with "silent periods" was already in operation and the CRE was told to make four wooden crossings of the Stroombeke between Albatross and York Farm. Reliefs were to take place during the night with 8/Warwickshire having to accept responsibility for most of the ground occupied by its three sister battalions; as there was to be no attack on 5 October, 5/Gloucestershire and the two Gloucestershire battalions of 144 Brigade moved back to Dambre Camp from their assembly positions on Canal Bank.

Reflecting later on the course of the battle, Brigadier General Sladen criticised himself for not having earlier moved at least one company of 8/Warwickshire behind the battalions attacking Winchester. He thought that "if properly handled" the company might have been in a position to take Vacher Farm and Burns House. Essentially, of course, it was a question of timing. Getting a battalion, company or platoon across such difficult and barraged ground to the right place at precisely the right time was probably impossible. The heavy and early loss of officers and the way the fall of the ground lay obliquely across the line of attack were blamed for the companies' frequent loss of direction. Like many other commanders, including two of his own COs, he also believed there had been an insufficient number of men available for the task. There was, they argued, sufficient men to take the first objective but they quickly became "too thin on the ground" to secure the second. Some of the supporting companies had followed too closely behind the leading units and had consequently become involved in fighting for the first objectives. They were thus thoroughly disorganized when they managed to disengage and attempted to advance towards their own objectives. There were doubts expressed, too, about the means of communications with the rear, the location of HQ and also of the quality of the protective barrage. The creeping barrage was thought to have worked quite well but the protective one fell short and was "rather thin" and "ragged" on some targets. Both the explosive and the smoke rifle grenades had proved useful but there were not enough of them available to provide effective cover for riflemen attempting to rush an entrenched or concrete position. This was especially the case if trench mortars and a good supply of ammunition for them had not been brought forward and if Lewis guns were clogged with mud. The simple but apparently novel expedient of tying breach and muzzle covers to rifles and Lewis guns so they could not be lost was thought to have been a major success in ensuring weapons could, in the main, still be fired. The COs all remarked they had tried to establish covering parties whenever possible in front of what served as a 'line' but owing to the scattered nature of the sections and the number of flooded shell holes, their existence and position was "more by accident than design." Lieutenant Colonel Knox of 7/Warwickshire believed the brigade staff had done a remarkable job because "everything we asked for we got without delay," but for Lieutenant Colonel Hanson of 8/Warwickshire, the most important lessons learnt from the operation were those which had been already endlessly stated and proved. He wrote of the "impossibility" of achieving a successful attack if there was insufficient time to reconnoitre the ground, explain the objectives and to brief the officers and NCOs.[24]

24 Major General Fanshawe circulated 39 questions to COs after the battle. One of these asked whether there was time to bury the dead. Lt. Col. Pryor, 6/Warwickshire, replied

After the relative quiet of 5 October, at 1630 on 6th, divisional HQ informed 143 Brigade there would be a "special operation" the next day with tanks to take Burns House and Vacher Farm. When Brigadier General Sladen learnt of the detail he objected to the divisional staff's plan to put smoke onto the objectives. In response, the GSO1 told him that Fanshawe insisted smoke was necessary because the GOC "did not want a large number of casualties and only get on a short way. He wanted the whole road or nothing at all." Sladen acquiesced and was to use 4/Ox&Bucks, which was still attached to his brigade, for the operation. This battalion sent out patrols during the night to ascertain whether the objectives were still actually occupied by the enemy but the patrols withdrew when fired upon heavily from the proposed objectives. Their efforts proved ultimately to be in vain because when the tanks failed to arrive next morning the operation was cancelled. 143 Brigade was finally relieved by the other two battalions of 145 on the night of 7-8 October and these were to hold the line in readiness for the next planned attack scheduled to take place on 9th. This was to be a three battalion operation by 144 Brigade, assisted by tanks, with once again the aim of securing Vacher Farm, Burns House, Inch House and Adler Farm.

Originally it was intended 144 Brigade should move up to the line on the night 7-8 October for the attack early on 9th. Owing to the heavy rain, however, it was decided the brigade should move on the night 8-9th and risk them arriving fatigued and late.[25] One officer and 16 NCOs were sent up ahead to reconnoitre the routes but the rain and darkness prevented anything worthwhile being achieved. Despite having most of the guides from 4/Berkshire knocked out by shelling before they even met 7/Worcestershire at the rendezvous point, the Worcesters on the right and 6/Gloucestershire in the centre managed to reach their assembly positions in good time. 4/Gloucestershire on the left had a far more difficult experience. Guides from 1/Bucks were supposed to rendezvous with 4/Gloucestershire but the guides themselves were unfamiliar with the featureless ground and became lost before they made contact with the Gloucesters. Tired of waiting for the guides Lieutenant Colonel Crossley,[26] CO of 4/Gloucestershire, decided to use a duckboard track which he correctly believed led to Hubner Farm; from there he moved on to Tweed House. On arrival at Tweed House at about 0145, he discovered three of his companies and one platoon had lost touch on the way up. Runners were despatched to find them while the remaining three platoons of C Company went to the jumping off positions. At 0430, A and B Companies and two platoons of D turned up just before zero but, as

that as there was only one shovel per section, 'and these mostly disappeared' no dead were buried; Lt.Col. Gell, 5/Warwickshire, replied, 'There was only time to bury officers.'

25 This decision was later heavily criticised. For example, Stacke, *The Worcestershire Regiment*, p297 described it as 'most unfortunate' while Falls, *Official History*, p. 335 states the men, 'Raked by fire from the start…already exhausted by the march up the previous night… [the men] were not in a fit state to meet the unexpected severity and suddenness of this opposition.'

26 In some sources Crossley is also referred to as Crosskey.

the brigadier's report later noted, the companies had already been under arms and in deplorable conditions for over 14 hours.

The Germans had been shelling the line of the Stroombeke since 0445 in anticipation of an attack. Four tanks were to have arrived at the British front positions by zero but as had happened several times before they had been unable to traverse the broken ground. Every known enemy strong point was supposed to have had a "certain and special" unit told off for its capture and each battalion was to have one company in reserve to meet counter-attacks. In addition, 8/Worcestershire was deployed behind the three front battalions to repel any major counter-attack which succeeded in breaking through the forward units. With a storm blowing on their backs and with the flooded ground having already dispersed the platoons, the three battalions began their advance. They immediately ran into fire.[27] 4/Gloucestershire was quickly held up by two machine guns, which were dealt with, but to their left there was no sign of troops from 11th (Northern) Division. In the centre, 6/Gloucestershire cleared the cemetery close to County Crossroads, passed through Vacher Farm, which they did not see, and then became mixed up with 7/Worcestershire. This battalion had been badly held up after 300 yards and by the time it had cleared that obstacle, the barrage was lost. The Gloucesters took a trench near Adler Farm while one company of 8/Worcestershire, which had been brought forward, advanced towards Inch House. It soon had to abandon the attempt because the protective barrage was firing short. Burns House was reported to have been captured and Oxford House captured and lost by two other companies of 8/Worcestershire. Two companies of 4/Berkshire were moved up to Springfield to replace the Worcesters, whose final company had been sent forward to support its sister battalion at either Adler Farm or Inch House. On arrival, it was instead used to hold existing posts. Adhering to their strategy of immediately counter-attacking, Germans were seen massing in front of the cemetery and Burns House but with the British protective barrage still falling, the threat receded.

The firing died away during the rest of the night and stretcher parties from both sides went out to collect the wounded. The first casualties were cleared through the DCP in St Julien to the ADS by 0830. 144 Brigade initially reported a casualty total of 30 officers and 745 other ranks, which later turned into a fatality list of probably 14 and almost 260 respectively. The brigade pushed out a few patrols and tried to establish posts east of Adler Farm until it was relieved by 9th Division on 11th. The inquests had already begun and quickly came to familiar conclusions: the opening barrage had lifted far too quickly; the creeping barrage should have proceeded at 50 instead of 100 yard intervals because this would have helped quieten the snipers and small posts in between;[28] the protective barrage often fired short; the men were

27 A new German division had just moved into the line. Its companies occupied shell holes so close to 144 Brigade's jumping off tapes that the barrage fell behind them.

28 One report stated: 'It started gradually and not suddenly as before; lack of this crisp beginning put the infantry off their stride.'

exhausted before they even arrived at the jumping off positions; the No.20 grenade was of no real use at short range; the ground made any advance almost physically impossible; there was insufficient intelligence on where the enemy strong points were and signalling lamps were too fragile for such conditions.

As Lieutenant Colonel Knox pointed out, one of the few successes of the two battles fought by the division in August and October was its own staff work.[29] It was commonplace for 'the staff', with no distinction made between divisional, corps or army personnel, to be derided and ridiculed by the troops in the trenches but very often divisional staff were at the mercy of those of corps and army. If the higher echelons were slow or late in issuing orders it meant even less time for the division's GSO1 and his staff to disseminate them to brigade majors and unit commanders. As we have seen, there were several occasions when attacks were rushed and little time allowed for preparation and assembly. The evidence suggests, however, that on the whole the delays in issuing orders were not the result of poor divisional staff work. There were, of course, occasions when messages and orders were late in arriving but that could have been caused by one or more of several factors. It seems extraordinary that if, as Knox, states, food and rations always did arrive (the war diary of 8/Warwickshire does have one entry which says "rations did not get up") but the infrequency of such comments suggests that coordination on the part of staff captains and brigade and divisional transport columns was sound. Although perhaps written with a degree of self-interest, during the division's three weeks in the rear the AA&QMG, Lieutenant Colonel Barnett, reported on how the division had been kept supplied during the August operations. He noted the pack transport train "worked well" and failed only once. That one occasion occurred because a pack convoy was apparently pushed into direct machine-gun fire from a strong point which had been reported to be in British hands.[30] Barnett had set careful but achievable rules and targets for how water, rations and small arms ammunition should be stored, transported, dumped and distributed, and had experimented with various methods of supplying hot food to the forward areas. He also made recommendations for the numbers to be employed in salvage and burial parties and of where and how what he considered the required number of trench board tracks for carrying parties, pack and wheeled transport should be laid and maintained.

The division's extant administrative work generally shows clarity and precision. Movement tables and daily orders which appear to have operated well in practice

29 Carrington, *War Record of 1/5th Warwick*, p. 58, concurred with Knox's assessment of the staff work, later recalling; 'This was the most highly organized of all attacks…all that was humanly possible had been done in the way of rehearsal, reconnaissance and preparation.'

30 The division seems first to have used pack animals for bringing up rations in November 1916. Infantry brigades had their own pack transport column organized into five sections of 18 animals, one for each battalion and one for the MG Company. In three weeks of August the pack transport train lost 94 animals killed and 102 wounded. About 50 percent of these casualties were sustained in camps and standings from bombs and shells.

followed familiar and widely-used formats. Timings of when heads of columns should be at a certain point and when battalions and brigades should rendezvous with lorries or trains will also have been worked out according to corps schedules and could, of course, be liable to disruption for a variety of reasons. There are very few references, however, to there being chaotic scenes on marches because transport arrangements had been badly designed. In the same way as the majority of divisions, the chief administrative positions within 48th Division remained throughout the war very much in the hands of regular officers. It is rare to find a TF officer in any division holding a permanent position as a brigade major but staff captains were sometimes drawn from TF personnel.[31] Similarly, battalion, field company and battery adjutants were TF officers, which is hardly surprising given the wealth of personnel within the TF with considerable commercial and industrial administrative experience. Unit war diaries were sometimes written by the adjutants and sometimes by unit intelligence officers. As would be expected, in the varying conditions in which they were written some diaries are more extensive than others. They can sometimes contain nominal rolls and medal recommendations but pages were often removed from the originals by clerks in record centres and not later returned to the file. The absence of such detail should not be seen as indolence or indifference on the part of battalion record keepers.

The divisional staff's administrative and coordination skills were to be tested again as the division rested and regrouped in the rear area. The formation was to travel quickly south to relieve 2nd Canadian Division and within the space of just over three days the division had moved from the swamps and desolation of Ypres to the quieter area of Vimy ridge. Since the Canadian success in taking the ridge in April and the closure of the Battle of Arras the sector, although by no means an inactive area, had stabilized. 48th Division took over the field ambulance sites, gun pits, RE dumps and accommodation areas from the Canadians and dared to hope that perhaps it had seen the last of the Salient. The line was thinned out so that battalions could again begin training although, as always, the need for working parties encroached upon periods out of the front system. There was also the opportunity to absorb new drafts and to reflect on the division's experiences of the previous three months.

The division had received several messages of 'thanks' from corps as well as from Major General Fanshawe; these wires were expected by formations and arrived regularly after operations. Battalions or brigades were usually paraded to hear the messages read to them but, as the war progressed, they were received with increasing degrees of sarcasm or indifference.[32] In its August and October battles the division had fought

31 One of the few exceptions of a TF officer holding the position of brigade major was actually in 48th Division. Captain the Hon. R.D. Kitson, 1/8th West Yorkshire Regiment, was appointed brigade major to 145 Brigade in February 1917.

32 When Lieutenant General Hunter-Weston addressed what was left of the four Warwicks battalions after the debacle of 1 July 1916, Carrington remembered: 'He strode into the midst of the brigade and poured forth such a wealth of what Stalky called "jelly-bellied flag-flapping" that our own general blushed in shame and the rear ranks shook with ill-

as part of General Hubert Gough's Fifth Army. Sir Douglas Haig liked Gough, who drove his staff, corps and divisional commanders hard and expected results. Even his own staff however, did not like him and belonging to Fifth Army was almost universally hated. Post-war condemnations of its organization and leadership were common and the later history of 4/Berkshire spoke for many. It assessed Fifth Army's staff work as being "thoroughly bad… [and] time after time units were set impossible tasks, with inadequate support from artillery and tanks, and with ludicrously small reserves."[33] The Bucks' historian also thought the objectives set by Fifth Army were "impossible of achievement."[34] Perhaps the division's most trenchant critic of Gough's management of the battles came from a captain who experienced the trauma at first hand. When writing of the attack on 27 August, he thought: "The plan… showed a great lack of imagination, and shook general confidence in the staff of Fifth Army. The lessons of 16th August seemed to have been entirely thrown away" and to have attacked at "the singular hour of 1.55pm…rendered concealment of all the final preparations impossible."[35] These aggressive, relentless and "ill-conducted"[36] battles fought by Gough, which had produced so little by way of territorial gain and which had threatened the morale of his army, were later contrasted with the less ambitious and generally well conducted engagements of General Plumer's Second Army. These combined a more realistic appreciation of the prevailing conditions and capabilities with rather more concern about preventing excessive losses. Plumer's 'bite and hold' tactics relied on the overwhelming fire power of the artillery to blast ahead of a deliberately limited infantry advance of about 500 yards. The artillery would then smash the expected counter-attack with yet more shell and shrapnel. The method remained expensive in terms of lives but Haig's objective of having the army wintering on the Passchendaele ridge was now seen as a possibility When Haig shifted the principal responsibility for continuing the offensive from Fifth to Second Army on 25 August, Plumer had asked for and been granted three weeks to prepare. In the meantime Gough was to continue with what were called "minor affairs", which explains why 48th Division and XVIII Corps continued to attack. Once Haig had made the strategic and operational decision to continue with the battle, however, there was little any commander could do by way of significant operational and tactical innovation. The physical component of Britain's fighting power had benefited enormously from the expansion of munitions manufacture and the radical improvements made in the logistical systems to get those munitions to the front. The conceptual component, too, had improved by means of the evolving doctrine and training pamphlets but the training manuals did tend to address tactics suited to open warfare rather than the

concealed giggles. The great man retired convinced that he had made a good impression.' Edmonds, C., *A Subaltern's War* (London, 1929) p. 32.

33 Cruttwell, *War Service of 1/4th Berkshire*, p. 122.
34 Wright, *First Buckinghamshire Battalion*, p. 82.
35 Cruttwell, *War Service of 1/4th Berkshire*, p. 126.
36 Ibid., p. 129.

means of taking objectives surrounded by swamps. Given the existing technology and the terrain, unless or until Haig decided to call off the battle even Plumer's more considered approach to operations had still to employ similar tactics to those which had already proved so costly.

It was, therefore, the morale component which was most severely tested during the British and Dominions forces' battles at Ypres. There was some unrest at the Etaples Base Camp but no outright mutinies, although the number of British and Canadian troops sentenced to death for various crimes continued to rise in 1917. Unsurprisingly, letters from the front did demonstrate that morale in an army now composed largely of conscripts was variable. There had been, for example, incidences from at least 1916 of companies discarding weapons and leaving their own wounded in trenches when relieved, of self inflicted wounds and deliberate attempts to develop trench foot. There is no evidence to suggest 48th Division as a whole suffered from particularly low morale, the incidence of crimes was very close to the average of other divisions and there was no more rapid a turnover of senior commanders than in other comparable formations. Except for his being wounded or killed, it is rare for war diaries to state why a CO was replaced. It is likely that some COs in the division were removed because they were not suited to command and their battalions knew it. It is conceivable that the remarkably low number of fatalities in 4/ and 6/Gloucestershire in August *may* suggest the battalions were used fewer times because morale or leadership was suspect, but there is nothing, such as quick changes in command or a comment in divisional or corps' war diaries, to prove it.

In none of its engagements in August or October did the division achieve all of its objectives on time. Several repeated attempts had to be made to secure the same broken area of ground or shattered farm and, while there were some localized and very hard-won successes, on every occasion the division's brigades withdrew having only partially succeeded. But this was no different to most other divisions fighting at Ypres.[37] There may have been times when men, sodden and chilled to the bone, decided not to attempt to climb their way out of the slime and into the teeth of a hail of machine-gun bullets. Staying where they were in a flooded shell hole did offer at least a modicum of protection. When he was trying to collect his company for another attempt on Springfield, Vaughan was told by two men in a flooded shell hole, one of them a sergeant, "we're staying here."[38] This was probably not an isolated incident. Self preservation, whether you were in 48th Division, 18th Division or 4th Australian Division remained, for many, paramount. Recruits who had only just arrived as drafts, possibly from a different regiment or part of the country and had had no time to integrate themselves into the close knit bands of survivors of earlier battles, had little incentive to throw themselves towards an objective that was just another patch of

37 Falls, *Official History 1917 Vol. I,* footnote citation p. 345 notes the Guards Division 'made the record of gaining the final objective allotted to it in every assault in the campaign.'

38 Vaughan, *Some Desperate Glory*, p. 224.

slightly lighter brown or red ooze than the mud which was already engulfing them. Even if they succeeded and survived in taking that small piece of tortured Flanders soil there would be another to take a day or two later and which, again, would seem to have no bearing on the eventual outcome of the war. In the same way as it is unusual to find criticism of commanders in war diaries there are few, and these generally vague and unspecific, critical comments about units. Brigade and divisional commanders may well have thought a certain battalion had not done well but were reluctant to commit themselves to paper because it might have reflected on their own ability to command and lead. The division's failures around Mon du Hibou, Springfield, Winnipeg and others *may* have been an indication of demoralization and of poor resolution and fighting spirit but they also certainly had a great deal to do with a determined and resilient enemy.

The period spent in the Salient had witnessed the departure of some long-serving personnel of the division and the re-appearance of others: Captain Crossley, a regular who had served for many months as adjutant to 5/Warwickshire, had been promoted to command 4/Gloucestershire in September but was wounded and evacuated the following month; the long-serving, and now Lieutenant Colonel Retallack, also of 5/Warwickshire, was severely wounded in August; Lieutenant Colonel Skinner of the Jodhpur Lancers commanded 5/Gloucestershire for six months before returning to the Indian Army in July; Major Hanson was transferred from his original 7/Warwickshire to command the 8th Battalion; Lieutenant Colonel Adams of 5/Gloucestershire was gassed in August but returned to command in October and Lieutenant Colonel Stephens of 4/Ox&Bucks was also wounded in August. There were three remaining TF commissioned COs in the infantry battalions: Lieutenant Colonel R.J. Clarke of 4/Berkshire; Lieutenant Colonel Langham of 5/Sussex, who had commanded his battalion since 1911, and Lieutenant Colonel N.M.Pryor of the Hertfordshire Regiment who had joined 6/Warwickshire in November 1916; he was promoted to its command in October 1917. Several other TF commissioned officers remained in command of the division's other units. It was noted above that Lieutenant Colonel Young, who had been ADMS since May 1915, had just been promoted and gone, but Lieutenant Colonel Green of 3/Field Ambulance, Major Eberle of 475th Field Company and, until he was killed as acting CRE in September, Major Clissold of 474th Field Company, remained. Major Todd of 240 Brigade RFA went home sick after having been with it since Plugstreet; two pre-war members of 2/Field Ambulance, Major Hingston and Captain Broderick were still with the unit; Captain Bindloss, a captain in 5/Warwickshire in August 1914 rejoined his battalion in May 1917 and was temporarily in command when the CO went on leave in September; QM & Hon Lieutenant Jeavons, a subaltern on the outbreak of war, returned to the UK in October. Among the other familiar faces to men who had been with their units for some time and who departed and returned were: Majors Alabaster and Whitehouse of 5/Warwickshire, and Aldworth, the second-in-command of 4/Berkshire. Majors Hall of the Bucks Battalion and Ward of 5/Gloucestershire, both long-serving members of their battalions, returned to them from a three month term at the Senior Officers' School in time for the battles around Ypres.[39]

Although 48th Division's October attacks, together with those of the remaining divisions of Gough's reduced Fifth Army, were in support of Second Army's larger efforts to the south, casualties remained substantial.[40] The three infantry brigades suffered just under 600 fatalities in October; the division's fourth worst monthly total. If we take the often accepted rate of 4.5 wounded and sick to one fatality, a figure of a further approximately 3,200 left the battalions during the month. In an attempt earlier in the year to maintain strengths there had been a medical re-categorization of eligible men. This process had allowed the home depots to clear out many of those men who had so far managed to remain at home either in particular jobs or because they had previously been deemed unfit for front line service. Eight officers' batmen of 2/Field Ambulance had already been replaced by men classed as Permanent Base, pioneer battalions were in the process of having many of their category A1 men sent off to line infantry battalions and A1 men of non-infantry corps in the UK were being transferred to the infantry and posted abroad. One such substantial draft arrived at 48th Division in October. It came from the Army Service Corps (ASC) and the men had either none or very little infantry training. Some battalions appear to have received at least 100 of these troops, many of who were understandably annoyed at having been transferred from the ASC. War diaries comment on the fact that as these men "required further training", they were often put into a special company where they underwent "recruits' training." It was generally felt, however, that they were "a good lot of men" but who were "naturally sore at being transferred to the infantry." They arrived in several batches during the month, often at the same time as a large number of new second lieutenants. The diarist of 4/Ox&Bucks expressed his astonishment at the "most unusual strength of officers" when 15 new subalterns were posted to his battalion. Among other large numbers, 5/Warwick received 10 and the Bucks Battalion eight.

The remainder of October was spent in adjusting to the changed local environment of Vimy. The trenches and camps were much superior to those of Ypres and not far from the front there were unspoilt villages and towns. The Germans were generally quieter than further north and, with winter approaching, an extended spell in the sector could be anticipated with almost a degree of satisfaction. One officer of 8/Worcestershire later described the sector as "the nicest place we ever knew in the trenches." While Sapper Roland Bishop,[41] who considered "everyone is fed up, infantry too," may have disagreed, other evidence suggests that most troops settled relatively happily into their new environment.

39 Lt. Col. Micklem, formerly CO of 6/Gloucestershire, had left the battalion to become an instructor at the school in January 1917.

40 Falls, *Official History 1917 Vol. I,* footnote citations pp. 311, 345, provide the division's casualties for the period 4-14 October 1917 as 2,085. This is the lowest divisional total for any Fifth Army formation. Considerable as this figure is, however, it is an underestimate.

41 R.Bishop, 'A Signaller's Diary'.

8

Italy

The Vimy Sector was certainly an improvement over the swamps and festering charnel house of Ypres. The deep, dry and generally well maintained trenches were named after the stars of music hall and stage[1] but although the conditions and the temperament of the enemy were different to those at Ypres, there was little time for real relaxation or levity. The field companies were occupied in the myriad tasks required in trench warfare such as building huts, laying tramways, burying cables, carting chalk, thickening parapets, knocking together trench boards and making latrines. The 7/Worcestershire undertook a minor raid in early November and a patrol of 6/Warwickshire pursued two Germans in no man's land who turned and fled when they spotted the Warwicks. The chase came to a halt when the Warwicks' officer tripped over some wire and hurt himself. 143 Brigade practised raids over marked trenches in the rear and there was much discussion about what types of training would be possible during the winter. The closest most of the division, however, came to any serious action was a largely passive role in support of a raid by 31st Division. 474th Field Company made dozens of dummy heads which were then attached to false bodies and propped up in a trench lying parallel to the British front line. Troops of 4/Berkshire operated the groups of dummies by pulling wires 300 yards long attached to the bodies. Helped by a smoke barrage and a demonstration by the guns of 240 Brigade RFA which had been well-coordinated with the battalion making the raid, the deception seems to have worked satisfactorily.

Leave for officers and men had been stopped soon after the start of the month. This was possibly in preparation for an impending move about which the troops themselves were as yet ignorant. Training progressed when possible, especially for the recent drafts of former ASC men still largely ignorant of the ways of the infantry, and there were occasionally further drafts of converted yeomanry. Casualties were

1 For example, Gladys Cooper and Gertie Millar.

few[2] and overall strengths of battalions were 650 – 800. The Third Battle of Ypres was officially closed down on 10 November[3] and 10 days later Fourth Army launched the Battle of Cambrai. Before the ruins of Passchendaele village had been occupied by the Canadians, however, an Austro-German offensive drove a huge wedge through the Italian defences on the Southern Front. In response to the rout of Italian Second Army, the *Commando Supremo* pleaded for the transfer of British and French divisions to help stem the potentially decisive surge by the Central Powers. Paris and London responded by agreeing to despatch a number of divisions to Italy but the reasoning behind why the particular ones chosen were actually selected is unknown. Sir Douglas Haig is reported to have decided the nominally regular 7th and the TF 48th Divisions, both of which had been reasonably heavily engaged at Ypres, should go and General Plumer, GOC Second Army, selected 5th and 21st Divisions from X Corps. In the end, 21st Division, and 47th Division which had also been warned to go, were both retained in France. This meant, ultimately, two regular, two New Army and one TF divisions were sent to help bolster the Italian forces and allow them time to reorganize after their shattering defeat.

Haig presumably made his decisions about which divisions should go to Italy on entirely pragmatic grounds. Following their struggle to take Passchendaele, he possibly considered it wise to send the Canadian Corps back to the Vimy sector, which it knew well. That move released divisions currently holding the sector, such as 47th and 48th, for deployment elsewhere.[4] It might have been politic to send the Italians at least one nominally regular division but as it is unlikely the Italians would have recognized any difference between New Army or TF formations, the South Midland went because it was a capable and steady, albeit unspectacular, division. If there were such things as superfluous divisions on the Western Front, 48th Division could have been considered to be one of them.

On 15 November, (the day before the newly-raised 251 MGC Company joined the division from the UK) the GSO1 and the AA&QMG left for Italy to begin

2 There was probably only one officer fatality among the infantry battalions during this tour: Captain R Fordham of 145 TMB was killed on 5 November. Later in the month 2Lt Rogers of 6/Warwickshire was reported to have been 'killed accidentally' on 24 November. Given the date of his death and his original place of burial Rogers, who had been commissioned from the ranks, was killed on the journey down to Italy.

3 The official dates for the start and finish of the principal battles were determined after the war by the Battlefield Nomenclature Committee. The troops on the ground would not, of course, have been aware a particular battle had been 'closed down'. Fighting continued, albeit often to a lesser degree.

4 The 31st Division had been line holding in the Vimy sector since the summer. The division had been used once in April during the Battle of Arras and had taken no part in either the Battle of Messines or Third Ypres. It was, therefore, rested and at reasonable strength. Presumably Haig had a reason for allowing it to remain in the quiet sector rather than despatching it to Italy and allowing one of those which was sent the opportunity to rest and refit after its Flanders trials.

coordinating arrangements for the departure and journey of the division. Six major entraining stations were selected on the St Pol-Arras line, an advance party of the artillery left on 16 November and the guns themselves began loading on 21 November. The following day the infantry brigade commanders confirmed to their battalion commanders entraining would begin shortly. The three infantry brigades each required a total of 11 trains, with battalions generally accommodated in two. Twenty-four men under a corporal were allocated to each truck, with sergeants travelling four to a truck in Third Class carriages. Each train was furnished with a canteen for providing tea at halts and a bugler to call men to the 'cookhouse'. Units were warned by the rail transport officer that as the operation was being organized at short notice, "improvisations" were to be expected. It was "feared" arrangements for feeding, ablutions and sanitation would be "primitive". Accounts vary as to how long the trip was expected to last, with some accounts suggesting four days and others detailing they were rationed for nine.

The journey itself was, according to the diarist of 3/Field Ambulance, 'tedious'. Accounts by some of the troops, however, suggest they enjoyed the scenery of snow capped mountains and vineyards, the chance to rest and sleep and the generally warm welcome they received en route. The reception accorded the troops varied depending on where they were. The area of Savoy was generally against continued Italian participation in the war while industrial and patriotic Milan welcomed the boost to employment and the chance the war offered to again to seek revenge on the Hapsburg enemy. Food could sometimes be bought from locals, French and Italians civilians gave them coffee, embraces and flowers but there were constant problems when dealing with local officials. The Italian station masters were unused to dealing with convoys of troop trains passing through their often single track stations and the language barrier meant little information could be gleaned as to the duration of halts or the route ahead. Horses, therefore, could only very rarely be disembarked to stretch their legs. For several frenetic days in early December the ADVS rushed about between the many detraining stations inspecting the condition of the horses and attempting to treat or cast any that had suffered during the journey. The two trains carrying the same battalion were often sent by different routes and arrived at different eventual destinations. There was no possibility of communication between the two halves on the way down and so coordination about where and when the battalion would be able to reassemble had to wait at least until they had arrived at their respective rail destinations. The personnel of DADOS, for example, were scattered over several trains and it took five days for all of them to be reunited. Similarly, the two halves of 5/Gloucestershire accidentally bumped into each other when marching through a town from different directions. The component batteries of the artillery brigades had concentrated by 5 December but Brigadier General Strong, the CRA, and Major Lyons arrived a few days later having decided to spend two days in Paris and then motor down through France before picking up a train at Savona.

In the wake of the Austro-German offensive, Italian military and civilian administration had degenerated into chaos. The consequent impossibility of acquiring up-to-date and relevant information from the Italians unsurprisingly seriously hampered the division's own staff work. According to Lieutenant Colonel Howard, GSO1 of 48th Division, "The Italian staff completely lost their heads" during the detraining process and while at first he had been "rather amused" to see retreating Italian junior officers riding on pony carts and the senior officers on phaetons and Victorias, he became increasingly irritated as the inefficiencies in Italian staff work became ever more apparent. He wrote of the "chaos", the Italian authorities' "quite deplorable…lack of knowledge" and their "complete failure to appreciate the importance of detail."[5] Despite the difficulties, the division finally completed detraining by 2 December and, gradually, the dispersed units sorted themselves. They moved from the Este and Isola della Scala region to Tezze, where the British and French formations were formed into two 'Groups'. Rather than relieve Italian divisions holding the forward lines, the groups' first function was to prevent any enemy breakout from the mountains. General Plumer, C-in-C British Forces in Italy, and his French counterpart had both warned the Italians that as they lacked mountain equipment, clothing and training they would be unable to hold positions on the higher ground and could act at least initially only as backstops. Together with four French divisions, the South Midland constituted part of the Left Group but as the possibility of a major attack through the mountains in the depths of winter receded and the British and French divisions began to acquire fur coats, boots, hot food containers and crampons, the Group System was broken up. In late January 1918, in preparation for eventually taking over a section of line, 48th Division began to move from its concentration area at Tezze to the reserve division area west of Treviso.

The time spent in the vicinity of Tezze had been devoted to training and becoming accustomed to Italy, its people and its methods. As the trains carrying the division passed through Northern Italy, the officers noted the apparent ill-discipline and dispirited nature of the Italian troops and the many refugees on the roads. At stopovers on the way to Tezze the Italian professionals and middle class, who were clearly pleased to see the British contingents, had entertained the officers with visits to the opera and dinner parties. While their officers enjoyed fine wines, the troops were treated to a strong black spirit, which "knocked them silly"[6] and was consequently supposedly banned. Their accommodation was also considerably less salubrious than the quarters occupied by their officers, with the men of 145 Brigade being crowded into three-sided barns. The open side was eventually patched up, which cut out some of the bitter winter wind, but as wood was in short supply there was almost no fuel for the oil drums and biscuit tins converted to braziers by the divisional tinsmiths. The field ambulances had been tasked with selecting sites for the construction of brigade bath houses but came across similar difficulties when trying to secure the means of heating water. The field companies also spent a great deal of their time erecting camps

5 TNA: CAB45/84: Howard to Edmonds, 10 Jan. 1944.
6 Greenwell, *Infant in Arms*, p. 202.

and laying on basic facilities. Most of the camps were of necessity begun from scratch and the field companies were short of much of their essential tools and equipment. Prefabricated huts were slow to arrive and the shortage of rock, gavel and concrete all added to the difficulties. In hopeful anticipation of future timber supplies becoming available, 475th Field Company took over a saw mill from a civilian owner and then experienced "great difficulty" in operating the plant.

For movement and billeting purposes the division had initially been split into what amounted to brigade groups. Each infantry brigade was supported by a field company, field ambulance and RFA brigade, together with a section of the divisional train. Nonetheless, all three of the division's brigade groups were billeted geographically close together. The infantry provided the inevitable working parties needed for the development of their own accommodation and facilities. They dug latrines, erected huts, laid paths, repaired roads and built assault courses and ranges. Large parties from 144 Brigade spent several days in early December helping in the construction of an airfield and battalion transport sections were sometimes used to supplement the divisional train and the RE in carting chalk and stores from railheads to dumps. When the South Midland left the Tezze region for the training areas allocated by the Italians to the incoming Allied divisions, it discovered the camps were primitive and largely undeveloped. 5/Warwickshire, for example, reported that when it reached what was known as the British GHQ Training Area near Padua, it found an excellent training area, good billets but no latrines "of any kind." The battalions trained when they could, undertaking route marches, PT, gas drills and sometimes brigade, battalion and company schemes. One particularly important element of the programme was to learn and practise the most efficient method of loading pack animals for mountain warfare. At least one attempt at a joint exercise between an infantry brigade and a RFA brigade collapsed when the guns became stuck in the mud and on other occasions the snow or mud on the fields precluded anything other than indoor lectures and "individual training." Major General Fanshawe seems to have been inspired by the location to deliver lectures on Napoleon's campaign in Italy and there were the inevitable inspections by the GOC, brigade commanders and General Plumer. A highly polished and gleaming 240 Brigade RFA paraded with men, horses and guns for an inspection by Plumer who then failed to turn up. The diarist restrained his frustration and annoyance by stating only that Plumer "unfortunately" was unable to attend.

A quick thaw in early January made road transport even more hazardous than it had been in the snow. The GOC, CRA and his brigade commanders watched a demonstration by Italian gunners on how to pull guns up a mountain on mule tracks. The demonstration was appreciated but when some of the division's own guns subsequently became stuck in road mud, the CRA complained that had the Italian authorities allowed his gunners to take the same thaw precautions as operated in France, the incident would not have occurred. Another group of gunners had a narrow escape when they were forced to leap from a lorry as it slid in the mud towards the precipice on the unfamiliar mountain hair pin bend. As the weather and a distant enemy conspired to provide little need or opportunity to fire throughout December and January the crews contented themselves with drills.

The ADMS was equally anxious about the state of the roads, regularly travelling forward to identify evacuation routes capable of taking lorries and likely sites for field ambulances. He convened meetings with his OC field ambulances and with sanitation officers and local Italian authorities in order to ensure water supplies and hygienic waste disposal. The local water was condemned as dangerous and was thought to be the cause of an outbreak of diarrhoea in December. Troops were quickly forbidden to wash out their mess tins in streams but a substantial number of men reported sick with quickly festering cuts, poisoned hands and large, painful boils. There were various theories about the causes, water included, but tinned food and a lack of fresh vegetables were also thought to be possible culprits. It had been difficult to obtain rations when the division first arrived at the villages around Tezze and there was little by way of supplement available in the divisional canteen, but by the second week of December fresh meat and bread became more readily accessible. The arrival of parcels and post from home towards the end of the month also helped to ease the position and contributed, together with food bought from local farmers, to the successful Christmas festivities. Because all units were well to the rear, troops enjoyed being waited on by their own NCOs on the correct day, uninterrupted by working parties or other duties. Despite the boils and diarrhoea, Greenwell believed the health of the troops was "far better" than it had been in France.[7] This is supported by the low numbers reporting sick in December and January. From a ration strength of over 17,400 in January 1918, only 854 men were admitted to the field ambulances; of these, 549 were sufficiently ill to be passed down the medical evacuation chain. There was considerable concern of possible contagion when outbreaks of cerebra-spinal meningitis and typhoid occurred in nearby Italian units but with villages placed out of bounds and fraternization temporarily prohibited, the outbreaks were quickly contained.[8]

A considerable amount of liaison and reconnaissance work was undertaken by unit officers with their Italian counterparts. Conversations were usually necessarily conducted in French but relations between the allies were invariably reported as cordial and productive. Like January, most of February was also spent in the reserve areas, although occasional staff rides for senior officers to study the possible deployment of advanced guards and rapid movement towards the forward areas were organized. The gunners experienced a short period at the front when they went into 5th Division's sector to calibrate guns and fire briefly in support of an Allied raid. Meanwhile, the

7 Greenwell, *Infant in Arms*, p. 210.

8 At a higher level, an important conference was held in January attended by the DMS Corps and representatives from the Italian Army, civilian authorities and the French Army. The discussion covered prophylactic and hygiene measures especially with regard to the spread of typhoid. Agreement was reached on preventative measures and on keeping each other informed. A ban, for example, was placed on the sale of milk to troops from infected farms. TNA: WO95/4198: WD of Director of Medical Supplies.

infantry continued to train in peace. About 30 of those who could not stand the pace were weeded out by the ADMS and trained as "water men". The idea was that these men would replace the hard-pressed RAMC orderlies who had formerly been responsible for testing the quality of locally sourced water. The field companies and pioneers continued to work on improving camp facilities and constructing gun positions for the heavy artillery, but 5/Sussex did possibly suffer a blow to morale when the battalion's long-serving CO, Lieutenant Colonel Langham, went sick and was invalided to the UK. While it was still a conventional infantry battalion, Langham had created a section of observers and signallers known as Langham's Scouts. Despite its conversion in 1915 to a pioneer unit and then the later subsequent transfer to Italy, this group had been retained and was to continue useful intelligence work in the mountains. With news that it would soon move to a forward area and take over front line trenches, a new sense of urgency was generated within the division towards the end of the month. Following agreement between Allied commanders, various Italian formations were to shift position and be replaced by French and British. Two of the British divisions had already moved to what was known as the Montello and, as part of the process of change, 48th Division was transferred to XIV Corps. It began relieving 7th Division on 2 March.

The Montello is a tortoise-shaped mound rising to about 150 metres and offering observation over a plain extending about four miles northwards to the mountains. To the south, the plain stretches to Venice. The mound is roughly six miles long and three miles wide and lies on the south bank of the Piave. The southern side and western end have reasonably gentle slopes but the northern face drops sharply to the river. The lie of the land and the elevation required to clear the higher northern face made it difficult for field artillery firing from protected positions in the centre of the hill to drop shells easily on the river itself. Austrian positions a little behind the northern bank and further into the plain could be targeted with ease but substantial woodland in that area masked any build up of Austrian forces and their artillery positions. As the hill was the last natural obstacle to the Venetian Plain, if it fell to the Austrians the way to the coast would be open; Italian forces on the Isonzo to the east would potentially then become trapped. In quiet times the river flows eastwards along several channels but when in flood it can become a savage torrent, filling the entire course with treacherous, raging water. The bed, which varies in width from 200 yards to 2,000 yards, is interspersed with small gravel islands around which surges a current strong enough to sweep men away in the icy snow melt water.

At the end of February, 145 Brigade became the first of the division's brigades to garrison the Montello front line. A patrol of 5/Gloucestershire managed to cross the river but 143 Brigade, which relieved 145 a few days later, had the unfortunate experience of taking over the front just as a storm over the mountains was reaching its climax. On the night of 3 March, the river rose by almost three feet and the outpost positions which lay on the southern bank of the river were quickly washed away or made uninhabitable. A number of fallen trees and other boughs were swept down colliding with the wire and sandbag defences but apart from being flushed with cascading rain

Taken from the Asiago plateau looking south towards the woods through which the front lines of British XIV Corps ran in June 1918. (Photo: P.Capanni)

Looking west along the vestiges of British trenches of June 1918. (Photo: S. Jones)

water, the main line at the top of the cliff remained intact. The divisional artillery, the machine-gun companies and the trench mortar battery had been tasked to fire in support of a deception scheme by 5th Division intended to convince the Austrians it would cross the Piave simultaneously as the Italian division to its right. The rise in water levels, however, put paid to any possible offensive operation and troops on both sides of the river concentrated on salvaging what they could from their flooded positions. 48th Division's learned soon afterwards that its stay on the Montello was to be very brief because on 12 March divisional HQ was warned to begin preparations for a move. British divisions of XIV Corps were subsequently ordered to relieve Italian XXVI Corps on the Asiago plateau to the north-west of the Montello. Divisional staff and unit commanders were instructed to begin immediate reconnaissance with a view to taking offensive action.

The division assembled between Cittadella and Padua and by the end of March was in the Agno valley about 10 miles west of Vincenza. The new position on the Asiago necessitated improving and developing some of the basic mountain warfare skills the division had been learning since its arrival in Italy. 145 Brigade experimented in finding the most practicable way of covering the 7,000 yards and the 3,000 feet climb to the front line; other schemes included "hill climbing combined with musketry."[9] At least one RE officer was sent to a course at the Italian Military School of Engineering. On his return he lectured his fellow officers who then, in turn, disseminated the newly acquired knowledge to infantry and artillery brigades. The field companies were heavily engaged in improving dugouts and shelters begun by other units whose workmanship, they considered, was "deplorable." According to 475th Field Company, their predecessors had shown "great carelessness" in selecting the positions because they were "quite impossible to drain [and in] imminent danger of collapse." The disposal of spoil had been thoughtless and the timbering, "if any" was weak and insufficient. In contrast, and in a rare appreciation of the skills of others, 477th Field Company was happy to leave the completion of a drainage scheme and an incomplete camp in the hands of "some very good infantry tradesmen." The move to the mountains also required learning the skills of rock drilling and blasting, the means of erecting cable ways up mountains and the maintenance and operation of *teleféricas*. Because six of the division's gunners had been electrocuted when the barrel of their gun touched the railway's overhead power cables, dire warnings had subsequently been issued about the dangers of Italian electricity cables and of the cable ways in general.[10] The *teleféricas* were certainly a novel experience for British engineers and required special skills but so, too, did blasting mule tracks up a mountain side and, probably for some sappers of the South Midland, the art of dry stone walling.

9 The division learnt that the Italians allowed one hour for every 300 metres (c.1000 feet) for climbing. Barnett, *With the 48th Division*, p. 39.
10 Greenwell, *Infant in Arms*, p. 201.

The constant work and the acquisition of new skills in a new and challenging environment was clearly an exhausting experience for the field companies. Their morale was not improved by the occasional lack of cooperation between the divisional staff and the Italian military authorities. When 474th Field Company was ordered to pack up and move at very short notice the company was allocated two roads for its transport. Delays were almost immediately encountered: "It was discovered after much questioning that both roads were prohibited after noon, a fact which apparently was not deemed worthy of notice by the authorities organizing the move." The adjutant next discovered they had already driven three kilometres beyond the allowed boundary for three ton lorries and then, to add further to the confusion, the lorries could neither proceed nor turn around because an Italian division had spread itself along the same stretch of tarmac. One fortunate section did eventually reach its destination in two lorries but the remaining three sections had a six hour march along congested roads.

The infantry spent the first three weeks of April training below the mountains. None of the formation's war diaries makes any specific mention of the detail of the syllabi followed, if indeed actual syllabi were available. Doctrine for warfare on the Western Front was constantly being updated and improved but the diaries never refer to any training pamphlets or instructions for mountain warfare. They record the occasional attachment of interpreters but do not note the presence of Italian training personnel. It is probable that discussions on what conditions might be expected in the mountains were convened but the apparent absence of recorded advice on, for example, Austrian tactical methods, operational doctrine and philosophy, equipment, structural organization and cultural and racial differences within the Hapsburg Monarchy's forces does seem strange. As far as the diarists were concerned, the infantry went on route marches, did physical training, rehearsed procedures for packing mules, grew accustomed to wearing Yukon packs, attended Italian classes and practised musketry, rapid tactical deployment and specialist skills. It is likely that battalions also practised Major General Fanshawe's interpretation of the concept of elastic defence. The divisional ammunition column was reorganized,[11] 48th Battalion MGC received two field kitchens and four dozen Ross rifles, and over 100 Winchesters were issued to battalions.[12] Unit commanders engaged in TEWTS, trips up to the plateau and brigade and divisional conferences. Since its arrival in Italy the signal company had tried testing lamps and heliographs in the mists of the mountains and had been connecting air lines to the Italian civil system. To prevent enemy eaves dropping, there were strict regulations about when telephones and telegraphs could be used but increasing

11 This involved the return to the base in the next two months of 29 GS wagons. The division received 400 additional mules, managed to borrow 200 pack saddles and was also able to call upon 60 of the smaller, lighter and more manoeuvrable limber general service (LGS) wagons and 120 mules from an auxiliary transport company.

12 Canadian Ross and Winchester rifles were utilised as sniping weapons.

numbers of wireless sets were becoming available and, as the low clouds and mists of winter passed, visual signalling became more practicable.

Similarly, when the artillery, which had spent much of April practising limbering up and quickly decamping, took up forward positions its observers could more easily see its fall of shot. It began to fire a daily programme of wire cutting and harassing fire on the rear areas. The three field ambulances all received 11 pack animals and began experimenting with how they could most efficiently be used to transport the kit and equipment of the ADS and MDS. The mules and handlers were taken out daily under the eye of the transport officers, with the men reportedly quickly acquiring "a lively interest in the animals and their peculiarities." Orderlies and bearers practised carrying stretcher cases up and down the mountains and determined relay posts needed to be at 800 yards intervals on the descent and 300 yards on the ascent. They also realized the old type of Talbot motor ambulance was not equal to the task of mountain driving. These vehicles were gradually replaced with a newer version but these, too, were generally thought to be inferior to the Fiat.

The staff captain of 145 Brigade decided the roads were of such good quality that lorries could be driven to within 100 yards of battalion HQ of the units holding the forward system. He added that the front trenches could be reached reasonably safely in daylight but condemned the unhygienic state of the trucks on the rack and pinion railway. Meat and other rations transported in them were too frequently covered in filth and discarded. Rations carried on the *telefericas* were also lost to pilfering. Despite sentries placed on rock ledges en route, stores of bully beef, sugar, jam and milk were taken as the cages and sacks ascended and by the Italian workers loading them at Calverne. To dissuade theft it was quickly decided one particularly vulnerable *teleferica* should carry only ammunition and the other three systems under British control should have their loads covered by tied tarpaulins. On the whole, however, these were tiring but enjoyable times for the division in the drying spring weather. The post was arriving regularly, there were concert parties, an inter-brigade football competition for the General Montuori Cup and there were still considerable numbers of civilians and cafes in and around the rest areas. Furthermore, a leave train capable of carrying 96 officers and over 800 other ranks to the UK was scheduled to re-start. Nevertheless, on 22 April, 143 Brigade together with 144 Brigade, whose last tour in front trenches had been at Vimy five months earlier, began the move into the British trenches on the Asiago.

Taken in by the stunning mountain scenery and looking down on the village of Asiago, the diarist of 8/Warwickshire thought it was "probably the most interesting line ever held by the British Army." While the accuracy of this observation might be open to interpretation, it was certainly different to the desolation of the Gravenstafel ridge or the barren approaches to the Hindenburg Line. The Asiago plateau was essentially a basin with the Allied line on the southern rim, a no man's land of up to two miles wide and a range of mountains rising to 6,000 feet behind the Austrian forward positions. The Allied support and reserve lines were on the southern side and on the crest of the highest ground at about 4,500 feet; from there the ground sloped northward down to the front line at 3,000 feet. Patrolling began immediately and several raids were undertaken on groups of abandoned houses close to the Austrian main line. 6/Warwickshire suffered 33 casualties when it raided a position known as the Sec Salient and 7/Worcestershire sent two platoons into the enemy's front line but returned without a prisoner. A sizable attempt by 4/Berkshire brought back one prisoner but another by 144 Brigade was abandoned when the swollen Ghelpac river surging between the opposing lines proved impossible to cross. Intelligence had clearly failed to identify what were changed enemy dispositions because a company raid by 5/Warwickshire bumped into resistance from an unexpected direction. A patrol of 4/Ox&Bucks was pleased with its work when it encountered an enemy patrol and took a prisoner but as the Oxfords were bringing the captive through the British wire a grenade in the unfortunate man's pocket exploded. Enemy patrols were, in fact, something of a rarity. The Austrians were prepared to defend their lines if attacked but showed little offensive spirit or adventure. The division's raids were covered by the artillery which also fired frequent dummy barrages on the Austrian lines to simulate an attack. On several occasions all British and Italian heavy guns that could bear fired 30 minute destructive shoots at maximum rates The CO of 4/Berkshire expressed his appreciation of the work done by the artillery in having successfully cut the wire but most of the tour was spent in maintaining a heavy but irregular fire on Austrian approach routes.

Battle casualties were minimal during March, April and May. Because the pioneers often worked while the rest of the division rested or trained, 5/Sussex did, however, suffer five dead and five wounded in March; Major Pridmore of 240 Brigade was killed in the same month and one of his gunners died accidentally in April. Two men were killed and 45 wounded in April, mostly from 6/Warwickshire, and one of the division's traffic control unit was accidentally killed. One of the very few fatalities in May was that of Second Lieutenant Aldrich of 8/Worcestershire who died when he and his horse slipped over a cliff. Although combat casualty statistics remained low, in the spring and early summer the number of men reporting sick soared. One company of 5/Sussex seems to have been the first unit to have been struck by a "pyrexia of unknown origin" (PUO) which caused temperatures of up to 104 degrees, sore throats and other flu like symptoms. The company was placed in isolation but other units also soon reported their men to be succumbing. The ADMS investigated possible causes, which were initially and tentatively ascribed to the unsatisfactory methods of refuse disposal and lack of proper sanitation at a particular camp. The number admitted to the ambulances did decline from the 5.8 percent of ration strength in March to 3.85 percent in April[13] but in May, 8/Warwickshire reported a large number of men complaining of high temperatures and pains in their backs and legs. This was quickly followed by identical reports from 2/Field Ambulance and a battery in 240 Brigade. Sufferers

13 Average ration strength in April was 13,812; in May it had risen to 14,476. The percentage of sick had fallen marginally to 3.54 percent.

were bathed, issued with clean clothes and given doses of potassium permanganate. They usually recovered after three days but if symptoms persisted they were evacuated to 39th CCS which had been designated the receiving facility. Orderlies from the division's field ambulances were sent to assist the CCS but in early June, when the PUO had been confirmed as a strain of flu, a convalescent camp with an entirely inadequate capacity of 300 beds opened at Grumolo. This new facility was in addition to the 200 bed DRS which had been opened by 3/Field Ambulance in February. While the convalescent camp dealt with flu victims, patients at the DRS suffered from a variety of minor physical and mental ailments or simple exhaustion. There were the usual baths, fumigation units and chiropodists' huts, with the treatment deliberately focussed on getting the men back to full fitness and work as quickly as possible. The standard regime was for a man to have three days of rest and assessment before being sent either to a CCS or enrolled on a three-day programme of physical fitness and musketry. The maximum stay was seven days and once out of their beds and taking part in the physical sessions the men were required to be smart and clean. It was made clear to all that the DRS was not intended to replace or emulate the work of hospitals or CCS; it was meant simply to get men who were capable of front line service quickly back to their unit. In mid-June, however, the persistence of the flu outbreak did cause something of a re-role for the DRS. Corps QMG acquired from the Italians an additional 150 shelters capable of accommodating 1,000 patients. He issued the shelters to the Corps DDMS who, in turn, allocated them to 48th Division's DRS. The DRS was then instructed to take all of the division's convalescents from 39th CCS, leaving 3/Field Ambulance to accommodate up to 800 patients from 7th and 23rd Divisions.

Once ensconced on the plateau, Lord Cavan, the C-in-C British Forces in Italy, was eager for his corps to take the offensive. Intelligence suggested the Austrian forces opposite the British and French divisions were of poor quality and suffering from a lack of munitions and rations. General Diaz, who had replaced General Cadorna as C-in-C Italian forces following the Caporetto disaster, was less enthusiastic about launching what he considered to be a premature offensive. He wanted time for his broken Second Army to reorganize, re-equip and rebuild morale. The British High Command was also reluctant to sanction an attack unless it could be reasonably assumed it would be successful and would not result in large numbers of British casualties. Although now contained, the German offensives on the Western Front had cost the British a significant percentage of its diminishing reserves of manpower. Lloyd George continued to advocate a strategy of "knocking away" Germany's allies, but he, too, appreciated the impracticality of diverting considerable numbers of Britain's troops to the Italian Front at the expense of further reducing divisional strengths in France.

Cavan wanted to secure a greater area of land between the British front line and the descent to the plain. An advance of about a mile and a half would create more space for future manoeuvre and push the Austrians back to their *Winterstellung*. He also argued an offensive would boost Italian morale and by forcing the Austrians further back against the mountains might perhaps pre-empt a future enemy attack. The British positions were far from ideal. Some of the forward trenches ran through pine forests and the distance between the outpost and front lines was, by Western Front standards, excessive. To add to the difficulties there were few communication trenches connecting the two lines. Further back were the Marginal and Intermediate Line and then, finally, the so-called Line of the Hills. As it wound and meandered across the landscape, the front system contained a considerable number of re-entrants and salients; in places this made observation from one sector of the line to the next extremely difficult if not impossible. Where the line ran clear of the woods there was a stretch of dead ground, which in some sections was further protected by rocks and scrub; the outpost positions were often isolated and impossible to support quickly. Observation of the line of approach was, of course, hindered by the woods and the areas of dead ground but, at the western end of 48th Division's sector, there was some good high ground protected by a steep ravine which followed the Ghelpac river. Forward artillery officers could, however, position themselves on the northern edge of the woods overlooking no man's land and call down observed fire on the Austrian lines. With the extreme width of no man's land field artillery pits were dug in the woods but considerable thought had to be given to the charges used so that shells could clear the trees and be able to put down a curtain of fire in front of the division's trenches. Lanes of fire were cleared through the woods for some batteries but with the steep descent to the plain so close behind them if the Austrians did secure a penetration of the front system the gunners would face the difficult decision of either trying rapidly to withdraw the guns down the mountain or abandoning them. On reflection, one CO in the division thought the line represented a "classic example of how not to hold a front."[14]

Accommodation in the front sector was unsatisfactory. There were few shelters available to protect trench garrisons from shell fire and the billets behind the front were inadequate in design and structure. 475th Field Company spent much of May weatherproofing and gas proofing dugouts and erecting water catchment tanks. Securing an adequate water supply in summer was a constant problem and one which much occupied the engineers. Water was pumped from the Ghelpac but because the pipes had to be laid above the rocky ground they were susceptible to shell fire. Further down the mountain, billets in the rest and reserve areas were cramped and sparse but with no current possibility of UK leave for other ranks, the British Army did have the use of villages on the shores of Lake Garda for rest and recreation. The units of 48th Division had been issued with khaki drill and pith helmets in May and, with parcels arriving reasonably regularly from home, morale appears to have been satisfactorily maintained.[15]

14 TNA: CAB45/84: Lt. Col. Pryor to Edmonds, 14 Jun. 1944.

15 The arrival of mail was interrupted in early May when 108 bags of parcels sent from home were destroyed. The bags were reported to have come into contact with sulphuric acid in the hold of the merchant ship transporting the cargo. TNA: WO95/4197: WD of XIV Corps A&Q.

With the village of Asiago in the distance and the Austrian mountains beyond, the photo looks north across the position of Ave from XIV Corps' line on the San Sisto ridge. (Photo: S. Jones)

Granezza British Cemetery contains the remains of 142 British servicemen killed on or near the Asiago, of who three are unidentified. There are fatalities of the June offensive in the cemetery but most of the casualties here fell in the months following. (Photo: S. Jones)

Preparations for an Allied offensive continued into early June. Divisional conferences covered topics including the allocation of roads, the sites of forward dumps and the ability of the artillery to limber up and advance quickly. Initially, the plan was for 48th Division to assist an attack by 23rd and 7th Divisions by providing two brigades as reserves but, by June, 48th rather than 7th Division was nominated as one of the two spearhead formations. Meanwhile, continuing emphasis was placed on developing the troops' mountain skills and improving visual signalling but there remained a shortage of important equipment such as hot food containers, anti-gas clothing and alpenstocks. Considerable time was devoted to practising counter-attack procedures and the rapid movement of reserve and support troops up the mountain to the forward positions. If Fanshawe's concept of 'elastic defence' was to work, all units had to be confident of their ability to fulfil the role of front line, support and brigade reserve troops. It took about five hours for a battalion to climb the 3,000 feet from the plain to the front of the plateau so the correct positioning of reserve troops was vital. Furthermore, the construction of an additional support line between the existing widely separated front system and the Marginal Line was essential if counter-attacks were to be well-timed and executed. Time and the lack of labour were to mean that few new positions had been excavated and prepared by the time of the Austrian assault.

A controversial issue aired at several corps conferences was the manner and detail of the corps' defence scheme. Concern about the strength and possible robustness of the various defence lines were discussed but the particularly difficult matter to be decided was how and where any SOS barrage should fall. After the war, Lieutenant Colonel Sandilands, GSO 1 23rd Division, remembered long and "rather heated" discussions centred around whether the barrage should fall in no man's land or between the outposts and the front line.[16] Sandilands recalled that several of the commanders present expressed doubts as to whether the outpost garrisons would hold their positions if the barrage fell behind them. This was countered by the "more ruthless" who advocated the barrage should fall behind the posts but that their garrisons would not be informed of the fact. Sandilands argued it would be a betrayal if the secret arrangement were made and that if word of its existence leaked out it would inevitably cause a slump in morale. If the troops *were* told, he believed, they would "stand their ground and take their chance." The issue, recalled Sandilands, "had a direct effect on the artillery action of 15 June." Sandilands' hindsight was perceptive as Fanshawe's alleged failure to order an early defensive barrage on 15 June was one of the reasons used implicitly to explain his subsequent dismissal.

Unknown to the troops in the forward positions, Cavan was facing something of a dilemma. While there remained a possibility of an Allied offensive he had to prepare his formations for that eventually but, at the same time, intelligence was accumulating on the probability of an Austrian attack close to the Asiago. Cavan

16 TNA:CAB45/84: Sandilands to Edmonds, 17 Jun. 1944.

expressed his concerns in a note to the CIGS, General Sir Henry Wilson: "My troops are being kept in a constant state of tension; reliefs become difficult, and the necessary preparations for [the] offensive conflict with the demands for defensive work."[17] Effectively, however, the decision was made for General Diaz by the Austrians who, under pressure from their German allies, were making advanced preparations for their own offensive. By early June the intelligence gathered by air reconnaissance and from deserters was becoming compelling.[18] There were reports of German divisions moving from the Western to the Southern Front and of a considerable build up of enemy forces along the Piave river to the south. Cavan attended a conference chaired by his army commander, General Montuori, and then briefed his divisional commanders on the situation. The intelligence was interpreted as suggesting no attack would be made against the two British divisions in the line on the Asiago but that the Austrians might make a demonstration in their direction. Prisoners brought in by patrols confirmed an attack was imminent. On 14 June Fanshawe held a conference for his brigadiers to ensure all gas precautions were in place and to order troops be put on the alert. The divisional commander was confident his brigades were fully conversant with the divisional defensive plan and that all units were in their battle positions. All preparations to fight a defensive battle appeared to have been in place but on the same day further instructions were issued about the temporarily postponed British offensive. According to war diaries and personal reminiscences, this was now to be launched on either 16 or 18 June.

The *Official History* notes that owing to the flu epidemic and what was called "mountain fever", in May and June British divisions on the Asiago had up to 30 percent of their manpower out of action. 48th Division had been hit particularly hard by the outbreaks with the consequence that battalion fighting strengths ranged from the 617 of 8/Worcestershire to the meagre 379 of 6/Warwickshire. These figures included men who were suffering from the infections but had not been evacuated to the rear. Many senior commanders had also been struck down by the virus. In view, therefore, of the apparent knowledge of the attack to come, it does seem strange that several commanders had also been allowed to go home on leave. Lieutenant Colonel Adams of 5/Gloucestershire returned to the UK sick, but two of the three infantry brigade commanders and several battalion COs went on leave. This meant that through the combination of sickness and leave, six of the 12 battalions were commanded by their second-in-command and two infantry brigades were commanded temporarily by battalion COs. For a few days at divisional HQ, only Major General Fanshawe and his intelligence officer were available for duty; all three senior staff officers were

17 Cavan to Wilson, TNA: WO106/85: 10 May 1918. Cited in Cassar, *The Forgotten Front*, p. 143.

18 British control of the air was complete. In the first two weeks of June, which included some days when the weather prevented any flying, 23 enemy aircraft were reported destroyed for the loss of one British machine. TNA: WO95/4194: WD of XIV Corps General Staff, Jun.1918.

indisposed by flu.[19] It was a similar picture of absence among the staff at the HQ of the divisional artillery. The artillery brigades themselves had been equally badly affected with, for example, C/240 having been unable to go up to the line with the other batteries on 3 June. There were sufficient crew members to man the battery's guns by the time the Austrians attacked but the overall shortage of fit men, together with the preparations made for the Allied offensive, meant that the brigades of 7th Division's artillery were also in the line. In addition, there were 44 batteries of British and Italian heavy guns whose roles were divided between counter-battery work and bombardment.

The British front on the Asiago was manned by 23rd Division on the right and 48th Division on the left. 7th Division, less most of its artillery, was resting on the plain. In 48th Division's sector, two battalions of 145 Brigade, 4/Oxford and 5/Gloucestershire, held the right and centre, and one battalion of 143 Brigade, 5/Warwickshire, held the left.[20] The Bucks Battalion was in its battle positions in the Lemerle Switch and Polderhoek Trench and the remaining battalion of 145 Brigade, 4/Berkshire, was in reserve at Carriola. In 143 Brigade, 8/Warwickshire had one company in the Cesuna Switch and three in or around Brusibollo Camp, 6/Warwickshire was close to M.Pau and 7/Warwickshire was down in Magnaboschi as divisional reserve. The divisional trench mortar batteries and the companies of the machine-gun battalion were partly scattered about the line and partly in reserve. During the short night of 14-15 June, sentries kept watch as their colleagues huddled in scrapes and rock trenches. They had been warned to expect gas and shelling but there was still the widespread belief that an infantry assault on their front was unlikely.

The enemy bombardment crashed down at 0300, just as dawn was breaking. Shells of all calibres fell on the front, reserve and rear positions. Suspected battalion and brigade HQ were among the areas targeted and the largest shells fell in the plain below the mountains. The forward gun pits in the woods were straddled as were the tracks and roads leading through the trees towards the rear. Shell dumps, some of them very far forward, had been assembled in preparation for the proposed Allied advance and were hit by the Austrian guns. Because the ground was so rocky, telephone wires tended to be strung from trees and these were quickly cut. 4/Ox&Bucks, for instance lost communication from battalion HQ to the front trenches in five minutes and

19 TNA: CAB45/84: Major Morshead, Cavan's GSO2, recalled being 'sent forward to take charge of that unfortunate division [48th] at a critical moment' because so many of the staff were ill. Morshead was despatched to administer the orders for the proposed offensive rather than the eventual defensive action. Morshead to Edmonds, 9 May 1944.

20 The sources are not entirely in unison with regard to the division's dispositions. 4/Ox&Bucks had either two or three companies in the outpost positions and the front trench (Pelly Trench) with one or two behind in a sunken road near battalion HQ; 5/Gloucestershire probably had one company in the outposts and two in the front line, with the fourth about 300 yards behind; 5/Warwickshire had two companies in the front positions (Thinle Trench) and two in support.

those to the rear within three-quarters of an hour. Amidst the confusion, messages did get through at about 0500 to withdraw the outposts and at 0530 others told of Austrian deserters announcing an infantry attack would begin at 0600. The bombardment was certainly devastating but there was some disagreement about its overall effectiveness and intensity. The *Official History* recorded it was largely unregistered and widely dispersed, relying on volume and luck rather than judgement to hit key British targets. Many of the gas shells failed to detonate, with one officer describing the deluge as "almost innocuous,"[21] and there was a significant percentage of duds in conventional artillery munitions. Shells exploded in the trees and while they could send down deadly splinters of wood, the overall impact of the bombardment was lessened. Similarly, although men could be killed by rock fragments loosened by the shelling, the unevenness of the rock sections and fissures allowed troops some shelter. Initially the bombardment was still thought to be a demonstration but as it continued it became "more than mere thoughtlessness on the part of the enemy."[22] The *Official History* believed it had "neither the volume nor the accuracy" of bombardments experienced on the Western Front, but Greenwell, who had, of course been involved in both the Somme and Third Ypres, thought it "the most intense I have ever known."[23]

After nearly two hours, divisional HQ must also have realized the duration of the shelling suggested something more than a demonstration. As per the prearranged scheme, at 0445, 8/Warwickshire was ordered to send another two companies up to the Cesuna Switch, keeping the fourth as reserve close to battalion HQ, and 6/Warwickshire moved from M.Pau to a position about one mile behind Cesuna. Fanshawe was, however, still not convinced that the shelling was a preliminary to an infantry assault and delayed ordering a barrage on the SOS lines. He later reported he did not want to order the barrage to commence unless an attack was actually seen and in progress. The reasoning behind this assessment was, he argued, that until it was certain enemy infantry were on the British wire, it would merely be a waste of ammunition hoarded for the British offensive. Furthermore, he added, it would make the enemy believe he had "diverted our artillery from the real attack [which] may be going on against the Italians" to the east. Attacks were indeed taking place along other sections of the line but it was not until just after 0800 that runners arrived at divisional HQ with messages confirming enemy infantry had appeared at the British front positions at about 0700; they were now in the process of "pouring" through gaps made in the British wire and defences. The forward battalions had apparently fired their SOS flares but they had either been lost in the mist or had not cleared the tree tops. Now convinced this was a serious assault, at 0811 Fanshawe ordered the CRA to put down the SOS barrage. Seven minutes later, the GOC 145 Brigade, who had been out of communication with both of his forward battalions almost since the bombardment

21 Cruttwell, *War Service of 1/ 4th Berkshire*, p. 140.
22 Compiled, *History of 1/6th Warwickshire*, p. 50.
23 Greenwell, *Infant in Arms*, p. 226.

began, was informed of what divisional HQ thought was happening. 4/Berkshire was also ordered to move up from Carriola to its battle position in case of a breakthrough. At 0835, the GOC 144 Brigade was told to move 6/Gloucestershire from Serona Camp to Carriola; 15 minutes later he was ordered to bring 4/Gloucestershire and 7/Worcestershire up from the plain. Lorries were provided and the battalions arrived during the early afternoon. Fanshawe was clearly acquiring a more detailed picture of what was going on and implementing the rehearsed divisional scheme of defence but the almost total collapse of cabled communications meant his overall situational awareness remained patchy.

At the front, the Austrians had made solid progress and were infiltrating the weakest parts of the British defences. The junction between 145 and 143 Brigades, which lay in an area known to the British as Happy Valley, was especially suspect owing largely to the nature of the ground and the consequent dubious positioning of the posts. It was a problematic choice of ground to station an inter-brigade boundary but there was also difficult terrain on 145 Brigade's inter-battalion boundary between 5/Gloucestershire and 4/Ox&Bucks. The attackers had taken advantages of the morning mist and reached as far as the British wire before being spotted. The division's right battalion, 4/Ox&Bucks, was attacked by seven battalions carrying flamethrowers and their own version of the Bangalore torpedo. The enemy's advance was made easier by the fact that the Oxfords' positions cut across a tongue of woodland which extended some 1,000 yards in front of their front line. This cover allowed the Austrians to "crowd" initially almost unmolested into the Oxfords' positions.[24] Surprise and sheer weight of numbers forced the Oxfords gradually to withdraw towards battalion HQ which lay in the sunken road about 500 yards behind the line. On their right, 11/Northumberland Fusiliers of 23rd Division had also been pushed back and contact was lost with them. By about 0900, the survivors of the Oxfords formed what was effectively a semi-circle around Hill 1021, forward of Pelly Crossroads, and tried to hold on until help arrived. One company of Bucks in Lemerle Switch managed to prevent the complete disintegration of the division's right flank but there remained a dangerous hole between 48th and 23rd Divisions. Aware of the threat, Fanshawe ordered 477th Field Company to move up and plug the gap. A young subaltern of the field company had been sent to divisional HQ at about 0330 to seek orders but nothing was decided until 1000 when the company began its trek towards Boscon Switch. The entire company, save five orderlies, left camp but the sappers failed to get in touch with 23rd Division.

To the left of the Oxfords, 5/Gloucestershire, experienced an equally torrid time. The enemy broke into its line after two posts near Perghele were destroyed in the bombardment; the invaders next wheeled round to take the Gloucesters' forward company from behind. All communications to battalion HQ were quickly severed and the left company was overrun. The support company was also enveloped on its left but with the help of a battery of trench mortars delayed the enemy until it was

24 TNA:CAB45/84: Lt. Col. Bartlett to Edmonds, 16 Jun.1944.

compelled to retire to the Cesuna road.[25] There the survivors bumped into a group of isolated 5/Warwickshire and two very advanced 4.5" howitzers. These weapons were hauled from their pits and fired over open sights. The entire group was soon forced back again, this time managing to maintain a position close to the railway where they found some 18 pdrs of 7th Division. These guns had been man-handled through the woods in an attempt to prevent the enemy debouching into the open ground near Cesuna. Contact between the two right companies of 5/Gloucestershire, A and B, and the Oxfords had been lost and penetrations through the resultant gap threatened to completely cut off what was left of the two forward battalions. Two companies of the Berkshires, however, arrived in support of the Gloucesters and managed to restore contact with the Oxfords. This action was assisted by a lull in fighting in the immediate area because, it was later assumed, Austrian troops had discovered a store of rum and had paused to refresh themselves.

In addition to the dead ground in front of the position, the penetration at the junction of the two brigades was also eased by the apparent obliteration of the particularly weak D Company of 5/Warwickshire. Two of the company's posts must have been destroyed or overwhelmed quickly, with the assaulting troops then turning inwards to both left and right. Two guns of the division's machine-gun battalion were also quickly subdued.[26] On the left, B Company held an area of ground which commanded the company's approaches and onto which they could bring concerted Lewis, rifle and Stokes fire. Austrian troops approaching the British lines up the ravine of the Ghelpac were slaughtered in substantial numbers and the company's position, which at the suggestion of the GOC 12th Italian Division on its left had been shortened by some 800 yards, was not directly threatened. On the right, however, it was a different story. Battalion HQ was badly sighted, being only 100 yards behind the trench held by D Company, and was under immediate threat from the advancing Austrians. The acting CO, Major Bindloss, despatched his adjutant and intelligence officer forward to garner information but neither returned. Realizing how desperate the situation was, and with all communications back to brigade HQ down, Bindloss led a party to try to regain the captured visual signalling station. He was killed in the attempt and with no other officer present, RSM Townley organized a stubborn defence of the HQ huts with a party of about 13 cooks, clerks and orderlies. Although the Austrians swirled past this isolated band, Townley's defence disrupted their advance and was to last for at least four and a half hours. "Ignorant of the situation [to their front], with no orders and no communications,"[27] 5/Warwickshire's remaining two companies manned the Cesuna Switch and brought heavy fire to bear on the advancing Austrians. The Lewis

25 TNA: CAB45/84: Lt.Col. Tomkinson to Edmonds, 3 Jul.1944. The former claimed that the crew of an Italian trench mortar battery on the left of 145 Brigade 'ran like hell and were not seen for days.'

26 The 48th Machine Gun Battalion had been formed on 22 March 1918. It comprised 143rd, 144th, 145th and 251st MG Companies.

27 Carrington, *War Record of 1/5th Warwick*, p. 73.

guns of one platoon alone fired over 4,500 rounds but the Warwicks could do little to save some of the 18 pdrs which, like the 4.5" howitzers, had been brought forward for the intended British offensive.

Cesuna and Lemerle Switches, which were almost connected by Polygon Trench near the hamlet of Guardiana, were the key to the division's integrity. These defences constituted the division's Red, or Intermedite Line of defence and by about noon the Austrians were within 200 yards of them. If the enemy could penetrate the narrow gap caused by the track of the light railway the way to the plain would be all but open. 6/Warwickshire moved into the sector and waited as "news trickled back, bearing the usual high colour of moments of agitation" in support of 8/Warwickshire which had one company in the Cesuna Switch. Further south, 7/Warwickshire, in reserve, sent scouts forward to glean information as to what was happening and despatched ammunition forward to 8/Warwickshire. Word then arrived announcing the enemy was through the front defences and additional bandoliers were issued to the battalion. Shortly afterwards, at about 1000, orders were received from divisional HQ for the battalion to advance and "drive them back and hold the Cesuna Switch." Fanshawe was working mainly on instinct. His situational awareness remained poor but his understanding of the progress of the battle was developing as reports from scouting brigade majors and officers returning from the front came in and began to fill some of the gaps in his overall appreciation. The order of 0830 to bring two battalions of 144 Brigade up the mountain had set the train in motion and now the order to 7/Warwickshire to counter-attack and secure the Cesuna Switch, a move which the battalion had twice previously rehearsed, was the next positive step in trying to wrest the initiative from the Austrians. Just before midday, 6/Warwickshire was also ordered to undertake a small counter-attack with two platoons in the direction of the farm buildings of Perghele which dominated the Warwicks' communications to the rear. In the confusion of not knowing who was where, little ground was gained but the attack did successfully regain contact with RSM Townley and his small group of defenders. Despite this relatively minor setback, however, as reports continued to come into divisional HQ, there was evidence to suggest that the enemy's attack had about culminated.

As they fought their way through the woods, the limited visibility had both helped and hampered the Austrian advance. When they emerged from the trees they were sometimes halted by relatively small parties of infantry, occasionally supported by the odd field gun. After already nearly six hours of often strenuous and often hand-to-hand fighting, when the Austrians bumped into these parties the attack increasingly lost momentum. This loss was exacerbated by the prompt action of Lieutenant Colonel Knox of 7/Warwickshire when he arrived with his battalion. Knox discovered that the gap between Cesuna Switch and Polygon Trench was defended by two 18 pdrs of 7th Division and the rifles of their crews. Knox used his troops to fill the gap, gaining contact on either flank and then at 1400 launched a counter-attack to take two houses and some out buildings occupied by the Austrians close to the railway. One 18 pdr of D/240 battery was man-handled close to the house at Guardiana to fire over open sights before the Warwicks rushed the building. Clo station was also secured but any further advance from either of the re-captured positions was prevented by Austrian machine-gun fire. The Warwicks were within about 500 yards of the original front line but when Knox learnt that 6/Gloucestershire would arrive by 1800 with orders to continue the advance, he decided to call a halt and await that battalion's arrival. Although unrecognized at the time, these actions, which coincided with the closure of two other gaps in the line by the Berkshires, marked what might be described as the battle's fulcrum. There was still hard fighting to be done but the pendulum of battle was now beginning to swing in favour of 48th Division.

Lieutenant Colonel Tomkinson, currently in temporary command of 144 Brigade, arrived at divisional HQ soon after midday. His brigade had still to concentrate, with 7/Worcestershire and 4/Gloucestershire on their way up from the plain in lorries and 8/Worcestershire in reserve about half a mile behind Fanshawe's HQ. The fourth battalion, 6/Gloucestershire, was just about to reach Magnaboschi having managed to negotiate a route of relatively safety around the burning and exploding ammunition dump at Handley Cross. Tomkinson was apprised of the situation by Fanshawe and his divisional staff and was informed his brigade would be used to counter-attack and drive the Austrians from the pocket into which they had fallen. Unless they could restore tempo and offensive action, the Austrians were now effectively trapped in this salient. Rather than send his brigade major, a staff officer from divisional HQ or even

The memorial to Lieutenant Colonel J M Knox DSO and Bar of 7/ Warwickshire and to the men of 143 Brigade who fell on the Asiago in 1918. Knox, who was a captain in the battalion in August 1914, was killed in September and lies in the cemetery. (Photo: S. Jones)

a senior officer from one of his brigade's battalions, for some reason which is not altogether clear Tomkinson volunteered to go himself to consult with Lieutenant Colonel Reynolds, the acting commander of 145 Brigade. It seems probable that Tomkinson, acutely aware of his 'acting' capacity, did not wish to rely purely on second-hand intelligence acquired by divisional HQ which was still out of wireless touch with Reynolds. In order to be as precise and as fully-informed as possible in his preparations he probably wanted to garner the most current information which would only be available at brigade HQ. Tomkinson's trip forward to Reynolds' HQ, which was housed in huts to the south of Oxford Trench, was swift and he reported back to Fanshawe within the hour.

Fanshawe had another visitor that afternoon. Lord Cavan, the corps commander, had already warned a brigade of 7th Division to be ready to move quickly into the mountains if ordered. After the war this decision was condemned as "alarmist" by an officer of 48th Division who considered it to have been made by a commander who was removed from the action and did not comprehend what was going on.[28] Rather than "alarmist" it should be seen merely as a sensible precaution made by a corps commander who was not yet in full possession of the facts. The official historian later reported that Cavan's visit to Fanshawe's HQ was "encouraging" but noted that Cavan made no attempt to interfere with the plans being conceived by the divisional commander.[29] In his usual 'hands on' fashion, during the afternoon Fanshawe undertook a 90 minute tour of his three infantry brigade HQ to consult and confer. He then issued orders for a counter-attack to go in at 1800 by 7/Warwickshire and 6/Gloucestershire; Tomkinson left immediately to discuss the proposed operation with his battalion COs. Following Tomkinson's brief, Knox of 7/Warwickshire then conferred with Lieutenant Colonel Schomberg, CO of 6/Gloucestershire. They agreed that as their combined objective was to advance and clear the Austrians from the pocket and make contact with 143 Brigade on the left and 145 Brigade on the right they would each attack on a two company front. Owing to intense Austrian machine-gun fire progress was limited and only about 150 yards were retaken. Touch was not made with the Oxfords on the right but with the added strength of 7/Worcestershire in support, the attack was renewed at 2000 and advanced another 300 yards. The absence of any enemy bombardment on the British positions and the area across which the battalions were to advance was encouraging. It suggested the Austrians had become disorganized and that communications to the rear and with their artillery had been disrupted. Rifle and machine-gun fire, however, remained intensive. With that, and with many platoons losing direction in the woods, the advance stalled but 7/Worcestershire had managed to gain contact with the Oxfords a little to the south-west of Pelly Cross. Equally important was the knowledge that the right flank of the Oxfords which was bent back towards Boscon was now again in contact with 23rd

28 Barnett, *With the 48th Division*, p. 78.
29 Edmonds, *Official History Italy*, p. 212.

Division. This meant that 48th Division now manned an almost continuous line from about Pelly Cross to just south of Perghele Farm.

This constituted a reasonable success but Fanshawe was frustrated by the failure of the attacking battalions to get on further and eliminate the pocket entirely. It had been a long, hard day of sometimes hand-to-hand fighting, however, and he realized the troops need to rest and reorganize. Men and supplies were being brought up the mountain but movement remained restricted by the burning ammunition dump at Handley Cross and by intermittent enemy long range shelling. The night allowed more small arms ammunition to be delivered to the forward units and for some of the more isolated trench mortar teams, machine-gun crews and 18 pdr guns and gunners to rejoin their batteries or to seek better protected positions. Throughout the night the Austrians maintained heavy rifle and machine-gun barrage on the wood which further hampered movement but the fire was generally wild and erratic. At 2130 the three battalion commanders whose units had been involved in the evening attack met to discuss the situation and agreed the existing line should be held and consolidated in preparation for renewing the attack next morning. There is no mention of any of the brigade GOCs being present and it is unknown whether Fanshawe actually knew of the conference. It is probably reasonably safe to assume that Fanshawe was confident his COs knew their commander's intent and believed they would act accordingly. Nevertheless, he issued orders following another meeting with Tomkinson that evening. It was decided 8/Worcestershire, Tomkinson's last battalion, should move up from behind divisional HQ and join in a combined attack by all three brigades to retake the original front line. Orders were swiftly issued to battalions and a fire plan aimed primarily at the enemy's gun lines and communications devised for the artillery. The attack began at 0430 but progress was uneven. The furthest advance was made on the right by the Oxfords and the Berkshires but the lack of progress in the centre and left, which had much to do with incessant machine-gun fire and the physical obstacles created by blasted and fallen trees, prompted Fanshawe to undertake a quick tour of the forward positions at 0700. After consultation and briefings he ordered the attack be renewed at 0730.

The coordinated attack met "scarcely a shadow of resistance."[30] The old British front and outpost lines were quickly retaken, with Austrians surrendering freely and others observed "streaming back" to their own lines where many then proceeded to "wander about" behind their unoccupied trenches.[31] Unmolested, the Bucks brought in a pair of mountain guns from no man's land and patrols from 143 and 144 Brigades went out to try to persuade yet more Austrians to surrender. A combined patrol of 5/ and 6/Warwickshire raided and took an isolated Austrian redoubt in the farm buildings of Ambrosini[32] and one of 8/Worcestershire reported the enemy was disorganized and sought permission

30 Barnett, *With the 48th Division*, p. 84.

31 Ibid.

32 The 6/Warwickshire was supposed to have relieved the much battered 5/Warwickshire but the war diaries suggest members of 5/Warwickshire were involved in the raid.

to advance further. The troops were "bursting with keenness"[33] to exploit the situation while the Austrians were clearly off balance and demoralized but the army commander, General Diaz, ordered caution. When news of the capture of Ambrosini redoubt reached Lord Cavan in the afternoon of 16 June he ordered more patrol activity but insisted that if or when they met stiff resistance they should halt on the positions which had been the objectives for the postponed Allied offensive.[34] The French, too, were anxious to follow up the Austrian withdrawal but Diaz thought the time was not yet ripe for a full pursuit. Instead, the troops had to content themselves with rounding up prisoners. The total collected by the division is open to some dispute but the number was probably a little under 1,000.[35] Furthermore, Barnett noted that 576 Austrians were buried on the division's front.[36] According to the historian of 6/Warwickshire, the burial of such numbers and also those of the division's own dead took five days.[37]

The division's three field ambulances were kept busy treating the wounded and coping with the still exceptionally high number of men suffering from flu or mountain fever. The successful counter-attack on 16 June meant that none of the ambulances had had to move to the rear but the units were stretched because many of their own men had succumbed to flu. The convalescent camp had been literally washed away by a storm on 12 June so all wounded, which included a large number of Austrians who had been left behind by their withdrawing comrades, had to be treated by the divisional ambulances or evacuated to the CCS on the plain. 2/Field Ambulance was the forward of the three and dealt with almost 500 from the division, more than 100 from other units and about 200 Austrians. The evacuation of the more seriously wounded was aided by the lie of the land which allowed Ford motor ambulances, several of which were loaned by 23rd Division, to get quite close to the front unobserved. 3/Field Ambulance had sent up all available bearers and a tent sub-division when it became clear the Austrians were attacking and pre-arranged relay posts were quickly put into operation. Evacuation appears to have been done speedily and efficiently, with bearers working in shifts up and down the mountain tracks.

Divisional battle casualties were, in fact, surprisingly light. The A&Q branch recorded figures of 16 officers and 153 other ranks killed, with 44 and 490 wounded and nine and 21, respectively, missing.[38] Later figures suggest the total number from

33 Barnett, *With the 48th Division*, p. 84.
34 Cavan's report to the CIGS stressed he ordered that patrols should not be undertaken until they were 'thoroughly organized' and that the original front line should remain the 'Line of Resistance.' TNA: WO106/852: 15 Jun.1918
35 Captain Keane, the MO of the corps' pontoon park, was responsible for the vaccination of prisoners, particularly against typhoid.
36 Barnett, *With the 48th Division*, p. 84.
37 *History of 1/6th Warwickshire*, p. 58.
38 Another table, probably compiled somewhat earlier than the one reproduced in the A&Q war diary, relates 16 and 134 killed; 42 and 446 wounded; 9 and 256 missing respectively. TNA: WO106/852.

the 12 infantry battalions who were killed and those who died of wounds sustained between 14-16 June are 16 and 128. Of the total number of 922 casualties, at least 196 were gunners[39] and it is known that two of the signal company and at least seven of the machine-gun battalion were also killed. 4/Oxford and 5/Gloucestershire, who bore the brunt of the attack, suffered the largest number of fatalities, with 42 and 36 respectively. The third battalion in the front line on 15 June, 5/Warwickshire lost a total of 14 other ranks dead. Of these, only three were later unidentified.[40]

As relief was not immediate for the division, casualties from Austrian artillery fire continued to arrive at the ambulances. Work was begun on replenishing ammunition stocks (a task made more difficult because the rack and pinion railway had been severed by shellfire), re-establishing the line's defences and collecting the detritus of battle.[41] Amongst the booty discovered were several of the trench mortar battery's own hastily hidden tubes and two of the machine-guns of D Company 48th MGC Battalion destroyed when the positions were overwhelmed.[42] The signal company began to untangle broken cables from the trees and buried as many replacement circuits as possible, rations were taken up the mountain or drawn from undamaged dumps and new wire was laid in front of the outposts and front lines. On regaining his former front line company HQ dugout, Greenwell was particularly annoyed at the Austrians for having plundered his personal belongings. Cavan later reported the Austrians' proclivity "instantly [to] set about looting"[43] had severely disrupted their momentum and slowed their advance but on a personal note, Greenwell cursed them for exchanging their lousy shirts for several of his own freshly laundered.[44] Baths and a change of clothing for all would be available when the troops returned to the plain but for three to four days the bulk of the infantry had to make do with those they wore.

When the division was eventually relieved, troops were able to enjoy some rest and relaxation in the camps at the foot of the mountain. Senior officers wrote reports of

39 TNA: WO95/4200. The war diary of CRA gives: three and 20 killed; 19 and 154 wounded. Interestingly, the numbers are almost equally split between the heavy and field batteries.

40 As testament to how quickly the division's lost positions were regained, of the 144 infantry fatalities only 12 bodies were not later identified and have no known grave. The names of these soldiers appear on the memorial to the missing in Giaverra British Cemetery. The majority of the division's dead were buried in Boscon British Cemetery, with those who died of wounds in the CCS interred in Dueville and Montecchio Precalcino. Most of the other dead of the battle are buried in Cavvaletto British, which is a small concentration cemetery.

41 A&Q Branch issued 1 million rounds of SAA, 17,000 grenades and 8,000 Very lights to replace those blown up or used. Fresh meat and bread was carried up the mountain by Italian pack animals. TNA.WO95/4197, 15 Jun. 1918

42 ADOS despatched a total of 14 Vickers and 19 Lewis guns to replace losses by 23rd and 48th Divisions. TNA:WO95/4200: WD of XIV Corps ADOS, 17 Jun. 1918.

43 TNA: WO106/852. Cavan to CIGS, 15 Jun. 1918.

44 Greenwell, *Infant in Arms*, p226-27

the battle to illustrate where things went right and wrong and some of the officers who had been absent from the battle rejoined: for example, Lieutenant Colonel Gell of 5/ Warwickshire, who had been on leave in Italy, reported back on 18 June, and others, such as Lieutenant Colonel Howard the GSO1, departed sick for the UK. What dumbfounded the division was, however, the almost immediate sacking of Major General Fanshawe. On 19 June, Fanshawe received orders to return to the UK; the following day Brigadier General Steele was appointed temporary GOC division. The departure of Fanshawe, who was clearly a popular and respected commander, appears to have significantly shocked the officers of the division and possibly also many of the other ranks. Lieutenant General Ivor Maxe, one of the most innovative and capable commanders in the BEF, knew Fanshawe well and had been his corps commander during the Third Battle of Ypres. Not a man quick to praise, Maxe described Fanshawe as "a good average divisional commander and trainer."[45] Fanshawe had commandeered 48th Division since May 1915 and the tales of his humanity and concern for his troops are legion. In post-war battalion histories it is impossible to find anything remotely critical of the general. In his account of the division's time in Italy Barnett has a photograph of Fanshawe as a frontispiece and describes his departure as the "heaviest blow to the division it received during the war."[46] The history of 4/Ox&Bucks also has it as a "very heavy blow", while that of the Buckingham Battalion says it was "received with the greatest dismay."[47] Several of the books describe Fanshawe's personality and character in the most favourable, sometimes almost fawning, of words and record their genuine disbelief that the commander could have been degummed.[48] Carrington pursued the issue long into the post-war years and was never reconciled to the sacking, while Vaughan was just one of several later authors who recalled his contacts with Fanshawe with pleasure and admiration. It is unlikely at this distance ever to come to any firm or definitive conclusion as to why he was sent home but it is worth making a few points from the available evidence.

Fanshawe's dismissal was seen by some as a reflection of the way the division must have performed on the Asiago. The troops themselves seem to have been proud and pleased with the way they fought, a view supported by some of the junior officers who later went into print. The men's behaviour was described as "simply magnificent"[49] and as having fought "splendidly". Carrington thought it to have been a "brilliant little victory"[50] and, although such cables were an accepted element of command, Cavan sent a highly appreciative message to the division which talked of the "resolute

45 Cited in S.Robbins, *British Generalship on the Western Front 1914–1918* (Routledge, 2005) p. 62.
46 Barnett, *With the 48th Division*, p. 95.
47 Pickford, *1/4th Battalion Ox & Bucks*, p42; Wright, The *First Buckinghamshire Battalion*, p. 114
48 See, for example, Corbett, *1/8th Worcestershire*, p. 15.
49 Greenwell, *Infant in Arms*, p. 226.
50 TNA: CAB45/84: Carrington to Edmonds, 28 Jun. 1944.

staunchness of 23rd Division and the determination of 48th Division."[51] All ground that had been lost in the initial enemy surge was regained and considerable numbers of the enemy had been killed and captured. If the troops had done what was expected of them, what in Cavan's eyes had gone wrong? Post-battle reports appear in several war diaries which outline some of the problems faced by the division but are generally positive and stress that despite the difficulties success was achieved. Fanshawe wrote two reports almost immediately after the battle: the first was for the CIGS dated 19 June; the other, possibly as evidence for the "careful enquiry into the exact reasons for the break into the 48th Division's line"[52] Cavan declared he would establish once the battle was over. This second was dated 21 June. The first report is brief, but jubilant in tone. Fanshawe wrote that the CIGS "may wonder how we managed to take over 1,000 prisoners, 75 machine guns and seven mountain guns in a purely defensive action" and describes the men as having "the time of their lives" as they pursued the fleeing Austrians.[53] The second is equally brief and also avoids going into detail of the tactical actions. It concentrates on the early loss of communications and how the effective use of the artillery and trench mortars, despite the morning mist, helped to stem the Austrian surge. It must have been written after he knew he had been sacked but apart from the sentence "this was the first defensive battle fought by the division", which might be seen as justification for the early loss of trench lines, it is perhaps strange that he does not make more of a case in his own defence.[54] It was not until after the war that he decided to explain his position further.

Recollections in later accounts suggest the Austrians significantly over-reached themselves. Their objectives were described as "almost impossible to obtain,"[55] the scheme was "ambitious to the verge of lunacy,"[56] and there was a "lack of push and enterprise."[57] Some of the units used in the first wave could be described as *sturmtruppen* battalions which by using infiltration tactics and assisted by the mist at first did show "considerable tactical ability and initiative", but even the humble signaller, Sapper Bishop thought, "They had no heart or go in them or they would have swamped us."[58] The resistance displayed by often isolated parties such as RSM Townley's did certainly help to undermine Austrian morale and faith in success and this is perhaps suggested by the comparatively low number of fatalities sustained by

51 TNA: WO95/4194: WD of XIV Corps General Staff, sent 1310 hrs, 16 Jun. 1918.
52 TNA: WO106/852. Fanshawe to CIGS, 15 Jun.1918.
53 TNA:WO106/852: Fanshawe to CIGS. 19 Jun. 1918.
54 TNA: WO95/4244: WD of 48th Division, General Staff. *The Ghelpac Battle, 15-16 June 1918*
55 Wright, *1/Bucks Battalion*, p112
56 H.Sandilands, *The 23rd Division 1914-1919* (Blackwood & Sons, 1925), p. 268.
57 Wright, *1/Bucks Bn*, p. 112. Edmonds, *Official History Italy*, p. 218 makes a similar point: '…had the Austrians pressed their attack with determination they would have penetrated far deeper without much difficulty.'
58 Bishop, 'A Signaller's Diary'.

the division. Eye-witnesses later recorded that the wounds of many of the British dead were testament to the ferocity of the hand-to-hand fighting but the percentage of dead and wounded to the numbers involved does seem relatively light. In particular, the 14 dead of 5/Warwickshire seems to be a very low number for a battalion which had two companies in the front line, two in support and which was in the thick of the fighting for the first few hours of the battle. The war diary reports casualties as 15 dead, 28 wounded and 30 missing. B Company on the left was not assaulted and must have suffered little except perhaps from the original bombardment. It managed to maintain a steady fire on the attacking units to its right during the morning. If, as Carrington suggests, the bulk of the casualties came from the unfortunate D Company, it may be that the two support companies did not put up much of a sustained resistance in their forward positions. It is possible they withdrew to the Cesuna Switch rather more quickly than they might have done. If this is the case it probably explains why Townley and his small group remained isolated for so long in the HQ position.

Comments, rather than formal reports, in some war diaries draw attention to certain features of the battle. For example, 143 Brigade believed "old lessons were brought out but no new ones" while 5/Gloucestershire considered the "undesirability" of forming ammunition dumps at cross roads was "forcibly demonstrated." The rather more considered post-battle reports, however, go into greater detail about how the engagement developed. There is criticism of the failure of the SOS flares to do their job in the poor visibility and of the fact many were virtual duds; animal casualties could have been reduced if unit transport sections had practised withdrawal procedures more assiduously; brigade transport sections should have had special groups designated as mobile reserves to carry small arms ammunition and grenades quickly to the forward positions; water reserves in petrol tins should have been available at brigade dumps and those dumps and others should ideally have been smaller and more widely spaced. It was thought communications could have been improved by having mounted orderlies and motor cycle despatch riders available from brigade transport sections to report immediately to brigade HQ. In addition it was pointed out that signalling lamps might have been more effective if used to signal through slits in strong point defences or pill boxes, and there was the usual complaint that unburied telephone cables could too easily be cut by shelling and wheels. There were recommendations that Lewis guns and 18 pdrs should be positioned to cover tracks through the woods and that every gun crew should be provided with rifles.[59] The lack of sufficient strong points behind the front line to where garrisons could withdraw and continue to fight was noted, as was the need for every company and battalion HQ to be themselves islands of resistance.

59 One report recorded that an officer of one battery fired seven shots from a rifle at an enemy machine-gun team only 40 yards away and missed every time.

A report by XIV Corps[60] echoed the criticism of the lack of strong points in the forward zone and that outposts had to be garrisoned by troops who should have been in the front line. The outposts were accused of not having closed the wire barriers behind them as they withdrew and, more seriously, of entire garrisons in the front positions having withdrawn into shelters when the bombardment started. Furthermore, when the shelling stopped there was "every evidence" to suggest they remained in the shelters rather than emerge and take position on the fire step. The report did admit it was possible to hold the line thinly but if that were the tactic employed, the garrisons must be able to bring fire to bear all along the front to cover the protecting wire. Given the lie of the land, the restricted view from many of the fire bays and the steep slopes down which the riflemen had to fire from often inadequate fire steps, not all 48th Division's wire could be covered. It was pointed out earlier than much of 48th Division's positions ran through woods and the report stressed that all wire in forests must be checked regularly and that adequate lanes of fire be cleared and maintained. Although it does not specify the thinly held trenches of 48th Division, these and other sections are clearly meant as criticism of Fanshawe's 'elastic defence.' To emphasize further how well 23rd Division performed in comparison to the alleged poorer showing by 48th Division, the former was praised for having sent out patrols soon before the Austrians attacked which did, so the report believed, disrupt the enemy's assault. Other sections in the report dealt with the performance of the artillery and the support branches. These very much reflect the evidence, information and suggestions relayed to corps from individual units, with the conclusions applying equally readily to both 23rd and 48th Divisions.

Most of these points raised by unit and corps HQ reports were more or less stating the obvious and would have been readily understood by any observer. The divisional area was short of strong points, the trenches were generally badly sited, dumps were too close together, batteries positioned in woodland are generally ineffective, telephone cables were far too exposed and visual signalling in mountains in poor weather is always problematic.[61] All these faults and problems were, however, already evident when the division moved into the sector. 23rd Division had held the line and inherited the existing system from the Italians before 48th took it over. 48th Division had had only two weeks in the area to work on any improvements which may have been begun by 23rd Division. With the preparations for the Allied offensive already underway, and with the numbers of troops available for work affected by flu, this timescale proved completely inadequate. The infantry, pioneers and field companies did what

60 TNA: WO95/4194: WD of XIV Corps, General Staff, June 1918.

61 Barnett, *With the 48th Division*, p 61, noted they could only observe 'the folly' of placing such a large dump as Handley Cross within about 2,000 yards of the front line. A corps conference of divisional commanders recorded 'we may learn from the Italians who have reduced their [communication] system to a fine art' by the way they protected their scarce power buzzer and wireless personnel. TNA: WO95/4194: WD of XIV Corps General Staff. 20 Jun. 1918.

they could but, unlike the chalk downlands of the Somme, the rock of the Asiago prevented trenches from being dug and constructed almost overnight.

Having been a brigade, divisional and corps commander on the Western Front, Lord Cavan was familiar with German defensive doctrine. German 'elastic defence' had evolved on the Somme and developed further during Third Ypres. Their practice of immediate counter-attack had, however, played into the hands of the British because the counter-attacks had been smashed by massed artillery fire. It is unclear for how long 48th Division had been training in the tactics necessary to execute Fanshawe's operational concept of elastic defence but the basis on which it was founded differed significantly to the reasons why the Germans employed it at Third Ypres. The purpose of the German counter-attacks had been to regain their lost line but the underlying purpose of Fanshawe's concept was to turn defence into attack and then into a pursuit. Allied intelligence knew the Austrian artillery was growing desperately short of munitions and the quality of its crews diminishing. Although still a potent force, as the Austrian guns were believed to be incapable of sustaining fire over any lengthy period of time they would be unable to crush counter-attacks in the same manner as British artillery had done at Ypres. A major difficulty for 48th Division's utilization of elastic defence was, however, the lack of space to manoeuvre. The divisional frontage, the limited area between the front lines and the descent to the plain and the general lie of the land, determined that any counter-attack would come from an obvious direction and aim towards an equally obvious objective.

This lack of available space did, paradoxically, work to the advantage of 48th Division's defences. In 1916, the Austrians had attacked the Italians in the same area during the so-called *Strafexpedition*. Because they offered the best approach to the Allied line, the channels down which they attacked in 1916 were those they used again in 1918. On 15 June 1918, these two principal lines of operation coincided with the boundaries between 23rd and 48th Divisions and between 145 and 143 Brigades. Allied commanders realized that any attack was likely to thrust at these two points. Happy Valley, the area marking the boundary between 48th Division's two forward brigades, led directly towards the so-called Valle Gap which, if penetrated and held would allow the Austrians to reach the Val Magnaboschi. Once in possession of that position, they could then sweep west to Campiello or surge south to Carriola. Being so critical to the corps' overall defensive scheme, the crucial importance of Happy Valley and the Valle Gap was clearly understood by Cavan. He later recorded that the enemy was to be "contained by a series of switches which had been constructed to meet this eventuality."[62] Once the enemy thrusts had been contained in the pocket, the attackers would then be softened up by concentrated artillery and trench mortar fire. The final stage of the plan was for the now weakened and trapped forces to be wiped out by counter-attacks from battalions in positions selected for that specific

62 TNA: WO106/852: Cavan's *Official Report on the Battle of the Piave River*, September 1918.

purpose. The trouble was that the defences designed to funnel and trap the enemy were incomplete. The switches, which in places were inadequately strengthened, did not completely connect with each other and several significant gaps in the wire had been made in preparation for the proposed Allied offensive.

Fanshawe's tactical decision to deploy only a limited number of men in the front line was later condemned because, his critics argued, the garrisons were insufficient to prevent a breakthrough towards the incomplete defences of the pocket's intended killing zone. His deployments were compared unfavourably to the numbers retained in forward positions by the French and by 23rd Division but Fanshawe will certainly have known the front line defenders faced difficulties of forward observation and of mutual fire support. He will have realized thinning the line might involve a degree of risk (while at the same time minimizing casualties) but reasoned that provided the artillery and the counter-attack battalions were well positioned and active, the attackers could still be held by the garrisons in the switch lines. What is in doubt, however, is whether the flu epidemic had caused the front to be thinned rather more extensively than Fanshawe had intended.

Battalions of 23rd Division, to the right of 48th, had been affected by the flu outbreak but by mid-June fighting strengths had been restored to pre-epidemic levels. These were still not close to the supposed establishment of infantry units but were stronger in numbers than the battalions of 48th Division. Furthermore, 23rd Division's fields of fire were superior to those of the South Midland and its counter-attack battalions were well placed to prevent any break-in developing into a breakthrough and break out. The division's line was penetrated in two places but well-organized counter-attacks quickly restored the situation and earned the division two Victoria Crosses. Furthermore, it is likely that the rate and intensity of machine-gun and rifle fire achieved by 23rd Division's troops caused the attacking Austrians to veer to their right in order to evade that fire. This took them into the more sheltered approaches to 145 Brigade's front. The front of 48th Division was then broken in three places and at all three points the enemy had the advantage of concealment and of hitting battalions which were exceptionally weak in numbers.

At the time of the attack the four battalions of 144 Brigade, the reserve brigade, constituted the strongest brigade in the division. It had just under 100 more than 145 Brigade and over 500 more than 143 Brigade. 5/Gloucestershire holding the left front of 145 Brigade was not the weakest battalion in the brigade but it was weak enough for the GOC brigade to "hesitate" whether the battalion was too weak to take its turn in the line.[63] On its right, 4/Ox&Bucks was almost 100 men stronger. To the left of 5/Gloucestershire, 5/Warwickshire was even weaker than 5/Gloucestershire and

63 Edmonds, *Official History Italy*, footnote citation p. 195. This volume does not specify whether it was the permanent GOC brigade, Brigadier General Watt, or its temporary commander, Lt. Col. Reynolds 1/Bucks, who 'hesitated'. That there was concern is confirmed in a letter from Lord Arnedale to Edmonds in TNA: CAB45/84: 6 Jun.1944

its adjoining D Company was reportedly especially low in number. It was against these positions the main thrust of the Austrian attack fell and with the similarly under strength 6/ and 7/Warwickshire, the counter-attack battalions of 143 Brigade, it was hardly surprising that the overwhelming number of Austrians, aided by the mist, the dead ground to the front, the early breakdown on 143 Brigade's communications and the absence of a British protective barrage, penetrated the Warwicks' defences. It could be argued that either Brigadier General Sladin or Fanshawe himself should have ordered D Company of 5/Warwickshire to be reinforced with at least one company from one of the three other Warwicks battalions to stiffen the front line. It seems remiss that such an obvious channel of possible attack should have been so lightly defended but putting more men in the front line reduced those available for the switch lines and for counter-attack. Furthermore, Fanshawe was, of course, not convinced an infantry attack on his front was imminent. He continued to believe the intelligence supplied by corps that the assault would fall on the Italians and French. Given this intelligence, Fanshawe probably remained focussed on the intended Allied offensive and for that reason kept his strongest formation, 144 Brigade, in reserve to rest because it was tasked to spearhead the counter-offensive. Like any commander, Fanshawe had, however, to achieve the right balance between being able to cope with the unexpected and conserving strength but also of remaining capable of exploiting opportunities should they present themselves. With hindsight, Fanshawe was at fault and perhaps guilty of a lack of overall situational appreciation but he believed that even if his front were assaulted his practised divisional defence scheme, and the faith he had in his senior commanders' capacity to implement it, would contain and then repel any penetration.

In less than modest fashion the war diary of 48th Battalion MGC claims its guns were "largely instrumental" in checking the attack on 143 Brigade's front and that they also inflicted heavy casualties on the enemy assaulting 145 Brigade's sector. The CO drew attention to several short comings that had become apparent during the two-day battle, several of which, such as maintaining a larger reserve of ammunition at the gun positions and ensuring all men were trained in the use of the Mills bomb, could have been resolved at divisional level. Others, however, such as the number of officers and signallers attached to each company, were largely structural issues which could only be addressed by the Army Council or the War Office. Fanshawe cannot be held responsible for those apparent failings. That the machine-gun crews and trench mortar batteries fought hard to disrupt the initial enemy advance is evident from the records but what was equally important was the work done by the divisional artillery.

It was noted earlier that the question of where and when SOS barrages should be fired had aroused considerable discussion between corps and the divisional commanders. A compromise had been reached in April by which divisional commanders were permitted to order counter-preparation barrages to be fired beyond their outpost lines; no fire was to be allowed in the portion of land inside the British outpost line until 90 minutes after divisional commanders had received the order to call in the outposts. Importantly, the actual timing of the order to shell the area within the outpost line was to be decided by GHQ rather than divisional HQ. Field artillery firing on SOS lines, but at counter-preparation rates, was to be ordered by GHQ one hour before the time GHQ believed the infantry attack would take place. Once that had been decided, the batteries were to fire for 10 minutes and then sweep the ground between the Austrian front and the British line in 300 yards lifts. In view of the possibility of poor visibility and a break in telephone cables, the infantry were ordered to blow a bugle and send up flares if they wanted the SOS barrage brought down.[64] Cavan may well have felt that Fanshawe had delayed ordering the CRA to fire on the SOS lines for too long after the Austrian bombardment had begun but the division's guns had fired their counter-preparation, which effectively meant a counter-battery programme, as soon as the Austrians began shelling. There are no reports of any bugle being blown anywhere along the division's front but Fanshawe's hesitation not to fire on the SOS lines meant the Austrian infantry enjoyed a shell-free approach to the British front positions. It was, in fact, Italian batteries on the left of 48th Division which opened fire on Austrian infantry advancing towards 143 Brigade's sector. Of course, the fracture of communications between the forward infantry and the batteries behind did not help Fanshawe's understanding and control of the battle but he could have despatched more runners and officers to obtain situation reports. At the start of the war the onus had been on the staff to request reports from the fighting positions but doctrine had changed and it was now the responsibility of the forward officers to report back to HQ. As those reports were not arriving, Fanshawe should have sent runners to discover why.

During the first few hours of the attack when communications between the infantry and their supporting batteries were frequently disrupted, battery commanders acted on their own initiative. The counter-preparation programme was continued until visibility improved sufficiently to permit observed shooting. Individual officers volunteered to go forward to make contact with the infantry and to telephone back with targets of opportunity. This allowed the heavy batteries in the rear at times to bring down crushing fire on enemy reinforcements crossing the plateau. This action did much to demoralize the Austrian follow up battalions and must have played a part in the eventual Austrian decision to abandon the assault. Several 18 pdr batteries in the woods were compelled to abandon their guns and withdrew after firing at point blank range on infantry pouring towards them but they, too, had taken a heavy toll of the attackers. Some gun crews subsequently picked up rifles and joined the infantry in Cesuna Switch. C/241 "had a very bad time…constantly shelled by all nature of shell" but once the battle began in earnest the artillery, from positions which had been prepared for the proposed Allied advance rather than sited to fight off an Austrian assault, did what it could to disrupt the attack.

Some defenders of 48th Division's performance during the battle point to its lack of experience in mountain warfare. This argument can be readily dismissed because

64 TNA: CAB45/84: Orders from GHQ dated 20 Apr. 1918.

23rd Division had not had any greater experience and its conduct was not questioned. Furthermore, the battle took place on a plateau of rolling woods and pasture rather than in more conventional mountain scenery. The division had not, however, had any experience of wood fighting, an environment in which troops can easily become disorientated and overly-cautious. The Austrians were probably more accustomed to this environment and the troops which attacked 48th Division were certainly well trained and efficient. This was in contrast to the divisions which assaulted the French on the right of 23rd Division.[65] The argument that had Fanshawe manned the front line with the same density of troops as that used by the French the enemy would not have broken through is unproven because even the Austrian *Official History* is scathing about the quality of its divisions deployed against the French.[66]

Lord Cavan never had publically to justify his dismissal of Fanshawe. It may be he wanted a scapegoat for the fact that the Italians had helped to halt the Austrian attack on 48th Division's front, or he may have felt Fanshawe had shown indecision during the morning of 15 June. If Cavan did, however, believe that Fanshawe was showing a lack of resolution when he visited the divisional HQ in the afternoon, the corps commander could have acted to rectify the situation. He did admit to experiencing "an anxious half hour about 0930"[67] but later used the rather vague excuse that he declined from issuing counter orders because he believed it would have only confused the issue. Fanshawe was 55 years old, an age which was not exceptional for a divisional commander in 1918 but close to when he might expect to be given a less strenuous command.[68] He had, however, commanded the South Midland for over three years and perhaps Cavan believed he was exhausted and that the division needed fresh blood. Another reason could simply be that because 48th Division had been penetrated more deeply than 23rd Division, had required four counter-attacks to regain captured land and had lost more men than its neighbour, something had to be done to demonstrate lessens were being learned and change was in hand.

By that stage of the war it was not unknown for GOC divisions to be sacked if it was thought their division had not performed to expectations. Total casualties of 23rd Division were recorded as 556 compared to the 922 of the already numerically weaker 48th. Unit diaries rarely mention the arrival of drafts during the summer and although this may be simple clerical omission, the critical situation on the Western Front meant very few reinforcements were actually despatched to Italy.[69] It is difficult to accept that the normally parsimonious Fanshawe completely threw caution to the

65 Edmonds, *Official History Italy*, pp. 217-18.
66 A French battalion held 800 yards of front; a British battalion held up to 1,145 yards. Ibid., p. 217.
67 TNA: WO106/852: Cavan to CIGS, 15 Jun.1918
68 Fanshawe's two elder brothers, Edward and Hew, had both been corps commanders at 56 and 55 respectively.
69 In one of the very few mention of drafts in war diaries, 6/Warwickshire recorded the arrival of 48 men in June.

winds and risked his reputation and philosophy by deliberately launching inadequately resourced counter-attacks during the afternoon of 15 June. He presumably, therefore, believed the resources were sufficient to eject an enemy whose assault had clearly lost momentum but, as the counter-attacks foundered, this assumption was shown to be a miscalculation. Cavan underscored this fact when he later claimed Fanshawe acted prematurely. Cavan also criticized Fanshawe's timing of the attacks, suggesting that he should have waited until 144 Brigade had ascended the mountain.[70] Commanders do have to take calculated risk but in a bid to regain the initiative and create tempo, Fanshawe did launch his three afternoon and evening counter-attacks with insufficient strength and inadequate artillery support. With drafts unlikely to appear and with current philosophy being "to risk incurring casualties lightly or with insufficient reason would be more than ever a crime,"[71] Cavan could have used this as ammunition against Fanshawe. Yet, according to the Corps Defence Scheme drawn up in April, Fanshawe had deployed his forces as directed. He had, as required, one brigade in reserve, the main defensive system was held in depth, with as many "ample resources" as his depleted manpower allowed for counter-attack and plans were in place to "contest every yard of ground between the varying systems."[72] Despite the gaps left in the wire in and around the Valle Gap, it is unknown, however, whether sufficient paths had been left through belts further back to allow the "rapid forward move of reserves."[73] Furthermore, a later discussion at corps agreed that divisional commanders should use "considerable judgement" about whether they should fight or draw back, although it was also stressed that because the ground was considered favourable for defence, the defences "should be able to stop any attack without losing much ground."[74] The conference concluded small scale local counter-attacks were usually ineffective and costly and should, if possible be avoided. But, there was agreement that the decision to launch such an attack "must rest with the local commander." Larger, organized, counter-attacks were thought to be more advisable but, as these were deemed to require "careful preparation", they were "usually" to be ordered by the GOC division. The corps commander further exhorted divisional commanders to ensure all counter-attack troops regularly rehearsed their counter-attack schemes, paying special attention to preventing the enemy from working up gullies and valleys, but that they should also had a definite, allocated defensive role[75] Fanshawe had adhered to all of

70 TNA: WO106/852: Cavan to Wilson (Chief of the Imperial General Staff) 15 Jun. 1918. Cavan must have written his note to Wilson following Cavan's visit to Fanshawe's HQ in the afternoon of 15 June. Cavan later wrote he believed Fanshawe should have 'softened' the pocket with mortars before launching the counter-attacks. TNA: CAB45/84: Cavan to Edmonds, 26 Jun. 1944

71 Sandilands, *The 23rd Division*, p240

72 TNA: WO95/4194: *XIV Corps Defence Scheme*, 7 Apr.1918

73 Ibid.

74 Ibid. Notes from a conference, 15 Apr.1918.

75 Ibid.

his corps commander's expectations, instructions and stated objectives. Moreover, during the battle, Fanshawe employed General Diaz's strategy of *defence a outrance* and respected General Montouri's insistence that ground should not be permanently yielded. Nevertheless, Cavan presumably felt there was sufficient evidence to warrant the dismissal of his divisional commander.

Major-General Sir Harold Bridgwood Walker. (Private collection)

In a later series of letters to the official historian Fanshawe wrote a marginally more erudite defence of his actions than he had managed in his two post-battle reports.[76] Former subordinates also wrote to Edmonds defending the performance of the division and of its commander. Tomkinson accepted the division was "for some time mud to GHQ Italy" but insisted there "was never any serious peril" the Austrians would break through and that he had never held any "anxiety" about their own lines not being recaptured.[77] Carrington disputed the belief that the division had "done badly" and emphasized: "We did exactly what we set out to do, or rather what General Fanshawe set out to do. There was much ill-feeling against GHQ when we got no credit for it."[78] In response, and in sympathetic vein, Edmonds agreed that Fanshawe had been "very badly treated" and claimed "Cavan was, and is, too stupid to understand elastic defence in depth."[79] This is a harsh judgement because Cavan was, overall, a reasonable corps commander but the question remains why he decided to degum Fanshawe. If the allegation that he first learned of the Austrian attack from the Italians rather than from Fanshawe is true, he may have felt embarrassed and sought retribution.[80] The extant signals evidence for this is, however, inconclusive and it is difficult to imagine that reports from both 23rd *and* 48th Divisions failed to reach Cavan before his telephone call from General Caviglia. It is more likely that Cavan used the temporary penetration of 48th Division's line as an excuse to appoint a proven general, Sir Harold Walker, who was more in sympathy with Cavan's own

76 TNA: CAB45/84: Letters dated 23 Jul. 1943, 14 Feb. 1944 and 18 Aug.1944.
77 Tomkinson to Edmonds, 3 Jul. 1944.
78 TNA:CAB45/84: Carrington to Edmonds, 28 Jun. 1944.
79 Edmonds to Carrington, 4 Jul. 1944. Carrington Papers 81/11/3. Cited in Cassar, *The Forgotten Front*, p164
80 Wilks & Wilks, *The British Army in Italy 1917-1918*, pp. 115-16

preferred tactical methodology.[81] That the decision caused considerable disquiet and anger to Fanshawe's former subordinates in the post-war years is incontestable but not all of them were quite as prepared as Carrington to continue the fight for appropriate recognition. Lieutenant Colonel Pickford decided in 1944, "I suppose this is a controversy that had better not be revived."[82]

81 Fanshawe's successor, Major General Sir Harold Walker, was one year older than the man he replaced.
82 TNA: CAB45/84: Pickford to Edmonds, 30 May 1944.

9

The Closing Phase

July was a period of rest and recuperation for the division. It moved down into what Greenwell called the "Promised Land"[1] of the plain where there was fresh food, bathing facilities and civilians. Arriving at divisional HQ on 4 July, Major General Walker assumed command but found swift acclimatization from France difficult. He was, apparently, "unpleasantly astonished by the heat and the enervating effect of the plains"[2] but did immediately begin to visit all units and make himself familiar to the officers and other ranks. Battalions undertook training schemes, which included instruction in how to use Austrian-issue infantry weapons, and organized inter-unit sports and other competitions. Walker held several conferences for his senior commanders and passed on to them instructions received from corps HQ. At least one set of these was a direct consequence of the temporary success of the Austrian offensive. Anxious to increase his divisions' fire power, Lord Cavan ordered ground in front of all trenches to be cleared of undergrowth, some overhead protection to be removed, the construction of additional trench traverses and the frequent rehearsal of counter-attack procedures. A thorough and expansive GHQ Defence Scheme was published which stressed that officers were expected to use their own initiative to improve sector defences and which also drew attention to the doctrinal pamphlet *SS. 210 The Division in Defence*.

While Cavan correctly emphasized the importance of substantial dugouts and correctly sited trenches with good fields of fire, he was also concerned about the reducing availability of sawn timber and about the number of accidental personnel injuries. The types of injuries are not specified but the numbers involved were enough for Cavan to urge his commanders to ensure they were reduced. No doubt having been warned of the dangers of carelessness when cleaning weapons or wielding picks, the division prepared for a return to the line. By a series of early morning marches which, although still intensely uncomfortable avoided the scorching heat of the day,

1 Greenwell, *Infant in Arms*, p. 229.
2 Barnett, *With the 48th Division*, p. 99.

the division climbed up to the plateau. The infantry relieved that of 23rd Division on 23 July with ration strengths of about 560 per battalion. A small number of drafts had arrived during the rest period and, fortunately, casualties when back in the line were light. 4/Gloucestershire, for example suffered only two killed and five wounded during the month but also had 51 struck off strength for various reasons. The artillery spent most of its time wire cutting to remind the Austrians that the corps was still intact and aggressive. This sentiment was reinforced by patrols which went out almost nightly to dominate no man's land.

In early August, a raid by the neighbouring French division assisted by the South Midland's batteries of 240 Brigade RFA, captured an Austrian general. Under questioning he helpfully disclosed his troops were to raid the following night. 5/Warwickshire sent out two small patrols after dark to establish whether this intelligence was true. With the guns on alert, the patrols heard the Austrians preparing for their raid and signalled the artillery to open fire after the Warwicks had had time to withdraw. The division's batteries were thought to have hit something like 60 percent of the 80 Austrian raiders as they crossed no man's land. That many Austrians still had fight in them had also been demonstrated the previous night. Two companies of 8/Worcestershire had been sent to raid the enemy positions and had become involved in a "desperate" hand-to-hand encounter with the defending Bosnians. The raiders captured about 26 prisoners but all were described as "very stubborn [and] refused to come quietly." Eventually only three prisoners reached the Worcesters' lines; the battalion suffered 15 dead and wounded.

Intelligence gathered from deserters and prisoners suggested the Austrians were preparing to withdraw to their *Winterstellung* positions on or around 10 August. General Montuori, GOC Italian Sixth Army to which the British divisions belonged, wanted to launch a pre-emptive strike to demonstrate that the withdrawal was forced rather than voluntary. Lord Cavan agreed in principle but argued that such an attack would leave the new forward positions exposed and difficult to supply across a wide stretch of open plateau. Furthermore, he told Montuori that only about two-thirds of his artillery would be in place by the time of the proposed assault. This sensible and cautious argument was accepted by Montuori who asked instead that the British and French undertake two large-scale raids in order to maintain pressure, weaken Austrian morale and discover whether the Austrians were actually in the process of withdrawing.

The planning process for the raids was slick, efficient and prompt. By now it followed something of a template developed from the experience gained in previous enterprises. The template could be quickly adapted to suit the various terrains, objectives and conditions. This facility allowed staff to produce a set of orders within a matter of hours of them being requested. The effort was to be coordinated by corps HQ, which was to arrange the corps artillery for the whole front, but divisional commanders had the freedom to decide the formations in which their men were to attack, their specific objectives and the lifts and box barrages needed as cover for their companies. The divisional signal company prepared for its part by carrying rolls of cable to brigade HQ, worked out how to link the front line with the raiders' control centres and organized the positioning of power buzzers between battalion HQ and the report centres. 7th Division was also to undertake simultaneous raids as part of this major demonstration of Allied aggression. In 48th Division, the scheme agreed was for three companies of 5/Warwickshire and three of 7/Warwickshire to work in cooperation with three of 8/Worcestershire and three of 6/Gloucestershire.[3] A section of RE was attached to each of the brigades but the sappers were ordered if possible to avoid blowing in dugouts because they could be used by the Allies in any later advance. To achieve surprise there was to be no preliminary bombardment but at zero, firing gas and explosive, several batteries would immediately concentrate on counter-battery work while others dealt with the wire and enemy strong points.

The raids went almost exactly to plan. With the defenders surprised and stunned by the intensity of the sudden bombardment, 7/Warwickshire entered trenches near Ave, attacked the nearby dump, cleared dugouts, shot mules of a ration party, destroyed machine-gun nests and mountain guns and returned with about 100 prisoners for the loss of 13 wounded. The left company of 5/Warwickshire was constrained by its own bombardment falling short and did not get into its objectives, but the other two companies penetrated and wrought considerable damage before withdrawing.[4] 6/Gloucestershire passed through the enemy wire easily enough and then ran into some machine-gun fire before clearing dugouts in a railway embankment. Telephone cables had been cut within 30 minutes of zero but touch was maintained with battalion HQ by means of signal lamps. 8/Worcestershire met with little resistance, killing over 60 and capturing 40 in return for three dead and 20 wounded. In a subsequent post-action report the episode was thought to have proved the "immense advantage of highly-trained and determined troops over a half-trained and demoralized enemy."[5]

In view of the "most successful" nature of the raids, it is unsurprising there were few suggestions as to how the enterprises might have been improved. Divisional HQ noted that "consequent upon previous experience" there were some tactical amendments made as to where and how the enemy line was to be hit but the two nights allowed for reconnaissance were considered adequate. 144 Brigade did record that scouts covering the passage of the assault companies needed to be in sufficient numbers and to be familiar with the lie of the land or, it was thought, they were likely to become more of a danger than a protecting force to the main body. Scouts of 6/Gloucestershire had, for example, completely missed one enemy post and its garrison was able to fire on the assaulting companies as they passed en route for the enemy front line. Technical faults with power buzzers convinced the divisional signal company it was not worth the

3 The number of companies employed in the raids varies in the corps' and individual unit war diaries. Those of the latter have been used here.
4 The 5/Warwickshire sustained 20 dead, with another two dying of wounds the following day. It seems likely that a proportion of the dead were killed by their own barrage.
5 Stacke, *The Worcestershire Regiment*, p. 394.

effort taking them forward for short, sharp raids. A useful and successful innovation involved the raiders taking coloured lights across no man's land. Having worked out the Austrian SOS system the lights helped to confuse and delay the enemy's artillery response. For the first time on the division's front bonfires were lit at a pre-arranged time in the British lines which not only acted as the signal for withdrawal but also guided the troops back to their own trenches. Unlike the raiders of 7th Division, however, and for reasons which are nowhere explained, 48th Division did not employ searchlights to indicate the way back to the British positions. The only other apparent criticism by those directly involved is a rather cryptic note by 144 Brigade. This suggested, "Either ample time must be allowed for getting out, or else the party must expect the unexpected and be prepared to deal with it vigorously and immediately." Continuing a practice which had become increasingly widespread in the BEF since 1916, corps HQ also analyzed the ways and means of the simultaneous French raids. It was apparent the French had suffered fewer casualties in their enterprises because, it was concluded, they had concentrated their artillery on a narrower front. Eager to acknowledge best practice and incorporate it within developing doctrine, Lord Cavan ordered the French tactic to be trialled by British divisions.[6]

Momentum and pressure was maintained by more very successful French raids the following night. Two undertaken by 143 Brigade in support of the French failed when the Warwicks' platoons were driven back by intense machine-gun fire. The success of the French and news of the advance of the Allied armies at Amiens prompted several of the senior Italian commanders to advocate an immediate offensive. Preparations on the Asiago were begun but, as Cavan had pointed out earlier in the month, ground and operational conditions remained unfavourable. If anything, they had worsened. British counter-battery work had been so effective the Austrians had been compelled to withdraw their larger guns beyond the range of British six inch pieces. This meant enemy heavy guns could now target the British lines with impunity. Various rumours abounded as to where the prospective offensive might take place but at a conference held by Cavan in late August all he was prepared to tell his GOC divisions directly was that it might be launched in September. Cavan was clearly worried about what an attack on the Asiago would mean for his troops. As they could not advance "blindly" through the heavily wooded areas he ordered "battle patrols" to leap frog through each other; tactical manoeuvre and leadership would thus need to be of the highest order. The advance would have to be made up hill and into the fire of Austrian guns positioned on commanding slopes beyond the range of British counter-batteries. The only hint he did give was a warning that GHQ schools would be closed four days before any attack and that officers and staffs would be called back from leave. Preparations for what was explained as an expected pursuit of an Austrian withdrawal were begun as cover but Barnett at least was unconvinced. With probably a degree of hindsight he looked back on the proposed role of 48th Division, which was to pass through 7th and

6 TNA: WO95/4195: WD of XIV Corps General Staff. Conference of 12 Aug. 1918.

23rd Divisions and take Monte Erio, with serious misgivings. The mountain lay on the far side of the deep Val d'Assa whose cliffs soared majestically but intimidatingly above the Assa river. Barnet described the scheme as "fantastic and contrary to the elements of common sense."[7]

While these proposals were being discussed at higher levels of command, raids continued. 144 Brigade undertook two small ones on 24 August and netted six prisoners, but a larger effort was planned by 145 Brigade for the night of 26-27 August. The instruction was for it to be on a "big scale" and was to involve two battalions. The objective was still to ascertain whether the Austrians were withdrawing and was to employ the recent lesson learned from the French of keeping the penetration on a narrow front. Security was to be kept exceptionally tight and training for the raid was to be conducted under the auspices of a doctrinal pamphlet published recently by the Training Directorate. Planning was again completed quickly and effectively. The Bucks and 4/Berkshire were both to use most of their fighting strength against the ruins of Asiago village which, despite some complicated tactical manoeuvre and initial resistance, was executed with almost clinical efficiency. The two battalions returned with about 100 prisoners for a cost of five dead. 7/Worcestershire was ordered to follow up this success with a raid the following night but the enterprise was cancelled when a deserter brought news that the Austrians were to raid themselves that night. The enemy attempt did not materialize and 4/Gloucestershire subsequently proceeded with its scheme. The two platoons killed or wounded about 40 of the enemy and returned with prisoners.

Drafts remained difficult to source from the UK. In September, the seemingly inevitable decision was made to reduce the size of brigades from four to three battalions.[8] There were sufficient reinforcements in the Corps Reinforcement Camp to bring the remaining battalions to an establishment of 900. Unlike the procedure followed in France, however, rather than lose some of their men to units which were to remain with the division, it appears the battalions despatched to the Western Front went intact. It is likely 8/Warwickshire and 8/Worcestershire from 143 and 144 Brigades were selected on the grounds of regimental seniority but it is less clear why 5/ Gloucestershire was the unit chosen from 145 Brigade. It may be that the geographic origin of the battalion was considered to be the least homogenous of the brigade's units and was selected for that reason. The three battalions left the division in late September and were incorporated within the reconstituted 25th Division. Somewhat surprisingly, there is no comment other than sheer matter of fact entries in any of the divisional or corps war diaries about the decision or the action of the authorities. By that stage of the war it was possibly simply accepted that the War Office was capable of caprice.

7 Barnett, *With the 48th Division*, p. 102.
8 British divisions on the Western Front experienced the unit reduction during February 1918.

It seems likely that most of the remaining nine battalions received between 200-250 men as drafts during the month.[9] September was relatively quiet but the division continued to lose a significant proportion of its strength to disease. An outbreak of diarrhoea resulted in the evacuation of 260 of the 915 affected and in the first 10 days of September, there were 16 deaths alone from flu. Cases were sent to a CCS and isolated, billets were sprayed and all men who had come into contact with infected cases gargled three times daily with potassium permanganate. The ADMS remained in constant communication with the field ambulances and unit MOs in order to coordinate the preventative measures and, with a beneficial reduction in the number of flies, by the end of September the diarrhoea outbreak had been contained. There were still, however, over 1,500 cases in October and almost 700 of flu. The laundries were working well and general health and hygiene was considered to be good. Scabies was, however, evident in the drafts and there was still official concern about the "extraordinary number" of accidental injuries. At least one man is known to have died from such injuries during October but overall casualties for September were remarkably light.

The ADMS and his staff made regular visits to brigade HQ in order to ascertain how many stretcher bearers and relay posts might be needed for the continuing series of raids. Blankets, hot drinks and motor lorries to evacuate the wounded were organized by the field ambulances, arrangements which came into their own after 5/Warwickshire met determined and unexpected resistance during a raid on the railway cutting close to the enemy front line. The preparation and planning was sound, but the barrage fell short and caused casualties among the raiders, a miscalculation which the CRA caustically noted meant the effort was "not a great success." This was in sharp contrast to the accuracy of the fire during the raids of 26-27 August when the raiders were able to start cutting the wire before the guns had shifted fire from the enemy front trenches. An enquiry into why the shelling for 5/Warwickshires' attempt was in error reached no firm conclusion.[10] The battalion reported eight deaths and 87 wounded but the post-war figure suggests 19 fatalities and another two dying from wounds. This raid, which had been in conjunction with one by 23rd Division, was followed three hours later by another involving almost the entire fighting strength of 4/Ox&Bucks.

Apart from the numbers engaged, the raid was typical of those conducted by the division and other British and French formations on the Italian front. The objective was a former farm which had been so well visited by British patrols and raids that its confines and characteristics were well known. A model of the area was constructed which company and platoon officers studied before they in turn briefed their men. The usual coordinating meetings were held with representatives from the artillery,

9 It appears that 7th and 23rd Divisions received the lion's share of the reinforcements because in October, Cavan reported 48th Division was 700 men under strength. TNA: WO106/852: Cavan to CIGS, 6 Oct. 1918

10 British, French and Italian batteries were involved in this barrage.

machine-gun company and trench mortar battery. The field ambulances were notified and a section of sappers detailed to assist if required. Platoons were told off to give flanking protection, the colours of flares agreed for their several purposes and a report centre established. Tapes were laid to indicate the forming up line in no man's land and at 0400, with the platoons having moved silently into position some time before, the barrage opened. The wire had been cut on so many previous occasions that it provided only a limited obstacle to the raiders who were able to make their way easily into the trenches. They worked along them with phosphorous and conventional grenades, gathering prisoners and despatching those Austrians who resisted. The signal for withdrawal was fired and by 0630 the well-executed raid was over. It was a swift, efficient and effective enterprise which, for a cost of probably four dead or died of wounds and fewer than 10 wounded, captured 37 prisoners. The post-raid report claimed that not a living enemy remained in the sector, with the raiders and the artillery estimated to have killed about 60. That there were not more enemy troops killed or captured was probably indicative of falling morale in the Austrian forces. The trenches were reported to be lightly held and the resistance sporadic at the best of times. It is likely many other defenders fled from what was a vulnerable and oft-raided salient in their lines to the greater safety of their front line system. They had not yet quite reached the stage of running towards the attackers to surrender, bringing their blankets with them,[11] but the fighting power of the Austrian Army was clearly on the wane.

One of the reasons why the division's raiders were pushing at an increasingly open door was because the Dual Monarchy's forces, as well as their families, were critically short of food. The manpower shortage was becoming acute and discontent at home was also affecting the troops at the front. In contrast, the Allies appeared to enjoy inexhaustible supplies of munitions and rations. Yet, while the Allies certainly did have the advantage in logistics and supply, they were not without their own difficulties. Owing to the U-boat threat and the shipping shortage, until the *SS Millars* docked in early August carrying 3,500 tons of meat, XIV Corps had suffered from reduced rations of fresh meat. The arrival of a small American contingent of troops, with apparently bottomless pockets, exacerbated the position because the price of Italian commodities soared. The supply of sawn timber had improved but only because the Foreign Office had become involved to secure supplies from Switzerland, and the ever increasing demand by the Italians for British munitions was absorbing excessive railway capacity and limiting the number of shells available for British guns. Corps HQ was concerned about alleged "slackness" in horsed transport on the mountain roads, the regular technical failures of the *teleferica*s, which often reduced daily tonnage by 50 percent, and about the lack of suitable lorries. Frequent requests to replace the inadequate British vehicles with Fiats were met with refusal until August when corps HQ was granted permission to purchase 25 Fiats. That, however, was only

11 Greenwell, *Infant in Arms*, p. 240.

one of the problems. Italian mountain roads were generally in reasonable condition and the better the lorry, the faster speeds the drivers maintained when descending. Excessive speed had caused a reported 18 Italian-driven lorries to have gone over the edge of one hairpin bend in one morning alone. Corps was astonished and worried by such losses and ordered experiments to be undertaken which would mechanically limit lorries' speed There were no complaints about the quality of the roads themselves. The British were impressed by the ability and efficiency of the mixed civilian and military maintenance gangs, many of which employed women and boys and girls of very tender years.

Another difficulty was deciding what clothing should be issued to troops on the plateau. By September, nights were growing increasingly cold and frequent thunderstorms could cause temperatures to drop 15 degrees in 30 minutes. This was possibly why so many men continued to catch flu and chills but it took several weeks of prevarication to decide that winter clothing would replace serge from the start of October. The worsening weather then caused the date to be brought forward and by the start of the month the issue was complete. The date coincided with growing speculation that the relatively fresh divisions in Italy were to be exchanged with exhausted formations from France. 7th Division was the first to be notified it would go to France and that it would be replaced by 48th Division's sister TF formation, 47th (2nd London) Division. As rumours spread that the exchange was to be the first of several it appeared possible that 48th Division might return to the Western Front. This possibility was considered even more likely because 5th and 41st Divisions had earlier returned to France and 7th and 23rd Divisions had left the Asiago to become part of the new Italian Tenth Army.[12]

According to XIV Corps HQ, it was General Diaz who first suggested 48th Division should stay on the Asiago to shield the move of the other British divisions to Tenth Army. This may have been the case but it would seem more likely that Diaz merely suggested *a* British division should remain and allowed Cavan to choose which one it should be. If that was the sequence of events it is tempting to suggest that Cavan selected 48th Division to stay because it was the one he least wanted in his own command. When ordered to lose one of their divisions, units or even men it has never been unusual for commanders to select the ones they considered to be the weakest or most troublesome. For reasons of seniority it is unlikely he would have chosen the regular 7th Division to stay on the Asiago. Of the other remaining two divisions, and with his negative perception of the South Midland's performance in June, he probably considered 23rd Division to be better suited for his new command. Although it remains unclear who did make the actual selection, corps HQ recorded Cavan only agreed to leave one division behind with the stipulation that it would join Tenth Army "at the earliest opportunity."[13] 48th Division certainly daily expected to

12 Lord Cavan was appointed GOC Italian Tenth Army.
13 TNA: WO95/4195: Summary, November 1918.

rejoin the two British divisions on the Piave front, and Cavan did several times petition the *Commando Supremo* to allow the British corps to reassemble. On 26 October he wrote: "The sooner I can get the 48th Division back the better but I can hardly ask for it at this exact moment." A few days later he was more forthright and requested the *Commando Supremo* return the division because "the enemy has withdrawn on the Asiago."[14] General Diaz declined Cavan's request and the South Midland was to remain the only British formation within Italian Sixth Army. This was a posting which was thought both to "profoundly puzzle the enemy"[15] and also to provide a constant source of irritation to the division.[16]

In October, the weather turned very autumnal. Frosts and ferocious rain added to the difficulties faced by the field companies and pioneers. They had performed fairly routine tasks throughout the summer: improving the defences, building ranges and assault courses, constructing flash spotting positions for survey teams, making kilns to salvage solder from discarded tins, concreting horse lines, preparing winter quarters and the inevitable work on roads. It is evident, however, that the engineers, echoing their experience in 1915, were once again frustrated by the attitude of the infantry. Four sappers had been attached to each battalion to advise on trench maintenance but they complained they were really teaching the infantry basic skills which they should already possess. "The infantry as a whole have been too completely nursed by the RE" and, as a consequence, had grown into the habit of allowing "the sapper to run the work completely, simply providing him with a fatigue party." The RE considered this to be a waste of their skills and time because "being on fatigue [the infantry] naturally take as little interest with the work as compatible with its completion." Responsibility for completion of the work and for its quality had thus devolved upon the capability of the sapper and, "in these days of wastage and incompetent reinforcements this quality is very often very difficult to ensure." Field company strengths appear to have been reasonably well maintained but it is evident that the engineers did consider themselves to be over-worked and compelled to accept responsibility for tasks which should have been the remit of others.[17]

Apart from the occasional bombardment, which tended not to last for any substantial length of time, the Austrians remained quiet. Their patrols were rarely encountered but deserters continued to come in. These were men who had had enough of fighting for what to them seemed a lost cause. In contrast to the irregular firing of their own artillery, they were daily deluged by French, British and Italian batteries and by swarms of aircraft staffing and bombing them. In July alone, XIV Corps HQ reported

14 TNA: WO106/852: Cavan to CIGS: 26 Oct.1918; 31 Oct.1918.

15 Stacke, *The Worcestershire Regiment*, p. 434

16 In a letter to Edmonds, Lt. Col. Howard the division's GSO1, recalled the discontent: 'I could write quite a lot … especially when the 48th Division was left behind on the Asiago Plateau and put into an Italian Corps, but fear that most of it would be quite unsuitable for an official History!' TNA: CAB45/84: 10 Jan.1944

17 The 477th Field Company went with the two other divisions to the Piave front.

the destruction of 66 enemy aircraft for the loss of only four British machines.[18] As summer turned to autumn the aerial balance swung even more in the Allied favour. The division raided and patrolled most nights, sometimes taking with them deserters from Austria's subject nationalities who called on their former comrades to leave their lines and surrender. This patrol tactic had some success but most raids kept to the tried and tested template and returned with a growing number of prisoners. Ave and Sec were each visited several times, with most of the events "working like clockwork"[19] and against little opposition. "Prisoners everywhere abounded"[20] and sweepstakes were organized to gamble on the numbers brought in.[21] In view of the frequency of raids undertaken since the June battle, it is surprising that 7/Worcestershire only managed its first big enterprise on 10 October. To cover the battalion's advance the CRA used every available battery of field artillery for the creeping barrage while the heavies concentrated on counter-battery work. Trench mortars and at least 28 machine guns were used to provide protection while the companies advanced across the wide expanse of no man's land. When they reached Sec, which was again the objective, platoons lost direction because many Austrian trenches had been so flattened as to be unrecognizable. 4/Gloucestershire of the same brigade raided nearby Ave on 23-24 October and brought back 217 prisoners many of who had been persuaded to surrender by Serbian and Romanian prisoners attached to the Gloucesters. This raid was thought to have been particularly successful for several reasons: the companies displayed excellent discipline when forming up, the state of the ground was ideal, there was a useful amount of moonlight and the barrage was "all that could be desired." Officers and NCOs had thoroughly studied and understood their objectives and, although there had been no interpreters to work with the Yugoslavs and Romanians, the prisoners had shown "great gallantry"; one was even recommended for an award. Fearing cruel treatment by their captors the enemy were reportedly reluctant at first to come out of their dugouts. This suspicion of the Allies' behaviour may have had some justification as there are suggestions that any hesitation on the part of prisoners to cross no man's land resulted in short shrift from their captors.[22]

The generally weak Austrian response to the numerous raids meant that divisional casualties remained light. Three gunners of C/240 were killed in the retaliation fired for a raid by 6/Warwickshire, but the battalion itself had lost only three killed and under 30 wounded in return for the capture of five officers and over seven score other ranks. The low casualty figures were fortunate because battalions seem to have averaged about 100 other ranks below establishment and drafts remained slow to arrive. The number of men lost to what are described as "injuries" continued to be higher than

18 TNA: WO95/4195: Summary, July 1918
19 Carrington, *War Record of 1/5th Warwick*, p. 77.
20 Ibid.
21 Greenwell, *Infant in Arms*, p. 240.
22 See, for example, Cruttwell, *War Service of 1/4th Berkshire*, p. 148.

might be expected but as they are not always recorded as self-inflicted it is difficult to ascribe them all to the consequences of possible low morale. When references are made in the sources to the spirit or determination of the troops they are usually of a positive nature. Furthermore, there does even seem to have been surprise that the weakening Austrian resolve was not encouraging divisional HQ to demand greater activity by the brigades. Cruttwell recorded, "The absence of any great concerted attempt to destroy them seemed almost inexplicable to our troops."[23] As a counter-balance to this apparent desire for action, however, 4/Ox&Bucks was thought to have "had enough and were glad to get out" after what was described as a quiet tour.

Significant developments involving the two other British divisions in Italy were about to be made down on the plain. Cavan certainly did want 48th Division returned to his command as quickly as possible but in the meantime he was concerned that it might be drawn into an unnecessary battle on the Asiago. General Pennella, GOC Italian XII Corps, announced without any prior consultation with his French and British divisional commanders that his corps would attack within four days. This lack of inter-Allied liaison caused consternation among the French and British commands. When questioned by Major General Walker's GSO1, the British liaison officer at Sixth Army HQ denied knowing anything about Pennella's proposed offensive, an opinion confirmed immediately by his French counterpart. An astonished Walker declined to agree to the proposal, declaring he needed to consult and contacted Cavan for advice. Walker pointed out to Cavan the very short notice given by Pennella and the fact that the plans appeared to be almost a carbon copy of those which had been prepared for the earlier, abandoned offensive. Cavan decided the proposal would involve "an entirely unnecessary sacrifice of life" and told Walker he could agree to the use of British artillery but not to the involvement of his infantry.[24] General Diaz agreed the plan should be shelved but asked that the British and French conduct raids as a diversion to the major attack which was about to be made on Mount Grappa. The eventual British contribution to the demonstration was a successful enterprise by 4/Gloucestershire on the night of 24-25 October.

It seems unlikely that the raids on the Asiago had any influence on the fighting on Mount Grappa. The inexperienced Italian Fourth Army made little progress in very hostile terrain and against resolute Austrian defence. Elsewhere the Allies had greater success, with British 7th Division leading the way for Italian Tenth Army to gain a footing on the Austrian side of the Piave by 29 October. As the Allied forces then headed north towards Veneto, Austrians on Grappa, and ultimately also on the Asiago were threatened with being cut off. The first 48th Division knew of a general Austrian retreat was during a raid by 1/Bucks and 7/Worcestershire on the night of 29 October. One section of 475th Field Company accompanied the infantry who met with so little opposition it was "presumed the long awaited withdrawal of the

23 Ibid., p. 145.
24 TNA: WO106/852: Cavan to CIGS, 26 Oct. 1918.

enemy had taken place." The Bucks moved on into the village of Asiago and reported they had found one solitary enemy soldier. This unfortunate man's job was, apparently, to light flares to deceive the Allies into believing the line was still held. On 30 October, when each brigade moved one company forward almost as a skirmishing line to test the strength of the Austrian will, they did encounter some resistance. A Company of 7/Worcestershire, for example, advanced two miles in utter darkness and over numerous delaying obstacles and then spent the day in bitter fighting for the village of Camporovere. In the face of such determined resistance the company withdrew, leaving behind the wounded Second Lieutenant Wenham, to wait for the rest of the battalion to come up.[25] Meanwhile, 18 pdr batteries were moving forward and 5/Sussex was ordered to improve the roads from the British front line across the former no man's land.

On 31 October, French and British patrols pushed northwards, occasionally running into small arms fire from the positions in the mountains beyond and from some erratic Austrian shelling. Major General Walker agreed to support an attack by the French but there was hesitancy at Pennella's HQ as to how prompt and swift the pursuit should be. Frustrated by Pennella's indecision, Walker informed the French he would attack whether the corps commander agreed or not. Unfortunately, over the next few days there was almost a complete lack of coordination and exchange of intelligence between the Italians and the British. To go on the offensive was a new scenario for all concerned but the lack of efficient liaison between corps HQ and its units should have been quickly addressed and resolved. Despite the absence of control from Sixth Army HQ, when 48th Division and French 24th Division moved forward soon after 0500 on 1 November cooperation between the two allies was good and well maintained. Progress was made, especially by 145 Brigade who pushed through the *Winterstellung*, but the two Gloucestershire battalions of 144 Brigade ran into stiff opposition in difficult terrain. They were forced back into Camporovere to regroup and organize a fresh barrage. Eager to establish momentum, Walker decided to accept a degree of risk by exploiting the advance made by 145 Brigade before clearing up the situation in Camporovere. By a turning action from the north, pressure on Camporovere would be automatically eased by this threat to cut off the Austrians in the village. Walker attached 7/Worcestershire to the brigade to strengthen its fire power and ordered 143 Brigade forward to Asiago. Once the position at Camporovere and Bosco had been recovered 143 Brigade, supported by a section of 18 pdrs, two tractor hauled 4.5 inch howitzers and a half company of RE, would become the advance guard and work its way up the Val d'Assa. By dusk on 1 November the brigade had assembled and was ready to move forward from Asiago.

The dawn attack on 2 November allowed both 145 and 144 Brigades to take important positions on the high ground. Efficient staff work and good communications

25 Stacke, *The Worcestershire Regiment*, p. 437 reports that when Wenham's body was found four days later, 'There was little doubt he had been foully murdered.'

ensured that 143 Brigade was quickly ordered to move and by 1000, 7/Warwickshire, the lead battalion, had entered the semi-darkness of the Val d'Assa. 145 Brigade protected its right flank from the mountains above the gorge, with Italian 20th Division assumed to be performing a similar role on the left. The one road, with a drop of about 1,000 feet to the river on its western side, climbed towards Vezzena and widened onto a plateau before descending eventually to Caldonazzo. It was difficult terrain and was severely to curtail the division's logistical train. Unsurprisingly, once they had improved the routes into Asiago, 5/Sussex and 475th Field Company continued their labours towards and into the valley. Ahead of them linesmen of the divisional signal company established forward visual stations and report centres, linking them to the rear with cabling and relay stations; behind them, field artillery limbers were readied to keep the advanced batteries supplied with shells. The ADMS had already prepared plans detailing the position of RAPs, the movement of stretcher bearer squads and their relay and collecting posts. On 2 November, several tent subdivisions went forward, as did a party from 1/Field Ambulance whose task was to test water quality in captured areas. The bulk of the field ambulances' work in the next few days was, however, caring for the hundreds of exhausted Austrian prisoners.

Meeting only occasional resistance, battalions of 143 Brigade advanced towards Vezzena. The Austrians made little attempt to withdraw their artillery and heavy equipment and the number of troops willing to give themselves up increased as the advance progressed. On one of the rare occasions when they were halted by fire, troops of 6/Warwickshire slid down an old *telefericas* track to the valley bottom and then made a two company charge up a mountain to silence a machine gun. 7/Worcestershire climbed through dense woods, ideal country for rearguards, but came across only the debris of retreat and the "astounding signs" of an army in collapse:[26] dead horses in harness, discarded personal equipment and weapons and an abandoned park of over 100 guns. Hordes of prisoners came in freely but having just become the first British troops to enter home territory of the Central Powers, 7/Warwickshire came under fire from scattered isolated positions. 143 Brigade halted for the night and regrouped. On the flanks of 48th Division, Italian 14th and 20th Divisions were also advancing but, again, there was no meaningful contact between the Allied formations. The Italians did not send out patrols to gain touch with the South Midland, but neither, it appears, did Walker or his brigade commanders. The mountain terrain made communications difficult, but there is little excuse for this failure to keep Allied forces coordinated and informed of each others' movements. Fortunately, given the chaotic nature of the Austrian retreat this neglect was not as crucial as had there been prolonged and organized resistance. It is likely 48th Division was more concerned with ensuring it could maintain its supplies than worrying too much about what its ally was doing.

Walker was acutely aware of the difficulties of bringing ammunition and essential supplies from railhead on the plain, up the mountain, across the Asiago and then

26 Stacke, *The Worcestershire Regt*, p. 436.

onwards in the wake of the advance. Sufficient heavy and light lorries did become available by 3 November when lorryhead was established at Asiago; horsed transport then took the supplies forward into Val d'Assa and beyond. At anytime, however, snow or the deliberate blocking of the single road by the Austrians could have seriously jeopardized the pursuit. Nevertheless, and still in ignorance of what the Italians were doing on both flanks, the reinforced 143 Brigade, followed by 144 and 145 Brigades, resumed the advance at 0430 on 3 November. 5/Warwickshire formed a mounted patrol using captured horses to round up an entire battalion and to gallop after escaping wagons. Lieutenant Colonel Pryor of 6/Warwickshire drove ahead of his battalion in a requisitioned car to conduct a reconnaissance and bumped into three Austrian battalions. They refused to lay down their arms, declaring that an armistice had come into force and that they were withdrawing that night the three kilometres required by the terms to prevent them from being taken prisoner. Hopelessly outnumbered, Pryor sensibly refrained from doing anything except drive on towards Pergine. When an Austrian party under a white flag appeared on the road in front of Brigadier General Sladen, who was accompanying 7/Warwickshire, its senior officer insisted the armistice was in force and that the Warwicks had advanced beyond the agreed line. Although considerably outnumbered, Sladen was in a stronger position than Pryor and quickly disillusioned the would-be negotiators by sending Lewis gun teams around the flanks and giving the battalion commander 10 minutes to surrender. A nearby strong point was also bluffed into capitulation when threatened with bombardment from guns which Sladen knew were still miles behind his infantry.[27] The number of prisoners collected was so considerable that when 144 Brigade appeared, 4/Gloucestershire was attached to 143 Brigade to help manage the masses.

The confusion on the part of the Austrians as to when the armistice came into force was the result of deliberate obfuscation by the Italians. In the early hours of 4 November, 48th Division learnt hostilities would cease at 1500 hours; Penella's HQ later sent details of where the line of demarcation between the opposing forces should be drawn. 6/Warwickshire piquetted the line but soon the whole area was invaded by thousands of Italian troops who had left their own sectors to celebrate the end of the war. They abandoned their hordes of Austrian captives who were at the end of their tether, demoralized, exhausted and without rations. 48th Division stepped in to feed and organize the prisoners. The diarist of 475th Field Company thought the smell of so many "close-packed Austrians was simply indescribable" but there were also civilians needing to be fed. Groups of them thronged several battalion HQ declaring the

27 The GSO1, Lt. Col. Howard motored to 3rd Austrian Army HQ at Trent on 3 November. He informed General Romer that 48th Division had received no orders to cease hostilities and demanded unconditional surrender. Romer was told his army should provide rations for all British troops in newly occupied areas and that he would be held hostage. Romer accepted the terms but pointed out that feeding British troops would be difficult as supply trains had been pillaged. TNA: WO95/4244: WD of 48th Division, General Staff. 3 Nov.1918

Austrians had long since requisitioned all the available food. The division's supply lines back to the plain were stretched to the limit and although even military rations had not always managed to keep up, the division accepted responsibility and did what it could to assist the civilians. Much to their own relief many Austrian officers were quickly removed from the supposed authority of the Italians and fed and guarded by the division. The hostility felt between the Italians and Austrians was such that the latter feared retribution at the hands of their pre-war, and now wildly celebrating erstwhile ally. With "almost the last remnant of self-respect" the Austrians were determined not to become prisoners of the Italians.[28]

The behaviour of the Italian troops created problems for the South Midland because their unregulated transport blocked the roads and strayed onto those which had been designated for the division. Furthermore, the Italians' celebrations caused general mayhem. Frustrated as the division was by the prevailing indiscipline, it could look back on what the diarist of 4/Ox&Bucks described as "four amazing days" with a deal of satisfaction. At Tenth Army HQ, Cavan wrote "I am glad 48th Division had its little show"[29] but it was, in reality, rather more than that. The division had undertaken an improvised advance across tortuous terrain, with potentially tenuous lines of communication and with little or no knowledge of what was happening on its flanks. The staff had worked out a plan involving the *ad hoc* attachments of units and which included complicated tactical manoeuvre with limited situational awareness. The units had demonstrated flexibility, resilience, adaptability and determination and had advanced almost 40 miles in two days. They had coped with thousands of enemy prisoners, a potentially hostile civilian population and a corps commander whose method of disseminating intelligence and orders was underdeveloped. According to the official historian, the division's total haul for 2-4 November was over 22,000 prisoners, 63 guns, 161 howitzers, a park at Caldonazzo of over another 200 guns, one 17 inch howitzer, a train loaded with field guns, and an uncounted number of guns in the neighbourhood of Vezzena.[30] All this had been achieved for a remarkably low number of casualties. Initially A&Q reported a total of six dead, 108 wounded and six missing for 1-5 November; the Official History revised those figures up to 26, 129 and seven respectively. Post-war, other ranks fatalities 30 October – 5 November were eventually computed to have been 42. Sixty-six percent of this total was lost by 4/Berkshire and 1/Bucks.

Prisoners had to be fed, protected from disease and have any wounds treated. The ADMS was fully employed in the last few days of conflict and then well into the post-armistice era in organizing makeshift hospitals and prisoner of war camps. On his

28 Cruttwell, *War Service of 1/4th Berkshire*, p. 148. Greenwell, *Infant in Arms* p. 244 also noted the difference in the way the British and the Italians treated their prisoners. He thought the Austrian officers were 'charming fellows and great sportsmen' who much appreciated the care provided by the division.

29 TNA: WO106/852: Cavan to CIGS, 2 Nov.1918.

30 Edmonds, *Official History Italy*, p. 345.

own authority he requisitioned a former Austrian hospital and sent RMOs forward to establish sick rooms and accommodation in occupied villages for the wounded and flu victims. As 24th CCS was repositioning, for the time being only the most serious cases were allowed to be evacuated through Asiago and down the mountain. 2/Field Ambulance took responsibility for clearing a stranded Austrian ambulance train whose patients had received no treatment or drugs for some days and the ADMS left with a small team to search for British prisoners of war in Innsbruck. By 8 November, 24th CCS had completed its move but was quickly overwhelmed and working to more than capacity. There was an obvious need for more accommodation, especially when increasing numbers of troops fell victim to flu and from diarrhoea contacted by the use of contaminated Austrian flour.[31] A divisional rest station was eventually opened in late November but while this did to some extent ease the difficulties, they were again immediately worsened by a telegram from DDMS GHQ Italy ordering the posting of 12 of the division's doctors. Billets for the troops were often squalid and unhygienic, which caused an increase in vermin-related conditions, but gradually messing and rations improved. The flu outbreak was contained by placing several villages out of bounds and when baths and laundries were installed in the prisoner of war camps, they, too, became more manageable.

By this time, however, 48th Division had withdrawn from the mountains and was reunited in XIV Corps with the two other British divisions. The division's march back from the armistice positions began on 8 November and was completed in several stages until all units reassembled in the Trissino area. It was here that the drawn out process of demobilization began, with the first significant trainload of men departing for the UK on 23 December. There were the inevitable complaints about the slow and inequitable progress before the system began to work smoothly but as a distraction education classes and a seemingly never-ending series of football matches for the Walker and the Cavan Cups absorbed much of the time. 'Pig boards' were established to purchase animals at highly inflated prices in preparation for Christmas dinners but before the festive period began 7/Worcestershire and a machine-gun company were sent as a precaution to Taranto where members of the British West Indies Regiment were involved in small-scale unrest. Although the troops were not used, the battalion stayed at Taranto until March 1919. In the divisional area troops were treated to lectures by Sub-Lieutenant Davis RNVR on 'The Right and Wrong Type of Recitation' and by Lieutenant Gamlen on 'The Franco-Prussian War.' In the attempt to prepare troops for the return to civilian life and to explain why the war had been fought, teams of War Office approved personnel did the rounds lecturing on topics ranging from how Germany had intended to conquer Europe and the inherent dangers of Bolshevism, to citizenship and post-war reconstruction. Probably of more use and interest to the men were sessions on how the demobilization system was working, classes on the maintenance of motor engines and a number of 'controlled' dances with

31 Flu was reported to be endemic amongst the civilian population.

48th Division's official 1918 Christmas card. By the time the families of some soldiers received the card, their demobilized brothers, sons or fathers had already arrived home. (Private collection)

nurses and selected locals. Canteens were opened but there was an acute shortage of cigarettes and supplies of other comforts were slow to arrive.[32]

Routine work had still to be done by the ever-decreasing numbers of men. Field ambulance orderlies were kept occupied in treating the sick and the usual testing and inspection of camp facilities, field companies maintained the huts and water supplies and the veterinary section was involved in the sale of animals. In February the War Office decided on the size of the British contingent to remain in Italy and instructed corps HQ to choose appropriate units. From 48th Division, 7/Warwickshire and 6/Gloucestershire were selected, together with a company of the machine-gun battalion, a battery from 241 Brigade RFA, 3/Field Ambulance and the MVS. Men who had enlisted in 1916 and afterwards could choose which of the two battalions they wanted to join. The Gloucestershire battalion was soon despatched to Scutari in Albania as part of the Allied Control Force while 7/Warwickshire went in April to Genoa. The two battalions, together with 22/Manchester and 8/York & Lancaster, were sent to Egypt in May 1919. In 48th Division's area, by March the majority of men had left and in that month the remaining cadres returned to the UK. Cavan had gone in January and two months later Major General Walker assumed command of what was left of XIV Corps. He took the opportunity to say "goodbye" to the remnants of his

32 Edmonds, *Official History Italy*, p. 383, notes there was an abundance of Austrian cigarettes but that they were 'too nauseous for British palates.'

former division as they left for the UK. The cadres arrived in their home towns, often to be met by the mayor, former and already demobilized officers and other ranks and the towns folk. Receptions were held in town halls, colours were retrieved from parish churches and then, with little more ado, the men resumed their civilian lives. The war became a memory which for some tormented their nights and constricted their days; for others, the comradeship of service would be renewed in 1920 when the Territorial Force was reconstituted as the Territorial Army.

10

Finally

As the troops of 48th Division returned to the UK, handed in kit and equipment, shuffled through the laborious demobilization process and said their mutual farewells, some would possibly begin to reflect on the overall experience of war and their particular part in it. Some may even have wondered how well or otherwise their division had fought. Those who had been posted into the division from other regiments or from distant parts of the country may have given their former service little public thought, but those who lived in the areas from which the division's units had traditionally recruited could occasionally relive their earlier comradeship in regimental old comrades' associations and later in the Territorial Army. Others no doubt wanted simply to forget the army and the war and get on with their family and civilian lives. Probably unknown to most of the former soldiers, committees and enquiries were being established to investigate how the war had been conducted and what lessons might be learned from the experience. Scrutiny tended to fall on the functions, machinery and efficiency of the War Office, the Admiralty and the civilian administration, the command and control systems and the cultures of the component elements within the three armed forces. The conclusions were studied as part of the process by which post-war strategies, arms procurement, establishments, doctrine and tactics were to be informed. Decades were to pass before any real consideration was given as to how well particular formations or units performed during the conflict and into the reasons why some appeared to be more successful than others.

Recently, an increasing number of studies have been made into how the British Army disseminated lessons and experience. These have examined the effectiveness of commanders and their staffs, the importance of group cohesion on morale and performance, and the influence of the evolving doctrine and technology on operational and tactical outcomes. There is a growing consensus that the British Army was not as inflexible and resistant to change as its critics have traditionally suggested. It proved itself to be responsive to technical development and to the influence, suggestions and ideas of serving soldiers and civilian expertise. By adopting various ways and means this expanding experience and knowledge was shared across armies, corps and divisions. 48th Division fought in seven different corps and worked alongside or in close proximity to possibly 20 divisions. It shared its knowledge with, and learned from, these other formations in what is often termed horizontal learning. Higher authority issued a growing number of training and doctrine pamphlets but within the division itself through means of courses, senior officers' conferences, unit lectures, formal and informal discussions and simple trial and error it also learnt both from top down and from bottom up. That a learning process was underway within 48th Division is apparent in the manner it matured and honed its patrolling, raiding, offensive and defensive activities. But, it was not, of course, unique. The British Army as a whole was analyzing its doctrine and practices and although misjudgements and mismanagement could never be entirely eliminated, by mid-1918 the army was efficient, adaptable, flexible and innovative.

Recent studies have examined the extent and consequences of the learning process and have produced a degree of agreement over which divisions were perhaps 'better' than others. The assessment is sometimes based on the number of occasions the divisions were used in major offensives and how successful they were in achieving their objectives. 48th (South Midland) Division does not appear in any of the studies' lists of most "successful" British divisions. This volume has attempted to offer several theories as to why the division was used in the manner it was during its more than three and a half years abroad; given its comparatively restricted activities in that period it is hardly surprising it does not figure in those lists. In many ways the division was simply a typical British trench division. Like the bulk of BEF formations it underwent changes in its composition and character but despite its transition from a division of TF volunteers to more of a hybrid formation comprising surviving volunteers and conscripts, it remained reliable, steady and essentially predictable.

The division experienced approximately the BEF's average number of changes in senior personnel during the 52 months of mobilization. Few GOC divisions remained in post as long as Fanshawe but his dismissal was certainly a blow to the long-serving officers. It was also one which left a distinctly bad taste in their mouths. The fact that Lord Cavan chose to import a brigadier general from a neighbouring division rather than to appoint temporarily one of the existing brigade commanders until Major General H.B. Walker arrived suggests he wanted to make an emphatic point to the division.[1] Walker came with a glowing reputation and did well in the remaining months but as is evident from the abundant tributes in post-war memoirs Fanshawe was missed by all who had known him. Criticism of Fanshawe is rare but one of the few adverse comments recorded of him was that made by Brigadier General G.W. Howard. He was brought into the division in October 1918 as GOC 145 Brigade to

1 Brigadier General J. Mc.C.Steele Coldstream Guards had been GOC 22 Brigade since August 1915. He was to return to 7th Division as GOC after a short spell with 48th Division in February 1918.

replace the short-lived appointment of Brigadier General W. Pitt-Taylor.[2] Howard was promoted from GSO1 of 7th Division and before coming to 48th Division appears never to have commanded even a battalion. In a letter to Edmonds he rejoiced at Fanshawe's dismissal because it 'put an end to the Divisional Commander feeding his troops with pieces of chocolate when inspecting the front lines.'[3]

For the fortnight between Pitt-Taylor's departure and the arrival of Howard, Lieutenant Colonel L.L. Reynolds acted as temporary GOC 145 Brigade. The practice of temporarily appointing TF officers to 'acting' positions was not, however, unusual in British divisions, but the bulk of permanent senior positions remained very securely in the hands of regular officers. In 48th Division all brigade commanders had been regulars, albeit with Sladen having served time as an adjutant and CO of a TF battalion; two others in the early months of mobilization had also previously worked with the Volunteers. The division's six GSO1 had all been regulars, as had Lieutenant Colonel G.H.Barnett, the long-serving AA&QMG. Barnett had at least served nearly three years as adjutant to a TF battalion. The one senior divisional officer in 1918 who was TF commissioned was the CRE. Following the departure of the aging former regular and later Indian Army Lieutenant Colonel Giles, the equally aged Major G.S. Eberle, who had been with 2/South Midland Field Company since at least 1904, acted as temporary CRE. He remained in post until the younger Briggs, who had been a captain in Eberle's own company in 1914, arrived.

Of more immediate relevance to the other ranks was the continued presence in the battalions of several very long-serving unit officers. The Buckinghamshire Battalion later recorded that promotions to second-in-command had "invariably" been made from within the battalion. Furthermore, it added that of those officers who had embarked in March 1915, three had become CO of other battalions, two others had been appointed second-in-command elsewhere and four had left to take up staff appointments.[4] The actual number of the division's August 1914 officers who were killed later in the war is low and reflects the number of existing officers who either did not go abroad or whose health broke down soon after arrival in France. With five fatalities 8/Warwickshire lost the largest number of August 1914 officers; four of those were killed in the ill-fated attack of 1 July 1916. 5/Gloucestershire and 7/Worcestershire both lost only one, with Captain Homfray of the latter battalion having died at home seemingly from natural causes. Slade of 4/Gloucestershire and Thorne of 4/Berkshire, both captains at the outbreak of war, were killed while commanding battalions in other divisions[5] but, with the exception of Innes of 8/Warwickshire who was CO on embarkation, the five battalion COs killed during

2 Brigadier General W. Pitt-Taylor was appointed to replace the long-serving Brigadier General Watt who went home in August 1918
3 TNA: CAB45/84: Howard to Edmonds, 16 Apr. 1944.
4 Wright, *First Bucks Battalion*, p. 120.
5 8/Gloucester and 12/Royal Scots respectively.

the war had all been promoted from within. Parkinson of 4/Gloucestershire, Bindloss of 5/Warwickshire and Knox of 7/Warwickshire had all been captains in August 1914; Nott of 6/Gloucestershire having been a mere second lieutenant. Another second lieutenant who was also promoted to command by 1918 was W.C. Gell of 5/Warwickshire. Four 1914 lieutenants, four captains and two majors of August 1914 were also battalion or unit commanders within the division by 1918. While it can usually be seen as a significant advantage for units to be commanded by other TF officers from within either their own regiment or the same division, the appointment was not always universally applauded. In a very rare example of implied criticism of a CO, the historian of 4/Berkshire noted that Lieutenant Colonel P.H.Whitehouse, a 1914 major in 8/Warwickshire, "succeeded, but did not replace Colonel Lloyd-Baker." Whitehouse was apparently, "a brave man, but of a narrow and unsympathetic school, staled by continuous service throughout the war."[6]

There had been something of an incestuous promotion system in those TF divisions which had served in theatres other than the Western Front. This practice had helped 48th Division to retain an above average percentage of TF commissioned officers because in 1918, it appears that only one of the 13 battalion COs was a regular. Schomberg of the East Surrey Regiment had served with 5/Gloucester and 4/Ox&Bucks during 1917 before being promoted to CO of 6/Gloucestershire. There had been, of course, a number of regular COs in the earlier years, especially when the division first went overseas, but with the exception of Schomberg all had gone by 1918. The seemingly only TF CO transferred into the division was Pryor. He had been posted into 6/Warwickshire from 2/1st Hertfordshire in 1917 and became the Warwicks' CO in 1918. There was also a handful of long-serving original officers who had come out with their battalion in 1915 and who remained in some capacity, often as the second-in-command. Pickford, for example, who was later to write his battalion's history, was a lieutenant in August 1914. He was to serve almost continuously and occasionally act as CO of 4/Ox&Bucks when the colonel was on leave. Officers such as Pickford provided an essential link to the ethos and character of their pre-war battalions and helped to maintain some of its original identity. Probably the longest continuously serving unit commander in the division was, however, Green of 3/South Midland Field Ambulance. A captain in August 1914, Green was promoted to command when the existing CO did not embark. Green remained as CO until he returned home from Italy in March 1919.

It is difficult to give an accurate figure for the total number of officers who died whilst serving with the division. From 1916, large numbers of junior officers were posted in

6 Cruttwell, *War Service of 1/4thBerkshire,* p. 145. Lloyd-Baker, an old Etonian, had been a captain in 1/Bucks in August 1914. He had from time to time been seconded to other battalions in the division before being appointed CO of 4/Berkshire in April 1918. Vaughan, *Some Desperate Glory*, p. 105, thought Whitehouse was 'not quite so objectionable' as his brother who had gone home earlier, but was nonetheless 'full of hot air.'

from other regiments and they are generally listed in the rolls of their original rather than their adopted regiments. Similarly, it is almost impossible to identify all other rank fatalities, especially those in the RFA brigades, RAMC field ambulances and RE field companies. The rolls of the dead in the supporting arms in the volumes of *Soldiers Died* do not always give the unit to which the soldier belonged but the proportion is generally accepted to be about one to 10 of the infantry. Soldiers who served in the 13 infantry battalions, however, are more easily identified. There are certain limitations and inconsistencies in the records but the number of other rank deaths in the infantry amounts to approximately 5,200. This works out to an average of about 400 fatalities per battalion which, when compared to average losses in other battalions of their own particular regiments, is very low.[7] Unsurprisingly, therefore, the total is also low in comparison to the numbers of men killed in other divisions. During its 32 months on the Western Front, 48th Division lost an average of a little below 160 infantry fatalities per month. In contrast, 41 British divisions suffered more than 200 per month, 17 of which lost more than 300.[8] Such a low figure for 48th Division can be accounted for by its good fortune in not taking part in any of the several 1915 battles, having only two battalions involved on 1 July 1916, not being engaged at Arras, Bullecourt, Messines or Cambrai, and entirely avoiding the German spring offensives of 1918. Although it spent longer on the Somme, and is recorded as having been involved in more 'Battles' during the campaign than the majority of divisions, it was not engaged in some of the offensive's most bloody encounters.[9] Similarly, it was engaged on more occasions during Third Ypres than most divisions but escaped with approximately only average casualties for the campaign as a whole. This is not to suggest that the division did not press on to its objectives any less determinedly than other divisions but the lower casualty lists must have aided the maintenance of collective and unit identity and morale.

By late 1917 it is clear that the composition of the division's integral battalions had changed. Thirty-four percent of the deaths occurring between August and December 1917 were of men not resident in the traditional recruiting counties of their regiment. Battalions contained men from the South-East, the Northern counties and the South-West. Furthermore, 24 percent of the total fatalities are known to have been posted to their battalion from other regiments. By 1918 the percentage of those from outside the respective regimental county boundaries was even greater. The numbers of those who died in Italy between December 1917 and demobilization in 1919 were not large in comparison to earlier casualty rolls but 53, 57 and 51 percent of deaths in 143, 144

7 See, for example, M. Middlebrook, *Your Country Needs You* (Barnsley: Pen & Sword, 2000) pp. 162-67

8 D.Tattersfield, *Divisional Usage in the BEF on the Western Front 1916-1918* (Unpublished MA dissertation, University of Birmingham, 2006).

9 E.A. James, *A Record of the Battles and Engagements on the British Armies in France and Flanders,1914-1918* (London: London Stamp Exchange, 1990).

and 145 Brigades respectively came from beyond the regiments' peacetime catchment areas.[10]

Williams' analysis of the origins of the personnel of the Warwickshire Brigade suggests that of the 70 percent of soldiers identified, nearly seven percent were commissioned, 21 percent were killed, 31 percent discharged and 32 percent were still with their battalions at mobilization. By the close of 1 July 1916 he calculates that about one third of the identified 610 men of 8/Warwickshire who had embarked in March 1915 had gone, and that by the armistice a total of 455 men of the battalion had been killed, commissioned or discharged. That meant, he believes, about 125 originals remained with the battalion in November 1918.[11] Because the battalion had been involved on 1 July 1916 and because it been transferred to the costlier theatre of France in September 1918, the battalion suffered a greater number of casualties than the three other Warwickshire 1st Line battalions.[12] It is likely, therefore, that a slightly larger number of original 1914 men remained with the other three battalions at the armistice. Similar evidence is suggested elsewhere: 200 men of 6/Warwickshire were recorded as having served continuously from embarkation until dispersal and a photograph taken in April 1918 of the original survivors in 4/Ox&Bucks shows a total of 165 all ranks.[13] Transport sections and orderly room staff often retained larger groups of 1914 men than the rifle companies and, from the army numbers of men awarded medals in the closing weeks of the war, it is clear that many of the recipients were long-serving individuals. In the same way as the 1914 officers, these men provided a sense of continuity and coherence to the battalions. Although their numbers may have been diluted by the arrival of men from different regiments and areas of the country, these survivors will have retained something of the original ethos of the volunteer pre-war South Midland territorial soldier.

The British Army has long depended on fostering unit identity as a means of maintaining and improving efficiency.[14] Morale can be defined many ways but essentially it is a state of mind which empowers the individual to endure hardship, display courage and determination in order to maintain the will to win. It grows from personal and

10 These figures are calculated from the fatality rolls of the three battalions in each of 143 and 144 Brigades which stayed with their brigades from September 1918, and from 4/Berkshire and 1/Bucks in 145 Brigade. It is generally more difficult to determine the regimental origins of men who were killed in 1918 than for fatalities in the earlier years of the war. It is clear, however, that there were still substantial numbers of survivors of the earlier drafts drawn from the Hunts Cyclist Battalion and the RASC.

11 R.D. Williams, *A Social and Military of 1/8 Warwickshire Regiment in the Great War* (Unpublished MPhil)

12 The totals are roughly: 419, 580, 393 and 702 for 5th, 6th, 7th and 8th Battalions respectively

13 Compiled, *History of 1/6th Warwickshire,* p. 82 ; the photograph is mentioned in F.MacKay, *Touring the Italian Front* (Barnsley: Pen & Sword, 2002) p. 142.

14 See, for example, D.French, *Military Identities. The Regimental System, the British Army, and the British People, c.1870–2000* (Oxford: Oxford University Press, 2005).

group élan and esprit de corps. In the pre-war era, regular divisions did occasionally concentrate to undertake manoeuvres but most exercises were conducted at the battalion or brigade level. Loyalty was generally to the regiment and sometimes the brigade rather than the division. New Army divisions had to capitalize on the local identity of their constituent units to generate a larger and wider loyalty, but this took time and cohesion could be broken when brigades were dismembered or swapped between divisions. Territorial Force divisions and brigades might not have been able often to undertake combined or joint manoeuvres but the local and provincial identities of the formations provided a bond or alliance which which was not always evident in Regular and New Army divisions. Much of the motivation for continuing to fight must have come from what are today considered to be the principles of moral cohesion. These factors provide a group with resilience and endurance. In turn, these characteristics rely on elements such as continuity of service to develop collective bonding, shared experience of success and failure to build confidence or learn lessons, sound preparation and training for hardships to come, a common purpose and shared values. These components help to reduce antisocial attitudes and behaviour within the group and to build trust in its collective ability. The TF as a whole relied on such virtues and had done what it could to foster and encourage them in the pre-war years. Once war broke out the county associations were in place to provide a ready-made support system to help maintain morale and will by overseeing welfare for the troops and their families.

At the root of this bond was the innate rivalry fostered in pre-war days through trade, commerce and sport between units from neighbouring towns and cities. Drafts joining the South Midland's units from outside the traditional recruiting areas might not have known a great deal about the nature and character of the division's internal rivalry but with good leadership and management at all levels of command they could be drawn into and thus perpetuate its sense when many of those who had understood its nuances were no longer serving. Unsurprisingly, and this was not of course unique to the South Midland Division, battalion histories and personal memoirs are replete with comments which emphasize the bond within units. For example, the diarist of 4/Ox&Bucks was one of several scribes who wrote along the lines of how an "excellent spirit of entente prevailed between officers and men." This continued to be the case even when the "old crowd", who were "so awfully different" had been replaced by those whose "initial enthusiasm has disappeared and [which had been] succeeded by a sort of dumb and disciplined resignation," As late as July 1918, Greenwell recorded his fury at being appointed OC of the Brigade School because it meant being "torn from the regiment."[15]

Henry Ogle's earlier[16] self-deprecating assessment of the division's status in 1915 was contradicted by several comments made later in the war. Carrington noted that a

15 Greenwell, *Infant in Arms*, pp. 170, 231.
16 See Chapter 3.

German of *2nd Guards Reserve Division* captured in a raid in June 1917 stated troops of 48th Division were regarded as *schrecklich,* and when a captured German general ranked British and Dominion divisions in order of merit, he put 48th Division in fourth place.[17] In view of the division's record these two assessments are difficult to justify. Rather than basing them on any sound factual foundation, the comments may simply have been prisoners telling their captors what they believed the captors wanted to hear. Wright adds, however, that General Gough considered the division to be "dependable", which was probably praise indeed, and after witnessing the attack by 6/ and 8/Warwickshire on the *Heindenkopf,* Brigadier General Prowse is reputed to have said, "I did not think much about Territorials but by God, they can fight."[18] In addition, the war diaries contain the usual 'thanks' telegrams from army and corps commanders expressing their appreciation of the invariably good work done by the division when under their command. The question remains, however, why was 48th Division used, in relative terms, so sparingly in major offensives? Was it because there was a feeling that it was not a good division, or was it simply fortunate to be in the right places at the right time?

During the mobilization and training period in the UK, the division was certainly fortunate not to have been dismembered and its units despatched abroad independently. 1st and 2nd London, West Lancashire, Highland, Lowland, Welsh, Wessex, Home Counties, Northumbrian and East Anglian Divisions all lost at least one of their units to other formations. Furthermore, 2nd London, North Midland, Northumbrian and Highland Divisions were quickly engaged in major offensives soon after they landed in France. Only South Midland and West Riding Divisions were retained as trench holders for a substantial period after their arrival on the Western Front. Following its period of trench acclimatization, 48th Division was sent as part of the vanguard of British divisions to the Somme front. It was to stay in this quiet zone for 10 full months doing little other than patrolling and instructing New Army divisions in trench warfare. While other TF divisions were mauled at Festubert and Loos, rather than being despatched to relieve its weakened sister TF formations, South Midland led a relatively peaceful life. There may have been sound operational reasons why the reasonably strong South Midland was not sent to an active front but what seems more difficult to understand is why the division was not employed in the diversionary operation at Gommecourt on 1 July. The division knew the area better than any other formation but instead of being used on the southern flank of the assault, the reconstituted 56th (1st London) Division was brought down to undertake the attack. By common consent the London Division was composed of battalions of huge potential

17 Carrington, *War History of the 1/5th Warwickshire*, p52. Roughly translated, *schrecklich* means 'troops to be afraid of'. Corbett, *War Story of 1/8th Worcestershire*, p. 78. The German general in question placed 48th Division behind 51st (Highland), an unspecified Canadian division and 1st Australian Division.

18 Wright, *The First Buckinghamshire Battalion*, p. 88 and Caddick-Adams, *By God They Can Fight*, p. 67.

but as it had been deliberately instructed to ensure the Germans knew an attack would be made against their salient, casualties would inevitably be enormous. 46th (North Midland) Division, which had been deemed by many in high places to have performed badly at Loos under a commander who was unpopular in the War Office, was to operate as the northern arm of the Gommecourt pincer. As the attack was not designed to be anything more than a diversion 46th (North Midland) Division was perhaps considered expendable. Given this premise, therefore, it is surprising South Midland Division, rather than the highly esteemed 56th (1st London), was not used or at least exchanged with the New Army 37th Division as the third division within VII Corps. The main Somme offensive was deliberately intended to be very largely a Regular and New Army campaign but any radical decision to make VII Corps a formation of entirely TF divisions would not have impinged on this intent because, as part of Third Army, it was not an integral element of Fourth Army's principal operation.[19] Although in the early hours of 1 July, with the exception of troops in 6/ and 8/Warwick, members of the division may have been disappointed not to be about to attack, 12 hours later they were probably relieved their formation had not been selected. Whether the authorities' decision not to use the division was purely a reflection of their prejudice against the TF, or whether despite General Sir Ian Hamilton's ringing endorsement of its qualities only 20 months earlier, because it was not considered to be a good division is obscure. It was, however, to be given the opportunity to prove its worth as a complete division in the following months.

The Battles Nomenclature Committee later designated the division's actions in July and early September around Ovillers and Skyline Trench as 'tactical actions'; the division's tours in the trenches near Le Sars in October and November were classified in similar manner. The division did not take place in any of the real set-piece battles of the Somme campaign but, as a consequence, spent longer in the line than most other divisions. Its bombing operations on the Pozières and Thiepval ridges made slow progress and involved considerable hand-to-hand fighting in confined positions. Battalions frequently took a German post or trench only to lose them when the enemy counter-attacked. Cooperation with units on its flanks and even between its own brigades and battalions was not always as secure as it should have been, but this did improve with experience and with the regular appointment of liaison officers. The divisional artillery's performance was erratic. It could sometimes place barrages with commendable accuracy just ahead of the advancing companies; on other occasions battalions were savaged by their own shelling.

In the tortuous conditions of the Somme, reporting and signalling remained haphazard; this made effective command and control in battle particularly difficult. Most of the small-scale actions were those where success depended very much on the leadership and initiative of platoon and section commanders but, as losses amongst

19 Only twice during the war were corps comprised entirely of TF divisions: XVIII Corps in September 1917 and XI Corps during October-November 1918.

these junior officers and NCOs were high, attacks were often led by inexperienced commanders who had only limited knowledge of their objectives and the ways and means of achieving them. What is clear, however, is that despite the length of time it spent in the line there were substantial periods in the summer of 1916 when it had time to train and rest. The BEF was as a whole embarking upon a learning process but conditions on the Somme uplands made it difficult to utilize the lessons being learned. The results of the encounters experienced by the division frequently boiled down to the personal and group determination of attacker and defender, the ability of carrying parties to maintain the supply of bombs and light trench mortar shells and the means of signalling to the artillery where precisely the infantry wanted the defensive barrage to fall. In November and December the division was once again fortunate in having its intended attacks near the Butte de Warlencourt cancelled; if they had taken place the results and casualty lists would undoubtedly have been similar to those suffered by 50th Division. This would not have been a reflection on the capability of the division because there is no evidence that the division did any better or any worse than other formations in the same corps or those which were undertaking similarly localized and limited operations. It is simply a matter of fact because the terrain and weather made significant success for *any* formation unlikely.

In the early months of 1917, when the division manned trenches south of the Somme river, it conducted a series of raids with varying degrees of success. It does seem to have taken rather a long time to expel enemy raiders from trenches occupied by 6/Warwickshire and 6/Gloucestershire in February but the organization and staff work during the German withdrawal to the Hindenburg Line worked efficiently. The field companies performed sound work in quickly bridging the Somme river and canal and touch was generally well maintained with the retreating Germans. The attack on Ste Emilie by 4/Gloucestershire was a rushed and ill-prepared affair which produced predictable results. The assaults on Épehy and the three villages to its south were, in contrast, well-planned with effective coordination between artillery and infantry in less than favourable conditions. The attacks on Gillemont Farm and the Knoll did not, however, always demonstrate the same degree of situational awareness. The strength of the enemy garrisons, the ground and weather conditions, the predictable tactics employed and the disrupted communications between the infantry and their supporting batteries ensured any gains were generally quickly counter-attacked and lost. In modern terms the attacks lacked flexibility, security and innovation and were usually characterized by insufficient concentration of force. The assault by 4/Berkshire in mid-April, for example, should never have been allowed to take place without greater preparation, specific training and greater understanding by all ranks of the difficulties the operation presented. To have ordered it to proceed in such appalling conditions and with inadequate coordination between flanking units and the artillery was a grave misjudgement on the part of corps, divisional and brigade commanders.

The division employed a consistently aggressive policy of patrolling when stationed in the Beaumetz sector. The constant nocturnal activity appears to have sufficiently intimidated the enemy into eventually surrendering control of no man's land. This relatively quiet period, and the month spent in training behind Ypres, allowed the division to absorb new recruits, rest and prepare tactically for the forthcoming offensive. When it came, 48th Division was not used on the first day, XVIII Corps HQ preferring instead to have 51st (Highland) and 39th Divisions as the assault formations. It is understandable the corps commander wanted to use the tried and tested Highland Division to start the offensive but it was probably the luck of the draw rather than any particular preference which put 39th rather than 48th Division in the front lines. The division's involvement in Third Ypres was heavy but it did also have several periods of recuperation and training in the rear. Corbett later claimed that at Ypres, 8/Worcestershire "always made our objective, and clung to it"[20] which in the case of that battalion is probably correct. There were many other instances, however, when battalions were unsuccessful. Again, it is difficult to condemn individual units for a lack of drive or determination for their failures to gain their objectives because the weather, terrain and resolute defence were sufficient to frustrate the best of divisions. 48th Division was active in some of the worst areas of the Salient, where even reaching the jumping off line at the scheduled time was in itself an achievement. Although the division's staff work appears to have been sound, the impossible conditions, the unstable gun platforms, the difficulties of re-supply, the frequent loss of direction, the broken communications between companies, battalions and brigades and the concrete blockhouses meant tactical lessons learned from earlier battles were largely inapplicable to the swamps the infantry were compelled to negotiate. There were times, for example 143 Brigade's attack on 4 October, which could have been handled and executed better than they were but, overall, advances made by 48th Division are comparable to those made by the other division in XVIII Corps.[21] Objectives were rarely reached and even more rarely secured at the first attempt, enemy counter-attacks were frequently successful in limiting the division's gains and for predictable reasons cooperation between armour, infantry, air and artillery was at times impossible.

It was probably good fortune again which determined 48th Division should be sent to Italy. Vimy was a convenient and familiar area where Canadian divisions could recuperate after Third Ypres; South Midland was one of the divisions already in occupation, at reasonable establishment and which could easily be moved. It was able to enjoy a substantial period of rest and familiarization before it saw any significant action in the Italian mountains and subsequent fatalities were light in comparison to those the division would have suffered had it stayed in France. Its defence of the Asiago in June 1918 was criticized and it probably retained for some months the stigma for the perceived poor performance. It is possibly significant that Lord Cavan elected to leave the division on the Asiago and instead take 7th and 23rd Divisions to

20 Corbett, *War Story of 1/8th Worcester*, p. 69.
21 11th (Northern) Division.

the plain as part of Italian Tenth Army yet, during the final offensive, albeit against a severely weakened enemy, the division covered a great deal of ground in a short time and captured an enormous number of prisoners. Its performance here was efficient and commendable. When the Territorial Army was formed in 1920, Major General Sir Harold Walker, the division's last commander, was pencilled in for command of a regular division. It is extremely unlikely he would have been on the short list for such a prestigious appointment if the authorities believed he had not been an able GOC of a good division.

During the course of the war the division's learning process had been acute. As the second strongest TF division in 1914 and with a pre-war reputation for efficiency, once Kitchener had invited the TF to accept foreign service the division expected to be sent quickly overseas. It could have had few complaints at the easy time it experienced in the Ploegsteert sector and the months of quiet activity on the Somme before the offensive opened. The training schemes during that lengthy period were probably based on the existing doctrine of *Field Service Regulations 1* and similar, essentially pre-war, pamphlets. Like all doctrine, *FSR 1* was intended to be a framework of best practice around which commanders could plan their campaigns. Because, however, it was aimed at what would now be termed the strategic and operational levels of warfare it demonstrated little concern for tactics. Battalion and company officers, sometimes under the guidance of divisional and brigade commanders, used their own judgement, experience and training to decide how their troops should be instructed. Although there is little evidence to confirm it, like other divisions on the Western Front before the Somme, 48th Division appears to have used its training periods to practise the putative tactics required in any return to a war of movement. In addition to the division's internal training processes, the establishment of corps and army schools and the gradual formulization of the training programmes at home and overseas enhanced the developing doctrine and best practice. The division used its earlier experiences and the tactical doctrine enshrined within the Training Directorate's circulars at Third Ypres but it had, in conjunction with the other British divisions posted to Italy, to develop and learn new doctrine applicable to mountain warfare. Aspects of Western Front doctrine, such as defence in depth could, of course, be adapted to the changed environment. It was the misapplication, however, of that concept to terrain which did not offer the space to the rear and the forward fields of fire integral to its effectiveness, which partly explains why the division was later thought to have performed badly.

Something like 1,850 British gallantry and service awards are thought to have been awarded to men of the division.[22] These included the Victoria Cross to Corporal Arthur Hutt of 7/Warwickshire. When foreign awards are added the total comes close to 2,200. This figure is roughly in line with other divisions which served a similar amount of time overseas. Three soldiers, two in 5/Warwickshire and one

22 Several of the battalion histories used as sources for this volume contained medal rolls as appendices.

in 4/Berkshire,[23] had been executed and the division as a whole had accrued battle honours for its time on the Somme, at Ypres and the Asiago. Troops of the division had shown endurance, fortitude and bravery during the four years of conflict and had contributed substantially to the final victory. It was, however, essentially a line-holding division which had not particularly distinguished itself in battle. Nonetheless, it had proved to be a stolid, generally reliable and resilient formation which despite the influx of conscripts and geographically disparate recruits had maintained its motivation to fight and its TF ethos. It had demonstrated an ability to learn and had shown adaptability, versatility and resourcefulness in order to sustain its conceptual, physical and moral components of fighting power. By a combination of good fortune, steady morale, sympathetic leadership and effective command, it emerged from the war with a record of competence and efficiency.

23 Statistically, TF divisions had a substantially lower number of executions than Regular and New Army divisions.

Appendix

South Midland Division's Drill Halls and Out Stations, 1914

Pre-war Territorials could, in theory, enlist in any unit they wished but the constraints of geography often determined which one they did actually join. If they were to take their membership of a unit seriously they usually had to work or live within easy striking distance of their drill hall or out station. Rural recruits had sometimes to travel considerable distances to attend their drill night or weekend exercise but most yeomanry, infantry, gunners or engineers of the South Midland Division had the opportunity to enlist in a regiment, battalion, battery or field company which was fairly close to their residence. There were occasional spats between county associations about the right to recruit in another's traditional catchment area but these were usually settled by good sense and reciprocal arrangements.

The divisional HQ was located in Warwick. In addition to the units listed below, the county associations were also responsible for administering the yeomanry regiments and associated units, 1st, 2nd and 3rd General Hospitals and South Midland Clearing Hospital.

The information below is garnered from Becke's *Order of Battle of Divisions*, Territorial Force County Association Minute Books and Westlake's *The Territorial Force*.[1]

Royal Field Artillery

I South Midland (Gloucestershire) Brigade: 1st and 2nd Gloucs Batteries at Clifton; 3rd in Gloucester: Ammunition Column in Clifton.

1 A. Becke, *Order of Battle of Division, Part 2A* (London: HMSO, 1936); R.Westlake, *The Territorial Force* (Newport: Ray Westlake – Military Books, 1988). Because 1st and 2nd South Midland Mounted Brigades were not technically part of the pre-war South Midland Division, the yeomanry regiments, the RHA battery, the two Army Service Corps Mounted Brigade Transport and Supply Columns, and the mounted field ambulances are not included in this list.

II South Midland Brigade: 1st Worcs Battery in Worcester; 2nd Worcs Battery in Kidderminster and Malvern; 3rd Worcs Battery in Redditch; Ammunition Column in Malvern.

III South Midland Brigade: 1st, 2nd and 3rd Warwicks Batteries and Ammunition Column in Birmingham

IV South Midland (Howitzer) Brigade: 4th Warwicks (H) Battery in Coventry and Rugby; 5th Warwicks (H) Battery in Rugby; Ammunition Column in Coventry.

South Midland (Warwickshire) Heavy Battery, Royal Garrison Artillery: Birmingham and Wednesbury; Ammunition Column in Wednesbury.

Royal Engineers

1/and 2/Field Companies in Bristol. Divisional Signal Company. HQ in Bristol

Infantry Brigades

Warwickshire Brigade, HQ in Warwick: 5/Warwickshire, Thorp St., Birmingham; 6/Warwickshire, Thorp Str., Birmingham; 7/Warwickshire in Coventry, Rugby, Leamington, Kenilworth and Nuneaton; 8/Warwickshire in Aston Manor and Saltley.

Gloucestershire and Worcestershire Brigade, HQ in Cheltenham: 4/Gloucestershire and 6/Gloucestershire in Bristol; 7/Worcestershire in Kidderminster, Tenbury, Bockleton, Stourport, Kinver, Oldbury, Halesowen and Dudley; 8/Worcestershire in Worcester, Pershore, Malvern, Upton-on-Severn, Elmley Castle, Fladbury, Evesham, Badsey, Droitwich, Stoke Works, King's Norton, Rubery, Bromsgrove and Redditch.

South Midland Brigade, HQ in Oxford: 5/Gloucestershire in Gloucester, Stroud, Cirencester, Tewkesbury, Kemerton, Cheltenham, Dursley, Wotton-under-Edge, Camden, Blockley, Shipton-on-Stour and Moreton-in-March; 4/Ox&Bucks L.I. in Oxford, Thame, Banbury, Brackley, Henley-on-Thames, Culham, Chipping Norton, Kingham, Charlbury, Shipton, Stow-on-the Wold, Witney, Woodstock, Burford, Eynsham, Banbury, Bicester and Woodburn; Buckingham Battalion, The Ox&Bucks L.I. in Aylesbury, Marlow, High Wycombe, Winslow, Buckingham, Tingewick, Chesham, Slough, Datchet and Wolverton, 4/Royal Berkshire in Reading, Englefield, Wantage, Wallingford, Windsor, Newbury, Bucklebury, Aldermaston, Hungerford, Abingdon, Maidenhead and Wokingham.

Army Supply Corps Divisional Transport and Supply Columns

Brigade Companies at Aston, Harborne, Wallbridge, Strood and Taplow.

RAMC Field Ambulances

1/ and 2/South Midland in Birmingham and Sutton Coldfield; 3/South Midland in Bristol

Bibliography

National Archives (Kew)

Army, corps, divisional, brigade and unit war diaries of the WO95 classification.

48th Division's war diaries during its deployment in France and Belgium commence with the General Staff diary in WO95/2745 and work down through the various HQ departments, infantry brigades and units of the supporting arms. For the division's subsequent deployment in Italy the run begins with WO95/4244. Other relevant WO documents can be found in the WO106 and CAB45 classifications.

County Record Offices

Buckinghamshire: T/A: 1/22 Annual Reports; T/A/1/4 General Purpose Committee; T/A/1/13 Committee Minute Books
Gloucestershire: D2388/1/1, Association Minutes 1908-1912; D2388/1/2 Association Minutes 1912-21; D2388/3/1 Committee Minutes 1908-1912
Oxfordshire: 011/1/A1/1; 011/1/A1/2; 011/1/A1/3; 0011/1/N1/1
Warwickshire: CR1141/4 General Purpose & Finance Committee 1908-1924; CR1141/8 HQ & Range Committees 1908-34
Worcestershire: BA5204/5 General Purposes Committee 1908-1922

Official Publications

Army Doctrine Publications, *Operations* (Shrivenham: DCDC, 2010)
A.F. Becke, *Order of Battle of Divisions: Part 2a* (London: HMSO, 1936)
Compiled, *Officers Died in the Great War,* (London: HMSO, 1919)
Compiled, *Soldiers Died in the Great War* (Polstead: Hayward & Sons, 1984-1986)
J.E. Edmonds, *History of the Great War: Military Operations France and Belgium 1916 Vol. I* (London: HMSO, 1932)
J.E. Edmonds, *History of the Great War: Military Operations Italy 1915-1919* (London: HMSO, 1949)

C. Falls, *History of the Great War: Military Operations in France and Belgium 1917 Vol. I* (London: HMSO, 1940)
E.A. James, *A Record of Battles and Engagements of the British Armies in France and Flanders, 1914-1918* (London: London Stamp Exchange, 1990 reprint of 1924 edition)
W. Miles, *History of the Great War, Military Operations in France and Belgium* 1916 *Vol. II* (London: HMSO, 1938)
War Office, *Organization and Training of the New Armies* (London: War Office, 1917)
War Office, *Field Service Regulations* (London: War Office, 1909)
War Office, *Training and Manoeuvre Regulations* (London: War Office, 1913)

Published Memoirs & Biographies

G.H, Barnett, *With the 48th Division in Italy* (Edinburgh: Blackwood, 1923)
C. Carrington, *Soldier from the War Returning* (Barnsley: Pen & Sword, 2006)
C. Edmonds, *A Subaltern's War* (London: Peter Davies, 1929)
J. French, FM Sir, *1914* (London: Constable, 1919)
G.H. Greenwell, *An Infant in Arms: War Letters of a Company Officer 1914-1918* (London: Allen & Lane, 1972)
M. Glover, (ed) *The Fateful Battle Line. The Great War Journals and Sketches of Captain Henry Ogle* (Barnsley: Leo Cooper, 1993)
G. Sheffield, & J. Bourne, (ed) Douglas *Haig. War Diaries and Letters 1914-1918* (London: Phoenix, 2006)
E.C. Vaughan, *Some Desperate Glory* (London: Macmillan, 1981)

Formation & Unit Histories

H. Adderley, *The Warwickshire Yeomanry in the Great War* (Warwick: W.H. Smith & Son, 1922)
C.T. Atkinson, *The Seventh Division 1914-1918* (London: Murray, 1927)
F.W. Bewsher, *The History of the 51st (Highland) Division 1914-1918* (London: Blackwood, 1921)
J. Boraston, & C. Bax, *The Eighth Division in the War 1914-1918* (London: Medici, 1926)
P. Caddick-Adams, *'By God they can fight': A History of 143rd Infantry Brigade 1908-1995*, (Shrewsbury: Private Printing, 1995)
C. Carrington, *The War Record of the 1/5th Battalion, the Royal Warwickshire Regiment* (Birmingham: Cornish Bros, 1922)
T. Carter, *Birmingham Pals: 14th, 15th and 16th (Service) Battalions of the Royal Warwickshire Regiment* (Barnsley: Pen & Sword, 1997)
J. Cobham, *The Yeomanry Cavalry of Worcestershire 1914-1922* (Stourbridge: Mark & Moody, 1926)

Compiled, *The History of the 1/6th Battalion the Royal Warwickshire Regiment* (Birmingham: Cornish Brothers, 1922)

Compiled, *The 21st Battalion Manchester Regiment: A History*. (Manchester: Fleur de Lys Publishing, 1994 reprint of 1934 edition)

J.C. Coop, *The Story of the 55th (West Lancashire) Division 1914-1919* (Liverpool: Daily Post, 1919)

E. Corbett, *War History of the 1/8th (Territorial) Battalion the Worcestershire Regiment*, (Worcester: Herald Office, 1921)

C. Cruttwell, *The War Service of the 1/4th Royal Berkshire Regiment (TF)* (Oxford: Basil Blackwell, 1922)

P.H. Dalbiac, *History of the 60th Division (2/2nd London Division)* (London: Allen & Unwin, 1927)

F.W. Dopson, *The 48th Division Signal Company in the Great War* (Bristol: Arrowsmith, 1938)

C.H. Dudley Ward, *The 56th Division* (London: Murray, 1921)

C.H. Dudley Ward, *The 74th Yeomanry Division in Syria and France* (London: John Murray, 1922)

C.H. Dudley Ward, *History of the 53rd (Welsh) Division (TF) 1914-1918* (Cardiff: Western Mail, 1927)

E. Fazan, *The Cinque Ports Battalion* (Chichester: Regimental Association, 1970)

F.P. Gibbon, *The 42nd (East Lancashire) Division 1914-1918* (London: Country Life, 1920)

P. Hurd, *The Fighting Territorials* (London: George Newnes, 1915)

A. Hussey, & D. Inman, *The Fifth Division in the Great War* (London: Nisbet, 1921)

J. Jeff, *The 5th Battalion the Royal Warwickshire Regiment TA* (Kingwinsford: Dulston Press, 1986)

A. Keith-Falconer, *The Oxfordshire Hussars in the Great War 1914-1918* (Oxford: John Murray, 1927)

A. MacDonald, *A Lack of Offensive Spirit? The 46th (North Midland) Division at Gommecourt, 1st July 1916* (Ross-shire: Iona Books, 2008).

L. Magnus, *The West Riding Territorials in the Great War* (London: Kegan Paul, 1920)

A.H. Maude, (ed) *The 47th (London) Division 1914-1919*, (London: Amalgamated Press, 1922)

K.W. Mitchinson, *Pioneer Battalions in the Great War* (Barnsley: Pen & Sword, 1998)

K.W. Mitchinson, *Amateur Soldiers: A History of Oldham's Volunteers and Territorials 1859-1938* (Oldham: Jade, 1999)

F. Loraine Petre, *The Royal Berkshire Regiment* (Reading: Reading Barracks, 1925)

P. Pickford, *The War Record of the 1/4th Oxfordshire and Buckinghamshire Light Infantry* (Banbury: Banbury Guardian Office, 1919)

R.E. Priestley, *Breaking the Hindenburg Line: The Story of the 46th (North Midland) Division* (London: Fisher Unwin, 1919)

H.R. Sandilands, *The 23rd Division, 1914-1919* (London: Blackwood, 1925)

H. Stacke, *The Worcestershire Regiment in the Great War* (Worcester: Cheshire & Sons, 1929)

J. Stirling, *The Territorial Divisions* (London: Dent, 1922)
R.R. Thompson, *The Fifty-Second (Lowland) Division 1914-1918* (Glasgow: MacLehose, Jackson & Co., 1923)
P. Wright, *The First Buckinghamshire Battalion 1914-1919* (London, Hazell, Watson & Viney, 1920)
E. Wyrall, *The History of the Fiftieth Division 1914-1918* (London: Percy Lund, 1939)
E. Wyrall, *The Gloucestershire Regiment in the Great War 1914-1918* (London: Methuen, 1931)
E. Wyrall, *The Story of the 62nd (West Riding) Division 1914-1919* (London: Bodley Head, 1924)

Secondary Sources

R. Baden-Powell, *Quick Training for War* (London: Herbert Jenkins, 1914)
J. Baynes, *Morale: A Study of Men and Courage* (London: Cassell, 1967)
I.F.W. Beckett, *The Amateur Military Tradition, 1558-1945* (Manchester: Manchester University Press, 1981)
I.F.W. Beckett, & K.Simpson, (ed) *A Nation in Arms* (Manchester: Manchester University Press, 1985)
T. Bowman, & M. Connelly, *The Edwardian Army* (Oxford: Oxford University Press, 2012)
I.M. Brown, *British Logistics on the Western Front 1914-1919* (Westport & London: Praeger, 1998)
G.H. Cassar, *The Forgotten Front: The British Campaign in Italy 1917-1918* (London: Hambledon Press, 1998)
P. Dennis, *The Territorial Army 1907-1940* (London: Boydell Press, 1987)
K.R. Grieves, *The Politics of Manpower 1914-1918* (Manchester: Manchester University Press, 1988)
P. Griffith, (ed), *British Fighting Methods in the Great War* (London: Frank Cass, 1996)
P. Griffith, *Battle Tactics on the Western Front* (New Haven & London: Yale University Press, 1994)
A.P. Herbert, *The Secret Battle* (London: Collector's Library, 2015 edition)
E.A. James, *British Regiments 1914-1918* (London: Samson, 1978)
P. Liddle, (ed) *Home Fires and Foreign Fields* (London: Brassey, 1985)
P. Liddle, (ed) *Passchendaele in Perspective: The Third Battle of Ypres* (London: Leo Cooper, 1997)
F. MacKay, *Asiago* (Barnsley: Leo Cooper, 2001)
F. MacKay, *Touring the Italian Front* (Barnsley: Leo Cooper, 2002)
C. Messenger, *Call to Arms: The British Army 1914-1918* (London: Weidenfeld & Nicholson, 2005.
K.W. Mitchinson, *Defending Albion: Britain's Home Army 1908-1919* (Basingstoke: Palgrave Macmillan, 2005)

K.W. Mitchinson, *England's Last Hope: The Territorial Force 1908-1914* (Basingstoke: Palgrave Macmillan, 2008)

K.W. Mitchinson, *The Territorial Force at War 1914-1916* (Basingstoke: Palgrave Macmillan, 2014)

G. Oram, *Death Sentences Passed by Military Courts of the British Army 1914-1924* (London: Francis Boutle, 1998)

R. Prior & T. Wilson, *Command on the Western Front* (Oxford: Blackwell, 1992)

R. Prior & T. Wilson, *The Somme* (New Haven & London: Yale University Press, 2005)

J. Putkowski, & J. Sykes, *Shot at Dawn* (Barnsley: Pen & Sword, 1992)

W. Richards, *His Majesty's Territorial Army* (London: Virtue & Co., 1911)

S. Robbins, *British Generalship on the Western Front 1914-18* (London: Frank Cass, 2005)

G. Sheffield, *Leadership in the Trenches* (Basingstoke: Macmillan, 2000)

G. Sheffield & D. Todman (eds), *Command and Control on the Western Front* (Staplehurst: Spellmount, 2004)

P. Simkins, *Kitchener's Army* (Manchester: Manchester University Press, 1988)

A. Simpson, *Directing Operations, British Corps Command on the Western Front 1914-1918* (Staplehurst: Spellmount, 2006)

M. Strohn, (ed) *The Battle of the Somme* (Oxford: Osprey, 2016)

E. Wallace, *Kitchener's Army and the Territorial Forces* (London: George Newnes, 1915)

R. Westlake, *British Battalions in France & Belgium 1914* (Barnsley: Leo Cooper, 1997)

R. Westlake, *British Battalions on the Western Front, January to June 1915* (Barnsley: Leo Cooper, 2001)

J. Wilks & E. Wilks, *The British Army in Italy 1917-1918* (Barnsley: Leo Cooper, 1998)

Unpublished Theses & Dissertations

D. Tattersfield, *Divisional Usage in the BEF on the Western Front 1916-1918*, MA dissertation, University of Birmingham, 2006.

A. Thornton, *The Territorial Force in Staffordshire 1908-1915*, M. Phil, University of Birmingham, 2004.

R. Williams, *A Social and Military History of the 1/8th Battalion the Royal Warwickshire Regiment*, M. Phil, University of Birmingham, 1992.

Electronic Sources

R. Bishop, 'A Signaller's Diary'. This source was discovered on-line as a downloadable file <https://europeana19141918.s3.amazonaws.com/attachments/41053/3356.41053.original.txt> It contained no references as to its origin other than "Sapper Roland Bishop" served in an unidentified 48th Division's signal company.

Index

PEOPLE

GENERAL

FORMATIONS & UNITS